NAPOLEON'S SHIELD AND GUARDIAN

The Austrians took one of my legs. Let them return it, or come take the other one. In the meanwhile, I advise you to stay clear of my guns, if you do not wish to feel their effect. General Daumesnil's reply to a Russian summons, on 31 March, 1814, to surrender the fortress of Vincennes.

DAUMESNIL. *Il n'a voulu ni se rendre ni se vendre.*
Dupin

An engraving of Daumesnil, by Maurin, Bibliothèque Nationale de France. The handwritten text reads: *"Il n'a voulu ni se rendre ni se vendre."* It is signed by Dupin, the president of the Chamber of Deputies, who spoke this phrase at Daumesnil's funeral. See *Notes on Illustrations*, p. 396, no. 4.

NAPOLEON'S SHIELD AND GUARDIAN

THE UNCONQUERABLE GENERAL DAUMESNIL

Edward Ryan

With the collaboration of
Henri de Clairval

Frontline Books

To my loving, and beloved, wife

Napoleon's Shield and Guardian: The Unconquerable General Daumesnil

A Greenhill Book

First published in 2003 by Greenhill Books, Lionel Leventhal Limited
www.greenhillbooks.com

This edition published in 2015 by

Frontline Books
an imprint of Pen & Sword Books Ltd,
47 Church Street, Barnsley, S. Yorkshire, S70 2AS
For more information on our books, please visit
www.frontline-books.com, email info@frontline-books.com
or write to us at the above address.

ISBN: 978-1-84832-841-9

CIP data records for this title are available from the British Library

Printed and bound in Malta by Gutenberg Press Ltd

TABLE OF CONTENTS

PRÉFACE

D écembre 1813. L'Empereur Napoléon Ier inspecte les défenses du fort de Vincennes, qui est le grand arsenal de la France, et dont le gouverneur est le général baron Daumesnil. Un peu moins de deux ans auparavant l'Empereur a signé le contrat de mariage de son ancien colonel-major des chasseurs à cheval de la Garde avec une jeune fille de seize ans, Léonie Garat.

Après la visite du fort de Vincennes, Daumesnil présente à l'Empereur son fils âgé de quelques mois.

— Que désirez-vous pour lui, demande Napoléon Ier à la jeune mere après avoir donné un baiser au petit Léon.

— Rien de plus, Sire, répond Léonie.

Avril 1884—Une dame très âgé s'éteint. C'est Léonie Daumesnil. Entourée de sa famille elle a aupres d'elle son arrière-petit-fils, Pierre de Clairval, mon père.

J'avais un peu moins de dix ans, me disait celui-ci, j'habitais rue Bayard à Paris chez mon arrière-grand-mère et je me souviens fort bien d'elle. Elle évoquait ses souvenirs, la vie glorieuse de son mari, l'époque du Second Empire durant laquelle, pendant dix-huit ans, elle avait été surintendante de la Maison de la Légion d'honneur.

Ainsi, par l'intermédiaire d'une seule personne, le passé prenait une étonnante présence et me rejoignait, comme si j'avais moi aussi vu vivre mon ancêtre, le général Daumesnil. Et c'est cette présence qui m'a incité, il y a plus de trente ans, à écrire labiographie de celui qui "n'a voulu ni se rendre ni se vendre."

A présent Edward Ryan *prend le relais.*

HENRI DE CLAIRVAL

PREFACE

December 1813—The Emperor, Napoleon the First, carries out an inspection of the defenses of the Fort of Vincennes, France's greatest arsenal, whose Governor is General Baron Daumesnil. Barely two years earlier, the Emperor had signed the marriage contract between his former Colonel-Major of the *Chasseurs à cheval de la Garde Impériale* and a young lady of sixteen years of age, Léonie Garat.

After the visit to the Fort of Vincennes, Daumesnil presents his son, who is no more than a few months old, to the Emperor.

"What do you wish for him?" asks Napoleon of the young mother, after giving a kiss to the young Léon.

"Nothing more, Your Majesty," answers Léonie.

April 1884—A very old lady is passing away: Léonie Daumesnil. Surrounded by her family, she has her great-grandson beside her. This is Pierre de Clairval, my own father.

"I was little less than ten years old," said my father to me. "I lived in Rue Bayard, in Paris, at my great-grandmother's home, and I remember her very well. She would recall her memories of the past, the glorious life of her husband, the days of the Second Empire, during which, over a period of eighteen years, she was the superintendent of the *Maison de la Légion d'honneur.*"

Thus, through the intermediary of one single person, the past would come alive astonishingly, as though I, too, had known my ancestor, General Daumesnil, in his own lifetime. It was this very presence of the past, which led me, more than thirty years ago, to write a biography of the one who "would neither surrender nor sell himself."

Now Edward Ryan is holding up the torch of memory anew.

HENRI DE CLAIRVAL

LIST OF ILLUSTRATIONS

Colour plates: pp 97–104

Black-and-white plates: pp 201–216

INTRODUCTION

The pages of Napoleonic histories are illuminated by the names of innumerable soldiers of every rank, who, imbued with indomitable courage and a fierce desire to earn for themselves a share in the glittering honors in the gift of one of the greatest military leaders of all time, singled themselves out on hundreds of battlefields by their extraordinary feats of arms. Thanks to the flood of volumes in which the exploits of these exceptional individuals have been recorded, the names of scores of them—from Desaix, saving the day for Bonaparte at Marengo to Cambronne, defying the British from within the last square at Waterloo—are common currency for those of us for whom this extraordinary chapter of history holds endless fascination.

Doubtless destined to remain unsung, however, are the accounts of an equal number of valorous deeds performed by other members of those legendary regiments who, with unquestioning devotion and indefatigable courage, followed and fought for their emperor until time ran out on them all. Recently it was my good fortune to happen upon one such story—an account of the life of a soldier, whose extraordinary character and exceptional career earned for him a unique place in his countrymen's hearts and his nation's annals. With that discovery came a conviction that fellow enthusiasts of Napoleonic history would share with me the particular pleasure that I had found in learning of the remarkable role played by Pierre Daumesnil in that saga.

I say "happened upon" because that is literally true, notwithstanding the fact that Daumesnil occupies a high place of honor in the Pantheon of heroes of that epochal time of remarkable men and in the memories of his countrymen, even if they are more likely to think of him as *la Jambe de Bois*[1] rather than as General Baron Pierre Daumesnil. How, then, had I

---

1 "Wooden-leg." Preoccupation with political correctness seems not to have been of much concern in those bygone days. In this case, the term served rather as a badge of honor.

failed to learn of him during so many years?

The explanation is simple: there are no biographies of Daumesnil in English, and precious few references to him even in the best known English-language texts on the Napoleonic period, although you will find some mention of him in Lachouque's monumental *Anatomy of Glory*. But you will search in vain for his name in such standard reference works as David Chandler's *Dictionary of the Napoleonic Wars*. I will freely acknowledge that I myself was unaware of his existence until I started my research in preparation for writing the text for *Napoleon's Elite Cavalry*. Then, as I proceeded to put together the account of the creation, evolution, and campaigns of the elite cavalry regiments of the Imperial Guard, I kept running across the name Daumesnil, as he rose through the ranks of Napoleon's "dear children"—the *Chasseurs à cheval*—winning new laurels and honors with each campaign. I learned that his promising and brilliant career path had been abruptly and devastatingly interrupted by the severe wound he had sustained at Wagram in 1809, which earned for him the soubriquet, *la Jambe de Bois*, and that subsequently Napoleon had made him governor of the fortress of Vincennes. Other than that, all I had learned was that, after the Allied occupation of Paris in March 1814 and the capitulation of the French army, Daumesnil had rejected a Russian summons to surrender that fortress. (I should note in passing that, in referring to that episode in the Introduction to *Napoleon's Elite Cavalry*, I unwisely stated that "history does not reveal how that stand-off was resolved." That, of course, is nonsense, as I was later to realize to my chagrin.)

It was my chance spotting of a book in a dealer's catalogue that enlightened me on that score, and this launched me on a serious study of Daumesnil's entire life and career. That book was *Le Blocus de Vincennes en 1815*, by Adjutant Bénard. From that small volume I learned that Daumesnil had been governor of Vincennes for a <u>second</u> time, in 1815, and that there had then been a second, longer-lasting blockade of the fortress. The more I learned about the man, the more persuaded I became that his story was an extraordinary one, well worth recounting for those of us who are always hoping to discover some hitherto unexplored aspect of that heroic period.

There are a number of elements in the story of Daumesnil's life that have persuaded me that an account of this Napoleonic officer's career make it of particular interest. I believe that those elements and circumstances, together with the unusual nature of his character, combine to make the story of his career well worth the telling once again, and this time for what our French friends would call "an Anglo-Saxon" readership. Against the background of Revolutionary France, Bonaparte's rise to power, the establishment of the Empire and its fall, Daumesnil's character steadily evolved from that of a feckless youth, who ran away from home to volunteer in the army of the Revolution, to that of a renowned cavalry leader and, finally, to the status of a national hero, at a time when France badly needed one.

It seems clear that, from the earliest days of his military career, Daumesnil was determined to make a name for himself by performing exceptional acts of skill and daring on the battlefield, and it was not long before he began to do so. As campaign succeeded campaign and new opportunities for achieving distinction came his way, Daumesnil made the most of them. His spectacular deeds were soon the subjects of campfire stories among his comrades. Soldiers like to give their fellows soubriquets, and by the time that Daumesnil had on several occasions played a role in rescuing Bonaparte from perilous circumstances, he was being called by his companions-in-arms "Bonaparte's guardian angel." One may be certain that the young chasseur did nothing to discourage the use of that highly flattering appellation. But that is not to say that Daumesnil was any different from thousands of other young French soldiers, who were imbued with the realization that the Revolution had opened for them the path to military rank and honor that for centuries had been blocked by the notion that such rewards were the exclusive preserve of the ennobled. They were certainly very conscious of the fact that many of their own leaders had risen to prominence from a wide variety of humble beginnings, having been the sons of farmers, old soldiers, shopkeepers, and professional men.

I believe that the exceptional nature of Daumesnil's character gives a special quality to his story. The most evident element of that character was his unshakable loyalty, first of all to his emperor, but no less to his comrades, which constantly governed his actions in the face of the most severe tests. A man of enormous energy and resourcefulness, he was as undaunted by the blow that an unkind fate had dealt him in a physical sense as he was by the stature and characters of the enemies that confronted him in the latter phase of his career. His manifest courage, resolve, and exceptional qualities of leadership, demonstrated repeatedly on many battlefields, stood him in equal stead when circumstances placed him on a political stage at the highest level. With a warm, generous, outgoing personality and a quick wit, Daumesnil had a sort of swaggering self-confidence about him, which endeared him to his soldiers and peers, and seems to have astonished and baffled his adversaries, and even evoked their reluctant admiration. Never at a loss for a memorable phrase when the situation called for one, he coined a number, which have become hallmarks of his legend.

One of the most appealing aspects of Daumesnil's character is the extraordinary affection that he displayed toward his wife, Léonie Garat, and the three children that she bore him, an affection which was reciprocated in full measure. Given her remarkable character and the vital role that Léonie played in her husband's career, one could easily make the case that there are really two "heroes" to this story. A less admirable facet of Daumesnil's personal qualities, which was to cause his wife continuing difficulties, was his impecuniousness, the consequences of which were greatly magnified by Napoleon's final fall and exile.

The story divides itself into two almost equal parts: the years of Daumesnil's steadily rising career, starting as a regimental trooper and gradually earning by his exploits the position of a senior officer among the "elite of the elite"—the *Chasseurs à cheval de la Garde Impériale;* and a radically different second half, as a consequence of a disabling wound he received in 1809 at Wagram, which brought to an end his life as a brilliant cavalry leader, and embarked him upon a course which would lead to even more remarkable events, and ensure for him enduring fame among his countrymen.

I have noted that there are no biographies of Daumesnil in English. In fact, there are no more than two in French, which deal with his entire life. The first of these, *Le Général Daumesnil "L'Ange Gardien de Napoléon"*, by Roger Baschet and published in 1938, makes for very entertaining reading, being written in a highly romantic fashion. It is just that quality, however, that makes it unwise to accept this account at its face value, tempting though it may be to do so. It is clear that the author has repeatedly created dialogues from his own imagination, and, in at least one instance, he recounts a seemingly extraordinary episode involving Daumesnil, which, however, has no factual foundation.

The second of these biographies is *Daumesnil*, by Henri de Clairval, a great-great grandson of Pierre Daumesnil. Published in 1970, this volume's text differs sharply from that of Baschet's in that it is strictly factual, to the extent that any biography written almost 150 years after the death of its subject can be said to be. In fact, it is Monsieur de Clairval's account of his ancestor's life and career that forms the framework for this volume, which could not have been written without that essential foundation stone.

When I first had the good fortune to meet Monsieur de Clairval, and to tell him of my intention to write this book, he unhesitatingly assured me of his full cooperation, which he has since consistently extended to me in the most generous way possible. As a consequence, I have had complete access not only to his own extensive personal records, but to the archives of other members of the family as well. At the same time I have had the great advantage of being able to draw on his own extensive research in such critically valuable documentation centers as the *Service Historique de l'Armée de Terre (S.H.A.T.)*, at Vincennes, the archives of the Foreign Ministry, the National Archives and other such centers.

At our first meeting, I explained to M. de Clairval that I did not wish simply to translate his own work, however much I admired it, but rather to try to add something of my own to it. It should be absolutely clear, however, that in many instances I am, in fact, translating passages from his book quite literally, simply because there is no other source for the information in question. In many instances footnotes will serve to identify specific documents from the family's archives, while in other cases the source of quotations will be obvious. Probably the single most valuable source for the events in Daumesnil's life, subsequent to his marriage in 1812 to Léonie Garat, is the diary, *Journal de mes souvenirs*, which she kept throughout their marriage, and which was the basis for the memoirs, which she wrote in later years. M. de Clairval has drawn extensively on that *Journal*, as have I, in his footsteps.

Among the documents of a personal nature preserved in M. de Clairval's archives is a number of personal letters, exchanged between Daumesnil and Léonie whenever they were separated. Their very affectionate nature provides a touching insight into what obviously was a very happy marriage, notwithstanding the many rocks and shoals through which their little family was forced to navigate.

As for Daumesnil himself as a source, although he had fifteen years of retirement in which to have composed his memoirs, he was no Marbot. His formal education had been interrupted at the age of 17, when, as a result of an impetuous action with fatal consequences, he felt forced to leave home and "go for a soldier." The turbulent and distracting years of his youth may account for what was apparently an indifferent performance as a student, but his native intelligence and quick wit would ensure that, as he rose through the ranks to increasingly senior and responsible roles in the most prestigious of the French army's regiments, he would successfully assimilate the skills in composition expected of a senior officer, almost continuously in the company and society of Napoleon's glittering entourage.

I am also in debt to others who have made significant contributions to this work. First among them is the late John Elting, who had previously done so much to provide me with assistance while I was writing *Napoleon's Elite Cavalry*. Even toward the end of his life, when his strength was ebbing, John never failed to respond promptly to a query of mine, or to comment on a point that I had raised with him. I have had complete access to the exceptionally fine library of John and Katherine Hart, both deeply versed in matters relating to the Allied occupations of Paris in 1814 and 1815, and it has proved to be an exceptionally valuable resource. I am especially indebted to *Le Général* M. Berlaud, *Chef du Service Historique de l'Armée de Terre* (S.H.A.T.), at Vincennes, for his kindness in facilitating my access to the invaluable archives of that institution. I am grateful as well to Madame Monique Pergeline, treasurer of the society, "Patria Familia," for her very helpful research in my behalf in those archives. Guy Démoulin, of Toulon, has been of great help to me with respect to the historical background for this narrative. My thanks also go to my indefatigable editor, Dr. Paula Turner.

In an effort to gain an understanding of the image of Daumesnil formed by the Allied commanders of the blockades of Vincennes during the two occupations of Paris and their reactions to his tactics and strategies, I sought the help of a Berlin friend and research specialist,

Angelika Iwitzki, who had ready access to, and familiarity with, the various military archives in that city. Her industrious search revealed nothing that was not available in more easily available records. (This apparent absence of any record of the Prussian involvement with the two blockades of Vincennes suggests to me that the principal officers involved, from Blücher down, didn't regard those experiences as being among their finest hours.) However, the eminent authority on Prussia's role in the Napoleonic wars, Peter Hofschröer, was kind enough to provide me with extremely useful information relating to the blockade of Vincennes in 1815. It was from within that information, in fact, that I was able to prove to my satisfaction— and I hope, to others'—that in 1815 the Prussian high command did attempt to bribe Daumesnil to surrender Vincennes to them.

The best insight into Allied attitudes with respect to the problem of French fortresses which did not submit after the capitulation of the French army in the wake of Waterloo and its withdrawal to Paris— Vincennes was far from unique in that respect—is provided by the Duke of Wellington's contemporaneous dispatches. On the other hand, not all of Wellington's biographers have portrayed accurately the Duke's role with respect to Daumesnil's refusal to surrender Vincennes to the Allies in 1815. A notable example of an overly worshipful—and entirely fictional— account of the Duke's actions in that regard may be found in *The Age of Wellington*, by Leonard Cooper, in which the author describes the supposed summary capitulation of Vincennes at the mere sight of British troops drawn up outside the fortress's walls. I need hardly say that there isn't a word of truth to it.

Now it's time to let the story tell itself. I can only hope that the reader will find it as absorbing and moving as I have.

CHAPTER ONE
A TUMULTUOUS YOUTH

O n the façade of a small house on La Place du Gras in Périgueux, once the capital of the province of Périgord and now the principal city in the Department of Dordogne, there is affixed a marble plaque, on which are inscribed the words:

Maison Daumesnil
Ici naquit
Le Général
Daumesnil Lieut.
Général des
Armées du Roi
Le 27 juillet 1776[1]

The infant given on that day the characteristically Périgordian name, Yrieix, would, before many years had passed, have ceased to use that baptismal name in favor of the more traditional "Pierre," and it is with the latter name that the subject of this volume has come down to us through history. Perhaps it was deference to his adopted region that prompted Jean-François Daumesnil to give his son a name in consonance with his birthplace, but Jean himself was a native of Normandy, having moved to Périgord from a small town in Calvados, Fresney-le-Puceux, where he had been born and grown to manhood. Daumesnils can be found in that town's parish records as far back as the end of the sixteenth century. There is reason to believe that they were farmers. In nearby Saint-Aignan, there had existed for centuries what may have been another branch of the family, whose members, belonging to the nobility, took their name from their lands—d'Aumesnil.

In 1758, at the age of 29, Jean Daumesnil left Fresney-le-Puceux and

---

1 Daumesnil House—Here was born—General—Daumesnil Lieutenant—General of the—King's Armies—on 27 July 1776.

established himself in Périgueux as a shopkeeper, dealing in fashionable goods such as gloves, ladies' hats stockings, fabrics, and jewelry. A widower, he had no children from his first marriage. In April 1766 he would marry again, this time to a young woman from Clermont-Ferrand, Anne Pietre. The following year he bought the house on La Place du Gras, on the ground floor of which he installed his shop, reserving the upper three floors and attic for family use. Jean seems to have enjoyed a modest commercial success, since, on his death in 1811, he left the house on La Place du Gras, a small farm, and some acreage to his children.

The Daumesnils had five children: Honorée, Léonard, Arnaud, Jean-Louis, and the youngest, Yrieix, called Pierre. Both Léonard and Arnaud died in their childhood, and Jean-Louis, three years older than Yrieix, preceded the latter into the army. A local tradition has it that Yrieix spent several years of his childhood in Saint-Priest-de-Mareuil, with the Pindray family, but little else is known of his earliest years.

A childhood friend of Daumesnil's later described him as a charming boy, tall and slim, full of energy, and resolute in his behavior. He was deemed a good comrade by his schoolmates, who liked and admired him for his forthright frankness and good heart. He had a mischievous streak in his character, however, which seems to have given him the reputation of a scapegrace among some of the townspeople and peasants from the nearby countryside, who were the unsuspecting targets of some of his tricks. One of the pranks that he greatly enjoyed playing on them involved his cutting out silhouettes of monkeys, dogs or birds from cloth or felt, which he then whitened and surreptitiously attached to the backs of his victims. By the time that he was 12, he had demonstrated to his comrades an unwillingness to tolerate any injustice in his presence, and he was consequently looked up to by them as a protector of those who might risk being victimized.[2]

While Daumesnil seems to have made an effort to apply himself seriously to his studies, his turbulent and impetuous character, no doubt aggravated by the atmosphere of political turmoil then sweeping over Revolutionary France, evidently won out over his good intentions, for he was never more than a mediocre student. A further distraction from his studies arose from the fact that in January 1790 his sister, Honorée, had married a squire of Périgord, Louis de Chastenet d'Eglise-Neuve, an officer in the regiment of *Chasseurs à cheval* of Hainaut. Seeing his brother-in-law in his brilliant uniform may well have encouraged in Daumesnil's mind whatever thoughts he already entertained about a military career for himself, rather than the role of a businessman envisioned for him by his parents.

The turmoil of the Revolution had not passed Périgueux by. There a Revolutionary Committee was hunting down supposed enemies of the

---

2   Renaud, *Souvenirs de jeunesse du général Daumesnil,* manuscript in the Clairval collection.

new regime and dealing severely with them.[3] With France threatened by invasion on all of its frontiers, in August 1793 the government proclaimed "*La Patrie en danger*" and decreed the *levée en masse* (mass conscription). All young men aged 18 to 25 were called up, and battalions of volunteers were formed in the Dordogne at the same time that a new wave of terror had descended on Périgueux. It is scarcely to be wondered at that young Daumesnil found it difficult to concentrate on his studies. An unforeseeable event was to bring his student days to an abrupt conclusion, and set his feet on the path that he would thenceforth follow.

Daumesnil was 17 when one day, having in some way been insulted by an artilleryman, he demanded that the affair be settled with weapons. Inexperienced as he was, Daumesnil attacked his adversary impetuously, running his sword through the soldier's breast and killing him. Appalled by what he had done and the probable consequences of his rash act, he decided that the only course of action open to him was to flee Périgueux at once, which he proceeded to do. With the intention of joining his brother, Jean-Louis, in the army, he set out on foot for Toulouse, some 200 kilometers away.

---

3 Louis de Chastenet had emigrated, leaving Honorée and their daughter, Julie, in Périgueux. For whatever reason, he never returned to France, even after the fall of the Empire, ending his days in Hamburg. Julie never married, and died in 1870.

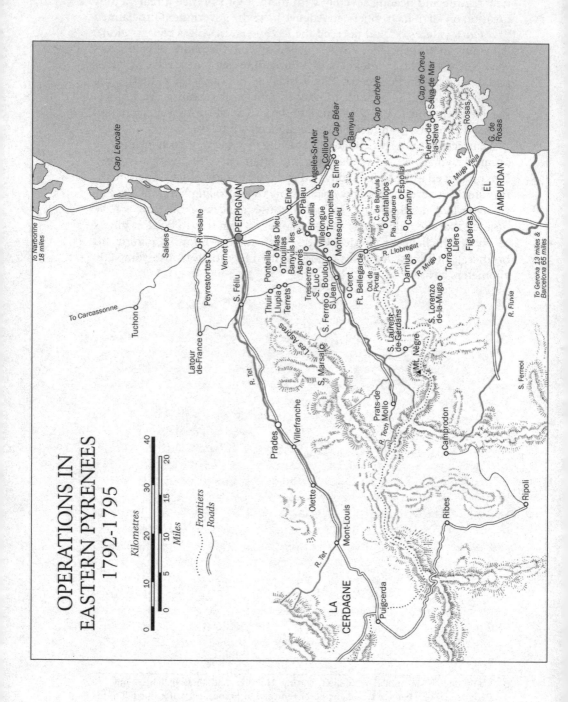

OPERATIONS IN
EASTERN PYRENEES
1792-1795

Kilometres

Miles

Frontiers
Roads

CHAPTER TWO
A GRIM INTRODUCTION
TO THE LIFE OF A SOLDIER

1793

France's Revolution had inspired in the Spanish monarchy the concept of a "crusade" to save the life of Charles IV's Bourbon relation, Louis XVI. Charles had set, as a condition for Spain's continuing neutrality in the wars of the Revolution, the preservation of Louis' life. Consequently, the execution of Louis in January 1793 had resulted in the *de facto* severing of the Bourbon "family compact" uniting Spain and France in opposition to England. On 9 March 1793 France declared war on Spain, and on 16 April 1793 a Spanish army advanced into France, quickly capturing Céret on the Tech, south of Perpignan.

An *Armée des Pyrénées* had been formed on 1 October 1792, and on 30 April 1793 it was divided into the *Armée des Pyrénées Occidentales* and the *Armée des Pyrénées Orientales* (Armies of the Western and the Eastern Pyrenees). The sector for which the latter was responsible extended from the mouth of the Rhône to the left bank of the Garonne, while the former's sector extended from that point to the left bank of the Gironde, well up France's Atlantic coast. It is the *Armée des Pyrénées Orientales* with which we are now concerned. R.W. Phipps[1] says of the *Armée des Pyrénées Occidentales* that it was the least interesting of the forces of the Republic, noting that it gave only one marshal, Moncey, to the Empire. In contrast, five marshals of the Empire emerged from the eastern army—Lannes, Bessières, Augereau, Victor, and Pérignon. The western army is also of less interest than its eastern counterpart because the Spanish strategy gave a much higher priority to their effort on the eastern front, where they mounted a very aggressive—and initially successful—drive to regain for Spain the one-time Spanish province of Roussillon. The Spanish court

---

1 Phipps, *The Armies of the First French Republic*, vol.1, p. 144. The map opposite is by Alex Jamison, and is based on one of Phipps' maps.

wished to remain on the defensive in the west, however, and to limit operations there to a demonstration.

Before we pick up the thread of Yrieix's story, it may be useful for the reader to know something of the status and condition of the army that he was to join in November of 1793. The *Armée des Pyrénées Orientales* had much in common with France's other Revolutionary armies, although in its case those characteristics seem to have been carried to an extreme degree. Together with their brothers-in-arms battling on France's other frontiers, many of its ill-clad, half-starved, and miserably armed soldiers were raw levies, lacking any but the most rudimentary training. It seems to have been, in effect, a poor relation of the other armies, overshadowed by the greater drama of the struggles in the east and south against the Coalition powers.

In May 1793 the army had 10,800 active troops, of whom some 2,000 were regulars. An additional 10,289 were in garrisons throughout its operational zone. There were critical equipment shortages, even among the active troops, seven-eighths of whose muskets lacked bayonets. 8,000 of their muskets were damaged or broken, and those that were functional were a mixture of ill-matched firearms of a great variety. Some of the men were armed only with pikes, and it was well into 1794 before muskets could be issued to them. Shoes were in acutely short supply, and some soldiers were forced to cut sections from their packs to fashion crude shoes for themselves. Finally, the army commissaries decreed that the local inhabitants would have to give their shoes to the soldiers, and make do themselves with wooden sabots.

The cavalry consisted largely of recruits lacking in training. Its commander, *général de brigade* André La Barre, wrote "I am sad to have cavalry so bad in every respect, and I see only dishonor for whoever commands it."[2] On the contrary, his own courageous and skilful leadership of the army's cavalry, before his needless death on the

---

2 De la Barre (he had dropped the nobiliary particle out of sensitivity to Republican prejudices) was born in a French fort in Louisiana in 1749, and from his boyhood he had been a soldier in a wide variety of cavalry regiments, initially royal and then Republican. He had served as a dragoon officer under Lafayette during the American Revolution, and in 1779 had been wounded during the siege of Savannah, Georgia. On 5 January 1794 he had come with Dugommier to the Army of the Eastern Pyrenees after the siege of Toulon, in which he had distinguished himself.

In that same year he had given himself, perhaps out of a sense of Republican zeal, the first name of *Pioche* (pickaxe), the name of his birth date on the Republican calendar. He was far from unique in doing so, however. When Edouard Milhaud, the most fiery and violent of the Representatives attached to the army, re-baptised himself "Cumin," it became obvious that that was the thing to do. Consequently, General Doppet became "Periwinkle" Doppet, General Peyron wanted to be known as "Myrtle" Peyron, and among the other officers of the army there appeared a few Rosemarys, a Limestone, a Hazel, a Maple, a Jasmine, a Chervil, a Zinc, and so forth. Sergeant-major "Coriander" Petit is witness to the fact that enlisted men were not immune to this madness. Apparently Dugommier felt no compulsion to so humiliate himself.

Llobregat in mid-1794, reflected only honor on him. In some instances, no sooner had the forward element of the army received additions to its cavalry arm than it was necessary to send them to the rear, for want of adequate subsistence. It was frequently necessary to reduce hay rations, and in the last week of January 1794 there were simply no oats for the horses. In late October and early November of that year, feed was almost totally lacking. Some horses were dying, and all the others were noticeably thinner. At one point, the commander of Daumesnil's regiment, Colonel Mamet, wondered aloud "if their horses were expected to become accustomed to not eating. Must we watch them die?" he asked. *Général de division* Charles-François-Joseph Dugua, who had replaced La Barre after the latter had been killed, replied that the horses of the artillery and train were no better off—that it was necessary to gather grass and straw to feed the horses. Mamet replied that there was none to be had where he was, and that, rather than stay and see his chargers dying, he would bivouac with the outposts, carbine in hand. As it happened, on 27 October of that year the army's commander-in-chief, *général de division* Jacques Dugommier, himself was unable to leave Boulou to review some troops because the commissariat refused to deliver more than half rations of forage to him and his staff.[3]

The command situation bordered on the chaotic, with the army's chiefs coming and going at a rapid rate—ten within the space of ten months during the first year of the war. Those commanders, such as they were, had to deal with the constant interference of the infamous Representatives of the People—which is to say, of the Committee of Public Safety—who often took into their own hands, sometimes with disastrous consequences, the conduct of military operations, while occasionally dispatching to the scaffold generals whom they deemed to be lacking in competence or revolutionary zeal. After one battle, Representative Fabre, who had been eager to conduct operations himself, wrote in a report to the Committee of Public Safety, "Fabre conducted himself heroically," and signed "Fabre." The French commander at that juncture, *général de division* Luc Siméon Auguste Dagobert, nearly went to the scaffold for smiling when he read that report. Fabre publicly stated that any commander-in-chief was useless, and demanded that the position be eliminated.[4] (When the Spanish drove the French out of Collioure and the coastal forts in December of 1793, Fabre's vainglorious ambition cost him his life in that disaster.)

The Spanish army concentrated on the eastern front, consisting of some 30,000 regular troops, had launched its attack from a base at Figueras. It was superior to its French opponent in both cavalry and artillery, as well as numerically and in terms of experience. Initially led by General Don Antonio Ramón Ricardos, it proved to be a formidable adversary during the first year of the war, until Dugommier took command of the *Armée des*

---

3 Phipps, *The Armies of the First French Republic*, vol.1, p. 175.
4 *Ibid.*, p. 169.

Pyrénées Orientales on 16 January 1794. At the outbreak of the war, the only French cavalry available to oppose the 4,000 elite Spanish cavalry were 50 dragoons and 300 *gendarmes* or National Guards.

In order for us to be able to visualize and understand Daumesnil's experience in this, his first campaign, we need to remember that at this point in his career he was merely a novice cavalry trooper, who brought to the army in which he had volunteered to serve nothing more than some familiarity with horseflesh, a high level of native intelligence, spiced with a sense of mischievousness and bravado, a modest level of schoolbook learning, an outgoing and warm personality, and a keen desire to make a name for himself by demonstrating reckless courage in the face of danger. Not a bad combination for success as a soldier, in fact. In his modest status as a chasseur trooper there is understandably little record to be found of the role that he played as an individual soldier. We have noted that Daumesnil was never a memorialist. In fact, it is in fair measure thanks to his wife's faithfully kept journal that we have knowledge of many important events of his life after their marriage in 1812.

For that reason, we must follow this first phase of Yrieix's career from, in the first instance, the broad perspective of the actions of the *Armée des Pyrénées Orientales* during this war, then from knowledge of the role played by the cavalry of that army, and finally, from the few specific references to his regiment's participation in the various skirmishes, combats, and battles of the war. From the French side, partly because of the materiel poverty of the army's cavalry arm and partly because of the nature of the terrain where much of the action took place, this was primarily an infantryman's war. Phipps observes that Bessières, being in the cavalry, had much less opportunity for coming to the fore than the four other future marshals in the army, although, even as a captain, he was beginning to be noticed. It seems possible that Yrieix found himself in the squadron with the then lieutenant Bessières not long after he joined the regiment. In any case, he was soon to attach himself to the rising star of that future marshal, forming a personal relationship that was to stand the young chasseur in good stead as his career evolved.

The war started badly for the French on both fronts. The commander-in-chief of the *Armée des Pyrénées Orientales* was *général de division* Deflers (in pre-Revolutionary days the Marquis de Flers), who had at his disposal to resist the Spanish invasion of Roussillon "the remnants of poorly organized units, undisciplined, ill-clad, badly equipped, and very badly armed."[5] An officer of limited experience and ability, Deflers was fortunate to have as his subordinate that valiant old soldier, Dagobert, recently joined from the *Armée d'Italie*. In anticipation of a Spanish attack, Deflers had placed Dagobert, with some 5,000 troops, in defensive positions south of Perpignan. When General Ricardos hit them with

---

5   Picard, *La Cavalerie dans les guerres*, p. 55.

15,000 men, Dagobert was compelled to pull back, but the Spanish general failed to pursue his advantage, instead withdrawing to his army's camp at Boulou on the Tech, still well north of the Franco-Spanish border.

The day ended ignominiously for the French when Dagobert's troops panicked and fled to the presumed shelter of Perpignan's walls, carrying with them troops that Deflers had been bringing forward as reinforcements. When this disorganized mob arrived before the walls of Perpignan, the city's garrison, mistaking them for the first wave of a Spanish assault, greeted them with a shower of case shot.

Ricardos, being unaware of the opportunity for the capture of Perpignan that his initial attack had created, instead set about besieging the French town of Bellegarde, on the border below Boulou. Deflers took advantage of six weeks of quiet on his immediate front to establish the large fortified *Camp de l'Union*, under the protection of the walls of Perpignan.

On 24 June, the small garrison in Bellegarde had surrendered, and Ricardos, believing that his rear was now covered, prepared a renewed assault on Perpignan, which he finally launched on 17 July. His formidable force consisted of 16,000 infantry, 6,000 cavalry, and 100 cannon, with which he counted on overwhelming the French defense. However Deflers kept his troops under the shelter of their fortifications, and beat off the attack. In the course of the battle, the then Lieutenant-Colonel Pérignon distinguished himself by his personal bravery, and thereby won a battlefield promotion to colonel.

Once again, the hesitant Ricardos pulled back his troops, and established a large, fortified camp at Ponteilla, to the southwest of Perpignon. On 3 August, the Spanish general, Crespo, coming from l'Île-sur-Têt to the west, had captured Villefranche above Perpignan on the Têt. While Deflers wished to remain on the defensive, some of his generals disagreed with him, and complained to the Representatives of the People about his leadership. The result was that the all-powerful Representatives removed Deflers from command, and sent him off to Paris, where in due course he was guillotined. In his place, they installed *général de division* Paul-François Puget, the former Marquis de Barbentane, who had professed himself as being "anxious to wash out his original sin" of having been a nobleman.

At the same time, the Representatives sent Dagobert with 3,000 men into the Cerdagne, off to the west, where on 28 August he drove the Spanish out of their camp at La Perche, thus relieving Mont-Louis, which had been under siege. In several cavalry clashes in the course of this affair, the Spanish lost almost all the 400 dragoons of the Sagonte regiment. On 4 September Dagobert re-captured Olette, seized earlier by the Spanish.

Meanwhile, back on the eastern sector of the front, Ricardos had not renounced his intention of taking Perpignan, and now began an encircling movement which enabled him to surround that town with four camps—

Argelès on the southeast, near the sea, Ponteilla to the southwest, Olette on the Tet above Perpignan (before its re-capture by Dagobert), and lastly Peyrestortes, on the left bank of the Tet and northwest of the town. Instead of perceiving, as Bonaparte would have done, the opportunity to strike at these Spanish camps in succession, Puget-Barbentane could only imagine being crushed between the Spanish pincers, and withdrew his head-quarters, along with some 4,000 men, to Salses, well to the north of Perpignan on the road to Narbonne, leaving the young *général de division* d'Aoust in command in the town. Puget soon decided that the responsibilities of high command were beyond his capacity, and submitted a letter of resignation saying as much to Lazare Carnot, the member of the Committee primarily responsible for military matters. He was immediately dismissed, but, surprisingly enough, ended his days in bed, rather than on the scaffold. The Representatives thereupon placed d'Aoust in temporary command of the army, and replaced Puget in Salses with a Doctor Goguet, who had now, by some chance, become a *général de division*.

The extraordinary tactical situation, with Spanish troops in Peyrestortes sandwiched in between Goguet's division in Salses and d'Aoust's main body in and around Perpignan, and with the French still holding Collioure and the coast forts south and east of the Spanish camp at Ponteilla, was broken on 17 September, when the Spanish advanced from Peyrestortes and took Vernet, near enough to Perpignan to permit Spanish artillery to bombard that town. D'Aoust reacted quickly, retaking Vernet with 2,000 of his best troops. When he hesitated to follow up this success, the Representatives made the decision for him, ordering that he continue up the road to attack Peyrestortes, in coordination with Goguet's troops, coming down from Salses. Despite a fumbled effort to achieve that coordination, the attack on Peyrestortes was a success, and seven flags, 43 guns, and 500 prisoners fell into French hands. Two days later, the re-capture of Villefranche further heightened French spirits, and an attack on the Spanish camp at Ponteilla, under d'Aoust's command, was quickly to follow.

On 19 September, the day on which the attack was to be launched, Dagobert and his men, fresh from their victories in the Cerdagne, arrived in Perpignan, where they were enthusiastically greeted. When Puget-Barbentane had submitted his resignation, he had recommended that Dagobert succeed him, and the Representatives had accepted that recommendation, while leaving d'Aoust in command at Perpignan until Dagobert could bring his troops there from the Cerdagne. Now Dagobert took command of the army.

Although he considered the plans for a frontal attack on Ponteilla ill-conceived, Dagobert let himself be persuaded that it should go ahead. With Goguet in command of the assault column on the right, together with all of the army's small body of cavalry, and d'Aoust leading the troops on the left, Dagobert and his Cerdagne division occupied the center of the assaulting force. Launched on the 21st, the attack went awry almost immediately, with Goguet bungling his assignment and d'Aoust making little headway on the left flank. Dagobert's valiant efforts to salvage the situation were unavailing, and after a disorganized withdrawal, the French found themselves back under the defenses of Perpignan, having lost 3,000 men (Bourdeau says 6,000), including some of the army's best troops.

When Dagobert insisted that the reluctant Goguet make a demonstration against Ricardos' left, seeming to threaten the bridge over the Tech, the Spanish general took this as evidence of an increase in the opposing French forces, and commenced a withdrawal to the fortified camp at Boulou. When the Representatives disapproved of a plan of Dagobert's to place his troops in the rear of the withdrawing Spanish, he furiously resigned his command, complaining bitterly to the Committee of Public Safety of the interference of their Representatives, and taking his troops back to the Cerdagne with him. The Representatives were glad to see him go, and put their favorite, d'Aoust, back in temporary command of the army. On 11 October, however, the command situation was again confused by the arrival in Perpignan of *général de brigade* Louis Marie Turreau, whom the Minister for War had appointed commander-in-chief. Seeing the state of disorganization in the army and the degree to which the Representatives were dominating its operations, Turreau, not wanting to become another of their tools, chose to leave actual command in d'Aoust's hands, while he undertook a detailed examination of the situation.

Free to act now, d'Aoust began a series of small-scale attacks on the Spanish, culminating in a major assault on the camp at Boulou during the night of 14–15 October. Successful at first, the obscurity frustrated the French effort to pursue the shaken Spanish troops, who were soon rallied by Ricardos and drove off d'Aoust's men, with no advantage gained. D'Aoust nonetheless persisted in his efforts to clear the Spanish posts along the Tech, and, after some success, on 26 November he was prevented from taking the important bridgehead town of Céret by the arrival on the scene of the Spanish general, La Union, with reinforcements for the beleaguered garrison.

We have now reached the point in our account of this first campaign of Daumesnil's at which he entered upon the scene. Before bringing him on stage again, however, I believe it is pertinent to quote some observations by Commandant Picard, since I believe they will help us to understand the circumstances under which Yrieix served his apprenticeship. This is what Picard has to say:

One thing that becomes clear with respect to the actions of our cavalry in the war with the Spanish is that the inexperience of our cavalrymen resulted in our not being able to take advantage of more than one favorable opportunity, whereas the Spanish cavalry, which always outnumbered ours in every encounter, was able on several occasions to restore the situation by itself, without, however, having been able to take advantage, to the degree they might have hoped, of the rout they had caused.

In a general sense, the progress of our cavalry on other frontiers is obvious, and if the regiments made up from the new *levée* are timid and uncertain in their apprenticeship, the other regiments, when they are well led, may already be compared advantageously with the best formations of the enemy. Less methodical in their manner of acting for want of instruction, and very different in accordance with their commanders, every day they enhance their tactical education by the lessons of experience in an unceasing war.[6]

Although the cavalry leaders of the *Armée des Pyrénées Orientales*— *général de division* André La Barre, *général de brigade* François Jean Baptiste Quesnel, *général de division* Charles-François-Joseph Dugua, and the commander of the 22nd *Chasseurs à cheval*, Colonel Mamet—are comparatively little known, it seems clear from their records and their actions in battle that they were brave and capable men, who cared for their men and their horses, and did the best that they could under extremely trying circumstances. As previously noted, Yrieix had the good fortune to be befriended by Bessières, whose qualifications as a cavalry leader need no elaboration here.

When the fugitive Daumesnil arrived in Toulouse, he found that an element of his brother's regiment was encamped near the city. At that time, the cavalry of the *Légion nationale des Pyrénées* consisted of the *Dragons de la Dordogne* and the *Dragons de Perpignan*. It seems likely that Jean-Louis was a member of the former. On 10 November 1793 Yriex enlisted in his brother's regiment, launching an extraordinary military career, which would draw to a close 39 years later, when he would die prematurely, a national hero rich in honors but in little else.[7]

For the first few months of Daumesnil's service, he was with the regiment's contingent garrisoned in Saint-Girons, and then in Rével-Sorèze, a fortified market town in the *Haute-Garonne*. Then, probably in April 1794, he was sent to join the regiment in the field. In the intervening months, there had been significant events at the front. On 26 November, Ricardos had pushed deeper into France, capturing Saint Féréol, north of Céret. Still another change in the French army's command had taken place, with General François Doppet, an incompetent former physician,[8] having been appointed by the Convention as Turreau's replacement, while d'Aoust nonetheless continued to exercise operational command. Attacks and counter-attacks continued to the east of the Spanish base at Boulou.

---

6 Picard, *La Cavalerie dans les guerres*, p. 60
7 On 21 November 1793 the two dragoon regiments were combined to form the 22nd Chasseurs à cheval, in which regiment Daumesnil would continue to serve until he became a member of Bonaparte's *Guides*, during the latter's first Italian campaign.
8 Chandler, *The Campaigns of Napoleon*, p. 25.

In one almost comical "ships-passing-in-the-night" incident, on the night of 6 December Ricardos prepared to attack the French defenses at Villelongue at daybreak on the 7th. As it happened, the French garrison at Villelongue chose the same moment to assault the Spanish post in the hills above them in the village of Montesquieu. 3,000 French from Villelongue and 5,000 Spanish groped past each other in the dark that night. The Spanish occupied Villelongue easily at daybreak, and the French, seeing themselves threatened by the Spanish force, broke and ran all the way back to Perpignan.

His forces depleted by this turn of events, the unfortunate Doppet could no longer hold the front as it then existed, and was compelled to pull back his troops to the *Camp de l'Union* before Perpignan. To cover the withdrawal of his heavy artillery, Doppet secured the Representatives' approval to launch a sudden attack on Villelongue. On the 19th, two French columns converged on the town, one under the command of d'Aoust, including a body of 500 picked grenadiers and chasseurs led by the then Captain Jean Lannes. The redoubt and camp were successfully carried, its Portuguese garrison massacred, and fifteen guns captured and removed. On 25 December Generals Augereau and Pérignon, who had recently joined the army, were promoted to the rank of generals of division, while Lanne's brave conduct in that engagement won for him the rank of *chef de brigade*, which equates to colonel. (Lest confusion arise, it should be noted in passing that in 1795 Lannes was dismissed for political reasons, but, nothing daunted, he re-enlisted as a private, and, rising rapidly in rank, in 1796 he was once again promoted to colonel, this time by Bonaparte.)

The final major action of the year ended with another serious set-back for the battered Army of the Eastern Pyrenees. With d'Aoust now formally in full command, on 20 December French positions on the coast at Fort Saint-Elme, Collioure, and Port-Vendres were seized by a Spanish force led by General La Cuesta. Once again the French were obliged to withdraw to the vicinity of Perpignan. Despite a stout rearguard defense by Pérignon, the French lost 7,700 men and 23 guns in this action. The boastful and inept Representative Fabre had fallen in the action at Collioure, his body found beneath a mound of corpses.

This humiliating climax to a year in which the Spanish more often than not bested their French opponents contrasted unfavorably with the successes of the Republic's armies on France's other frontiers, and the Convention was quick to conclude that treason must have played a role in this disastrous conclusion to the campaign of that year. D'Aoust had no sooner led his troops back to the *Camp de l'Union* than he was sent off to Paris, were the scaffold awaited him.

∞

1794

In January 1794, the fortunes of the heretofore luckless Army of the Eastern Pyrenees took a significant turn for the better, with the arrival from his victory at Toulon of *général de division* Jacques Dugommier. He brought with him 10,500 men from the force before Toulon, although, to his great regret, he was unable to include among them his friend, *lieutenant-colonel* Bonaparte, the commandant of artillery during that siege. (The latter was promoted to *général de brigade* and sent off to command the artillery of the *Armée d'Italie*.) Not only did his victory at Toulon confer on Dugommier a prestige and authority absent in his numerous predecessors in the army, but he had the additional advantage of being himself a member of the Convention, and consequently a colleague of the Committee's Representatives. Phipps comments that "this army had been in the hands of the Representatives to an extent unknown elsewhere." Now that deplorable situation was about to change. New Representatives, Jean-Baptiste Milhaud and Soubrany, had come with Dugommier, and he had already established good working relations with them. (Milhaud was to go on to become a famous cavalry general under the Empire.)

Dugommier was appalled by the condition of the army he had inherited. He found that half of his men had no arms or bad ones, that his artillery scarcely existed, and that the horses of the cavalry and train were starving for want of forage. Not surprisingly, he concluded that his first priority had to be a reorganization and re-equipping of the army before any serious offensive operations could be undertaken. He made a particular effort to bring the unfortunate cavalry into fighting condition, since that arm had suffered the most from the lack of adequate subsistence. At the beginning of April, the 22nd *Chasseurs* had 50 horses wounded, and its two squadrons were only fit for service by the end of that month. In the 19th Regiment, many of the men didn't even have spurs.[9]

On the Spanish side, a change in command had also occurred. The capable but irresolute Ricardos had died, allegedly after having been mistakenly poisoned in Madrid by a cup of chocolate intended for the queen's favorite, Godoy. His replacement was the Conde de la Unión, Don Luis-Fermin de Carvajal y Vargas, who had accepted the appointment with great reluctance, although he had already performed effectively in the campaign of the previous year. It turned out that he lacked the ability of Ricardos, thereby affording the French a further advantage in the forthcoming campaign.

Dugommier had as his principal lieutenants the two future marshals, Augereau and Pérignon, *général de division* François Franconin-Sauret, and a third future marshal, *général de brigade* Claude Victor. His cavalry commander was *général de brigade* La Barre. Popular with his men and known as a fine leader, he nonetheless maintained a strong sense of

---

9 Chuquet, *Dugommier*, p. 185.

discipline in the cavalry arm in the face of daunting logistic difficulties. Bessières was now Yrieix's squadron commander in the 22nd *Chasseurs*, while also serving as an assistant to the *adjutant-major-général des chasseurs*.

Dugommier gave command of the center, the strongest element of the army with 12,500 men, to Pérignon. Augereau was to lead the right wing, 6,300 strong and the best drilled and equipped troops of the army, and Sauret was given command of the 5,000 men making up the left wing. Victor had under him the 3,000-man reserve. The small cavalry force was divided among the three attack columns in this manner:

Sauret's *division de gauche*		100	men
Pérignon's *division du centre*	Brigade La Barre	1,357	"
	Détachement Quesnel	550	"
Augereau's *division de droite*		80	"
Total		2,087	"

For the first time in its brief existence, the Army of the Eastern Pyrenees was a formidable force, led by experienced, capable, and determined officers. Even the Representatives had accepted a less intrusive role in the army's operations.

The campaign of 1794 was opened by Dagobert, who had returned from Paris after successfully facing down the members of the Committee and on 18 March resuming command of the *division de Mont-Louis*, in the Cerdagne on the army's westernmost flank. On 7 April he crossed the border at Puigcerda and attacked and occupied Belver. He even managed to push on farther along the Segre to Urgel, but was unable to overcome its fortifications for want of any heavy artillery. Accordingly, he withdrew his force to Puigcerda, where on the 21st he died from a fever. Since Dagobert lacked any personal funds of his own, his men had to take up a collection to make possible a fitting funeral for the old soldier.

The Committee had ordered that the forts on the coast, which had been captured by the Spanish in the previous September, be retaken, but no fleet was available to support such an action, so Dugommier instead directed his attention to the Spanish camp of Boulou, which the Spaniards had been significantly strengthening. It had become clear that there was a significant gap between the Spanish force on the coast at Collioure and their main body based in the vicinity of Boulou. Dugommier therefore devised a plan by which Sauret's division, supported by the reserve, would hold the Spanish on the coast in check while Pérignon would lead the center division across the Tech to the east of Boulou and swing around behind the Spanish camp there. Augereau's role was to appear to threaten the Tech bridge at Céret, in order to draw Spanish troops away from the center of their line.

The operation was set in motion before midnight on 29 April, when the center division crossed the Tech below Boulou, aiming for the fortified Spanish post at Montesquieu. By 8 a.m. the following morning, Pérignon stood with his men on the ridge above that post, expecting that the Spaniards would evacuate their position as soon as they realized their predicament. When they showed no signs of doing so, Representative Milhaud impatiently precipitated a French assault, and by 2 p.m. the post was in French hands. Pérignon had been reinforced by Victor's reserve and had all of the army's cavalry, so he had two-thirds of the army under his command.

The battle was renewed the following day, 1 May, and, Phipps comments, "For the first time, the French cavalry had its chance." La Barre had gathered his regiments behind the *Trompettes Basses*, a low range of mountains to the east of Boulou. When he saw the Spanish beginning to withdraw from their camp there, he observed that the Spanish general Montforte had divided his force of 800 dragoons, sending half of them across the bridge at Boulou to the left bank of the Tech to protect the withdrawal of the Las Amarillas and the Mendinueta divisions, threatened by Augereau above the Tech. La Barre sent *général de brigade* Quesnel, with 800 men of the 15th *Dragons* and the 14th *Chasseurs*, in pursuit of those of Montforte's dragoons who had remained on the right bank of the river and were heading for Céret.

Taking "his two best regiments, the 1st *Hussards* and the 22nd *Chasseurs*"[10] and a half battery of light artillery, La Barre led them across the Tech at a ford below Boulou and dashed westward along the left bank of the river, crossing back again to the right bank at the ford of Saint-Jean between Boulou and Céret to cut off the retreating Las Amarillas and Mendinueta divisions and their supposedly protective force of Montforte's dragoons. By the time La Barre and his men reached the bridge, a number of the fleeing Spaniards had managed to get across it, but Bessières' squadron—in which Daumesnil was a trooper—broke down what resistance there was. When La Barre saw a small number of Spanish artillerymen attempting to evacuate their positions, accompanied by a column of some 800 infantry, he ordered his "flying artillery" to get off a few rounds at them, and the Spaniards quickly laid down their arms.

In the meanwhile Quesnel and his two regiments had dispersed those of Montforte's dragoons who had remained on the right bank of the river, who had then joined other Spanish troops flooding down the road to Bellegarde. There many of them fell into the hands of Martin's infantry brigade, which had been awaiting them at l'Ecluse-Haute.

The fruits of the victory were significant. 1,500 Spaniards had been killed and a like number captured. The fleeing Spanish had left behind all their artillery, tents, and baggage, 150 guns, and 1,800 horses and mules.

---

10 Phipps, *The Armies of the First French Republic*, vol.1, p. 176. Picard, *La Cavalerie dans les guerres*, p. 80, calls them "his two elite regiments."

French losses were astonishingly small, with almost none on the second day of the battle.

With Boulou in his hands, the road to Spain now lay open to Dugommier. However, he chose not to take it at that moment. With the smoke from the battlefield scarcely dispersed, Dugommier ordered La Barre to take 1,500 of his men to encircle Argelès-sur-Mer, and then to move on the Camp de la Justice, which protected Collioure from the landward side, in order to cut off its communications with other Spanish forces until the French infantry could arrive to undertake siege operations. When he was summoned to surrender Collioure, General Navarro, who had 7,000 fresh troops and 91 guns emplaced on strong walls, all supported by a naval squadron in command of the offshore waters, rejected the summons.

It was only on 4 May that Dugommier permitted Pérignon to advance beyond Boulou. Augereau, however, had not waited for orders to continue the pursuit of the withdrawing Spanish, and on the same day he had launched his troops across the border south of Saint Laurent-de-Cerdans. By 6 May he had penetrated as far as Saint-Lorenzo-de-la-Muga, where he seized the important foundry there, which had been supplying arms to the Spanish forces. Oddly enough, Dugommier was alarmed when he learned of this, exclaiming *"Nous voilà donc en Espagne!"* (But we're in Spain!) He thanked Pérignon for not following Augereau's example.

Leaving Pérignon to blockade Bellegarde, the fort on the border guarding the main road to Spain which the Spanish had captured the previous June, Dugommier went off to conduct the siege of Collioure and its related defenses, employing for that purpose Sauret's division and Victor's reserve. The first stage of the operation involved the investment of Fort Saint-Elme, which dominated Collioure and Port-Vendres. This was accomplished by carving out a path on its approaches sufficiently wide to permit the passage of siege artillery and ammunition. Orders were then given to haul the guns and hand-carry all the necessary supplies up the path, and generals, officers, *sous-officiers*, and privates set about doing so, urged on by patriotic songs and drums sounding the charge. In two days all was ready.[11] On 10 May, the garrisons of Collioure and Port-Vendres sortied at two in the morning in an effort to relieve Saint-Elme, catching the French sentries completely by surprise, and sending them fleeing in panic. The reserve came to their rescue, however, and order was soon restored. It may have been during this action that both Dugommier and Victor were wounded.

On 17 May, a breach was opened in the walls of the fort, and when Dugommier's proposed conditions for the capitulation of the fort were refused by its commandant, an intensified bombardment by the French began. Finally, on 29 May General Navarro, the commander at Collioure

---

11 Pelleport, *Souvenirs militaires*, p. 16.

and Port-Vendres, agreed to surrender all the Spanish positions to Dugommier. The next day, Navarro's 7,000 men laid down their arms at Banyuls-sur-Mer, and Victor was named governor of Collioure. In his terms for the surrender of Collioure, Dugommier had required that a corps of French *émigrés*, known as *La Légion de la Reine*, who were known to be among the garrison, be turned over to him. Navarro accepted that term, although he expressed doubt that there were any such men in the town. At the same time, he permitted the *émigrés* to be sent off by sea. This action did not escape Dugommier's attention, but he was just glad to see them safely away, rather than being turned over to the Representatives for a certain death.

A second Spanish action arising from the capitulation provoked a violent reaction from Dugommier, however. In accordance with the usual European practice of that period, the men of the captured Spanish garrison would in due course be exchanged for French prisoners. Both groups would thenceforth not be permitted to serve against France and Spain respectively. When General La Unión received his own men, he refused to turn over an equivalent number of French, declaring that the capitulation was null and void without his consent. He reasoned that, while it was true that prisoners returned to the French could not be used against Spain, they could well be used against Spain's allies, whereas Spanish prisoners returned to him were of no use to him. The French, he said, must be content with the possession of the forts and their stores.

Dugommier, the Representatives, and the men of the army were all outraged by La Unión's stand on the matter, and Dugommier sent him an angrily-worded protest. The Spaniard held his ground, making, however, the remarkable suggestion that the matter be referred to the United States for adjudication. In a fury by this time, Dugommier asked the Convention to declare the war with Spain to be "one of death," as had been previously decreed against England. On the eleventh of August the Convention accordingly decreed that no more Spanish prisoners would be taken. Augereau had been one of the strong advocates for this action, and his men, for the most part, took the decree literally. Dugommier seems to have intended it more as a threat, because he had earlier (at Toulon) demonstrated an awareness that such practices were two-edged swords.

Strangely enough, the Spanish, so merciless in later years in their struggle against the French occupiers of their land, in this instance refused to follow the French example. La Unión recommended to the king that, if such a decree were passed, it would be more dignified for Spanish generals to treat French captives more humanely than in the past, and the king approved.

With his left flank now secure, Dugommier went to Pérignon's headquarters at La Junquera, south of Bellegarde, where he resumed command of operations. It was only on 19 June he brought Sauret's division forward from Roussillon, where it had been resting, to

Cantallops, somewhat to the east of Pérignon's position. Augereau's division was still off by itself at Saint-Lorenzo-de-la-Muga, and consequently in an exposed position. After being driven out of Boulou, La Unión had managed to assemble a force of 15,000 infantry and 4,000 fresh cavalry, who had not been engaged in the disaster at Boulou. Believing that he would be able to destroy Augereau's much smaller force, on 19 May the Spanish general had launched a multi-pronged attack on that division. Augereau's well-disciplined and trained men had made short work of the Spanish, giving them no quarter, and leaving hundreds of their corpses strewn over the landscape. Once he became aware of the situation, Pérignon had assisted in pursuing the scattered Spanish force as it withdrew.

Having heard in early June that the Spanish were strengthening the defenses of Bellegarde facing Pérignon's front, Dugommier ordered him to reconnoiter them, and disrupt whatever activity was in progress. Dugommier apparently intended that this should be simply a demonstration, rather than a full-fledged attack on the Spanish positions. Perhaps for that reason he did not notify Augereau of this planned action, with unfortunate consequences for both of his divisions.

On the night of 6 June, Pérignon set forth on the main road leading toward the center of the Spanish positions on the right bank of the Llobregat, which he crossed on the bridge at Cabrénys. La Unión reacted vigorously, throwing his considerable cavalry force on Pérignon's flank. La Barre had accompanied the French reconnaissance with a small body of cavalry (probably including Bessières' squadron), and might have been able to delay or deflect the Spanish cavalry's intervention successfully. However, either in a thirst for glory or an excess of Republican zeal, Representative Soubrany, a former cavalry officer, took it on himself to take command of La Barre's 250 men in order to lead them in a charge across the Llobregat against the force of 1,200 Spanish cavalry, which was striking the flank of Pérignon's brigade of 1,700 men. Before Soubrany could carry out his intention, La Barre, his pride and honor piqued by Soubrany's vainglorious pretensions, put himself at the head of his handful of men, and plunged into the river with them behind him.[12] Splashing up the opposite bank of the river, La Barre led his men straight at the center of the Spanish squadrons. Hopelessly outnumbered, they were quickly engulfed in the mass of Spanish cavalrymen, and those who survived the brief clash managed to make their way back across the Llobregat. La Barre himself was fatally wounded, and was succeeded as

---

12 Another consideration in La Barre's mind may have been the number of "crimes" punishable by death that had been decreed by Representative Milhaud, which included "a general or officer who, in the course of combat, did not appear at the head of his division." Milhaud believed in the efficiency of having generals, who, in his view, had failed to demonstrate appropriate Republican virtues, shot in front of the troops they commanded, and this was done on more than one occasion.

the army's cavalry commander by *général de brigade* Dugua. The army had needlessly lost a brave and talented leader.

Pérignon's small force was still hard pressed as he tried to extricate it from a perilous situation. By chance, it happened that Augereau had been visiting an outpost of his at Torrados, almost in the rear of the force engaging Pérignon. Learning of his fellow commander's difficulties, he launched an attack on the Spanish camp at Llers, which relieved enough of the pressure on Pérignon to permit him to complete his withdrawal. Both divisions ended up back at their starting points, somewhat the worse for wear. Dugommier blamed Pérignon for having pushed matters farther than intended, but it is clear that the commander-in-chief's failure to coordinate the actions of his two divisions was in fair measure responsible for the unfortunate results of the operation.

The garrison of Bellegarde was still holding out, and on 13 August General La Unión made a determined effort to break the French siege of that key fortress. Dugommier had a force of 34,000 in hand—9,000 on each flank, and 16,000 in the center under Pérignon. For want of forage, the army's cavalry was reduced to 1,800. The Spanish had 45,000 men, including 4,000 good cavalry. 22,000 of those troops, formed in six columns, made up the attack directed against Augereau's division at the arms foundry near San Lorenzo-de-la-Muga. After an intense struggle, in the course of which the best of the army's brigadiers,[13] Mirabel, was killed, Augereau's men managed to gain the upper hand, giving little quarter, killing 80 officers and 1,560 men. Despite the "war to the death" decree, Augereau nonetheless spared 140 prisoners.

On the army's left flank, Sauret had successfully fought off the Spanish attack, while over on the coast at Col de Banyuls Victor had repulsed an effort by the Spanish to conduct an amphibious operation, forcing the landing force to be taken off the beach. Augereau's division had suffered significantly, however, and his position at San Lorenzo-de-la-Muga had become untenable. He therefore destroyed the arms foundry, and Dugommier called him back closer to the army's center and in touch with Pérignon on the main road to Figueras. Sauret's division had also been drawn to the center.

On 19 August, in a combat at Elne, Yrieix was struck by a bullet, which wounded him severely, fracturing his left thigh. He was taken to a dressing station, where a decision was taken by the surgeon to remove his leg. Before the operation could be performed, however, scurvy and putrescence had set in, and the surgeon concluded that, since the trooper was sure to die in any case, removing the his leg would serve no purpose and only increase his suffering. He therefore abandoned the idea of an amputation, and Daumesnil was made as comfortable as possible among the other wounded. Thanks to the young chasseur's robust constitution,

---

13 Phipps, *The Armies of the First French Republic*, vol.1, p. 184.

and doubtless to a determination on his part not to see his fledgling career so rudely cut short, Daumesnil survived this first of twenty wounds that he would receive during his career as a cavalryman.

When Yrieix had recovered sufficiently from his wound to be able to travel, he made his way back to Périgueux, where he had an emotional reunion with his parents. The circumstance that had prompted his hasty departure from the family hearth scarcely a year earlier seems to have been expunged from the town's collective memory by Daumesnil's return as a wounded hero. When his medical leave was about to expire and his parents were faced with the prospect of his return to the wars, it was arranged that he would be awarded by the General Council of Périgueux a "certificate of good citizenship." Its text read, "Before departing for the Army of the Pyrenees, Citizen Yrieix Daumesnil has been unanimously granted a certificate of good citizenship."

Traveling as best he could, Daumesnil made his way back to his regiment, probably rejoining it in early November. The army to which he returned was still desperately short of almost everything that an army in the field requires. Even the Revolutionary ardor, which had inspired many of the volunteers who had joined the colors, was flagging under the impact of the severe privations that the soldiers were being forced to endure. However, on 17 September the Spanish garrison at Bellegarde, consisting of only 1,000 men, had surrendered, thus liberating the last portion of French soil seized by the Spanish. Dugommier was able to persuade the Convention that the captured garrison should be spared, on the grounds that they might well have chosen to blow up the fortress and the French besiegers with it, if not promised their safety as prisoners. (As we shall see, a little more than a month later other Spanish garrisons employed that tactic, with devastating consequences for their French attackers.) On 21 September La Unión made an unsuccessful attempt to recapture Bellegarde. But there was till heavy fighting ahead before the arrival of the harsh winter, which would inflict severe hardships on both adversaries.

Driven by his determination to rid Spanish soil of the French, in a remarkable engineering feat La Unión had succeeded in establishing, over a period of some six months, 97 fortified positions of various types across the face of the French army's positions, evidently, as Phipps says, with the intent of "cannonading the French out of Spain." These "Lines of Figueras," bristling with 250 cannon and manned by 46,000 men, were also intended to thwart any French attempt to seize that major base for the Spanish army.

In preparation for an assault on the Lines, Dugommier had collected 24,200 men fit for battle. His plan called for his two flanking divisions to initiate the attack, with Pérignon remaining in reserve in the center with his own division and the cavalry. In a reorganization of the army in early November, detachments of the 1st *Hussards* and the 22nd *Chasseurs à cheval* had been assigned to Sauret's division on its left flank. Presumably the other squadrons of those regiments remained with Pérignon in the center. By this time Daumesnil would almost certainly have rejoined his regiment, but we have no information as to the location within the army of his squadron.

On 15 November there arrived at Dugommier's headquarters at La Junquera an individual who would in due course play an increasingly important role in Daumesnil's life—Surgeon-major Dominique Jean Larrey. That later renowned surgeon had come from Toulon, where he had been waiting to participate in a proposed expedition to liberate Corsica from the British that had been aborted when the blockading British fleet chased the expedition's ships back into the harbor at Nice almost as soon as it had sortied. Larrey had then been offered the assignment to replace two aging surgeons in charge of surgical services with the Army of the Eastern Pyrenees. He would go on in later years to become the principal surgeon to the Imperial Guard, and in that capacity he would have frequent occasion to provide services to Daumesnil, as we shall see.

A central strategic position south of the French headquarters at La Junquera lay between the opposing armies. Called by the French *la Montagne Noire* because of its dark woods, it was to give the ensuing three-day battle its name. When it had become evident that La Unión was planning to include this height in his line of fortifications, Augereau had anticipated him and occupied its crest, beating off a belated effort by the Spaniard to seize it. On 17 November Augereau opened the battle with an attack on Spanish positions on the Muga, from which he had recently been obliged to withdraw his own troops. By ten in the morning the Spanish left wing had collapsed, its troops in flight. Learning that the bulk of the army was not advancing, Augereau reined in his own troops and awaited orders from Dugommier.

No instructions would be forthcoming from Dugommier, however. At 7:30 that morning, when he had briefly absented himself from his position of command in order to breakfast, a Spanish shell had struck and killed the French commander-in-chief. An immediate decision as to his replacement had to be made, and Representative Delbrel, who was close at hand, decided that Pérignon was best suited for that role, since his central location on the battlefield gave him the best overall understanding of the tactical situation. On the left, Sauret's division, depleted by transfers of some of its strength to the center and to Augereau, was being hard pressed by a superior Spanish force, and had been forced to fall back, despite the arrival on the scene of Victor's men, coming from the vicinity of Banyuls and capturing two forts at Espola as they came.

It was clear to Pérignon that a pause in offensive operations was essential to permit a reorganization of the army now under his command. Accordingly, he instructed Augereau to hold the ground that he had gained, while the center and the left pulled back to their starting positions.

This break in the action provided an opportunity for a council with his commanders, and enabled his scouts to reconnoiter the Spanish dispositions. *Général de division* Jean-Baptiste Beaufort took Pérignon's place as commander of the center division.

By 20 November, Pérignon was ready to renew the battle. Again, the main weight of the attack was on the right, where Augereau's initial target was the great redoubt of Roure, which the Spanish had boasted could only be taken by God. Being unaware of that boast, Augereau's men took that position in stride, and in coordination with Beaufort's center force, they broke the Spanish line and sent its regiments fleeing in the direction of Figueras. On the left, Sauret's weak division had been hard pressed by Spanish General Vives' troops, but the rout of the Spanish center forced Vives to pull back as well. When it became evident that the retreat of the main Spanish body would not stop at Figueras, the right wing sent their artillery to Rosas on the coast due east of Figueras, while the rest of the troops of that wing marched south toward Gerona, passing west of Figueras as they did so.

While the Lines of Figueras had been broken comparatively quickly, the capture of its fortifications had not been without cost. When the Spanish saw their mighty redoubt and its associated works fall to the French, they touched off a mine which ran under several of the forts, and great explosions sent scores of French soldiers flying into the air. Larrey, who was in the midst of the advancing troops, gives a grisly description of the spectacle he observed at that moment:

> More than 100 of our volunteers were in those fortifications at the instant that those mines exploded. They were all lifted up with the debris of the stone parapets and of the artillery defending the forts. The fragments of that artillery, the stones, the men, or portions of them, were dispersed by the explosions, and fell here and there from considerable heights. Some of those victims of that frightful catastrophe ceased to exist at the moment of their ascension, while others died by falling on the rocks.[14]

Larrey and his surgeons went to work on the 76 men who had survived the explosions, as well as the other more than 600 wounded that the battle had cost the French. The psychological effect of the explosions of those mines on the French was to have deplorable consequences.

La Unión had made an effort to stem the flood of retreating men, but his escort had scattered, and the general was swept along in the confusion of the retreat. Shots were heard from a troop of Spanish cavalry passing by the spot where La Unión had last been seen, and the following day the French found his body, pierced by two balls. It was rumored that his own

14 Larrey, *Mémoires de chirurgie militaire* , vol. I, p. 91.

men had shot their general for the disgrace of the defeat inflicted on them. Phipps notes that this was a rare instance in which the commanders of two contending armies died in the same battle. The Spanish asked for their general's body, but the French, who had begun the battle intending to give quarter, had been enraged by the loss of their men in the mine explosions on the second day of the battle, and took their revenge by massacring 8,000 to 9,000 of their prisoners. When a Spanish general offered his sword to General Duphot, the latter ran him through. Eventually a sense of humanity prevailed, and La Unión's body was turned over to his father.

It was a great victory for the French. Since Captain Bessières and his squadron participated in the pursuit of the routed Spanish force, it seems probable that Yrieix was among them. When Pérignon learned that Figueras was only lightly defended by an ill-assorted group of fugitives from the routed Spanish army, he persuaded its governor to surrender the town. Over 9,000 men, 171 guns, herds of cattle, and an enormous quantity of supplies fell into the hands of the French. The "Hunger Offensive" had paid off. Larrey was astonished by the fine medical stores. He noted that the bandages were like cambric, and the lint was as fine as silk, made up in little packets tied with colored ribbons by the Queen of Spain and ladies of her court.

1795

There remained to be dealt with the Spanish garrison of some 4,000 to 5,000 men in the fort at Rosas, on the gulf of the same name. The commander at Rosas was made of sterner stuff than the governor of Figueras, and the French were consequently forced to lay siege to the town. Defended on the east by the sea, on the west by deep ditches and swamps, and on the northeast by a chain of snow-capped mountains, the defenses of Rosas posed a formidable challenge to Victor and his troops. By extraordinary efforts, however, they succeeded in dragging guns to heights above the town, rendering the town defenseless. On 3 February 1795 the Spanish fleet evacuated all but several hundred men, left behind to cover the withdrawal of the bulk of the garrison. When the Spanish admiral sent in boats to remove those men, Victor drove them off. The siege had been a cruel affair, carried out in freezing conditions in very difficult terrain. Larrey noted that some sentinels at advanced posts of both armies had been found by their reliefs frozen to death.

While the siege of Rosas was in progress, the new Spanish commander, General Don José Urrutia, had been pulling together, reorganizing, and reinforcing the shattered Spanish army behind the Fluvia, and on 16 January there had been a sharp clash on its banks. Cavalry encounters occurred on 1 March and on 21 March at Bezalu and Bascara, and again on 24 and 28 April at the same points on the Fluvia, as each army tried to establish bridgeheads on the adversary's bank. To cope with these Spanish harassing tactics, Pérignon was obliged to recall the 1,800 men of his cavalry who had been temporarily sent back into France, where the forage was better. On 6 May he launched a probing offensive, which precipitated a fierce but inconclusive cavalry action, after which the French were obliged to return to their positions.

Three weeks later, gunfire from the Spanish fleet, which was heard in the French headquarters, caused Pérignon to believe that a combined land-sea operation by the Spanish was underway, and when he sent his left wing eastward into the open country to deal with the imagined attack, Spanish cavalry, supported for the first time by horse-drawn artillery, succeeded in cutting the French army in two. With considerable difficulty, Pérignon extricated his divided force from its dangerous predicament, and withdrew his men to their initial positions. For their part, the Spanish re-crossed to the south side of the Fluvia.

Apparently because of the tensions existing between Pérignon and his fiery and strong-willed subordinate, Augereau, on 3 March the Committee had selected as a replacement for Pérignon *général de division* Barthélemy Louis Joseph Schérer, the commander of the Army of Italy, who in turn would be superseded in that latter capacity on 27 March by Bonaparte. Pérignon took the demotion like a gentleman—after all, he had only been the acting commander of the army—and simply asked to be given command of the reserve, which he was. It was only on 31 May, however, that Schérer finally arrived on the scene, with plans of his own for carrying the war deeper into Spain. He received no encouragement for such a campaign from the Committee, however, which turned down his request for reinforcements.

Settling for a more modest initiative, Schérer sent the center of his army south toward the rich farmland bordering the Fluvia to gather in as much of the harvest as might be possible. On 15 June, General Urrutia, sensing that the French were launching a major offensive, reacted strongly, and it was only Augereau's timely intervention, which compelled the superior Spanish force to disengage and withdraw. Nonetheless, the French had been able to gather some 300 wagonloads of wheat and to bring back a great many livestock. Schérer next imprudently attempted to establish a line of defensive positions in the inhospitable terrain of the Ampurdam. When his troops were brought down in large numbers by fevers arising from what Phipps refers to as "the poisonous marches" of that region, General La Cuesta drove the weakened and dispirited French back north for what proved to be the final engagement of the war.

Finally this pointless conflict was brought to a close by the Treaty of Basle, signed on 12 July 1795, which tied Spain closely to Revolutionary France. Paradoxically, the subsequent Treaty of Ildefenso (1796) was a virtual renewal of the "family compact," only on terms far more disadvantageous for Spain than had been such previous alliances. The French troops welcomed the end of a war which had inflicted great hardships on them, and been marked by almost as many humiliating setbacks as victories, while resulting in little in the way of tangible gains. But young troopers like Daumesnil and his comrades emerged from its rigors inured to hardships and battle-tested, having demonstrated repeatedly that they were able more than to hold their own against regular Spanish cavalry, almost invariably superior in numbers.

CHAPTER THREE
A FIRST GLIMPSE OF FAME

1796

At the beginning of 1796, the 22nd *Chasseurs* were transferred to the Army of Italy.[1] For the better part of a year, the commander of the Army of Italy had been *général de division* Schérer. At that time Bonaparte was employed in the Bureau Topographique in Paris, working closely with Lazare Carnot, the member of the five-man Directory of the French government responsible for military affairs. Orders emanating from Carnot, which Schérer considered did not take into account the actual capacity of the forces under his command, so exasperated the elderly general that he recommended to Carnot that the latter relieve him with the individual responsible for generating what he, Schérer, regarded as unrealistic instructions. Carnot took him at his word, and on 2 March 1796 Bonaparte was appointed commander of the Army of Italy. (As noted in the previous chapter, Schérer in turn was given command of the *Armée des Pyrénées Orientales*.)

Having married Josephine on 9 March, Bonaparte left for his command on the evening of the 11th. He arrived in Nice on the 26th, and took command the following day. He had brought with him Chauvet, paymaster of the Army of Italy, 8,000 livres in gold louis, 100,000 livres in bills of exchange, and 18,000 shoes. The shoes proved to be more useful than the bills of exchange.

The Army of Italy, which Bonaparte inherited from Schérer on 27 March, was in a deplorable state, with only some 37,600 men of its approximate total of 65,000 considered to be effective. Many of the Army's soldiers were in an openly mutinous mood, and instances of indiscipline were increasingly frequent. A week before Bonaparte took com-

---

1 In September 1795 Yrieix's brother, Jean-Louis, had been invalided back to Périgueux, suffering from a continuous fever caused by intestinal complications and pneumonia. He died soon thereafter.

mand of the Army of Italy, Sérurier's division had mutinied because its bread ration had been cut in half. In Augereau's division, the 69th demi-brigade had risen in revolt, saying, "Pay us, or you'll have no soldiers!"

The three senior commanders of the Army of Italy were *général de division* Jean Sérurier, *général de division* Pierre Augereau, and *général de division* André Masséna. The first two received their new, 26-year-old commander-in-chief with a mixture of astonishment, skepticism and apprehension. Masséna, however, had learned to respect Bonaparte during their service together at Toulon and during the campaign of 1794 in Italy. Sérurier and Augereau were nonetheless quick to perceive the mettle of their new commander-in-chief, and to accept without challenge his self-confident and tactically innovative leadership.

It was Bonaparte's good fortune to inherit as his chief of staff Louis-Alexandre Berthier, who had been appointed in that capacity to the Army of Italy early in March. For the next eighteen years Berthier would tirelessly—and usually uncomplainingly—serve Napoleon. Now he had as his *sous-chef adjutant général* Vignolles. The artillery commander was *général de division* Dujard. Among the officers who would rise to eminence in the meteor-like trail of the future emperor were, as his aides de camp, the flamboyant and fearless cavalry leader, Joachim Murat, the future marshal and Duke of Ragusa, Auguste Frédéric Marmont (whose title would in 1814 be transformed into a verb—*raguser*, meaning "to betray"), Major Jean Andoche Junot, and Louis Bonaparte. Another future marshal, Jean Bessières, who had come with the 22nd *Chasseurs* to Nice, was now also serving as an aide de camp to the commander-in-chief. To command his modest cavalry force, Bonaparte had the man reputed to be the Republic's best cavalry leader, *général de division* Henri Christian Michel Stengel.

By the 9 April 1796, the army, with a strength on paper of 65,402 men, was organized as follows: [2]

Advance Guard
    Commander, *général de division* André Masséna
        1st Division – *général de division* Amédée Emmanuel François La
            Harpe (8,614 men)
        2nd Division – *général de division* Jean Baptiste Meynier
            (9,526 men)

Corps de bataille
    3rd Division – *général de division* Charles Pierre François Augereau
        (10,117 men)
    4th Division – *général de division* Jean Sérurier (9,448 men)

---

2 Archives of the *Service Historique de l'Armée de Terre (S.H.A.T.)*, quoted by Col. Bernede in *Carnet de la Sabretache*, 1997.

Cavalry

Commander, *général de division* Henri Christian Michel Stengel

1st Division – *général de division* Stengel, assisted by *général de brigade* Marc Antoine Beaumont (3,090 men)[3]

2nd Division – *général de division* Charles Kilmaine (1,778 men)

Artillery and engineers – 4,770 men

Reserve – (5 divisions, 18,059 men).

The actual effective number of troops available was very considerably less than the army's nominal strength—perhaps as few as 37,600. For example, the supposed strength of Daumesnil's regiment, in the first cavalry division, was 900 men, but there were only horses for some 200 troopers. As it was, their mounts—fine horses from the Camargue—had been on half rations for a year or more, and were in correspondingly poor condition. (Soon additional cavalrymen were mounted on captured Austrian horses.) The cavalry consisted of chasseurs, hussars, and dragoons. The law of 8 January 1796 had denied heavy cavalry to the army on the grounds that the mountainous terrain in which the Italian campaign would be fought was unsuitable for the employment of such troops. The army's artillery consisted of 60 cannon available for field deployment.

There is some question as to whether or not Bonaparte's famous proclamation to the men of his new command, whom he reviewed in Nice on 27 March, was "touched up" after the fact by Napoleon at Elba. However, in the form that it has come down to us it so well describes the condition of the Army of Italy at that moment, as well as Bonaparte's vision of how he planned to employ this weapon that had been entrusted to him, that I believe it is worth quoting in full:

> Soldiers! You are hungry and naked; the government owes you so much but can give you nothing. The patience and courage which you have displayed among these rocks are admirable; but they bring you no glory—not a glimmer falls upon you. I will lead you into the most fertile plains on earth. Rich provinces, opulent cities, all shall be at your disposal; there you will find honor, glory and riches. Soldiers of Italy! Will you be lacking in courage and endurance?[4]

If anything had been needed to fire Yrieix's imagination and ambition and those of his comrades in arms, those words would have served to do so, and doubtless they did. Bonaparte had wasted no words in appealing to the Republican instincts of the soldiers, which had been largely submerged in the mens' minds by the hardships they had been forced to endure.

---

3 The 22nd *Chasseurs à cheval* were in this division.
4 Pigeard, *Les Campagnes Napoléoniennes*, vol. I, p. 7.

On 5 April Bonaparte moved his headquarters to Albenga, and set 15 April as the date for the commencement of the campaign against the combined Sardinian and Austrian forces, arrayed in an arc extending from north of Genoa on the French right almost to the Alps on their left. Facing the French left wing were 22,000 Piedmontese mountain troops under the command of Field Marshal Colli, an Italian-born Austrian officer seconded to the army of Sardinia. The Austrian forces, totaling some 40,000, were under the command of General Johann Peter Beaulieu. His subordinate commanders were Lieutenant Field-Marshal Sebottendorf, who held the left wing with 16,000 men, Lieutenant Field-Marshal Eugène Argenteau, whose force of 10,000 men was centered on Acqui, and a force of 6,000 Piedmontese, posted at Millesimo under the command of Lieutenant Field-Marshal Giovanni Provera, and intended to act as a *corps de liaison* between the former two. The only operations instructions given to Beaulieu by his masters, the Aulic Council, were simply to drive the French back into Provence.

The start of the campaign came four days before Bonaparte had planned to launch it, when, on 10 April, Austrian troops, under the personal command of Beaulieu, attacked a brigade of General La Harpe's division, commanded by *général de brigade* Jean Baptiste Cervoni, which had advanced as far as Voltri on the coast some 15 miles west of Genoa, at the time when Schérer was still in command of the army. Cervoni was able to withdraw his troops without serious loss, and Bonaparte, ignoring Beaulieu's thrust, sent 9,000 troops, under Masséna and General La Harpe, north to prevent the earth-fort at Montenotte, garrisoned by 1,200 French troops, from falling to attacking Austrian forces led by Argenteau. On 12 April La Harpe launched a frontal attack on Argenteau's 6,000 men, while Masséna struck them on the right flank and from the rear. The Austrian force was driven away from Montenotte, losing 1,000 killed or wounded and 2,500 men as prisoners. 1,000 of the Austrians' muskets were used to arm French soldiers, who had been forced to advance without firearms. Bonaparte had his first victory as commander of the Army of Italy.

Argenteau rallied what was left of his force, and withdrew northwest to Dego. At Beaulieu's request, Colli had sent four battalions of his men there, and Argenteau put the combined force to work fortifying the town. On the 13th, in order to pursue his strategy of separating the Austrian and Sardinian armies and eliminating the latter before dealing with the more serious opponent, Beaulieu's army, Bonaparte instructed Masséna to block any possible advance from Dego by Argenteau with half of his division, while he took the other half westward with Augereau's division in the direction of Ceva, held by Piedmontese troops. The French advance drew up before Millesimo, held at that point by a part of Colli's Piedmontese force. Colli's subordinate, Provera, commanding the Austrian auxiliary corps, had holed up with 1,000 picked troops in the ruined castle of Cosseria, a few kilometers northeast of Millesimo. On the 13th *général de brigade* Barthélemy Joubert led his troops in an attack on the castle, but they had to be withdrawn after the attacking force had suffered 900 casualties.

On 14 April, infantry of Augereau's division, led by *général de brigade* Jean François Ménard and supported by some of Stengel's cavalry from the reserve that Bonaparte had established at Carcare, captured Millesimo. On the same day the Austrian troops in Cosseria capitulated. The total French bag of these two engagements was an additional 2,500 Austrians killed, 9,000 prisoners, 22 cannon, and 15 standards captured.

With the fall of Cosseria, Bonaparte felt free to re-focus his attention on Dego, and ordered Masséna to launch an attack on it. The town, with most of its 5,000 Austrian defenders and nineteen of their guns, soon fell under an assault by La Harpe's division. This success proved to be short-lived, however, when the French troops, their spirits buoyed by their victory and driven by their impoverished condition, were soon scattered throughout Dego, looting and searching for food and drink. Unluckily for them, early on the morning of the 15th a force of five Austrian battalions, under the command of Major-general Josef-Philip Wukassovich, which had been ordered by Beaulieu to the defense of Dego, arrived belatedly on the scene, and quickly put to flight the French, sodden with sleep and celebrating, leaving the captured cannon once more in the hands of Austrian gunners. (Whether there had been time and guards to spare to send the prisoners back to the main French body is not clear.) Wukassovich sent off couriers to Beaulieu and Argenteau requesting reinforcements, and did what he could to prepare for a renewed French attack on the town.

The terms in which Bonaparte reprimanded Masséna and La Harpe for this fiasco may readily be imagined. Its consequence was that Dego had to be stormed once more later that day, at a cost of an additional 1,000 casualties. Wukassovich, and those of his men who had not been captured in this second assault, were driven northward toward Spigno by 400 men of the 22nd *Chasseurs,* the 7th *Hussards,* and the 15th *Dragons.* As they fled, Wukassovich's men abandoned 30 cannon in their traces, 60 caissons, 15 flags, and 6,000 prisoners, among whom were two generals and 24 senior officers. The 13 French cannon, which had fallen into Austrian hands at the beginning of the action, were recaptured, and on the battlefield and in the mountains around Dego a large number of muskets were collected. Meanwhile, Argenteau, having picked up two battalions sent by Beaulieu to Wukassavoch's assistance, had retired farther north to Acqui.

Having satisfied himself that his right flank was for the moment safe from any attack by the weakened and disorganized Austrian forces, Bonaparte shifted his attention and the main body of his troops eastward toward Ceva, aiming to destroy Colli's Piedmontese force, and thus compel Sardinia to break its alliance with Austria and sue for peace.

However, by the time the French reached Ceva and were preparing to attack the 13,000 Piedmontese, who had been occupying that town and its environs, they discovered that Colli had withdrawn his force to positions west of Ceva, and was moving them towards Mondovi.

Further fruitless maneuvers designed to bring Colli to battle occupied several more days, until finally, on the 21st, he was run to ground in Mondovi. In an attempt to cut off Colli's further retreat, Stengel had led his cavalry across the Ellero River south of Mondovi, planning to circle around behind the town. He had with him the 1st *Hussards* and two regiments of dragoons, about 1,000 men. Although an outstanding officer, Stengel had what proved to be for him a fatal flaw—he was literally short-sighted. When he launched his men in pursuit of the Piedmontese cavalry, which was well mounted and superior in numbers to the French, they turned about, obliging Stengel to fall back on his reserve, which was being brought forward by Murat, at that time an aide of Bonaparte's. Picard gives the following account of what happened next:

> Having received this reinforcement, Stengel wanted to resume the offensive, but, after having passed in close column order in a space between two rice swamps, he perceived the enemy formed in a line of battle, a half cannon-shot off on his left flank.
>
> Seeing that he had sufficient time, Stengel immediately took a decision and ordered "By the left in reverse order, line of battle!" Knowing that one of his regiments was composed entirely of men from Lorraine and Alsace, and that almost all of the officers of one of the other regiments came from the *Dragons de Lorraine*, he repeated the command in German. The movement that he had ordered was not in the regulations, although the regimental and squadron commanders would probably have understood it, if they had had a few moments to give it thought. But here the decision had to be instantaneous, followed by its prompt execution in proper order, which is difficult to achieve for an evolution performed for the first time amidst the dangers and tumult of the battlefield. The French column became entangled, and the enemy attacked its left flank, broke into it, and our regiments suffered considerable losses.[5]

Stengel threw himself into the midst of the Piedmontese squadrons, and was mortally wounded. (He would soon die, after having an arm amputated.) Murat, however, managed to rally Stengel's men, dispirited by the loss of their greatly admired commander, and restored the situation, leading a charge of the 20th *Dragons*, which earned him a citation in the commander-in-chief's report. In a letter to the Directory, Bonaparte made the point that it was above all the absence of horse artillery that had made it impossible for

---

5 Picard, *La Cavalerie dans les guerres*, vol. I, p. 116.

Stengel's cavalry to resist a superior force. Stengel was replaced as commander of the army's cavalry by *général de brigade* Beaumont.

On the 22nd, Sérurier's and Masséna's troops were able to occupy Mondovi without difficulty, its population having forced its remaining Piedmontese garrison to surrender. The rest of the day was devoted to re-forming the demi-brigades and cavalry regiments, whose pillaging soldiers had scattered through Mondovi and the nearby countryside. The morning of the 23rd Bonaparte sent Sérurier northwest to Fossano, and Masséna due north to Cherasco, dividing between them the bulk of the army's cavalry. On the 22nd, Augereau had already started his troops up the eastern bank of the Tanaro, with Alba as his immediate objective. Further splitting his forces, Bonaparte had sent La Harpe north to Niella, and Victor northeast to Scaletta. His succession of victories over the two opposing armies evidently gave him confidence that he was incurring no serious risk in so doing.

Obviously both Colli's and Beaulieu's intelligence resources were keeping them informed of these rapid deployments of the French forces, clearly intended to complete the separation of the Austrian army from that of Sardinia. The successive defeats of his forces, now retreating on every front and with the French driving them steadily deeper into his own territory, apparently convinced Colli's master, King Victor Amadeus of Sardinia, that it was time to call a halt to hostilities, and to make the best possible deal with Bonaparte. He therefore instructed Colli to ask for an armistice. Bonaparte's response was that, while he had no authority to conclude a peace, he would agree to an armistice if two of the three major fortresses of Piedmont—Alessandria, Tortona, and Cuneo—were sur-rendered to the French, and that, until he received a response, he would continue his operations. On the 26th, the king accepted Bonaparte's terms, and on the 28th Sardinian representatives signed the Armistice of Cherasco in their king's name. In addition to the surrender of the three fortresses, the French were granted free passage through Piedmontese territory, and the right to cross the Po at Valenza, should their commander wish to do so.

Bonaparte marked the conclusion of this phase of the campaign by issuing a proclamation to his soldiers, read to them by their *sous-officiers* at the daily morning parades. Their commander-in-chief exhorted them in these terms:[6]

Soldiers! In fifteen days you have gained six victories, taken 21 colors and 55 pieces of artillery, seized several fortresses and

---

6 I believe it's well worth reading the full text of this stirring proclamation, not only because in it Bonaparte outlines his further objectives in this campaign, intended to break Austria's hold on northern Italy, but also as an example of the remarkable rhetorical skills already at the command of this 26-year-old leader of men. See Annex B. (Its text is from Pigeard, *Les Campagnes Napoléoniennes*, p. 23.)

conquered the richest parts of Piedmont. You have captured 17,000 prisoners and killed and wounded more than 10,000....

The cost to the French of these victories had been 6,000 casualties.

At this point, the patient reader may say to himself—or herself—"That's all very well, but where does Yrieix Daumesnil fit into all of this?" And that's a fair question, although providing a precise answer to it is not easy, since it is even difficult to pin-point the specific actions in which his regiment took part, although we have noted above that his regiment participated in the pursuit of Wukassovich's men when they were driven out of Dego.

Several factors combined to reduce the importance of cavalry's role during this Bonapartist early version of a *blitzkrieg*: the mountainous character of the terrain in which it was fought, with little space for sweeping cavalry tactics; and the acute shortage of serviceable mounts, even of the half-starved variety. The government's refusal to assign heavy cavalry to the Army of Italy, in light of the first of these considerations, has been noted. The under-strength regiments of chasseurs, hussars, and dragoons which formed the cavalry component of the army were by no means idle, however, employed as they were in the traditional roles of light cavalry—advance post duties, reconnaissance, pursuit and harassment of enemy forces, and screening infantry movements. As captured Austrian horses fell into French hands, the regiments were gradually able to approach their nominal strength.

Specific, precise information regarding actions in which the 22nd *Chasseurs*—and, therefore, trooper Daumesnil—participated during this initial phase of the campaign is sparse, but some conclusions on that score may reasonably be drawn. On 11 April the army's cavalry were together with Masséna's and Augereau's divisions at Loano. When on the 12th the combined forces of Masséna and La Harpe turned Argentau's attempt to seize Montenotte into a rout, the Austrian survivors of that action were pursued by some 500 French cavalry northward though Dego, and almost to Acqui. On the 14th, when Colli was beaten at Millesimo, again the cavalry played a role in that victory. Stengel's fatal clash with Sardinian cavalry at Mondovi has already been noted. According to Henri de Clairval, the 22nd *Chasseurs* distinguished themselves at Dego, Millesimo, and then at Lodi on 10 May. Let us now follow events leading up to that last-named victory.

In the last days of April, Beaulieu had begun to withdraw behind the barrier of the Po, crossing to its north bank at Valenza before Bonaparte was able to collect and re-organize his battle-weary troops and prevent the Austrian from so doing. Rather than attempting a crossing of the Po at Valenza, with Beaulieu's troops entrenched on its north bank, Bonaparte directed some of his divisions to move eastward to Piacenza, their movement being screened by cavalry riding along the river's south bank.

Masséna and Sérurier were charged with staging a demonstration at Valenza, simulating a planned crossing of the river at that point, to try to hold as many as possible of Beaulieu's troops in their positions. The advance guard of the Army of Italy, as it hastened in a forced march toward Piacenza, consisted of 3,600 grenadiers and carabiniers, drawn from almost every demi-brigade of the army, 1,600 cavalry led by Kilmaine, and a battery of horse artillery, all under the command of *général de brigade* Claude Dallemagne, with François Lanusse and Jean Lannes as brigade commanders.

This advance force reached Piacenza by 09:00 on 7 May, and Dallemagne's men had begun to cross the Po, with Colonel Lannes leading the way. By 14:00 the French were across the river in strength. The following day an Austrian force of some 7,000 men, led by Liptay, had arrived in Guardamiglia on the north bank of the Po across from Piacenza, and was fortifying it, along with the nearby towns of Fombio and Codogno. With Augereau's leading elements across the river and in touch with La Harpe's division, Bonaparte ordered Dallemagne to drive Liptay's men out of those positions. As the Austrians fled from Guardamiglia and Fombio, Kilmaine's cavalry hastened them on their way, pursuing them into and through Codogno.

That night, La Harpe pulled his exhausted men back into Codogno, where they were unexpectedly attacked by advance elements of Beaulieu's divisions, converging with the remnants of Liptay's division. In the confused night action, La Harpe was fatally wounded by his own troops, and the French troops were momentarily thrown into a panic. Berthier, together with other senior officers, managed to bring matters under control, and the Austrians withdrew northward, joining the body of Beaulieu's force, which he had ordered to move toward Lodi, where he intended that they would cross and take shelter behind the Adda.

Bonaparte spent the 9th sorting out the elements of his army that had arrived in the vicinity of Casalpusterlengo piecemeal, almost all of them across the Po by that time. Kilmaine had been ordered to collect all cavalry at that point, except for those detachments with Dallemagne.

Early on the 10th, the bulk of Beaulieu's force had gained the eastern bank of the Adda, leaving only a small detachment of grenadiers blocking the road to Lodi north of Zorlesco and a detachment in the town of Lodi, evacuating supplies for transfer across the Adda. The Army of Italy's advance guard brushed aside the small blocking force, and, driving the surviving grenadiers before them, charged into Lodi itself. The Austrian commander, General Sebottendorf, either had not had time to order the destruction of the 200-yard-long wooden bridge across the Adda or had simply forgotten to do so. Dallemagne led his troops in a rush onto the western end of the bridge, where they were met by a withering fire from the Austrian cannon and infantry emplaced at the eastern end of the bridge, and forced to take shelter behind the town's ramparts. By this time, Bonaparte had arrived on the scene, and he promptly deployed the first cannons to arrive in positions to sweep away any effort by the Austrians to burn the bridge.

In order to be able to take Sebottendorf's force in one or both flanks, while the main body attempted to force its way across the bridge, Bonaparte sent Beaumont and Michel Ordener, with 2,000 troopers and some light artillery, half a league upstream from Lodi to a reported ford near Mozzanica, but the ford there proved to be less easily passed than had been anticipated, and consequently the attack on Sebottendorf's right flank was considerably delayed. Another regiment of cavalry, led by *général de brigade* Jean Baptiste Rusca, galloped off south of Lodi, where they were able to swim the Adda. Back in Lodi, Bonaparte had emplaced 24 of the army's cannon in positions to support the attempt by the main body to force the bridge. 3,000 of Dallemagne's grenadiers were formed into a dense column six men abreast, and, as the French batteries opened up on Sebottendorf's troops across the river, the spearhead of the column was launched onto the bridge, the army's leaders among the grenadiers and carabiniers.

The French were met with an intense fire from the Austrian infantry and cannon, and for a moment the column seemed to founder. Then Berthier seized a flag and, with Dallemagne, Lannes, and Masséna joining him, officers and men alike regained the momentum of their attack, and finally attained the eastern end of the bridge, driving its defenders off. As an Austrian counter-attack seemed to put the issue of the struggle in doubt and with darkness descending over the scene, Beaumont's leading squadron struck Sebottendorf's right flank, and almost simultaneously, Rasca's troopers sliced into his left flank, helping to render the Austrians' further resistance impossible.

Sebottendorf was able, however, to extricate his badly wounded force from the fracas, and withdrew eastward in the direction of Beaulieu's main body, leaving behind 153 dead, 1,700 prisoners, and 16 cannon. Beaumont's troopers drove the remnants of the Austrian force eastward through Cremona, with the French advance guard penetrating as far as the Oglio. While this was a noteworthy tactical victory for the Army of Italy and its fledgling commander, it had cost them some 350 casualties, and left the bulk of Beaulieu's force still in the field, undefeated and still constituting a significant obstacle to Bonaparte's ultimate objectives.

On 11 May Bonaparte gave his badly worn troops a brief respite, but the road to Milan was now open and the commander-in-chief was not one to dally. Beaulieu had withdrawn to Mantua, leaving only a small garrison in Milan's citadel, and on 13 May, when Masséna's division occupied the city, there was practically no resistance to its occupation. Two days later, Bonaparte made a ceremonial entry into the city at the head of his troops, acclaimed by much of the population as their liberator from the Austrian yoke. However, in the face of widespread looting by French soldiery—and officers—the bloom was soon off the bouquets with which the French had been welcomed.

Bonaparte soon had the army on the move again. Leaving 5,000 men to besiege the citadel, which was still holding out, on 22 May he set out with the bulk of the army in pursuit of Beaulieu's forces, by now disposed east of the Mincio, with small detachments left on its west bank to guard bridges. The French advance was temporarily arrested, however, by uprisings by the populace in Milan and in Pavia, where the French garrison's commander had surrendered the citadel. Bonaparte, hurrying back to Milan with 300 light cavalry and Lannes' grenadiers, found that *général de division* Despinois, commander of the troops besieging the citadel, had matters well in hand. Pavia was another matter, however, and there the revolt was suppressed with brutal measures. Bonaparte had the unfortunate officer who had surrendered Pavia's citadel summarily executed.

By the 28th, Bonaparte was ready to set in motion the river crossing. Augereau was to give evidence of preparations for an attack across the Mincio at Peschiera, while Kilmaine would swing down from Lake Garda with his cavalry on the 29th, leading the army's main thrust to Borghetto, still lightly held by the Austrians on the river's west bank At 0700 on the 30th, Kilmaine's force came up against a force of 3,000 Austro-Neapolitan cavalry screening Borghetto, and, flanked by grenadiers and carabiniers, drove the enemy back through Borghetto in disarray. As they retreated, the Austrian troops managed to break one arch of the bridge across the Mincio. This time there were no guns defending the un-damaged bridge's eastern end, however, and as soon as repairs had been made to the damaged arch, Murat led the cavalry of the advance guard across it in pursuit of the withdrawing Austrians. Almost simultaneously, *général de brigade* Gaspard Amédée Gardanne's grenadiers found a ford slightly south of Borghetto, and with little difficulty occupied the river town of Valleggio. Picard comments that this was the first time that the French cavalry, notwithstanding the poor condition in which it had been, had successfully gotten the better of Austrian cavalry. They had captured nine cannon, two standards, and 2,000 men, including the commander of the Neapolitan cavalry, the Prince de Cuto.

With his divided forces badly battered, Beaulieu collected them as best he could, and pulled back to Castelnuovo, shadowed by Kilmaine's cavalry. By 1 June, he had started to withdraw northward along the Adige, east of Lake Garda. With Beaulieu temporarily disposed of, Bonaparte established his headquarters in Vallegio, and turned his attention toward Mantua.

But Bonaparte's plans were very nearly rudely interrupted on 1 June, when scouts from Sebettondorf's division managed to make their way into the town's center and to reach his lodging, where he had paused briefly to bath his feet. The picket scarcely had time to give the alarm, and Bonaparte only avoided capture by taking flight over a garden wall, "one

51

boot on and one boot off." This incident made it evident that better protection was required for the commander-in-chief, and on the same day that the incident occurred an order of Bonaparte's prescribed the formation of an elite corps, to provide for his personal security and to serve as a guard for the headquarters at all times. Two battalions of grenadiers, under the command of Lannes, were given the latter responsibility, while the then Captain Bessières[7] was charged with organizing a mounted unit of 50 chasseurs, to be known as the *Compagnie des Guides à cheval du Général en Chef*, which would assure the commander-in-chief's personal security wherever he went. At the same time, it would form a permanent reserve under his immediate command. It was to be composed of men with no less than ten years' service, who had distinguished themselves in some manner. This order was the "birth certificate" of the *Chasseurs à cheval*, first, of the Consular Guard, and then, of the Imperial Guard.

The company of *Guides* quickly made a name for itself during the Italian campaign. When in September of 1796 its strength was raised to 136 men, each cavalry regiment was required to nominate eight of its bravest men. The records of the candidates were carefully examined, and only the best were selected. Not only were the candidates required to have given proof of unexcelled bravery, but also to possess exceptional moral qualities. On 14 June 1797 Daumesnil was made a member of the *Guides*, and raised to the rank of *brigadier* (cavalry corporal). Then, on 28 October, he was made a *maréchal des logis* (cavalry sergeant). It was probably at about this time that Daumesnil ceased to use the first name, Yrieix, or perhaps he had done so at the time of his enlistment. In any case, the roll of the Guard of the Consuls only gives "Pierre" as a first name for him. The same document gives as his physical description: hair and eyebrows auburn, high forehead, gray eyes, well shaped nose, average mouth, round chin, oval face.

In his *Etudes sur Napoléon,* Lieutenant-Colonel de Baudus, who came to know Daumesnil quite well in later years, has this to say about this critically important step in the young chasseur's career:

> Only men of proven reputations of courage and audacity were admitted to the *Guides*. Of all the brave men who made up the company of *Guides*, Daumesnil had the good luck to distinguish himself by the greatest number of battlefield feats.

In his *Les grands hommes de France. Hommes de guerre,* Edouard Goepp offers a complimentary assessment of Daumesnil:

> His character was made up of a combination of courage, audacity, a spirit of enterprise, open-heartedness, and chivalry. He never

---

7   On 4 September he would be made a *chef d'escadron* on the battlefield of Roveredo.

commanded *coups de main*, or surprise attacks. His role was to lead cavalry charges: that was his element. He outdid every one in a mêlée. He galvanized men, and led them by his example. He wasn't simply a general who led—he was an individual who acted.

Despite the string of victories that he had thus far achieved, Bonaparte had by no means inflicted a crushing defeat on the Austrian army as a whole, and he now found himself facing an imminent threat from Austrian reinforcements, under General Count Dagobert Würmser, who was coming down from the Tyrol to take over command from the battered Beaulieu. At the same time, continuing unrest in the cities of Lombardy had manifested itself in open revolts in Tortona, Pozzolo, and Arquarta. Then there was the problem of Mantua, manned by 12,000 men armed with 316 cannon, and situated among lakes and swamps, which rendered an assault well nigh impossible. So a siege was the only practicable means of taking it.

After two attempts in late May and early June to capture the city by surprise attacks had failed, Bonaparte accepted the inevitability of a siege. Initially Sérurier was simply ordered to establish a blockade of the city, but after the fall of the citadel in Milan on 29 June, it became possible to shift the army's siege train, together with cannon from the Milan citadel, to the vicinity of Mantua, and a proper siege of the city began. An attempt on 17 July to take the city by assault failed, and on the 31st, with growing concern over the threat posed by the continued Austrian advance southward along both sides of Lake Garda, Bonaparte reluctantly lifted the siege of Mantua, in the process being forced to abandon a good portion of the siege train that had been emplaced around the city.

In mid-July the army's cavalry had been distributed among its divisions in the following manner: Sérurier had with him the 8th *Dragons* and the 7th *Hussards*. Augereau, on the lower Adige, had the 10th *Chasseurs à cheval*, and Masséna, at Verona, had the 15th *Dragons* and the 25th *Chasseurs*. The army's cavalry reserve, under the direct command of General Kilmaine, included the 5th, 8th , and 20th *Dragons*, the 22nd and 24th *Chasseurs*, and the 1st *Hussards*. Encamped in the vicinity of Vallegio, it consisted of 1,535 men.

The next four months were marked by extraordinary marches and counter-marches by the still ill-clad and ill-fed French soldiers, fighting almost continuously against superior Austrian forces, initially under Würmser and his subordinate, General Peter Quasdanovich, and then General Josef Alvintzi and his lieutenants, as the Austrian generals endeavored to relieve the besieged Mantua and to drive the French completely out of northern Italy. For the first time during this campaign Bonaparte found himself on the defensive. The tactical skill which the 27-year-old commander-in-chief proceeded to display in the face of superior enemy forces, bringing the campaign successfully to a close at the end of the year, was characterized by Clausewitz as "one of the finest examples to be found in military history."

The extraordinarily complex story of the moves and counter-moves of both forces during this period has been told in exquisite detail by our most learned military historians, and therefore no attempt to retell it here is necessary, nor would it be appropriate, since the business of our story is the life and career of one individual in this epochal time—the formerly Yrieix, now Pierre, Daumesnil. Until now, as he has learned his trade, suffered his first wound, and repeatedly demonstrated admirable martial qualities, no particular feat on a battlefield has singled him out for special recognition by his senior commanders. But that was soon to change, as we shall shortly see.

For our purpose, it will suffice to sketch briefly the momentous events which followed the lifting of the siege of Mantua at the end of July. By 1 August Quasdanovich's advance down the west side of Lake Garda had been brought to a standstill. Kilmaine and Augereau had driven the small Austrian force out of Brescia, and the stage had been set for the French victories at Lonato and Castiglione. In the meanwhile, Würmser had reached Mantua and re-stocked it, before shifting his troops to the vicinity of Castiglione on 3 August. In the battle which took place there on 5 August, the French cavalry, led by Beaumont (Kilmaine had fallen ill) played a decisive role by sweeping around the left wing of the Austrians and assisting in the capture of the redoubt at Medolano, thus throwing the Austrians into confusion and causing Würmser's general withdrawal across the Mincio. By 7 August, he had led his force back northward, having left a reinforced garrison in Mantua. Würmser's first offensive had thus come to an end. It had cost the Austrians 16,700 casualties, but it had not been cost-free for the French, who had lost 6,000 killed and wounded, and suffered the loss of 4,000 men as prisoners. On 24 August Austrian outposts around Mantua were driven off and General Sahuguet re-invested the city.

By September Würmser was ready to confront Bonaparte again, and this time his advance took him well east of Lake Garda, to Bassano, where on 8 September his force was badly beaten by Bonaparte, with the combined divisions of Augereau and Masséna. Together with 3,000 prisoners, the French booty included 35 cannon, 2 complete bridge trains, and 200 wagons. Gathering what he could of his scattered forces, Würmser decided to take shelter once more in Mantua, and by the 12th he had entered the city with 10,000 men. Over the next three days a series of clashes took place as Würmser struggled in vain to break the siege of the city. His efforts cost him 4,000 men and 25 cannon, and left him with 24,000 men hemmed within the city's confines, 9,000 of them sick, and 150 a day falling ill or dying.

According to de Henri de Clairval, in the course of this campaign Daumesnil, always in the forefront of the action, himself captured six enemy flags. It was during the final, successful French effort to capture Mantua, on 15 January 1797, that Daumesnil managed to seize not just one of those six flags, but two on the same occasion.[8] When he presented the first of these to Bonaparte, the latter was intensely preoccupied with observing the progress of operations through a long glass, and paid no attention to Daumesnil or his trophy. A short while later, Daumesnil returned to the commander-in-chief with another Austrian banner, this time a rich and splendid standard of the Royal Volunteers given to them by the Austrian empress, which she herself had embroidered and decorated with a magnificent embroidered *cravate*—a broad knotted and betasseled ribbon. When Daumesnil presented it to Bonaparte, the latter noted that it lacked the usual *cravate*, and asked the young chasseur what had happened to it.

"*Mon général*," Daumesnil replied, "you granted me nothing for the first flag, so I rewarded myself for the second." As far as we know, Bonaparte did not insist on Daumesnil's handing over the splendid silken *cravate*, which, in any case, seems to have vanished in the mists of history.

This might well have been the second time that Daumesnil had succeeded in bringing himself to Bonaparte's personal attention—Arcola having been the first—as he strove by his audacious actions on the battlefield to single himself out as an exceptional soldier worthy of advancement. The episode serves to give us a glimpse into an aspect of Daumesnil's personality, which was to prove to be one of its most salient characteristics: he did not stand in awe of the high and mighty. (This insouciance would later very nearly prove fatal to him.)

Militarily October passed quietly for both the French and the Austrians, while the latter reassessed their options for evicting the French from northern Italy, and Bonaparte busied himself with political affairs. On 10 October a treaty signed with the Kingdom of Naples served, among other things, to detach from Austrian service a considerable body of fine Neapolitan cavalry. With the aim of stabilizing the political scene in French-occupied Lombardy, Bonaparte set up three new Republics: the Cisalpine, comprising the Milanese; the Cispadene, linking Modena and Reggio; and the Transpadene, which joined Bologna and Ferrara. He continued to badger the Directory for reinforcements, but with only limited success.

With the onset of November, the Austrians again resumed the offensive, this time under the command of General Baron Josef Alvintzi, who marched southwest in the direction of Bassano with Quasdanovich, while Davidovich headed down through Trento toward Roveredo. The possible junction of these two forces was an obvious cause for concern to Bonaparte, and he was determined to ensure that it did not take place. After failing, at the cost of 2,000 casualties, to drive Alvintzi back along the Verona–Villanuova road in order to remove the threat to Verona,

8   Verillon, *Les Trophées de France*.

Bonaparte rapidly revised his strategy, planning instead to attempt to swing around Alvintzi's left flank and take him in the rear.

Crossing back to the south bank of the Adige, Bonaparte entrusted the defense of Verona to *général de division* François Macquard and 3,000 men, while on the night of 14 November he set out with his main body toward the town of Ronco, on the Adige's south bank, where his chief engineer was already constructing a pontoon bridge to permit the French to cross into the marshy area north of the river. On the 15th, as soon as Masséna's and Augereau's divisions were across the Adige, Masséna moved his division west along one of the causeways—actually, more of a broad dike—though the marshes to protect the force's left flank, while Augereau led his division toward the bridge over the small tributary to the Adige, the Alpone, on the east side of which lay the town of Arcola. His mission was to cross the Alpone and march north to Villanuova. Although Alvintzi's advance guard was almost on the outskirts of Verona, the rest of his force was strung out along the road back to Villanuova, where his baggage train and artillery park were believed still to be positioned.

Alvintzi had left 4,000 Croatian troops to guard the Alpone crossing at Arcola. As Augereau's advance guard approached the narrow, wooden bridge across that small stream, they were obliged by the marshy terrain, which covered much of the area between it and the Adige, to proceed along a narrow dike parallel to the river for several hundred meters. As they did so, they were raked by an intense musketry fusillade, interspersed with cannon fire, from the Croatians arrayed on the opposite side of the small stream and blocking the far end of the bridge, itself no more than 20 meters in length. With some of his men already down, and seeing their comrades faltering and taking shelter under the dike's embankment, the commander of the advance guard, *général de brigade* Jean Antoine Verdier, ordered a drummer to beat the charge. Thus energized, some of the grenadiers regained the top of the dike, but at once the intense fire which met them drove them back under its shelter. Several more efforts to overcome the men's unwillingness to face almost certain death were fruitless.

Alerted to his advance guard's difficulties, Augereau arrived on the scene, and in their turn his generals placed themselves at the head of the French column, exhorting its men and ordering the charge to be beaten. And in their turn, Bon, Lannes, Verdier, and Verne were driven back by the hail of fire, bleeding from their wounds. Augereau passed through the ranks of the soldiers, calling on their pride and their love of glory. Then, suddenly seizing a regimental flag, he started toward the bridge. A handful of men followed him, while the rest stood shaken and uncertain. In a few moments, almost a dozen had fallen, and Augereau, too, was forced to fall back to the protection of the dike.

Two of Bonaparte's aides, Colonel Jean-Baptiste Muiron and Captain Joseph Sulkowski, had been sent forward with the advance guard, and had participated in several of the attempts to reach and cross the bridge. They now hastened to inform Bonaparte of the deadly impasse in which the advance guard found itself. He rapidly made his way to the bridgehead, followed by his staff and his *Guides*. A quick assessment of the situation persuaded him that more than a headlong rush into a storm of lead and cannon balls would be required to extract his army from the physical and moral morass into which it had stumbled. Accordingly he ordered *général de division* J. J. Guieu to take 3,000 men back to Ronco and then eastward, to try to cross the Adige at Albaredo in order to come back up on the far side of the Alpone and take Arcola from the rear.

Realizing that further delay might mean a lost opportunity, since it was obvious that Alvintzi would be hurrying reinforcement to "the sound of the guns" during the time that Guieu was seeking another crossing of the Alpone, Bonaparte reined in his horse in front of his shamefaced men. Passionately invoking memories of past victories, he called out to the downcast men, "Are you no longer the men of Lodi? Of Castiglione?" Then, perhaps sensing that his entire campaign was on the point of unraveling and that his grandiose visions for his own future were being dispersed like fog under a brilliant sun, he dismounted and drew his sword in preparation for yet another charge. At his sides, Muiron and Sulkowski, as well as his brother Louis and Marmont drew theirs. The rest of the staff and the *Guides* closed around their commander-in-chief.

At that moment a young grenadier rushed forward out of the ranks and clung to Bonaparte, exclaiming "You're going to get yourself killed, and if you're killed, we're lost! You shall not go farther—this is not your place!" Brushing the man aside, Bonaparte seized a flag and rushed toward the young drummer of the soldier's regiment, André Etienne, shouting at him to beat the charge.[9]

Marmont placed himself at the head of the small column, with Bonaparte behind him, flanked by Muiron and Sulkowski, with Louis Bonaparte close behind, and with other staff officers, all the *Guides,* and a few grenadiers clustered in their rear. But the rest of the soldiers hung back. Under a rain of fire, the little band managed to reach the approach to the bridge, where an increase in the storm of lead intensified and stopped them in their tracks. General Vignolle, Sulkowski, Belliard and two of his officers and a *Guides* lieutenant fell, badly wounded or killed. Muiron threw himself in front of Bonaparte, his own back to the enemy's fire, exhorting his general to go back. As he did so, Muiron was struck in the back by a projectile, killing him instantly and spraying his blood over Bonaparte.[10] Marmont managed to release Bonaparte from the dead

---

9   The little drummer's conduct on that occasion inspired his native town, Cadenet, to erect a statue in his honor.

10 Napoleon did not forget the sacrifice his young friend had made in no doubt saving his life. (Muiron was 22 at the time of his death.) When Bonaparte re-named the six vessels of the Venetian navy taken over by the French after their occupation of Venice in May 1797, he gave them the names of officers killed in battle, all of them generals except for

officer's embrace, and with the assistance of Louis and several others in a sort of frantic confusion they hustled their badly shaken general back toward the shelter of the dike's embankment.

In the confused struggle to draw Bonaparte to safety, his rescuers let him slip from their grasp into a deep mire-filled canal, where he was still exposed to the enemy's fire. Seeing their general's desperate situation, a number of soldiers rushed to his assistance. One of them, Sergeant Boudet, fell mortally wounded, calling out as he did, "I'm dead! Better me than the general!" Daumesnil, who never lost an opportunity to be as near as possible to the point of the action, had been hovering nearby with his friend and fellow chasseur, Michel-François Muzy. When a number of others plunged into the muck to rescue Bonaparte, Daumesnil and Muzy joined them, and were among those who succeeded in drawing Bonaparte to safety.[11]

While this drama was being enacted, Guieu and his men had managed to ferry themselves across the Adige in the vicinity of Albaredo, and had come back north on the east side of the Alpone, entering Arcola after dark without firing a shot, the exhausted Croatians having put up little resistance. When Guieu learned that Bonaparte had ordered Augereau's division back to Ronco, after the failure to get it across the bridge over the Alpone, he too withdrew his force to Ronco. At the same time Alvintzi was pulling his troops back along the Verona-Villanuova road and sending additional support to Brigido and Mitrowsky in the Arcola area.

Bonaparte had withdrawn the bulk of his force to the southern bank of the Adige, leaving two demi-brigades to guard the bridge at Ronco. At the same time he had sent orders to Kilmaine at Mantua to send him an additional 3,000 troops. The 16th passed with clashes between Masséna's division and Provera near Porcile, in the swampy triangle between the Adige and the Alpone, and between Augereau's division and Mitrowsky's force, coming from Arcola along the road to Ronco. Masséna got the best of Provera, taking 800 prisoners and 6 cannon, and Augereau drove Mitrowsky back into Arcola, but again was unable to get across the bridge. Once more Bonaparte withdrew both divisions back over the Adige at Ronco, leaving a guard force on the river's east bank.

That night Bonaparte set his engineer, Andréossy, to work constructing a trestle bridge across the Alpone, just above its junction with the Adige. His plan for the following morning called for Masséna to recross the Adige and seem to threaten Arcola from the west, while Augereau

---

that which bore the name of a colonel – Muiron. It was aboard *Le Muiron* that Bonaparte returned to France two years later. In his will, Napoleon left 100,000 francs "to the widow, the son, or the grandson of our aide Muiron, killed at our side at Arcole covering us with his body." Muiron's body apparently fell into the Alpone, and was never recovered. See Gourdin, *L'Ange Guardien de Bonaparte*.

11 In recognition of his conduct at Arcola, Daumesnil received a pension of 600 francs annually from the Cisalpine Republic.

would also take his division across the Adige at Ronco, and then eastward, crossing the Alpone on the new bridge so that he might come up on Arcola from the south, taking Alvintzi's force in its left flank. On the 17th Masséna got his men across the Adige at Ronco, sending one demi-brigade westward toward Porcile, another eastward toward the Arcola bridgehead, concealing a third near the Arcola dike, and posting two others at the Ronco bridge. Meanwhile Augereau's division successfully crossed to the east bank of the Alpone on Andréossy's bridge and started northward toward Arcola.

The Austrian reaction came quickly. Mitrowsky's men issued from the Arcola bridgehead, falling on Masséna's demi-brigade and driving it back. As the French fell back, Mitrowsky fell into the trap that had been laid for him, as the other demi-brigades of the Masséna division encircled his men and either killed or captured all of them. Across the Alpone, Augereau's advance toward Arcola had been held up by four Austrian battalions sent forward as a blocking force. To dislodge the stubborn Austrians, Bonaparte sent a platoon of 25 *Guides*, under the command of Lieutenant Joseph Domengo, called Hercule[12], to swing around behind the Austrians, instructing the officer to have his four trumpeters sound the charge, to give the appearance of a new French force arriving on the field. When Domengo succeeded in carrying out his instructions convincingly, the Austrians, believing that they were being attacked from their rear by a superior force, panicked, and shortly Augereau was able to push forward and occupy Arcola. Masséna then brought his men across that blood-stained bridge, and joined forces with his fellow division commander. On the morning of the 18th, the remainder of the Austrian force withdrew northward to San Bonifacio, and then to Montebello, on the road to Vicenza.

Alvintzi had lost 6,000 prisoners, 15,000 men killed, wounded, or missing, 18 cannon, and four flags. Bonaparte led his victorious troops back to Verona and sent Augereau to the support of the embattled *général de division* Charles Henri Vaubois, who had been hard put to prevent Davidovich from achieving his goal of joining forces with Alvintzi. Learning of the latter's defeat and faced with the reinforced Vaubois, Davidovich thought better of his strategic plan and withdrew toward the Tyrol, as he did so losing some 2,000 men as prisoners, along with a great part of his supply train. He finally drew up at Roveredo. For their part, the French occupied Rivoli and the plateau of La Corona.

At Mantua, Würmser had attempted a sortie on 23 November, but it had been easily repulsed. Alvintzi's first attempt to relieve Mantua and to loosen the French grip on northern Italy had ended disastrously.

---

12 A black man, Domengo rose to be a squadron commander in the *Chasseurs à cheval* of the Imperial Guard, despite being completely illiterate. When Napoleon refused to raise him any higher, Hercule felt ill-used because the Emperor had not made him a marshal of France.

Nonetheless, the Austrians showed great resilience in the face of their continued inability to regain control of their lost territory, and Alvintzi kept a substantial body of troops in the Bassano area, fleshing out its depleted ranks with reinforcements of varying quality sent down from Vienna. For its part, the French government was looking for a way to end the war. The offensive across the Rhine had failed and an armistice had been concluded there. The Directory sent *général de division* Henry Clarke to Bonaparte's headquarters, with instructions to open negotiations with the Austrian government, and, incidentally, to give the Directors his assessment of Bonaparte, whose increasingly independent ways were causing serious concern to the Directory.

It is not surprising that Bonaparte did not agree with the idea of settling at this point with the Austrians, whose armies he had repeatedly driven from the field, and his passionate arguments for continuing the campaign soon brought Clarke around. The result was that the Directory, having earlier considered Italy a secondary theater and the Army of Italy's role primarily to draw Austrian forces away from the eastern front, now accepted Bonaparte's argument that the main thrust against Austria should come from what Churchill would have called Austria's "soft underbelly." Accordingly, the Directory now promised to send Bonaparte 30,000 men from the Army of the Rhine. Those troops were not to arrive until the beginning of March, however.

1797

By January of 1797, the stubborn old soldier, Alvintzi, was ready to try once more to break through to Mantua and relieve its starving garrison. This time his plans called for a multi-pronged advance southward from the area of Trento on the eastern side of Lake Garda, and secondary thrusts toward Verona and Mantua from east of the Alpone and Adige. On 7 January the main Austrian force left their position along the Brenta, and the following day General Provera's men encountered Augereau's outposts east of Legnano. As reports came in to Bonaparte in his headquarters at Roverbella, he concluded that the main Austrian offensive would be down the Adige toward Rivoli, and he accordingly ordered a maximum concentration of his forces in the Rivoli area.[13] Under heavy pressure from Alvintzi's force at La Corona, Joubert had been forced to pull back to Rivoli. The French force which would converge on Rivoli would total some 23,000 infantry, 1,500 cavalry, and 35 cannon.

Bonaparte arrived at Rivoli at 02:00 on the 14th. It was a clear, moonlit night and the widespread pattern of Austrian campfires, together with his pre-existing knowledge of the terrain spread out before him, enabled Bonaparte to formulate his plans for the battle which would develop

---

13 According to Tranié (p. 238), one of Bonaparte's spies, Toli, had sold the Austrian plans to him, and then gone off to Alvintzi to report to him that the French were demoralized, and had no more than 10,000 men with which to oppose him.

during the morning hours of that day. The account of that victorious battle has been told many times, so it will suffice for our purposes simply to note that the comparatively flat terrain of the Rivoli plateau gave the cavalry a welcome opportunity to play a role on the battlefield. At the climax of the struggle between the infantry of Liptay, Knöblös, and Ocskay, and Masséna's and Joubert's men on the northern rim of the Rivoli plateau, the 21-year-old *chef d'escadron* Lasalle led a furious charge of a squadron of hussars in support of the hard-pressed French infantry, creating panic among the Austrian soldiers, and capturing an entire Austrian battalion. Clairval says that Daumesnil charged with his regiment at Rivoli, but more than that we do not know.

By midday, it was clear that the Austrians were beaten, so, leaving the pursuit of the broken Austrian forces to Joubert, Bonaparte started south, taking with him two of Masséna's demi-brigades in order to join Augereau in his effort to prevent Provera from slipping by him to reach the besieged Würmser in Mantua. The combined marching and fighting ability of the best of the infantry of the Army of Italy—and Masséna's men were certainly that—almost defies comprehension. They had fought at Verona on the 13th, then marched all night, arriving at Rivoli at dawn the following day, fought Alvintzi's columns that day, then ordered that afternoon to start south to Mantua, marched all that night and the next day. Finally, on the 16th they took part in a skirmish at La Favorita, on the outskirts of Mantua. Bonaparte's own seemingly inexhaustible energy was certainly a factor in motivating such extraordinary feats, but they still leave one in wonderment.

Austrian losses at Rivoli had been 3,300 killed or wounded and 7,000 taken prisoner or missing. French casualties amounted to 2,200. Of the 28,000 men that Alvintzi had led south from the Brenta in the first week of the new year, only some 7,000 were able to make their way back to Roveredo. 13,000 were prisoners, and the remainder were killed or scattered among the mountains and valleys of the region. General Gabriel Rey, who had performed poorly at Rivoli and had been reprimanded in front of his peers by Bonaparte, was given the dubious honor of leading a column of 20,000 prisoners back to France. Tranié says that Rey would never forgive Bonaparte for his treatment, and only continued to serve while awaiting the most propitious moment for treason. (Apparently a suitable occasion never presented itself.)

Now at last, the siege of Mantua was going to be brought to a successful conclusion. Provera had, in fact, managed to get around Augereau by 14 January, and by the 15th his force had reached the small town of San Giorgio, a few kilometers east of Mantua, and had established contact with Würmser. The following morning their combined forces struck at *général de division* Alexandre Dumas, in San Antonio, driving his men out, but Sérurier held La Favorita, while Masséna's demi-brigades began to arrive on the scene from the north, and Augereau's troops from the east.

Provera soon accepted the impossibility of his situation, and surrendered with 5,000 of his men. His inability to break through to Würmser, and the absence of any other possible relief force, made the capitulation of Mantua inevitable, and on 2 February Würmser surrendered the city. 16,000 of his men became French prisoners, although Bonaparte, in recognition of the Austrian's stubborn defense of Mantua over so many months, permitted Würmser to march out of the city with his staff, 200 cavalry, 500 men of his choice, and 6 cannon. The Directors had wanted to shoot Würmser, a Frenchman who had taken arms against France, but Bonaparte would have none of it. (Würmser died in Vienna two months later, "of a broken heart," according to Tranié) The Republic's conquest of northern Italy was now complete.

Bonaparte had not waited to accept Mantua's rendition in person, however: he had to make Pius VI see reason. The Pope, who quite naturally hated the Revolution, had made a serious error of judgment in allying himself with Austrian fortunes, and the Directors wanted Bonaparte to depose him. So on 1 February the commander-in-chief headed south once more, and in short order his troops had defeated the feeble Papal armies at Imola, Faenza, Ancona, and Loreto. Recognizing that Bonaparte would continue to Rome if this *commédia buffa* of a war[14] were not halted immediately, the Pope requested an armistice, which Bonaparte granted. By the Treaty of Tolentino, signed on 19 February, the Pope surrendered the Papal states of Bologna, Ferrara, and Romagna, plus 30 millions in gold. With that business handily disposed of, Bonaparte headed back north to prepare for his next campaign, this time against Austria itself.

Having been bloodied on the Rhine, the Directors were delighted by Bonaparte's spectacular victories, and now decided to give the primary responsibility for the defeat of Austria to the Army of Italy, acting in concert with Moreau's Army of Germany, coming through southern Germany. Reinforcements for Bonaparte now began arriving, including Bernadotte's and Delmas's divisions, and by early march the Army's total strength, not counting three Italian formations, totaled nearly 80,000 men, organized in two corps. The first, under Bonaparte's direct command, included the divisions of Masséna, Guieu (in replacement of Augereau, gone on leave to Paris), Sérurier, and Bernadotte, with Dugua's cavalry. The second corps, under Joubert's command, included his own division, and those of Delmas and Baraguey-d'Hilliers, and the 22nd *Chasseurs,* 5th *Dragons,* and 8th *Dragons*, under the command of General Dumas.

The Austrian *Hofkriegsrath* (Supreme War Council) had now entrusted to the Archduke Charles the task of cleansing northern Italy of

---

14 At one point Lannes, who was leading the advance guard escorted only by his staff, encountered several hundred Papal cavalry. "Halt!" he commanded them, and they halted. "Dismount!" was his next command, and again they obeyed. "Surrender your arms!" Lannes then called out, and to his astonishment, the Papal troops did so, and were made prisoners. Cronin, *Napoleon Bonaparte,* p. 125.

the French Republican presence. He had already demonstrated his superiority over Jourdan's *Armée de Sambre-et-Meuse* and Moreau's *Armée de Rhin-et-Moselle*, and the French loss of Kehl on 10 January and of Huningue on 2 February had freed 22,000 excellent Austrian soldiers for employment in Italy. Together with the remnants of Alvintzi's force, the men from the garrison of Mantua, who had been exchanged for French prisoners, and a considerable body of militia, Charles was gathering together behind the Tagliamento a force which would eventually total some 90,000 men. It would soon become evident, however, that the skills which had enabled the Archduke to discomfit Jourdan and Moreau were to avail him little against Bonaparte.

Apprised by his spies that Charles had not yet received all of his reinforcements and consequently had not managed to deploy his force in such a way as to block the three principal Alpine passes through which Bonaparte might advance into the Austrian heartland—the Brenner, the Tarvis, and the Adelsberg—Bonaparte decided to strike the Archduke without waiting for Moreau to move forward into the Tyrol. On 11 March he launched his attack, with Joubert remaining off to his northwest to protect the army's left flank, and Masséna heading north to cut the Austrians off from the Tarvis Pass, while Bonaparte led the main body of the army eastward toward the Archduke's forces arrayed along the east bank of the Tagliamento. On 16 March the French reached the river, the depth of which was then less than a meter. Bonaparte disposed his four divisions in a formation extending across a 3½-kilometer front, with Guieu on the left and Bernadotte on the right in the first line, Sérurier in the second line behind the gap in the first line divisions, and Dugua's cavalry to the rear of Bernadotte's division. Arriving at the shallow river's edge as though on a parade ground, the troops simply waded across it, under the cover of a heavy artillery bombardment

As soon as the French infantry reached the left bank, Charles ordered his cavalry commander, General Schultz, to charge them, but, seeing his men repulsed, the Archduke sent them galloping off to try to outflank Bernadotte's division at the right end of the French line. Observing this maneuver, Bonaparte ordered Dugua, commanding the cavalry reserve, and *adjutant–général* Kellermann to take their regiments across the river in support of the infantry. Arriving on the far bank, Dugua's troopers drove off the Austrians. In the face of that severe check, the Archduke decided that he had had enough, and he ordered a general withdrawal.

Bonaparte did not slacken the pace of his advance, however, and while Masséna pushed on toward the Tarvis Pass, Bernadotte and Sérurier's divisions followed the retreating main Austrian body as it withdrew eastward. In short order, Palmanova, Gradisca, and Gorizia fell to the French, while Dugua took his cavalry to occupy Trieste, with its important arsenal.

Off to the west, on the extended left flank of the army, Joubert had beaten Davidovich on the Aviso on the 20th, and had then moved on to Neumarkt, where he seized its bridge. When the fighting there, with General Laudon's force covering Davidovich's withdrawal, was indecisive, General Dumas led his staff and some of his dragoons across the bridge, charging the Austrian column in its flank and throwing it into disorder. In the action, all the French but Dumas were killed or wounded, leaving him fighting an Austrian squadron single-handed until one of his own squadrons came to his rescue. Leaving *général de brigade* Louis Baraguey d'Hilliers at Neumarkt to prevent any further interference with his advance, Joubert pushed on through Botzen, and by the 24th he was in Brixen. On the 28th he attacked some Austrian battalions coming from the Rhine as reinforcements, putting them to flight. With his cavalry Dumas pursued the scattered remnants to within 60 kilometers of Innsbruck, taking a good number of prisoners. It seems probable that Daumesnil's regiment participated in this action.

It was now time for Bonaparte to concentrate his widespread forces for a final drive against Vienna. The Directory had not as yet been willing to order Moreau's army forward into the Tyrol, so it was clear to Bonaparte that he would have to carry out the Directory's strategy on his own. Joubert was summoned from the west, and by 8 April he had made his way to Villach, slightly to the west of Klagenfurt, en route disposing of some Tyrolian levies, who had risen in his path. Under pressure from Bernadotte, Quasdanovich had withdrawn eastward from Laibach, leaving the former free to join Bonaparte at Klagenfurt.

On 31 March Bonaparte had proposed to Charles a suspension of hostilities, in the hope of winning enough time for Moreau to make his presence felt in the Tyrol. At the same time he continued to push forward so that it would not appear that his proposal derived from his own weakness. By 7 April he had reached Leoben, and on the same day the Austrians agreed to a five-day suspension of hostilities. On the 13th an extension of five more days was agreed upon, and on the 18th the Austrians agreed, in what became known as the Preliminaries of Leoben, to enter upon formal negotiations for a peace treaty. It was to be followed on 17 October by the signing of the Peace of Campo Formio.

After the provisional peace of Leoben, French troops had been withdrawn from Austrian territory, and Bonaparte had made his headquarters in Milan. On 14 November 1797 he bade farewell to the Army of Italy, saying to his men:

Soldiers, I leave tomorrow to attend the Congress of Rastatt. Finding myself separated from the Army, I only am consoled by the hope of seeing myself back among you soon again, contending with new dangers. Whatever duties the Government assigns to the soldiers of the Army of Italy, they will always be worthy supporters of liberty and of the glory of the French name.

Soldiers, in talking of the princes that you have conquered, of the people who owe you their independence, of the battles that you have won, say to yourselves, "In two campaigns, we would have done more."[15]

Leaving Berthier in command, Bonaparte went on to Rastatt, remaining there as briefly as possible before continuing to Paris. The Directory had offered him the command of the Army of England, and he now accepted it, if only as a form of interim employment until he would conclude that the time would come for him to give reality to the visions which were whirling about in his head. On 10 December the Directory gave him a magnificent reception, and a flag, on which were inscribed in letters of gold the achievements of the Army of Italy: "The Army of Italy has taken 150,000 prisoners, 170 flags, 550 pieces of siege artillery, 600 field pieces, five pontoon bridges, nine ships, a dozen frigates, 18 galleys, triumphed in 18 fixed battles, won 67 combats ...," and more.

We have noted in the pertinent contexts above the two specific instances during this campaign in which specific information regarding Daumesnil's exceptional battlefield deeds exists—his capture of two flags during the siege of Mantua, and his participation in the rescue of Bonaparte from the mire by the bridge at Arcola. He is said to have captured another four flags during this campaign, but specifics regarding those feats are lacking. These instances of military prowess and bravery would certainly have been sufficient to impress on his superiors, including Bonaparte himself, the quality and personality of the young chasseur trooper. Unequivocal evidence of that is his incorporation in the *Guides*.

Daumesnil's admission to the *Guides* brought him back directly under the eye of Bessières, permitting him to strengthen the relationship which had been established between them during the war with Spain, when he had the good fortune to be a member of Bessières' squadron. The latter's brother, Bertrand, a future *général de division*, was a *Guides* captain, as was Joseph Domengo (or Damingue), called Hercule, who had panicked the Austrians with his four trumpeters at Arcola and won a promotion for so doing. A close friend of Daumesnil's, Michel-François Muzy, who had been one of Bonaparte's rescuers at Arcola, was now a *brigadier-fourrier* (corporal quartermaster) in the *Guides*. He would be an inseparable companion of Daumesnil's until his luck ran out at Wagram, where, according to a popular legend, he was killed by the same bullet that shattered Daumesnil's left leg. His battlefield heroics had earned him steady promotions to the rank of captain by the time of his death. A lieutenant in the *Guides* at that time was Jean Barbanègre, one of three brothers who won fame for their family during the Empire. Jean was killed at Jena, as a colonel leading his regiment, the 9th *Hussards*. We shall have

---

15 Pigeard, *Les Campagnes Napoléoniennes*, p. 55.

occasion later to note the splendid final act of Joseph Barbanègre's career as a Napoleonic officer.

The French National Archives contain a curious document regarding Daumesnil and another *Guide*, which may have prompted by a request from the commander of the 22nd *Chasseurs* for the return of both men to their parent regiment. Dated 16 July 1797, a few days over a month after Daumesnil's entrance into the *Guides*, it is a letter from Bonaparte's chief of staff, Berthier, to the commanding general of the general staff at the headquarters in Milan. It reads:

> In consequence of the orders of the General-in-chief, the citizens Reboul and Dominique,[16] *Chasseurs* of the 22nd Regiment and at present non-commissioned officers in the *Guides à cheval* of the army, are authorized to remain in the places that they occupy at present. The order that they are to rejoin their regiment is consequently not in force.
>
> Signed: Alex. Berthier
> Copy to *chef de brigade* Bessières[17]

Even given Bonaparte's extraordinary capacity for what we call today micro-management, this may be taken as clear evidence that Daumesnil had impressed himself favorably on his future emperor. By the time Daumesnil was admitted to the *Guides*, the original squadron had expanded to the extent that there were now four squadrons—organizationally the equivalent of a regiment, although the Corps was still termed a company—and in May 1797 an artillery detachment, consisting of two field pieces served by 26 gunners, was added to its T/O.

By December Bonaparte was back in Paris, having brought his *Guides* with him. They were not to leave his company again until the fatal days of April 1814.

---

16 Even after Daumesnil became an officer, in various official documents his name was spelled "Dominique." Spelling peoples' names correctly at that time seems to have been something of a hit-or-miss proposition.

17 Archives Nationale, Bessières collection, 32 AP2.

CHAPTER FOUR
EGYPT—NEW PERILS AND NEW HONORS

1798

O ne can imagine the overwhelming impression that this first glimpse of Paris must have made on the newly minted *maréchal des logis*. His campaigning in the Roussillon had done little to awaken him to the character of large, sophisticated cities and their populations, but seeing and living, however briefly, in the cosmopolitan cities of northern Italy must have washed off the last vestiges of the country bumpkin that had marked him as a raw recruit in the *Armée des Pyrénées Orientale*. But now, in his new *Guides* uniform, with the chevrons of his new grade decorating the sleeves of his long-tailed green coat, tailored to display his braided red vest, he must have cut a figure bound to attract the attention of young Parisiennes eager to hear tales of France's new hero, the victorious General Bonaparte. It seems reasonable to assume that the swaggering young chasseur was fully prepared to satisfy their curiosity, no doubt interlarding his accounts of the feats of his commander-in-chief with an occasional reference to his own deeds of derring-do.

That commander-in-chief's mind and actions were focused on a considerably loftier plane, however. While his appointment by the Directory as commander-in-chief of the Army of England may have struck him simply as a tactic designed to move him from the center of the political stage, there was, in fact, a sense of reality to it, at least in the minds of the Directors. France was now at peace with its immediate neighbors, but a state of war still existed with that implacable enemy, England, and there were already troops and ships assembled in the Channel ports for the projected operation. Whatever Bonaparte's views on the matter may have been, he obviously felt it incumbent on him at least to seem to take the project seriously, so in February of 1798 he went to northwestern France to assess the concept first-hand.

He was not impressed by the quality and experience of the soldiers and officers who had been selected for the expedition, and the insufficiency of the ships and equipment earmarked for his army gave him serious concern. But the most obvious obstacle to such an undertaking—which seems not to have given the Directors pause—was the uncomfortable fact that the British had what amounted to absolute control of the sea. (Although that condition essentially still obtained six years later, that did not prevent the then Emperor Napoleon from considering, and even preparing for, a similar expedition.) So Bonaparte said to the Directors, "Thanks, but no thanks," and proceeded to sell them on an alternative means of striking at the English—an expedition into the Near East, commencing in Egypt and seeming to pose a threat to British-held India.

It is generally accepted that the Directors' agreement with this strategic *volte-face* was, at least in part, motivated by their desire to see Bonaparte as far removed from Paris as possible, given the fact that his exceptional popularity was already beginning to cast a threatening shadow over their own inept efforts at governing the nation. For his part, Bonaparte sensed that the time was not yet ripe for an attempt on his part to seize power, while at the same time he saw in a venture into the Near East an opportunity to add new laurels to his brow. He realized that the worst thing he could do would be to remain inactive. He observed to his secretary, Bourienne, "I know that if I stand still, I'll soon be ruined."

On 5 March 1798 the expedition to Egypt was officially authorized by the Directory. It was agreed that Bonaparte could take 36,000 men from his old Army of Italy, a certain number of generals and officers of his choice, and scientists and artists of various disciplines for the purpose of conducting a broad-ranging study of Egypt, almost totally unknown to the European world at that time. They made up the Commission of the Sciences and the Arts. An intensive effort was made to keep the destination of the gathering expeditionary force secret, even to the point of publicly designating Bonaparte's new command the Left Wing of the Army of England, while its secret title was the Army of the Orient. The mission given to its commander was to take possession of Egypt, to drive the English from all of their possessions in the East, to destroy their settlements on the Red Sea, and to open the latter to the ships of the Republic

The 400 merchant ships which would transport the army to Egypt would be protected by a fleet of 13 ships of the line, 9 frigates, and a swarm of smaller vessels, all under the command of Admiral Brueys, whose flag flew in *l'Orient*, a splendid 120-gun warship. The crews of these ships totaled some 10,000 men.

The five infantry divisions, made up of 15 demi-brigades, were commanded by Generals Bon, Reynier, Desaix, Menou (later, by Lannes), and Dumas. General Kléber commanded the 3,000-man cavalry contingent, which included seven regiments (including Daumesnil's former regiment, the 22nd *Chasseurs*), and *chef de brigade* Bessières commanded the *Guides*. Now there were *Guides à pied* as well as *Guides à cheval*, and Bonaparte took with him most of the latter, now organized as a regiment, and between 200 and 400 of the former.

On 19 May, the armada weighed anchor and put out to sea. The bulk of the army, 20,000 men, was in ships setting sail from Toulon, but smaller contingents set out from Marseille, Corsica, Genoa, and even Civitavecchia. Admiral Nelson had been cruising off Toulon with 13 ships of the line, but his fleet had been driven out to sea to ride out a violent storm, so Bonaparte's luck held, and the vast, lumbering convoy was thus able to slip by Nelson and set course for the first task of the expedition—the capture of Malta, seen by the Directory as a strategically important prize. The contigents from Corsica and Civitavecchia were able to rendezvous with the main body there soon after its arrival at the port of Valetta on 9 June.

Since the year 1000, Malta had been governed by a succession of religious orders of a quasi-military character—the Hospitallers, the Knights of Saint John, of Rhodes, and finally, of Malta. After a token resistance, the current Knights allowed the French occupation to take place, and on 17 June the French armada set forth once more, this time its soldiers and sailors no longer in doubt as to their ultimate destination. Bonaparte left in Valetta a garrison of 2,300 men, under the command of General Vaubois, but made up for the subtraction of this number from the Army of the Orient by forming the *Légion maltaise* from existing Maltese regiments and crews of the Order's ships, a total of 3,000 men. It seems unlikely that the Maltese were given any choice in the matter, so it is improbable that, man for man, the men of the new Legion were an even trade-off for the men from the two demi-brigades left at Malta.

Once again Bonaparte's luck favored him, as Nelson's efforts to intercept the French expedition were frustrated. He had visited Alexandria three days before the French fleet arrived, and, finding its port empty, he had hared off to the northwest, thereby missing his quarry. On 1 July Bonaparte began to put his army ashore in the Bay of Marabout, slightly west of Alexandria. Severe weather and sea conditions increased the difficulty of getting troops ashore in the small craft with which they had to be ferried from the large transports, and some drownings resulted, but the operation continued through the night.

As soon as there were enough men ashore to commence operations, Bonaparte divided them into three advance columns. He led the first of these through the night to Alexandria, which he stormed and captured during the morning hours. The second, under Menou, pushed on and occupied Rosetta, while Desaix put the men of the third column on the main road to Damanhur and Cairo. As soon as the main body had formed up, it set off in Desaix's tracks. Meanwhile, a commandeered flotilla of river craft started up the Nile to provide gunfire and subsistence support to the troops afoot.

Of two possible routes to Cairo, Bonaparte had chosen the most direct, which was to lead his army through 80 kilometers of unforgiving desert terrain under the searing July sun, their march trailed by bands of irregulars, who preyed mercilessly on stragglers. It was to prove a severe test for men and officers alike, and led to a few suicides among the troops, unaccustomed to such conditions.

On the 10th, the left wing of the army made contact at Rahmaniya with the flotilla coming up the Nile, where a body of Mamelukes had clashed with the advance guard. Desaix dispersed them with a few volleys of grapeshot. Three days later at Chebreïss, another attempt by Murad Bey's cavalry to interrupt the progress of the French failed when the Mamelukes had their first experience with the bristling wall of bayonets and the artillery batteries of infantry squares.

At dawn on the 21st, the French advance guard perceived a body of some 1,000 Mamelukes across their path, and prepared for combat. However, a few fusillades from the advance guard discouraged any attack by the enemy, who withdrew in good order, and the French continued their advance. Early that afternoon, the French came upon the main Mameluke force on the left bank of the Nile, deployed in a mass of some 40,000 of Murad Bey's troops, with their right flank anchored on the river at the town on Embabeh, about 2 kilometers north of Cairo. His experience at Chebreïss had convinced Murad that a fixed defense of some kind, in addition to his fearsome elite cavalry, would be necessary to stop the French. Accordingly, he had converted Embabeh into a strongly fortified position, in which were emplaced some heavy cannon in fixed mounts. Across the river, Ibrahim Bey, with 100,000 men and his treasure collected around him, awaited the outcome of the pending battle. Presciently, he was prepared for a swift withdrawal eastward in the event that the day went against Murad Bey.

The 25,000 men of the five French divisions formed into squares, with Desaix's on the right flank, then in succession Reynier's, Vial's, and finally Bon's, at the river bank facing Embabeh. Dugua's divisional square was placed slightly to the rear of Reynier's and Vial's, as a central reserve. (It would be more accurate to call the formations "rectangles," because, in the case of up-to-strength divisions, one complete demi-brigade formed the front of the formation and another the rear, while the flanks were each made up of one-half of the third demi-brigade. Being under strength, Reynier's and Vial's divisions were obliged to adopt smaller formations.) In addition, Desaix had sent a detachment of cavalry and grenadiers to take possession of the village of Biktil, on the extreme right flank of the French line. In the interval before engaging battle, Bonaparte rode among his soldiers, gesturing in the direction of the distant pyramids and declaiming, "Soldiers, from the heights of those pyramids, four thousand centuries look down upon you!" Then, together with his staff and escorted by the *Guides*, he took shelter within Dugua's square.

Finally the tension in the simmering glare of the Egyptian sun was broken at 3:30 in the afternoon, when, with little warning, the leading ranks of the 6,000 Mamelukes launched themselves with fierce cries against Desaix's and Reynier's squares. When the squares stood firm, bringing down scores of riders and their mounts with regular volleys of musketry and grapeshot from the cannon posted in each corner of the formation, the horsemen flooded around and past them, and then swept back for renewed attacks, as other of their fellows joined the battle. Those who had hurled their spears in the initial attack received additional weapons from their servants and spurred their mounts back into the fray. Desaix's men in the village of Biktil held off the Mamelukes by climbing onto the roofs of the houses and firing down on their attackers.

When it was clear to Murad Bey that his attempt to crush the French right wing had failed, the combat in the center of the battlefield intensified. In their efforts to breach the steel-tipped ranks of the squares, some of the Mamelukes forced their rearing horses to launch themselves onto the bayonets of the infantrymen. Those Mamelukes who succeeded in penetrating the squares by such tactics were immediately shot down.

In his *Etudes sur Napoléon*, Lieutenant-colonel Baudus, a companion-in-arms of Daumesnil's, describes an incident occurring at the height of the battle, which is of particular interest to us. He writes that one particular Mameluke "was sowing terror in our ranks." Then he goes on to say that Bonaparte, himself astonished by the seeming invulnerability of this man as his soldiers must also have been, called Daumesnil to him, and, handing the *guide* one of his own pistols, said, "Go kill that man for me!"

Daumesnil had one of the corners of the square opened for him, and, weaving his way at a gallop through the swirling mass of horsemen, enveloped in clouds of dust and smoke, with gunfire crashing around him, he reached his target and shot him down. Making his way back to Dugua's square, where the ranks parted to permit him to enter, Daumesnil rode up to his commander-in-chief and returned his pistol to him, saying, "That one won't come back again!"[1]

I believe that two conclusions may fairly be drawn from that episode: first, that Daumesnil was by this time making it his business to be in the immediate presence of his commander-in-chief as frequently as possible; and second, that his battlefield feats, going back to the bridge at Arcola and his capture of flags at Mantua and elsewhere, had made a lasting and very favorable impression on Bonaparte. Events would soon serve to make that impression well nigh indelible on the exceptionally retentive mind of the future emperor.

As the ranks of the Mamelukes and their supporting infantry and Arab allies were thinned by the relentless French musketry and artillery grapeshot, and as their frustration at their inability to come to grips with

---

1   Ambert, *Trois hommes de coeur*, p. 72.

their enemies grew, Bonaparte ordered the squares of Desaix and Reynier forward, with Dugua's closing in behind them. At the same time, Vial and Bon were ordered to form columns for an attack on Embabeh. Soon that town was in French hands, and the rout of Murad Bey's force was in full swing. As he sought to lead his men southward from the battlefield in the direction of Gizeh, however, 60 hussars led by Lasalle and a demi-brigade under Marmont's command cut around behind them to prevent their escape. In desperation, the Mamelukes sought safety by attempting to swim across the river to join Ibrahim Bey's forces, but as they did so, many were shot, and at least 1,000 drowned, dragged beneath the surface by their heavy clothes, body armor, richly decorated saddles, and bejeweled weapons.

The battle had lasted little more than an hour. Murad Bey had managed to extricate 3,000 of his Mamelukes from the disaster, and was leading them off to the south unmolested. French casualties were astonishingly low: 29 killed and about 260 wounded. Murad's losses amounted to 2,000 Mamelukes, plus several thousand infantry. Across the river, Ibrahim Bey was already leading his massive force, together with all his treasure and those men who had escaped across the Nile, eastward towards Belbeïss, on the road to Syria.

After the extraordinary hardships they had endured in order to arrive at the gates of Cairo, the French soldiers, buoyed by their success on the battlefield, engaged in an orgy of looting of the bodies of the Mamelukes and in gathering the richly decorated housings and harness of their horses, even fishing the bodies of their late opponents from the river. As was their custom, those formidable warriors had gone into battle with much of their personal wealth on their person, in one form or another. Bonaparte established himself in the palatial home of a Mameluke general in Ghizeh, and awaited the submission of the Cairo authorities. When a delegation of sheiks and imams came to him on the morning of the 22nd to proffer surrender, General Duphot was authorized to negotiate the terms, and on 24 July Bonaparte crossed the Nile and entered Cairo at the head of his troops.

The euphoria engendered in the army by its relatively bloodless victory over Egypt's most formidable military force, and by the subsequent exposure of its officers and men to the exotic and comparatively opulent character of Cairo, was dealt a rude blow when Nelson finally caught up with his quarry late in the day on 31 July. He had found the capital ships of the French fleet at anchor in Aboukir Bay, and, with his fourteen ships of the line and four frigates, he proceeded to sink or capture all but four of the seventeen French vessels, those four having managed to escape to Malta.

Mortally wounded during the battle, Brueys died when his flagship, the 120-gun *l'Orient,* was set afire and exploded. Altogether 2,000 French sailors were killed, 1,100 were wounded and 3,000 captured. English losses were 1,500 killed or wounded. The Army of the Orient was now effectively cut off from France, and would soon begin to experience all of the difficulties that flowed from that painful predicament.

Bonaparte learned of this disaster on the 5th or 6th of August, in a dispatch from Kléber dated the 2nd. At that point he was at the head of his main body, pursuing Ibrahim Bey on the road to Syria and approaching Belbeïss. If his iron will and his determination to accomplish what he had set out to do were shaken by this resounding set-back to his plans, he gave his officers and men no outward manifestation of such feelings. He contented himself with saying rather enigmatically, "Very well, we no longer have a fleet! Either we'll have to remain in these countries or leave them in a grand manner like the Ancients." This cheery "up-beat" assertion clearly did not afford all the reassurance that some of his generals wished for, and there ensued some unconcealed rebellious talk among them.

Writing of this affair, General Edouard Colbert says that, having been informed of the discontent among his generals, which was giving rise to rumors capable of causing discouragement and a breakdown of discipline in the army, Bonaparte instructed General Dugua to invite the principals among the malcontents to dinner.[2] Addressing his guests, Bonaparte said, "I know that several generals are fomenting discontent and preaching mutiny. Let them take care. For me, the distance from a general and from a drummer is the same, in certain cases, and if such a case were to present itself, I would have the one shot just as I would the other." One of those present was heard to mutter, "This fellow is a man who keeps his word." There was no more open challenge to the commander-in-chief's plans and intentions.

There was still the matter of dealing with the continuing threat posed by Ibrahim Bey's massive presence on Egyptian soil, even though he seemed to have decided to withdraw to Syria. There was also the possibility that vast booty might be collected if Ibrahim's troops could be dealt with as summarily as Murad Bey's had been. Consequently Bonaparte sent General Leclerc, at the head of an advance guard consisting of a battalion of infantry, 150 cavalry, and several guns, to locate and report on Ibrahim's movements. On 4 August Leclerc located Ibrahim's host at Belbeïss, but his little force was attacked by Arab tribesmen and forced to fall back to the town of Kankah. The next day he and his men were assailed by a larger body of Mamelukes, Arabs, and Egyptian infantry, while the inhabitants of Kankah fired down on them from the terraces of their houses. Leclerc was obliged to withdraw his battered force even closer to Cairo.

The main body of the French had been following the advance guard at a considerable distance, and its cavalry had been in the process of being remounted, Murat having been sent toward Belbeïss to look for horses. When he encountered the beleaguered Leclerc, he sent word of that

---

2 Picard, *La Cavalerie dans les guerres*, p. 150.

general's difficulties back to Bonaparte, who dispatched Reynier's division to Leclerc's aid, and on the 5th that division re-occupied Kankah. Two days later Bonaparte and his staff arrived on the scene, and gave the order to march on Belbeïss. Upon reaching that town, the French discovered that Ibrahim's force had already moved on, so the French army continued the pursuit.

On 11 August, when the French halted briefly half-way to Salahieh, they still had not seen a single Mameluke. Bonaparte therefore rode ahead of the main body accompanied by the cavalry, consisting of single squadrons of the 7th *bis Hussards*, the 22nd *Chasseurs,* and the 3rd and 15th *Dragons*—some 300 men. A patrol of chasseurs sent ahead to scout was greeted by a scattered flurry of shots as they came upon Ibrahim's entire force in a large encampment. A chasseur was sent back to alert Bonaparte to the presence of the enemy, and the commander-in-chief halted the cavalry until supporting infantry could be brought up. During this interval, the scouts observed that the encampment was in a state of great confusion. Tents were still pitched, camels had been relieved of their burdens, and horsemen were running about in disorder, apparently unsure as to whether they were expected to fight or to flee.

Bonaparte decided to launch his cavalry on the encampment: the chasseurs and hussars in the first line, led by Lasalle, and the dragoons following, commanded by Leclerc, the cavalry commander. By the time this had been arranged, however, Ibrahim had managed to get his massive body underway again, leaving a rear guard consisting of 1,500 Mamelukes and 500 Arab horsemen, and so the opportunity for capturing a rich booty was lost.

Unwilling to see Ibrahim continue his withdrawal with immunity, Bonaparte ordered a combined infantry and cavalry attack on Ibrahim's rear guard by four companies of Reynier's division and the available hussars, chasseurs, and dragoons. Picard[3] says that even officers without troop commands joined in the attack, eager to come to grips with the Mamelukes. A cavalry-to-cavalry encounter turned out to be quite a different affair from shooting Mamelukes out of their saddles as they hurled themselves in vain against solid walls of bayonets, and it soon became evident that the French cavalry were in danger of being over-whelmed. The *Guides* were sent into the fray, and other officers of Bonaparte's staff followed them. Before the fierce clash ended with the last Mamelukes tailing off to join their withdrawing fellows, Leclerc, Murat, Auguste Colbert, and Lasalle had all distinguished themselves. *Chef d'escadron* d'Estrées, of the 7th *bis Hussards,* had been thrown from his horse and was covered with more then twenty wounds. Of the 150 hussars and chasseurs who had formed the first line, 52 had been put out of action. Picard observes that this combat has become famous because it

---

3   Picard, *La Cavalerie dans les guerres*, p. 148.

was the first time that French cavalry had clashed with Mamelukes without infantry support. Had Mi' Lord Wellington been observing that confrontation from the sidelines, he might well have described it as "a near-run thing." But he wasn't, although a little more than sixteen years later his path would cross that of Daumesnil's under very different circumstance, soon after the Great Duke had actually coined that memorable phrase.

It was now clear that Ibrahim Bey would not in the immediate future pose a threat, so, back in Cairo again, Bonaparte proceeded to busy himself with reorganizing the government of Egypt and with the myriad other civil reforms and innovations which absorbed his attention. In some measure these initiatives were designed to persuade Egyptians of the sincerity of his professed intention to liberate them from tyrannical Turkish rule, but they were also intended to consolidate Egypt as a reliable base for his projected advance into Syria. In late August Bonaparte sent Desaix off up the Nile in pursuit of Murad Bey. He gave Kléber the responsibility for governing Alexandria and its hinterland, while he continued to exercise direct control over the rest of Lower Egypt himself.

The seemingly peaceful, if not entirely harmonious, relationship, which had been established with the citizens of Cairo and elsewhere, was shattered violently on 21 October, when, at morning prayers, the muezzins called for a holy war against the French. General Dupuy, governor of Cairo, and 300 troops were massacred. Bonaparte, absent from the city on a tour of inspection, hurried back to Cairo and quickly repressed the uprising with great severity. 4,000 of the rebels were executed, although Bonaparte pardoned a number of the dignitaries so that he might continue with his policy of rapprochement. His diplomatic efforts to keep the Turkish government on the sidelines had come to naught, however, since on 9 September, the Turks, strongly encouraged by the British and Russians, had declared war on France.

Far to the south of Cairo in his pursuit of Murad Bey, Desaix had been performing prodigies with 3,000 men, a small flotilla on the Nile, and a few guns. At Sediman on 7 October his force came up against a force of 10,000 infantry in emplacements, supported by 4,000 Mamelukes and several thousand Arab horsemen, with Murad Bey and his generals at the head of their troops. Desaix decided to attack them. Forming his division into one large square and two flanking smaller ones, he advanced on the enemy. It was a repetition of the Battle of the Pyramids, on a smaller scale, although the French losses were triple those suffered in that earlier battle. His own force seriously wounded, Murad Bey withdrew deep into the desert.

1799

By the time of the Battle of Samhoud on 22 January 1799, Desaix had received some reinforcements, and now had 1,200 cavalry, including the 22nd *Chasseurs*, the 7th *bis Hussards*, and the 15th and 21st *Dragons*, all under the command of the then *général de brigade* Davout, and nine guns, in addition to 3,000 infantry. Murad Bey had 14,000 of his own men, supported by 20,000 Arabs. Desaix formed his infantry in three squares, with Davout's cavalry in the square in the center of the line. Murad's Mamelukes threw themselves first on Friant's square, on the left flank, and then on Belliard's on the right, but they were all beaten off by the fierce fire from the infantry. As Murad's cavalry paused to regroup, Desaix unleashed Davout and the cavalry, who put the Mamelukes and their allies to flight.

Desaix continued to drive Murad Bey's forces deeper into Upper Egypt, although the latter continued to renew his forces, in part with reinforcements from Arabia. Finally, however, Desaix's relentless pressure wore down the Mameluke general, and when General Belliard captured the Red Sea port of Kosseir on 29 May, effectively cutting off further reinforcements from Arabia, the pacification of Upper Egypt was essentially complete.

As it became increasingly evident to Bonaparte that the Turks, urged on by the British, were assembling two forces for an attack on Egypt, he decided on what in today's terminology is called a pre-emptive strike, in the form of a march through the Sinai Desert with the objective of attacking and dispersing the gathering Turkish force in Syria under the command of Ahmed Pasha, called "El Djezzar" (The Butcher). The second Turkish force was being formed by Mustafa Pasha on the island of Rhodes, whence it would transported to Egypt by the British fleet.

Bonaparte now divided his small *Armée de l'Orient* almost in half. The larger portion, for the campaign in Syria, consisted of four infantry divisions, under the command of Generals Kléber, Bon, Reynier, and Lannes. The 900 cavalry, drawn from different regiments of the army, were led by Murat, while Bessières was at the head of the *Guides*, now totaling 400 infantry and cavalry. Attached to the latter were the 80 men of the recently formed Dromedary Corps. 1,755 artillerymen and engineers raised the total force to some 13,000 men. Siege artillery and 16 heavy cannon were to be sent along the coast by coastal craft as the army advanced. Left in Egypt were Desaix, far to the south on the Nile, Dugua in Cairo, Marmont in Alexandria, and Menou in Rosetta.

Having set out on 10 February 1799, on the 12th the army's advance guard, led by Reynier, arrived at El Arish, which unexpectedly turned out to be a fortified town, garrisoned by 600 Mamelukes and 1,700 Albanian infantry. It was clear that such a potential threat to the army's communications could not simply be by-passed. Reynier's initial attempt to take the fort by storm failed, and it was obvious that a siege would be necessary. When Reynier learned that a relief force of some 8,000 men from Ibrahim Bey's army was approaching El Arish, on the night of 14/15 February he turned the approaching army's position, attacked the encamped troops and drove them fleeing in panic. Many of their cavalry were massacred, and a large quantity of camels, horses, munitions, and food supplies fell into French hands. Finally, on the 19th a bombardment by the combined artillery batteries of the army brought about the surrender of the fort's 900 survivors. But this unanticipated delay of a week was to have drastic consequences for the entire expedition.

The dispersal of Ibrahim's relief force had left an additional 1,000 prisoners on Bonaparte's hands. Since he could neither afford to guard nor feed so many prisoners, Bonaparte turned them loose, having required them to swear that they would not serve again against the French. Whether he put much stock in such a commitment or not, it must not have been a great surprise to him when it turned out to be worthless, with terrible consequences.

Kléber now took the advance guard with his division and some of Murat's cavalry, heading for—he thought—Chan Junes, the first village inside Palestine on the road to Gaza, Jaffa, and St. Jean d'Acre. But, led astray by an ignorant or traitorous guide, Kléber and his division wandered blindly in the desert for almost two days, suffering from thirst and the heat. Believing that he was following his advance guard, Bonaparte had gone ahead of the main body, escorted only by his *Guides à cheval* and a small detachment of the Dromedary Corps. Arriving at Chan Junes, he was astonished to find only scattered remnants of the Mameluke force that Reynier had defeated at El Arish.

Hesitating as to whether to withdraw to the main body, possibly thereby inviting an attack by the Mamelukes, or to brazen it out by riding forward as though he was simply leading the army, Bonaparte chose the latter course, despite the advice of some of his officers. Putting himself at the head of the *Guides*, Bonaparte rode confidently toward the small town, and the Mamelukes reacted as he had hoped they would, disappearing at a gallop eastward toward the camp of Abdallah Pasha, visible in the distance on the road to Gaza. Before long Kléber and his men straggled in from the desert, and almost at the same time, the other divisions caught up with the commander-in-chief and his escort.

On the 25th, the army arrived at the approaches to Gaza, where found a Turkish force of 12,000 men, including 6,000 cavalry, arrayed in a line of battle before the city. A well-coordinated attack by Murat's cavalry and Kléber's and Bon's divisions broke through and scattered the Turkish formation. With scarcely a pause, Bonaparte pressed on to Jaffa, arriving at its gates on 3 March. When he sent a *parlementaire* to ask that the city submit, his answer was the emissary's head on a pike. After careful preparations and preliminary bombardment, which effected a breach in the city wall, Lanne's division broke into the city, and in revenge for their comrades massacred in Cairo, his men cut a bloody swath through the city's defenders and population, despite the efforts of their officers to restrain them.

Accounts as to what happened next differ. One version is that the 3,000

Turkish survivors in the citadel had surrendered, after having been promised by a subordinate French officer that their lives would be spared. (Apparently the officer was Eugène de Beauharnais.) However, when it was learned that a great many of the Turks were men who had been paroled after their capture at El Arish, Bonaparte decided that, not only could he not afford to feed these prisoners, no more could he afford to parole them again.

The only solution to this dilemma seemed to be to have the prisoners shot. However, Bonaparte did not wish to take so fatal a decision entirely on his own, so for two days he discussed the problem with his senior officers. The majority favored the prisoners' execution, so on 10 March he had them shot, along with 1,400 other prisoners. Other sources place the figure of prisoners executed at 2,000, or as low as 700. But Bonaparte justified his action on the grounds of military necessity, and one must recognize the dilemma with which he was faced without condoning his solution to it. It will be recalled that in 1794 the French government had declared the war with Spain to be a "war to the death," and that after the capture of the Lines of Figueras, 8,000 to 9,000 Spanish prisoners were massacred, simply out of revenge for French losses. At least Bonaparte had a certain grim logic on his side.

It was at Jaffa that the army was struck with an enemy that terrified it in a way that no scimitar-wielding Mameluke could—the plague. Immediately realizing the threat to the army's morale posed by this horror, Bonaparte resolved, after consulting with his chief surgeon, Desgenettes, to demonstrate to his troops that the disease was not readily transmitted. He proceeded to do so not only by visiting the ward where the plague's victims were being treated, but by assisting in the removal of one corpse, whose uniform was stained with pus. His courageous action was immortalized in the painting by Jean-Antoine Gros, which shows Bonaparte touching the bared chest of an afflicted soldier, while a dismayed officer shelters behind him, his handkerchief pressed to his face. While the commander-in-chief's dramatic act served its purpose, the disease was nevertheless to cost the army many more of its soldiers.

The army pressed on towards St. Jean d'Acre, finally arriving at their goal on 18 March. The 5,000 men defending the heavily fortified town were commanded by Ahmed Pasha, called "El Djezzar" (The Butcher), who had been on the point of abandoning the city when, on 15 March, a man who would prove to be a nemesis for Bonaparte—Commodore Sir William Sidney Smith —arrived on the scene with two British ships of the line. With him was a French *émigré* engineer officer, Colonel Phélippeaux, who, ironically enough, had been a classmate of Bonaparte's at the *Ecole Militaire*. Smith sent him ashore to bolster El Djezzar's morale and to improve the city's fortifications. On the 18th Smith compounded Bonaparte's problems by capturing half of the siege guns that were being brought to St. Jean d'Acre by sea, and adding them to the city's already formidable defenses. (A second French convoy successfully landed the other half of the army's siege train at Jaffa on 15 April, whence the heavy cannon were with great difficulty dragged to St. Jean d'Acre.)

While accepting the necessity for a classic siege operation despite the absence of his siege artillery, Bonaparte nonetheless simmered with impatience at the prospect of a long drawn-out affair. When his field artillery had managed to make a small breach in one wall, he ordered an assault on 28 March. When the storming party jumped down into the fortress's moat, they found that their scaling ladders were too short to reach the breach in the wall. Fascines were thrown down to support the ladders, but the effort was in vain, and the attack was repulsed with heavy losses. Seated at a safe distance from the action with a sack of Turkish pounds at his side, El Djezzar paid in gold for every French head presented to him.

Other assaults would follow during April, but they only cost the lives of irreplaceable officers and men. Meanwhile, additional Turkish troops, ammunition, and supplies were being brought to the garrison by British ships. From the narrow perspective of our story, however, the unremittingly grim tale of that foredoomed siege is brightened by two episodes, which, once again, brought Daumesnil to the future emperor's attention in a most favorable light. The first of these occurred early in the siege, probably on the first of April. In his *Mémorial de Sainte-Hélène*, the Count de Las Cases, one of Napoleon's companions in his exile on the island of Saint Helena to whom the ex-emperor dictated his *Commentaires*, recounts the incident in this way:

> During the siege of Saint-Jean-d'Acre, Napoleon received proof of a heroic and very touching devotion. While he was in a trench, a bombshell landed at his feet; two grenadiers immediately threw themselves on him; placing him between them and, raising their arms above his head, they covered him entirely. Luckily, the bomb spared the entire group, and no one was injured.
>
> One of these brave grenadiers later became General Daumesnil, who remained so popular among the soldiers as *la Jambe de Bois*. He lost a leg during the Moscow campaign, and commanded Vincennes during the 1814 invasion.

Las Cases is, of course, mistaken on two points: Daumesnil was not a grenadier, but a *Guide*, and he lost his left leg at Wagram, not in Russia.[4]

In his *Souvenirs et campagnes d'un vieux soldat de l'Empire par un capitaine de la garde impériale*, Charles Parquin gives his version of the

---

4   Las Cases says that the name of the other soldier was Souchon, while Bertrand gives his name as Carbonel. Other accounts of Daumesnil's heroic action appear in Dr. O'Meara's *Napoleon in Exile*, the *Journal* of Captain Gerbaud, and the *Mémoires* of Queen Hortense (see edition of Hanoteau).

incident. Having mentioned Daumesnil's defiance of the Russians in 1814 as governor of Vincennes, Parquin goes on to say:

> It was the same Daumesnil, who, as a simple *guide* of General Bonaparte at St. Jean d'Acre, risked his life to save his general's. He was a few paces behind the commanding general and Berthier, holding their horses and his own, when a shell fell four paces from the group. Instantly perceiving the danger to which the general was exposed, Daumesnil didn't hesitate; he left the horses and covered with his own body that of the individual who would later be his emperor. Fortunately, the shell, having buried itself deep in the sand, didn't explode, and Daumesnil went back to the horses. General Bonaparte spoke these two words, which, coming from him, were certainly worth any number of compliments: "What a soldier!"[5]

It was later, during one of the futile attempts by the French to break into the citadel at St. Jean d'Acre, that Daumesnil again won distinction, although at the cost of a painful wound. Although his duties as one of the commanding general's escort would certainly not have required him to participate in efforts to scale the walls of that fortress, Daumesnil had evidently volunteered to join one of the storming parties on this occasion. One of the first to mount one of the scaling ladders, he was met at its top by a blow from a scimitar to his head. Almost simultaneously, the explosion of a mine precipitated Daumesnil into the ditch at the base of the wall. His wound was soon patched up by the famous surgeon, Larrey, who would have a number of other occasions on which to perform similar services for his friend.

His conduct at St. Jean d'Acre earned for Daumesnil one of the first *sabres d'honneur* awarded to the Army of the Orient. Upon his return to Cairo with the army, however, his fortunes took a sharp turn for the worse, as we shall see.

In a larger sense, there had been one positive feature of the otherwise painfully depressing events in Syria during the siege of St. Jean d'Acre. By the end of March, Bonaparte was receiving reports of an Army of Damascus gathering in Galilee to come to the relief of the besieged city. To determine the character of the threat that such an army might pose, and with the intent of eliminating it altogether, on the 30th Bonaparte sent Murat off northwards to the town of Safed, northwest of the Lake of Tiberias and west of the Bridge of Jacob across the Jordan. At the same time, he sent Junot off southeastward toward Nazareth, with 400 men, including 100 cavalry and 70 mounted Druzes.

Murat returned to St. Jean d'Acre on 6 April without, however, having

---

5   Parquin wrote this in 1843, when he was imprisoned for supporting Louis-Napoleon's abortive landing at Boulogne. He died in 1845, while still in prison. A modern edition is Jones, *Napoleon's Army*.

discovered the large body of Turkish troops, which was gathering in the vicinity of Jacob's Bridge. For his part, when Junot reached Cana on 4 April, having passed through Nazareth, he was warned by the local sheik not to advance further, since there were several thousand mounted troops awaiting him. Before leaving Nazareth, Junot had taken the precaution of sending word back to Bonaparte that he was encountering elements of the Damascus army, but that he was pressing on while awaiting reinforcements, which he requested. Now he continued his advance, and on 8 April, back in the vicinity of Nazareth, he found his small band confronted with another several thousand Turkish and Arab cavalry, amidst the ranks of which a number of standards of senior pashas could be seen. The total Turkish force now amounted to 5,000 horsemen, clearly bent on overwhelming Junot's handful of men.

With his infantry deployed in a square of four-deep ranks, during the next six hours Junot's men beat off repeated cavalry charges by salvoes of volley fire, delivered at very close range. Against hundreds of the enemy killed, Junot had lost 12 killed and 48 wounded, all of whom were brought with the detachment as it withdrew to Cana. Meanwhile, Bonaparte had sent Kléber to Junot's aid with his small division of 2,000 men, and on the 11th the two forces came together in time for another pitched battle with 6,000 Turks, who were soon dispersed, disappearing into the desert. On 15 April, Murat, who had been sent back to Jacob's Bridge, achieved a notable victory by capturing a Turkish encampment, which he had caught unawares.

It almost immediately became clear, however, that the danger of an intervention at St. Jean d'Acre by the Army of Damascus had by no means been eliminated. On the 16th Kléber learned that there were about 30,000 Turkish troops 20,000 cavalry and 10,000 infantry—concentrated at the base of Mount Tabor. Fearing that his small force would be surrounded and overwhelmed by this horde, Kléber devised a plan for circling behind the Turks during the night and safely taking his men back to St. Jean d'Acre. He reported the situation to Bonaparte, advising him of his intentions. However, after attempting this maneuver under cover of darkness, at dawn on the 17th Kléber found that, instead of successfully slipping by the enemy encampment, he had been led astray during the night by his guides and was now, in fact, effectively surrounded by the Turkish force. He had no choice but to accept battle. His men formed in two squares, one under Junot and himself in command of the second, Kléber calmly awaited the enemy's onslaught.

The Turkish cavalry came at the squares in waves—4,000 at first, then another 3,000, then a third, and finally all those who had not yet joined the battle. In addition to the cavalry, there were infantry armed with muskets, who engaged the *tirailleurs*, whom Kléber had thrown out as a screen for the squares, in a lively exchange. Despite the heavy losses that the volley fire from the men of the demi-brigades had inflicted on the Turkish cavalry, they continued to swirl about the squares, unable to break through the fire-tongued hedge of bayonets. Soon the soldiers were firing from behind a parapet of bodies of men and horses.

After six hours of unrelenting combat, despite Kléber's orders to conserve ammunition the soldiers' cartridge pouches were almost empty. The odds were still enormously against the little French force, and its prospects seemed grim. Fearing that Junot's square was weakening, Kléber had merged it with his own. After consulting with his generals, he was on the point of spiking his guns and leading his men in an effort to break though the clouds of cavalry still biting at the sides of the enlarged square, leaving the wounded to their certain fate. "With death in his soul," as Tranié puts it, he was about to give the orders to do so, when, in a climax which Hollywood would have rejected as too absurdly improbable, "the cavalry came charging over the hill to the rescue," in the form of Bonaparte, who had announced his arrival on the scene by a salvo of cannon fire.[6]

Having guessed at the predicament that his lieutenant might have found himself in, the commander-in-chief had taken the 2,000 men of Bon's division, some cavalry—certainly the *Guides à cheval* must have been among them[7]—and some artillery, and marched without stopping throughout the night and the better part of the following day to reach his desperately embattled men. Now, caught between the two French forces, the army of the Pasha of Damascus were thrown into confusion, and the cavalry scattered in the direction of the Jordan, leaving the infantry to be massacred.

Many of the fleeing Turkish cavalry were drowned in the rushing waters of the Jordan, swollen by a sudden tempest. Others, heading north to cross the Jordan at Jacob's Bridge, ran into Murat's force, hastening southward to join their comrades at Mount Tabor, and hundreds of them were captured or slain. Total French losses were less than 200, as contrasted with an estimated 6,000 among the Army of Damascus. If there had been any question before Mount Tabor of the superior effectiveness of disciplined musketry from steady, confident troops in the face of disorganized attacks by undisciplined cavalry, now there no longer was.

With the threat from the Army of Damascus to the siege operations at St. Jean d'Acre eliminated, Bonaparte led his troops back to the besieged city, where several more efforts to take it by storm were made. During one of those assaults, an entrée was actually made into the city through a breach in the walls opened by the artillery. At the head of 200 grenadiers, General Rambaud, of Lannes' division, and his men were sowing terror

---

6 Tranié, *Les Guerres de la Revolution*, p. 355.
7 In his splendid panorama, *Bataille du Mont Thabor*, in the Musée de Versailles, Louis Lejeune places the *Guides* in the lower left corner of his painting, although he mistakenly puts on their heads colbacks, which did not become one of the characteristic signatures of their dress until after the Egyptian Campaign.

among the city's defenders, but the rest of the assault force was unable to follow them, and before long Rambaud's little band was surrounded. They took refuge in a mosque, but their situation was hopeless, and every one of the heroic band was slain.

It was now painfully evident to Bonaparte that time was working against him. On the first of May a sortie by the garrison was successfully repulsed, but at the cost of more French lives. With additional Turkish reinforcements continuing to arrive by sea, the scales were now badly out of balance—if they had ever been *in* balance. So Bonaparte decided to raise the siege. To spare themselves from having to carry their artillery ammunition back to Cairo, for three days Bonaparte had his gunners hurl their shells into the city. The army's departure, to be carried out in the utmost silence, was fixed for the night of 20/21 May. When dawn came, the besieged occupants of St. Jean were astonished to see the French camp completely empty. Fortunately for the French, in their excitement and jubilation, the city's defenders gave no thought to pursuing the retreating army.[8]

The siege had lasted 63 days, and eight assaults had failed to carry the city, while costing the lives of a number of senior officers and 1,200 men. General Bon had been mortally wounded in the last assault, on 10 May, and Bonaparte's good friend, General Caffarelli, already missing one leg, had died after the removal of his left arm, its elbow shattered by a Turkish cannon ball When the army set out on the road back to Cairo on 21 May, an additional 2,300 men were sick or wounded, and 1,000 had succumbed to the plague.

An achingly painful dilemma arose over the question of whether or not to attempt the evacuation of plague victims who might survive. Bonaparte suggested to Dr. Desgenettes that fatal doses of opium be given to the hopeless cases, but the doctor disagreed, and instead administered laudanum to 30 of the sick as a pain-killer. Surprisingly, this caused them to vomit, and some of them made it back to Egypt. Bonaparte issued an order that all horses, mules, and camels were to be given to wounded or sick able to travel, and to plague-stricken who still showed signs of life. When his groom asked Bonaparte which of his horses he would ride, the general stuck him with his crop, saying, "Everyone not sick goes on foot, starting with me."

The march through the Sinai and onwards to St. Jean d'Acre had been conducted by fresh troops, unburdened with sick and wounded, and in the comparatively mild early months of the year. Now the weary troops felt the full force of the mid-summer sun, and the endurance of all was put to a terrible test. In hindsight, it might be said that this retreat was a mini-

---

8   The famous military artist, JOB, did a marvelous illustration of Bonaparte striding resolutely across the parched waste at the head of his bedraggled army, his shoulders back and his head erect, his gaze focused on the dazzling future he envisioned unfolding before him.

preview of another, far more disastrous retreat thirteen years later, under very different climatic conditions. Although there had been no immediate pursuit of the retiring French by Ahmed Pasha's force, as the army slogged westward a continuous rearguard action was required to deal with swarms of Turkish horsemen, who swirled in the army's rear, hoping to pick off stragglers, just as the Cossacks would swoop down out of snow tempests on the remnants of the *Grande Armée*, also led on foot by the same man.

On 24 May the army reached Jaffa, and, after a four-day halt to permit the army to gather its strength, Bonaparte led it on to Gaza, arriving there on the 30th. But there was still the Sinai to cross, and that required another four days of marching through a sun-blasted oven, with temperatures reaching 54° C. At last, on 3 June those still able to walk staggered into Katia, and their ordeal was over.

His skill as a spinmeister already well honed, Bonaparte arranged for a "triumphal" entry to Cairo on 14 June. In the course of the ceremonies and exchanges of gifts which accompanied the celebrations on that occasion, Bonaparte was given the Mameluke slave, Roustam, who would remain at his master's side—or sleeping at the door of his bedroom—until the fateful days of 1814.

With the commander-in-chief back in his headquarters in Cairo, something like a normal daily routine was resumed. As a *sous-officier* of the *Guides à cheval*, Daumesnil was always one of the detachment which escorted Bonaparte when he left his headquarters. By this time Bessières knew the young trooper well, and liked him for his bravery and his proud manner, and would have liked to advance him rapidly. Unfortunately, Daumesnil's hot-headedness seemed at times to spoil his chances, and on one occasion very nearly cost him his life. In his *Etudes sur Napoléon*, de Baudus wrote, "Daumesnil told us many times that, often, after having earned the modest stripes of a *brigadier* and a *maréchal des logis,* he would then get himself broken."

Baudus goes on to tell the following story of what Daumesnil's undisciplined behavior led to on one occasion.

One evening in Cairo after the return from Syria, Daumesnil and several comrades had gone into a café for something to drink. After having imbibed heavily, the three young men became very noisy, despite the presence in the same room of some generals. When the troopers were told by their superiors to quiet down, the drink in them got the better of their judgment, and they replied coarsely to the generals, and insulted them. They were promptly arrested by military police summoned to the scene.[9]

---

9 Quoted by Clairval, *Daumesnil,* p. 44.

Insubordination and indiscipline had been a constant problem in the Republican armies, and there had been occasions in the Army of the Orient, as has been mentioned, when revolt had been just simmering beneath the surface. Thus it was that harsh punishments for such flagrant breaches of discipline were far from infrequent. So, when the three offenders were brought before a court martial, their fate was effectively foreordained: they were sentenced to be shot.

Informed of the court's judgment, Bonaparte expressed reluctance to see executed a man who had so courageously saved his life at St. Jean d'Acre—and perhaps he remembered Arcola, as well—so he instructed an aide to tell Daumesnil that, if he would ask for pardon, it would be granted to him.

"Never, without my comrades!" was Daumesnil's reply to the proposal. "Pardon me, or shoot me with them!"

The three men were taken out to the place for the execution, and the same proposal was once more made to Daumesnil. Again, he refused to separate his fate from that of his condemned comrades. Then, as he watched his companions being shot, one can imagine the wrenching agony of soul he must have felt, as he imagined his hopes for a brilliant career, crowned with glory, being blown away in a flash of musket fire. But, having administered this terrible lesson to the reckless young soldier, the commander-in-chief ordered that Daumesnil simply be imprisoned. It was a lesson that Daumesnil would never forget, and it served from that day on to temper his previous rash and impetuous behavior.

Soon, however, the march of events brought Daumesnil's release from prison: the need for the services of all good soldiers in the field was an overriding priority. (Presumably he had been broken again, to the rank of *brigadier*, if not to that of simple *cavalier*.) On 11 July a fleet of some 60 Turkish and Russian transports, escorted by British warships, appeared in Aboukir Bay and dropped anchor. The Army of Rhodes, under the command of Mustapha Pasha, had arrived. News of this sent by Marmont reached Bonaparte on the 14th, and he immediately sent off orders concentrating his forces. Desaix was brought north from Upper Egypt to Cairo, Kléber was ordered to march from Damietta westward across the Nile to Birket, just southeast of Alexandria, and Bonaparte established his own headquarters in that town.

On 15 July, in the absence of any opposition, Mustapha put ashore somewhere between 15,000 and 18,000 troops, most of them infantry. Almost at once the Turks attacked the Fort of Aboukir, which was held by a small French force under the command of *chef de batallion* Godart. For several days he and his men resisted fiercely, while praying for the arrival of the assistance that he had requested, but by the 18th the little band was being overwhelmed, when one of the fort's defenders threw a torch into the magazine, and Turks and French alike were buried in the debris of the resulting explosion.

For the next week Mustapha Pasha made no further aggressive moves, instead confining his army's activities to building two lines of defense across the base of the promontory at the tip of which stood the remains of the fort. The first line consisted of field fortifications built on three small hills in a concave pattern, but lacking connecting entrenchments. A second line, farther back toward the tip of the peninsula, was based on an existing fortification. The first line was manned by 8,000 Turks, the second, by another 6,000 to 7,000, and a reserve of some 5,000 men filled the village of Aboukir and the fort. Both Turkish flanks were protected by their gunboats.

Although Kléber and his men had not yet arrived by the 24th, the inactivity of his foe decided Bonaparte to strike first. Accordingly, before dawn on the 25th he launched his attack. Lannes was to hit the Hill of the Wells on the left flank of the Turkish first line of defense, while Lanusse, with the division of Rampon, would attack the Hill of the Sheik, at the right end of the Turkish defenses. Simultaneously, Murat would lead his cavalry, consisting of 2,300 men of the 7th *Hussards*, and the 3rd and 4th *Dragons*, down the center of the peninsula, splitting his forces in two to circle around the two hills and cutting off the retreat of the Turks being assaulted by the French infantry.

The quick success of this initial attack, which had sent the Turks fleeing in disorder toward their second line, and even seeking refuge by attempting to swim out to their ships, encouraged Bonaparte to continue the attack, rather than awaiting the expected reinforcements. He ordered Colonel Cretin to bring forward the 17 field pieces on hand to support the second wave of the attack. While Bonaparte was perched on one of those cannon, observing the enemy's movements through his long-glass, Daumesnil, who was nearby, perceived a Turkish battery shifting its aim to their location. Seizing Bonaparte in his arms, Daumesnil lifted him off the cannon and set him in a less exposed position, saying as he did so, "*Excusez, mon général!*" No sooner had he done so than an artillery officer took Bonaparte's place, bracing himself on the cannon, and at once he was struck by a bullet and killed.

When the French infantry hit the second Turkish defense line it was heavier going for them, and at first the men were unable to scale the defensive walls and ramparts, being forced to fall back to re-group. However, when they saw the Turks between the lines cutting off the heads of the dead and wounded French lying on the battlefield, they were enraged and flung themselves against the Turkish defenders. Murat led his cavalry forward again, and Bonaparte, seeing the difficulties that his troops were encountering, sent Bessières into the fray at the head of the *Guides*. It was during this action that Daumesnil managed to seize one of the standards of the Captain Pasha, the military commander of the Turkish army.

With Murat leading the way, the Turkish defenses were finally shattered, and by the thousands Mustapha's soldiers were either cut down, driven into the sea, where most of them drowned, or taken prisoner. When Murat himself reached the tent where Mustapha, at the head of 200 Janissaries, was striving to fend off complete disaster, the old Turk fired a pistol at his enemy, wounding Murat in his cheek. Undeterred, Murat struck the pistol from Mustapha's hand, cutting off two of his fingers and taking him prisoner. With that, the Janissairies laid down their arms. Turkish losses amounted to 2,000 killed, perhaps as many as 10,000 drowned, and 3,000 taken prisoner. The Army of the Orient had lost 220 killed and 750 wounded—a comparatively insignificant number, but all the dead were irreplaceable in the steadily dwindling numbers of that army.

In the course of negotiations with Sir Sidney Smith over the disposition of Turkish wounded, Smith made sure that European newspapers, in which reports of French defeats in Germany and Italy appeared, were conveyed into the hands of the French. Bonaparte had already concluded privately that there was nothing to be gained by his remaining any longer in Egypt, clearly no longer a theater of any importance to the French government. He was hoping to be recalled by the Directory so that he would not be seen to be abandoning his troops on his own volition. These news reports served, however, to precipitate his decision, and he decide to leave for France. He did not confide his plans to even his most senior officers until 17 August, when Admiral Ganteaume reported to him that the Turkish/British fleet had left Egyptian waters.

That same evening Bonaparte informed his generals and his staff of his intentions, and the small party left Cairo for Alexandria, where the frigates Muiron and Carrère and two other small vessels had been kept ready to put to sea. Of his senior officers, Bonaparte took with him Berthier, Lannes, Bessières, Marmont, Duroc, Murat, and, of course, one more junior officer, Eugène de Beauharnais. Kléber had the misfortune to be left in command of the army, and to his fate: eight months later he would be assassinated in Cairo. Being unable to take all of his *Guides à cheval* with him, Bonaparte picked 112 of the best of them, including Daumesnil, who had by that time earned back the gold lace chevrons of a *maréchal des logis*.

The little fleet sailed from Alexandria on 23 August, with Bonaparte aboard the Muiron. It was a long and highly indirect voyage, partly because of the vagaries of the weather and partly because of the necessity of avoiding the English fleet. Finally, on 9 October Bonaparte was able to set foot on French soil once more, disembarking in Saint-Raphaël in the Gulf of Fréjus. One hour later, he was in a coach and on his way to Paris. According to the famous trumpet-major of the *Guides* and later of the *Chasseurs à cheval de la Garde*, Elie Krettly,[10] Bonaparte was escorted to

---

10 Grandin, *Souvenirs historiques de Capitaine Krettly,* p. 134.

Paris by some twenty *Guides*. (Despite that escort, some of Bonaparte's baggage was stolen by bandits en route to Paris.) There is no record as to whether or not Daumesnil was among that select few. The remainder of the troops who had been brought back from Egypt were left to make their way to Paris on foot, on horseback, or by wagon.

Krettly says that the reception that those troops received during their long march by the officials and citizenry was very different from that accorded their commanding general. In some towns local officials refused to accept them, and they were therefore obliged to take detours to avoid towns. When they reached Valence, they nonetheless entered the town, and their officers asked that their men be billeted in the town's citadel, then guarded by a company of grenadiers. When their request was refused by the town authorities, Adjutant-major Dahlmann and Bessières's brother formed the *Guides* in battle formation, and simply took possession of the citadel, where the troops made themselves comfortable, while the town's grenadiers unresistingly gave way to them. Soon afterwards an order arrived from Paris ordering the troops to proceed thither immediately. It was signed by the First Consul. When they arrived in Paris on 17 December, the *Guides* were billeted in the *Caserne de Babylone*.

Bonaparte had arrived in Paris on the 16 October, and had been greeted enthusiastically as a victorious general, who could be expected to take the initiative on the battlefield against the increasingly threatening forces of the Second Coalition. The story of the events leading up to the *coup d'état de 18 brumaire* (9 November) and its success need no re-telling in these pages, so let us rather examine the organization of the Consular Guard that Bonaparte created soon after assuming the title and role of First Consul.

CHAPTER FIVE
A CHASSEUR À CHEVAL DE LA GARDE

1800

W hen Bonaparte set his feet on the path that would lead him to glory and immortality by declaring himself First Consul and thus the *de facto* ruler of France, there already existed two military guards for the existing government: the *Garde du Directoire executif*, the latest version of a body that went back to the earliest days of the Revolution, and the *Garde du Corps legislatif*. The first of these bodies included two companies of Foot Grenadiers, two of Horse Grenadiers, and a 25-piece band formed from musicians of the Paris Conservatory of Music. Not one to lose any time in exercising his new powers, on the evening of *19 brumaire* Bonaparte amalgamated the existing guards to form the *Garde des Consuls*. This action was formalized in a decree of 28 November 1799. The *Guides à cheval*, who had accompanied Bonaparte back from Egypt, were not mentioned in that decree, however, so their incorporation in the Consular Guard may not have occurred until a decree of 3 January 1800 prescribed the structure of the new Guard.

With an organizational strength of 2,089 men, the new Guard consisted of a general staff, two battalions of foot grenadiers, a battalion of foot chasseurs, three squadrons of horse grenadiers—at first, incongruously termed light cavalry—a company of horse chasseurs, a company of light artillery (including a detachment of horse artillery), and 50 musicians divided between the infantry and cavalry. The Guard's first commander was Joachim Murat, who was promoted in May to the position of commander of the cavalry of the *Armée de reserve*. Jean Lannes succeeded him as commander-in-chief and inspector general of the Consular Guard, and *chef de brigade* Bessières became commander of the Guard cavalry.

The initial strength of the company of *Chasseurs à cheval* was four officers and 113 troopers, under the command of Captain Eugène de

Beauharnais. Almost without exception, the chasseurs were the same men who had made up the *Guides* of the Army of Italy, who had followed Bonaparte from there to Egypt, and now to Paris. As a *maréchal des logis*, Pierre Daumesnil, already well known for his exceptional battlefield feats of bravery, must have been prominent among them.

Trumpet-major Krettly[1] says that their new status as members of the Consular Guard gave the former *Guides*—and certainly the other members of the newly formed Consular Guard—a foretaste of the jealousy and resentment that would be felt by many of the troops of the Line toward the Guard throughout its existence. This jealousy was in some degree exacerbated by the fact that all the soldiers of the Army of the Orient now in Paris were being paid, a month at a time, the seventeen months of arrears in their pay, which made it possible for them to savor the pleasure of the capital to a degree beyond that which their Line colleagues could afford. In the streets the chasseurs often found themselves targets of slurs and sarcastic comments on the part of soldiers whom they looked on as brothers in arms. One particularly galling taunt was to call them, in a play on their commander-in-chief's name, *les Guides de Bon-à-pendre* (good for hanging).

Doubtless another factor giving rise to resentment on the part of Line troops toward the men of the *Chasseurs à cheval* of the Consular Guard was the fact that the badly worn uniforms in which they had returned from Egypt had now been replaced by more striking—and therefore more visible—uniforms. If they were to escort the First Consul everywhere he went, the chasseurs had to be appropriately attired. Expert opinion has it that it was at this time that the colback became a distinctive "signature" for the uniform of the chasseurs, although the first design of that headpiece was conical and smaller than the one adopted several years later, and lacked a *flamme* (bag).

Krettly recounts an occasion when he was chatting with some comrades at the entrance of the Babylone barracks and they were approached by some *maîtres d'armes* (fencing instructors) from Line regiments, who asked to speak to the chasseurs' *maîtres d'armes*.

"They remained in Egypt," Krettly told the visitors. Finding this hard to believe, the others insisted to the point that Krettly, seeing that the strangers were seeking a quarrel, finally said to them,

"Gentlemen, go right on in. Close your eyes and put your hand on the first one you come to and you'll find a brave man who's the equal of a *maître d'armes*."

One of the "champions", as Krettly terms them, responded by saying to Krettly, "Very well, I put my hand on you!" His comrades followed suit, picking other chasseurs. Without the chasseurs ever having understood the basis for this challenge, both sets of soldiers left the barracks to find a

---

1   Grandin, *Souvenirs historiques de Capitaine Krettly*, pp 142–4.

suitable ground on which to settle matters. In the ensuing affray, eleven of the chasseurs' antagonists were wounded, some even dying of their wounds.

Two days later, another challenge was delivered to the chasseurs, inviting them to a meeting on the Champ de Mars. Despite strict injunctions by their officers to avoid such confrontations, the chasseurs' tempers were up, and they went to the rendezvous at the agreed time. They had scarcely arrived on the scene when a few score other soldiers, together with a crowd of town bullies, swarmed around them. In a few minutes some 150 men, divided more or less equally, were lined up facing one another. A serious brawl would have broken out in an instant if it had not been for the timely arrival of the Paris military commander, Marshal Lefebvre, at the head of a squadron of the 5th cavalry regiment.

It's not clear whether or not Daumesnil was personally involved in either of these fracas, although, given his fiery character, the odds would seem to make it probable that he was. Is it likely that a non-commissioned officer of the company, admired for his feats on the battlefield, who, as a youth, was incapable of standing idly by when a comrade was being bullied—is it conceivable that such a man would stand aside in the face of these circumstances? I don't think so. What we *do* have evidence of, however, is a somewhat analogous incident, described by Dr. Foissac, in his *La chance ou la destinée* (pp 648–9). Many years later the Baroness Daumesnil had told the doctor about this episode.

Daumesnil had conceived the fanciful idea of consulting the famous Paris fortune teller, Mlle. Lenormand. That lady had scarcely laid her cards out on the table when she exclaimed, "Oh, *mon Dieu*, what bad luck! This very day you're going to fight a duel!" The improbability of such a prediction's being correct struck Daumesnil as being laughable, but Mlle. Lenormand insisted that she was not mistaken, and that this fatal event was certain to occur.

Still shaking his head over such an improbable prediction, Daumesnil left the seeress, and, hearing the evening recall sounded, headed towards his barracks. He was halfway up the Rue Garancière, behind the church of St. Sulpice, when an officer of the Line barred his passage and addressed some provocative observations to him. Remembering the fortune teller's prediction, Daumesnil responded that he wasn't free to fight that day since his recall had been sounded. The officer would not agree, however, to grant Daumesnil any delay in settling the matter.

"You unfortunate man!" Daumesnil cried, "If we fight, I'll kill you!" The officer continued to insult him, however, and refused to let him pass. Forced to defend himself, Daumesnil drew his sword, and, despite trying merely to disable his opponent, he killed the man. We are left to guess what the consequences—if any—were for Daumesnil, but we know that this was not the first time that he had killed an opponent in a duel, and it may well not have been the last time. He was hardly unique in that respect however.

Duels among officers and soldiers were not infrequent, despite rigorous prohibitions of the practice. For some men, duels represented an opportunity to demonstrate their courage and martial prowess away from the battlefield. Others were simply bullies, spoiling for a pretext to draw their swords against one of their fellows, as seems to have been true of the notorious duelist, General Count Fournier-Sarlovèse, whose pursuit of one officer in a series of duels was the basis of Joseph Conrad's story "The Duel" (transferred to the screen as "The Duellists").[2] For others, they were simply an occupational hazard, to be avoided if possible without compromising one's honor. Senior officers were not immune to the practice. In 1815, General Count Philippe-Antoine Ornano, who had been a senior cavalry commander in 1814 and commander of the *Dragons de France* during the First Restoration, had rallied to Napoleon upon the latter's return from Elba, but he missed Waterloo because he was recovering from a wound incurred in a duel.

Bessières was now commander of the cavalry of the Consular Guard, consisting of the *Grenadiers à cheval* and the single company of the *Chasseurs à cheval*, the latter under the command of the 19-year-old Captain de Beauharnais. (On 5 March 1800 the latter was promoted to *chef d'escadron*, but continued to command the company of chasseurs.) From the outset of his command of the *Guides* and now of his Consular Guard cavalry, Bessières had been determined to develop their moral qualities. He wanted them to dominate the other corps, not only by their exceptional bravery, but also by the dignity of their daily lives, by their self-mastery, by their cult of honor, and their respect for the uniforms they wore. In short, he wanted them to serve as models for the rest of the army.

As a consequence of his extreme lack of concern and his impulsive character, Daumesnil had marked time in the lower grades. Six years after his enlistment, he was still a non-commissioned officer. However, bit by bit, the spirit that Bessières was striving to inculcate in men like Daumesnil, who already possessed the essential basic qualities, was having its effect. Once Bessières judged him to be worthy of promotion, on 3 May 1800 Daumesnil was made an *adjutant sous-lieutenant*, which is to say, a junior lieutenant attached to his unit's staff, a rank which existed only in the Consular Guard. The second Italian campaign would soon give the newly commissioned young officer an opportunity to demonstrate that he was worthy of the confidence reflected by that promotion.

At this time France's international position was precarious. Bonaparte

---

2   Although he was an exceptionally brave and skilled officer, who rose to high rank because of his exceptional martial qualities, Fournier-Sarlovèse's disputatious character continuously put him at crossed swords—both figuratively and literally—with his fellow officers. His general behavior won for him the unenviable soubriquet *le plus mauvais sujet de l'armée*, the worst person in the army. Ney, under whom he served at Gross Beeren and Leipzig, once said to Fournier (he did not pick up the "Sarlovèse" until 1816), "Monsieur, in my lifetime I've seen many poltroons, but until now I've never met one as dull as you."

and the French nation badly wanted peace. For the First Consul's part, to afford him an opportunity to consolidate his position and to bring some order to the chaotic governmental and financial situation in the country; and on the part of his countrymen, to win a respite from seven years of unremitting warfare. But Bonaparte's peace overtures to England and Austria had been rejected summarily, and their Coalition partners, Turkey, Würtemberg, Bavaria, Portugal, Sicily, and Sardinia, held fast. Out of pique over Austria's having given Russia little credit for the role played by the Russian army under Suvorov in making it possible for Austria to regain its Italian possessions, Tsar Paul I had withdrawn from the Coalition.

Astutely, Bonaparte had won the Tsar over to his cause by sending back to Russia without ransom 8,000 prisoners, dressed anew at the expense of the Republic. France's allies were a reluctant Spain, a passive Switzerland, and the new republics created by France's armies, which regarded the French cause as their own. Prussia remained neutral, and many of the small German states followed her example.

Strategically, *général de division* Jean Victor Moreau's Army of the Rhine of some 100,000 men was facing an Austrian army of roughly equivalent strength, under the command of General Baron Paul Kray, which posed a direct threat to French territory. Masséna's Army of Liguria of 36,000 men was spread over a roughly triangular area of the Maritime Alps, bounded by Mount Cenis on the north and Nice and Genoa on the coast. Masséna's headquarters was in Genoa, while Soult commanded the right wing of his army, and Suchet, its left wing. Poised menacingly to the east was an Austrian army of roughly 100,000 men, commanded by General Michael Melas.

Determined to regain for France the territories lost since his first Italian campaign, and to end the war by striking at the heart of the Second Coalition, Vienna, Bonaparte's strategic plan involved the creation of a new Army of the Reserve, which would interpose itself between the two main Austrian armies by way of a passage over the Alps, thus placing itself on the left flank of Kray's army and on the rear of that of Melas. Since the Constitution of the Year VIII did not permit a Consul to command an army, Bonaparte replaced Berthier as his Minister of War with Carnot, and sent the former to Dijon to form and command the Army of the Reserve. His own role would be that of the coordinator of the actions of the armies of Moreau, Berthier, and Masséna, while accompanying Berthier's headquarters.

Moreau was to attack Kray in mid-April. When he finally did on the 25th, within ten days he had administered a decisive defeat to the Austrians at Stokach. The Austrians, however, had surprised Bonaparte by striking first. Melas had struck at Masséna on 5 April, and by 7 April the Austrian had driven to the sea, splitting Suchet's and Masséna's forces. The latter had been told by Bonaparte that his strategic role was to hold out at least until 20 May—later amended to 4 June—to keep Melas preoccupied long enough for the Reserve army to cross through the Alpine passes and into the valley of the Po.

With the Army of the Reserve on the march, Bonaparte left Paris on the night of 5/6 May, accompanied by the Consular Guard, and arrived in Geneva late on the 8th. The Great Saint Bernard Pass had been chosen for the passage of the principal elements of the army, while smaller units would feint at entering the Little Saint Bernard, the Simplon, and the Saint Gothard passes. Bonaparte had moved on from Geneva to Lausanne, and on the 16th he left that town, escorted by a detachment of Guard *Chasseurs à cheval*, arriving at Martigny the morning of the 17th, where he put up at the convent of the Bernardins, in the center of the town. Three days earlier, Lannes had led the advance guard of the army up into the pass, followed in echelons by the divisions of Duhesme, Victor, Murat, Monnier, and, finally, Bessières with the Guard. On the 17th, Lannes had captured Aosta and pushed on to the formidable obstacle in the army's path represented by Fort Bard.

Here the advance halted, until mountain trails were found which permitted Lannes to bypass the unyielding defenders of the fort, which was then placed under siege. By the 22nd Lannes had reached Ivrea, designated by Bonaparte as the point of convergence for his several columns. Bonaparte had remained at Martigny until the 20th, when he left on horseback, changing to a mule at Bourg Saint-Pierre and arriving at the Hospice of Saint Bernard in the late afternoon. After a hasty meal with the prior, he pushed ahead, finally spending the night at Etroubles. The next day he went on to Aosta, where he would spend the next four days.

The complex maneuvers during the following three weeks, by Bonaparte on the one hand and by the Austrian commander-in-chief, General Michael Melas, on the other, led to the fateful meeting of both forces on the field of Marengo on 14 June. The French army had, under the command of Generals Victor, Lannes, Murat, and Desaix (who had managed to slip through the British blockade of the French troops still in Egypt and rejoin Bonaparte), five infantry divisions consisting of 45 battalions of 23,791 men, and five cavalry brigades, commanded by Murat, plus the Guard cavalry under Bessières—one squadron of Grenadiers and one of Chasseurs—a total of 40 squadrons of 3688 men. Guard foot and horse artillery and engineers totaled 618 men, and the Guard light artillery consisted of 72 men. The French therefore had just over 28,000 men in the field prior to the battle, although Desaix's two divisions were not present at its outset. On the 12th the bulk of the army's cannon had reached the army, after having been blocked on the road until after the garrison of Fort Bard had capitulated.

Melas' force in the field that day was roughly equivalent to that of the French. Its advance guard—or Corps of the Right Flank—led by General O'Reilly, consisted of the Frimont Division, which included 832 infantry, four squadrons of Mariassy Chasseurs, two squadrons of Imperial

Dragoons, and two squadrons of de Bussy Chasseurs—a total of 458 cavalry. The main *corps de bataille*, under Melas' direct command, included two infantry divisions, one cavalry division, and one of mixed infantry and cavalry. The Corps of the Left Flank, led by General Ott, consisted of two infantry divisions. The total force included 30,837 men.

Ten days before the meeting of the adversaries on the Plain of Marengo, the siege of Genoa had come to an end in an odd way. Concerned that the attention and the forces that he was devoting to trying to starve out the French garrison of that city might detract dangerously from his ability to confront the French threat posed by Bonaparte in northern Italy, Melas had decided to lift the siege to free his forces to help deal with that threat. His decision to do so was taken on 2 June, but that happened to be the very day that Masséna sent an emissary to General Peter Ott commander of the besieging force, saying that the French were prepared to capitulate. So the capitulation was accepted, and the French were escorted westward along the coast to where Suchet's troops were positioned on the west bank of the Var. No conditions were imposed by the Austrians which would prevent the troops of the garrison from immediately being incorporated in French offensive formations elsewhere.

Bonaparte had been puzzled by Melas' apparent inaction, and rather desultory French reconnaissance had failed to provide clear evidence of the Austrian commander's intentions. In fact, disinformation fed to the French by Austrian double-agents increased Bonaparte's uncertainty on that score. He was inclined to believe that Melas was planning either to move north across the Po or south to Genoa, but least of all was he expecting Melas to attack him across the Bormida, although when the Austrians had withdrawn a few days earlier across the Bormida, Melas had left a bridgehead on its eastern bank, manned by General O'Reilly's advance guard.

As a consequence, the movement of the Austrian army en masse across the Bormida in the early hours of the 14th caught the French completely by surprise. Since there was only one crossing available, it took Melas some time to deploy his troops on the eastern bank of the river in its attack formation, with Ott on the left flank, Melas himself commanding the main force in the center, and O'Reilly's advance guard now forming the right flank.

During the night of the 13th/14th Victor's Corps, consisting of Gardanne's and Chambarlhac's divisions, had taken up positions behind the small Fontanone River, and it was their troops who bore the brunt of the initial Austrian attack directed at the village of Marengo. The infantry assault was supported by an intensive shelling by the greatly superior Austrian artillery. Despite a fierce defensive stand, Victor's divisions were hard pressed to hold their line, and Bonaparte, who had at first not fully grasped the seriousness of the situation, now ordered forward Watrin's division of Lannes' Corps, and the cavalry brigades of Kellermann and

Duvigneau in support of Chambarlhac's division on the French left flank. At the same time he sent off an urgent recall message to Desaix, who at this time was some eight miles east of Marengo with the Boudet division, preparing to cross to the right bank of the Scrivia in accordance with Bonaparte's earlier instructions to scout south to Rivalta and Novi.

When it became evident that Watrin's division on the right flank was being cut up by Ott's troops, Bonaparte sent the Guard infantry, some 800 strong, to its support. Formed in a square, the men briefly stemmed the Austrian advance and helped prevent Ott from turning the French flank, but after their ranks had been severely reduced by Austrian shell fire, they and the remnants of Watrin's division were obliged to fall back. At the same time, the French center and left withdrew in order to maintain the integrity of the line. At this point, all of Bonaparte's reserves had been committed to the battle, and yet the Austrians kept coming. By three in the afternoon, the entire French force was arrayed in an inverted arc north and west of the village of San Giuliano, some four miles east of Marengo.

Melas, having concluded that he had won the battle, and being shaken from having two horses shot out from under him, gave responsibility for the pursuit of the French to his chief of staff, General Zach, and to General Kaim. Having retired to Alessandria, Melas dispatched a young officer named Radetzky (perhaps best known today for the march bearing his name) to Vienna with the news of his supposed victory over Bonaparte at Marengo. There ensued a break in the action while the Austrian troops were reformed into columns for the anticipated pursuit phase of the engagement.

While Bonaparte was redeploying his battered force, Desaix came galloping up to the group of staff officers clustered around Bonaparte, where he was enthusiastically welcomed. Calling out that Boudet's division was hard on his heels, Desaix dismounted. Bonaparte had been counseling with his generals as to the best course of action, and the majority had favored a further withdrawal. Turning to Desaix, Bonaparte asked for his opinion. Desaix pulled his watch and said, "Well, this battle is completely lost, but it's only two o'clock, so there's time to win another!"[3]

That settled the matter, and, as Boudet's division began to arrive, its men were deployed in line of battle across the road along which the Austrian columns were advancing, with Victor's and Lannes battle-worn men extending the right flank, supported by Champeaux's two dragoon regiments. The 450 troopers of Kellermann's cavalry brigade were positioned in support of Boudet's left flank. Bonaparte rode among his troops, "reminding them" that it was his practice to bivouac on the field of battle. Marmont had gathered into a single battery the cannon still in

---

3   Or "three o'clock" or "four o'clock," depending on which source you prefer to believe. Actually, it was probably closer to five o'clock when Desaix arrived on the scene, and his calling it two o'clock may have been his way of saying, "Buck up, boys, we've still got plenty of time to lick those buggers!" And he was right.

1 Pierre Daumesnil in the uniform of a major of the *Chasseurs à cheval de la Garde Impériale*, by Riesener. Anne de Menou collection.

2 Colonel Eugène de Beauharnais and the Chasseurs à cheval des Consuls, by Hoffmann. Anne S. K. Brown military collection.

3 Left: No.19: *Garde Impériale, Trompette des Chasseurs à cheval, Grande Tenue*, by Martinet.
Right: No. 17: *Garde Impériale, Officier des Chasseurs à cheval, Grande Tenue*, by Martinet. Author's collection.

4 *La Carga de los Mamelucos* (The Charge of the Mamelukes), by Goya. Museo del Prado. During the Revolt of *Dos de Mayo* in Madrid, the Mamelukes were attached to Daumesnil's squadron, which he led across Madrid twice that day. See *Notes on Illustrations*, p. 396, no. 1.

5 *The Battle of Wagram*, by H. Vernet. The wounded officer being carried off the field, lower left, may have been intended by the artist to depict Daumesnil. The fallen Marshal Bessières is depicted beneath the outstretched arm of Napoleon's aide. Musée de Versailles.

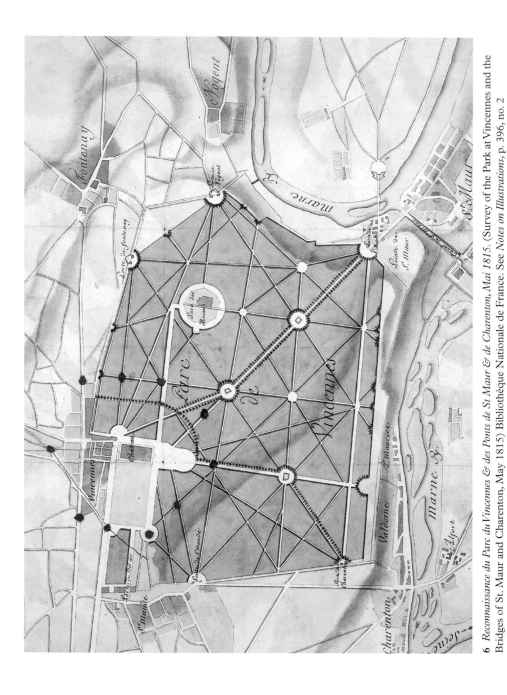

6 *Reconnaissance du Parc du Vincennes & des Ponts de St Maur & de Charenton, Mai 1815.* (Survey of the Park at Vincennes and the Bridges of St. Maur and Charenton, May 1815) Bibliothèque Nationale de France. See *Notes on Illustrations*, p. 396, no. 2

7 *Le Général Daumesnil à Vincennes*, by Gaston Mélingue. Vincennes town hall. Photograph Isabel Tabellion. See *Notes on Illustrations*, p. 396, no. 3.

DAUMESNIL.

8 *Daumesnil*, by Maurin. Author's collection.

French hands, and by 17:00 the French were prepared for the Austrian assault on their lines.

It came almost at once, when the leading Austrian formation, St. Julien's brigade, advanced on Boudet's 9th Light, which met them with volley fire, while Marmont's guns pounded them at close range with canister. The Austrian first line disintegrated, but the following grenadiers of Lattermann's brigade pressed forward determinedly, compelling Boudet's men to start withdrawing. Seeing the French line beginning to fracture, Desaix led forward the rest of Boudet's division, and as he did so, he was struck dead by an Austrian bullet in his breast. Suddenly an Austrian ammunition wagon exploded, throwing the leading Austrian brigades into a momentary state of confusion. Seeing an opportunity to catch the enemy at a disadvantage, Kellermann led his troopers in a looping charge behind and then between Boudet's two brigades, and then drove full tilt into the left flank of Lattermann's grenadiers.

In the brief clash that followed, 1,700 of Lattermann's men and General Zach himself were captured. As Kellermann then wheeled to his right to deal with an Austrian cavalry regiment, which had remained passively by, Bonaparte released the Guard cavalry to ensure the complete disruption of the Austrian left flank. Bessières led the 300 troopers of the Grenadiers and the Chasseurs forward across a terrain broken by vine-yards and deep ditches. With de Beauharnais at their head, the Chasseurs struck the first Austrian line head-on, and overwhelmed it. Kellermann then joined the mêlée with his men, and their combined force drove the Austrian dragoons back on their own infantry, quickly turning the battle into a rout. The French cavalry pursued the fleeing Austrian infantry and cavalry to the outskirts of Marengo, where Weidenfeld's grenadier brigade had managed to establish a defensive line, behind which the beaten Austrian troops struggled to cross the Bormida in order to gain the shelter of Alessandria's citadel.

It had taken the Army of the Reserve an hour to recapture the ground that it had taken Melas's army eight hours to occupy. The defeat cost the Austrians 6,000 dead, 8,000 captives, 40 guns, and 15 colors. French losses were 2,000 killed, 3,600 wounded, and 800 taken prisoner. That evening, judging it useless to prolong the struggle, Melas asked for an armistice. Although Bonaparte had hoped for a more brilliant and decisive conclusion to the campaign, he recognized the degree of attrition that his army had suffered and, feeling the political need to return to Paris, he probably welcomed the respite. Within 24 hours Berthier—maintaining the fiction that he was the commander-in-chief of the French army—had signed the Convention of Alessandria in the First Consul's behalf, thus sealing the armistice.

Captain Elie Krettly, at that time a *brigadier-trompette* of the Chasseurs, has this to say about the charge of the Chasseurs, which helped to break the back of the Austrian army:

Prince Eugène, seeing the dragoons of de Bussy coming toward us, ordered us to charge them. A large ditch separated us from our adversaries, but we were soon over it, and our charge was so rapid that in a moment we were among the leaders of that corps. In the midst of the mêlée, the general[4] commanding that corps was swept off his horse and found himself astride the neck of the horse of the brave Daumesnil, who had seized him vigorously and held him so tightly that it was impossible for him to move. In that manner he was brought to the headquarters.

The dragoons had been put to flight, and in our pursuit of them they had received on their backs some vigorous saber blows. This prompted the prisoner general (*sic*) to say to Prince Eugène, "Your chasseurs have strong fists, for my dragoons' backs are all slashed." "General," Daumesnil commented in good humor, "That's because we took them for Paris mackerel!"

Colonel de Frimont was an émigré who had entered Austrian service. In his *Gens de Guerre*, General Ambert states that Frimont, fearing mistreatment by his captor, quickly offered his watch to Daumesnil. "Oh, yes!" exclaimed Daumesnil. "*I'm* going to give *you* one!" In a box of jewelry that had been given to him that morning as his lot of some booty, he urged his prisoner to select a valuable watch.[5]

When the Allies entered Paris in 1814, Daumesnil was a general and the governor of the fortress of Vincennes. Frimont, who by that time had become a field-marshal and was one of the principal leaders of the Austrian army, came to Vincennes and complimented his adversary for knowing how to prevent all the Allied armies from entering the fortress. Wishing, in his turn, to leave a souvenir with the governor of Vincennes, Field-Marshal de Frimont offered him a pair of magnificent horses. When Daumesnil refused the gift, Frimont pulled out the watch Daumesnil had given him fourteen years earlier. "It has never left me," he said. It was impossible to refuse the horses.

In the course of the cavalry pursuit of the Austrians toward the end of the battle that day, Bessières demonstrated the chivalrous nature of his character. An Austrian trooper, who had until then been giving a very good account of himself, fell wounded from his mount. Dismounted, he feared he was about to be run down by the horses of the Chasseurs. He shouted, "Don't trample me!" Hearing the man's cry, Bessières quickly went to him and called out to his men, "Open your ranks!" The troopers,

---

4 Grandin, *Souvenirs historiques de Capitaine Krettly*, pp 154, 155. Actually, it was not a general, but rather Colonel Johann Maria Frimont, who had started the battle as the commander of the two brigades of O'Reilly's advance guard. Early in the afternoon of the battle, it had been Frimont who had led the horse chasseurs of Bussy in a crippling attack on the Foot Guard.

5 Quoted by Clairval, *Daumesnil*, p. 53.

charging at full speed, parted, and Bessières said to the man, "You're free!"

The evening of the battle, Bonaparte congratulated the commander of the Guard cavalry, saying, in the presence of all of the corps commanders, "Bessières, your cavalry covered itself with glory."

But Desaix was not there to savor the victory. During the battle, his body had been lost in the tumult of the battlefield, and that evening, in accordance with the usual practice, his body, along with all of the others, had been stripped of its clothing before being thrown in a common grave. A search by his officers, however, identified his body, which was then sent by post to Milan for embalming. It was later interred in the little church at the pass of Mount Saint Bernard. Bonaparte had lost another of his best generals on the same day, when Kléber was assassinated in Cairo.

During this campaign, one incident served to demonstrate not only Daumesnil's grasp of the nature of war, but also his indifference to the attraction of money. One day a detachment that he was leading on the track of a retreating enemy came to a bridge obstructed by overturned wagons intended to arrest the progress of the French pursuit. Some pieces of gold had escaped from a staved-in wagon and were flashing under the hooves of the troopers' horses. When some of his men drew up in the face of such riches, Daumesnil turned back to them, calling out "Let's go! Come on! We don't pay attention to mud splashes!"[6] So on they went.

Another day, when Bonaparte was in an advanced post, he gestured to Daumesnil: "Come here, I know your firm shoulder." Placing his long glass on the young officer's shoulder, he began to observe the position and movements of the enemy. An instant later, a bullet shattered his glass. "They must think we're in the Palais Royal and they want another shot," commented Bonaparte with a smile.[7]

The victory of Marengo marked the end of that campaign, and on 17 June the First Consul left for Milan, accompanied by the Chasseurs of the Guard. Arriving there at midnight, he was welcomed by Masséna and a jubilant population. During his stay there, Bonaparte issued a decree

---

6 *Éclaboussures*, in the French: an odd choice of words. Perhaps the image in his mind was that of the sun's rays glancing off the surface of a mud puddle. Or was this a half-remembered catechism lesson of his boyhood? The *Book of Wisdom*, Chapter 7, verses 1–11, says, "Because all gold, in her view, is a little sand, the spirit of wisdom came to me, and, before her, silver is to be accounted mire." A similar incident that occurred in October of 1805, when Murat was pursuing the retreating Austrian cavalry after the fall of Ulm, suggests that this may have been a commonly adopted tactic of retreating Austrian forces. On that occasion, Picard (*op. cit.* p. 277) says, Colonel Cochois's 1st Carabiniers, hastening to catch up with the Austrians, didn't pause in their course to collect prisoners, cannon, horses, or baggage, even though in the midst of the latter was a treasure chest containing, it was said, 200,000 florins, deliberately left open to tempt the pursuers. But the Carabiniers had been imbued with a thirst for glory, and those riches seemed to hold no comparable value for them.

7 Quoted by Clairval, *Daumesnil*, p. 54.

abolishing the Army of the Reserve as a separate formation and incorporating its men in the Army of Italy, under Masséna's command. He also presided over the re-establishment of the Cisalpine Republic, which had, of course, ceased to exist under Austrian rule. By 2 July Bonaparte was back in Paris, where he received a hero's welcome.

After having proceeded by forced marches, on the 14th the Guard arrived in Paris, where a triumphal reception awaited them. The First Consul, high dignitaries, and an immense crowd went to the Champ de Mars to greet the cavalry of the Guard, who brought with them the flags captured at Marengo.

On the recommendation of Bessières, who seems to have taken an almost paternal interest in the young officer, on 18 July 1800 Daumesnil was promoted to the rank of lieutenant[8]. From that point on, Daumesnil would rise rapidly in rank. On the first of August a year later, he became a captain. He was just 25, and a brilliant future seemed to be opening up for him.

---

8   In a list of proposed rewards dated 16 July, Bessières asked for a *sabre d'honneur* for *sous-lieutenant* Daumesnil. However, in that list the words *sabre d'honneur* had been crossed out and replaced in the margin by the word *lieutenant*.

CHAPTER SIX
YEARS OF EVOLUTION

1800

We know relatively little about the next four years of
Daumesnil's career, other than the fact that the Consular
Guard, which became the Imperial Guard on 10 May 1804,
remained in Paris almost continuously until the start of the German
campaign in September of 1804, since as First Consul and then as the
Emperor Napoleon, Bonaparte did not take to the field himself during
those years. They were marked by momentous happenings in France and
in Europe generally, but for the young officer of one of the most
prestigious regiments of the army, over whose unruffled head those great
events passed, it must have been an intoxicating time.

His days filled with routine training and escort duties, revues by the First
Consul, and parades on whatever occasion—or pretext—warranted
turning out the Guard in their increasingly splendid uniforms, Daumesnil's
evenings were no doubt equally taken up with his making his way in the
brilliant Consular society. In a modest way he was already something of a
celebrity, since accounts of his battlefield heroics had been brought back to
Paris with the armies of Italy and the Orient. At some point the tag,
"Napoleon's guardian angel," was attached to him, and it seems unlikely
that Daumesnil took any steps to disavow it. At the frequent receptions and
balls, which he doubtless attended, Daumesnil's outgoing and self-assured
manner, spiced with his quick-witted repartee, must have made him an
attractive and sought-after guest at such gatherings.

While Daumesnil was gaining in terms of his social skills and
broadening and deepening his relations with his companions in arms
during these years, the world in which he moved was certainly affected in
greater or lesser degree by significant developments both within France,
and abroad. The Convention of Alessandria had proved to be no more
than an armistice, since Emperor Francis was by no means ready to accept

the loss of Austria's Italian possessions, and, in any case, Austria's treaty with England ruled out any separate negotiations with France before February 1801. England was equally unwilling to accept passively France's increasingly dominant position on the Continent.

Conscious of the fact that the French people were weary of years of seemingly unending war, and anxious to profit by his role as a peacemaker, Bonaparte would have preferred to avoid a renewal of conflict. However, finally convinced that the Austrians were simply playing for time in order to reorganize their armies and strengthen their alliances, on 22 November 1800 Bonaparte denounced the armistice, and hostilities were resumed. This time Bonaparte remained in Paris, still concerned that his political position was not entirely secure, and with confidence in the military capacity of General Moreau, commanding the Army of the Rhine. Moreau was ordered to renew the offensive on Vienna, and on 3 December at Hohenlinden he defeated the Austrian army, commanded by the Archduke John and General Kray, practically ending the war with Austria. The Treaty of Lunéville, signed on 8 February 1801, brought to a conclusion Austria's participation in the War of the Second Coalition against France.

As one element of his effort to bring order into France's chaotic finances, early in 1800 Bonaparte gave his approval to the establishment of the Bank of France and the selection of Martin Garat as its first director general. At that time Garat was the director general of the *Caisse de Comptes Courants* (Office of Current Accounts), and in 1812 he would become Daumesnil's father-in-law and hence an individual of considerable importance in our story.

The year had ended with an event which served to demonstrate that Bonaparte had good reason for concern regarding the stability of his position. A plot to assassinate the First Consul, devised in England by one Georges Cadoudal with the participation of the Comte d'Artois and the Polignac brothers, involved the placement of a bomb at a spot on the Rue Saint-Nicaise, just north of the Tuileries Palace, on the route that Bonaparte could be expected to take during an evening at the theater. It happened that on Christmas Eve Bonaparte had been persuaded to attend the theater with Josephine, Caroline, Hortense, and General Rapp. Bonaparte set forth first, accompanied by Lannes, Berthier, and an aide-de-camp. Their escort was provided by a troop of Horse Grenadiers of the Guard. The ladies and Rapp followed several minutes behind. Just as the First Consul's carriage passed the emplaced bomb, one of the conspirators touched it off. Bonaparte and his escort of Grenadiers were shaken by the tremendous explosion, but not injured. The second carriage barely escaped being blown to bits, but, again, no one within it was seriously injured. However, nine bystanders were killed, and twenty-six injured.[1]

---

1   A "*plus ça change* ..." note: In 1962, members of the Secret Army Organization (O.A.S.) ambushed President de Gaulle on the road between Paris and his country home, shooting at the tires of his vehicle. However, special puncture-proof tires permitted the chauffeur

Although Bonaparte had made an effort to reinforce the Army of the Orient, which was still making a valiant attempt to maintain France's tenuous position in Egypt, he was unable to transport additional troops through the British blockade. On 8 March 1801 the British landed troops at Aboukir Bay, and after seven months of fighting, the French commander-in-chief, General Jacques François Menou, capitulated in Alexandria on 2 September. By the 15th the last French soldier had left Egyptian soil, thus ending three years and two months of Bonaparte's ill-starred attempt to sever England's communications with India.[2]

1801

Having satisfied himself that the French people wanted to be able to practice their Catholic faith freely, Bonaparte initiated lengthy and complex negotiations with the Vatican, which led to the signing of the Concordat on 15 July of 1801. On the first of October, negotiations between France and England culminated in the Preliminaries for the Peace of Amiens, which was signed on 25 March 1802, and France was—for the moment, at least—at peace with all of her neighbors. English tourists once more walked the streets of Paris.

1802–1803

On 26 April 1802 Bonaparte granted an amnesty—he chose to term it an armistice—to all French living abroad, except for those who had taken up arms against France. 40,000 émigrés accepted his offer, and many of them found their way into the ranks of officers in the army and into the professional classes. That summer, to honor Bonaparte's bringing peace to France and the achievement of the Concordat, the assemblies declared him Consul for Life. This action was overwhelmingly approved in a plebiscite on 2 August 1802. In the same year he created the order of the *Légion d'Honneur*, although it would be two years before the stars had been designed and produced, and the first awards made.

The fourteen months of complete peace which followed the Peace of Amiens were, however, marred by a series of territorial disputes between France and England, which, in sum, made it evident that anything like a stable peace between the two powers at that time was not possible. Finally, Bonaparte's efforts to avoid a rupture came to naught in the second week of May 1803. When two English frigates, acting on the basis of "letters of marque and reprisal against France" issued by the order of George III, seized two French merchantmen on 18 May, this action was judged to be a *de facto* declaration of war, and France declared war on England. For the present, the warfare between Europe's greatest sea power and its greatest

---

to drive safely away. A bullet which penetrated the limousine barely missed Madame de Gaulle.

2 By the end of September, the *Guides* who had remained in Egypt had been incorporated in the *Chasseurs à cheval de la Garde des Consuls.*

land power would be largely confined to the high seas and the Continent's ports, but England intensified her efforts to draw Russian and Austria into a Third Coalition against France.

1804

Plotting against Bonaparte from abroad—primarily England—had continued unabated after the failure of the Rue Saint-Nicaise assassination attempt. In 1804 the Duc d'Enghien, the eldest son of the House of Bourbon, was living in Ettelheim, across the Rhine from Strasbourg. On 14 February the acting chief of police reported to Bonaparte that Cadoudal had come to France and been captured, and that the Duc d'Enghien had been implicated in the plot. This was too much for the First Consul. On the night of 14/15 March he sent General Ordener across the Rhine to Ettelheim with three brigades of *gendarmerie* and 300 dragoons, their horses' hooves muffled with wadding cloth. There Ordener awoke the Prince, and brought him back to France.

The young prince was taken to Vincennes, which had long served as a state prison. As a Frenchman, in time of war he was subject to a military court, and Bonaparte ordered that he be tried by a court of seven colonels. He was found guilty of treason, and sentenced to death. Despite a plea from Josephine for the Prince's life, Bonaparte approved the sentence, and on 21 March the young man was shot by a firing squad in a dry moat of the château of Vincennes, and buried at the foot of the Queen's Tower.[3]

On 18 May 1804 Bonaparte's fellow Consul, Cambacérès, in the name of the Senate proclaimed him Emperor. Three and a half million Frenchmen voted in favor of the Imperial title's being hereditary, and less than 3,000 against the proposition. In the forefront of the new emperor's mind was the question of how to deal with England. It will be remembered that when he returned from his first Italian campaign, the Directory had appointed him commander-in-chief of the Army of England, but, even though some preparations had been made for a possible attack across the Channel, Bonaparte had judged it to be infeasible, and the idea had been dropped. Now he had convinced himself that striking at the heart of his implacable enemy was the only way to end the contest between the two powers for once and for all. Before dealing with the consequences of the newly minted Emperor's decision as to how to resolve the English question, however, let us come down to earth to take note of more mundane matters bearing more directly on Daumesnil's existence as a proud member of his elite corps.

In March 1800, Eugène de Beauharnais, still commanding the company of *Chasseurs à cheval de la Garde des Consuls*, was promoted to the rank of *chef d'escadron*. On 8 September the corps became a squadron of

---

3   In 1816 the body was taken from its grave in the moat and, at the request of Louis XVIII, placed in a tomb set in the east end of the château's chapel. In 1851 Louis Napoleon had the tomb and the body moved to a less conspicuous location in the chapel.

234 men, and on 9 May 1801 that squadron was attached to the *Grenadiers à cheval*, in the sense that they were henceforth expected to fight side by side. On 6 August of that year the addition of troopers carefully selected from Line cavalry regiments permitted the formation of a second squadron, each then consisting of two companies. Finally, on 14 November 1801 the corps became a regiment, with Beauharnais continuing as its commander.

A year later, the steady addition of men had brought the regiment's strength to 56 officers and 959 men, divided into four squadrons, and Beauharnais had been made a *chef de brigade*. The Senate proclamation which made Bonaparte an emperor also converted the Consular Guard into the Imperial Guard. At that time a company of Mamelukes, commanded by Colonel Jean Rapp, was added to the regiment[4]. Captain Edouard de Colbert, who would go on to win great distinction in the wars of the Empire, was in charge of administration.

It was by now evident that the Emperor's particular favorites were his *Chasseurs à cheval*, a preference he demonstrated in a striking manner by his habitually wearing their uniform during his normal activities. Before long the Chasseurs would acquire several nicknames: *les Enfants chéris* (the pet children), and *les Invincibles*—the latter a sarcastic comment on the fact that the Emperor seldom committed them to battle. Occasionally in later years their privileged status led some of the men in the regiment to foolish excesses, and then the Emperor reined them in sharply, but their fall from grace was always of short duration.

On 14 June Daumesnil was named a *chevalier* of the Legion of Honor. On 14 July, some 6,000 generals, other officers, soldiers of the Guard, magistrates, savants, and artists received stars of the Legion in a grandiose ceremony under the dome of the Invalides. Daumesnil received his star from the hands of the Emperor himself. Before long he had followed the example of many of his fellow officers in having his own letterhead stationery printed. At the top of each sheet one could read:

GARDE IMPERIALE
P. Daumesnil, Capitaine des Chasseurs
à cheval, Membre de la Légion d'honneur

Letters written by Daumesnil throughout his career reveal his ignorance of grammatical rules, but their contents most often convey a frankness and open-heartedness which give them a warm vibrancy. But there is no doubt, Henri de Clairval comments, that Daumesnil was more adept with the sword than with the pen.

Let us now enlarge our view again. Napoleon's decision to strike

---

4   On the occasion of a parade on 11 July 1802, which included the presentation of flags to some light demi-brigades by the First Consul, 100 mounted Mamelukes made their first public appearance.

directly across the Channel at England had caused the movement of many thousands of troops of every category to a number of camps in northwest France and Holland—at Utrecht, Ghent, Saint-Omer, Compiègne, and Brest—but the largest camp was at Boulogne, where the massive encampment became a small town in itself. The construction of a large flotilla of transport craft of various sizes began in a number of ports. To meet the need for sailors to man these craft, in September of 1803 the Emperor created within the Consular Guard a battalion of 737 seamen, divided into five crews of five squads each. Their pay was the same as that of the cavalry of the Guard. By May of 1804 they had been concentrated in the Camp of Boulogne.

During the months that this massive force was gathered on and near France's Channel coast, while hundreds of vessels of varying sizes and characters were being constructed in almost every northern French port, the troops were being trained in boarding and manning these craft and in conducting assault landings on a hostile shore. Napoleon periodically inspected the camps, observed training exercises, and reviewed his troops. Evidence that the cavalry of the Guard were not exempt from maritime training exercises is afforded by the fact that Captain Daumesnil took part in at least one such exercise aboard a gunboat commanded by Lieutenant Grivel of the Seamen of the Guard.

One review of a flotilla of vessels of the growing naval force took a disastrous turn when the Emperor insisted on the review's taking place despite the threat of an onshore gale. The result was that twenty of the small, shallow-bottomed craft, manned by seamen and filled with soldiers, were thrown upon the shore, with the loss of 2,000 men. Admiral Bruix, whose sound sailor's judgment and personal courage had led to his advising against conducting the review in the face of Napoleon's land-lubber's ignorance of the power of the sea, was rewarded for his sagacity by being sent into exile in Holland. He died in Paris less than a year later. Napoleon's sense of his own infallibility was gradually feeding on itself.

Wishing to place the second granting of stars of the Legion in a spectacular setting, Napoleon chose the Camp of Boulogne for the ceremony, since these stars were all to be given to men of the army. On 16 August 1804 100,000 men were aligned in a massive fan-like formation in a huge amphitheater, with an elevated throne for the Emperor before a flag-bedecked pavilion at its apex. The soldiers and officers who were to receive stars were brought out of the ranks and grouped at the foot of the dais. Napoleon then read the words of the oath of the Legion, and, to the accompaniment of trumpets and cannons, the legionnaires shouted in unison, "We swear it!" Then during the next two hours the men came, one by one, to receive their decorations.

An unplanned event lent extra drama to the occasion. A division of a flotilla, which had recently departed from le Havre, was just at that moment entering Boulogne harbor in the midst of a lively cannonade with

English ships off shore. From time to time the Emperor suspended the ceremony so that he could observe the progress of the action through a long glass. Finally the French ships made harbor safely and disembarked their crews, to the accompaniment of cheers from the spectators.

Before the end of the year the Imperial Guard would be called on to play prominent roles in two events designed by Napoleon to confirm, in religious and martial splendor, his imperial stature. The first of these was the Coronation, which took place in Notre Dame cathedral on the second of December. Three days later there took place the ceremony of the *Champ de Mars*, in the course of which Napoleon, standing in a pavilion before the *École Militaire*, gave the colonels and standard-bearers of his regiments their eagles, then declaring to them:

> Soldiers, here are your flags! These eagles will always be your rallying point. They will be wherever your Emperor deems necessary for the defense of the throne and his people. Do you swear to lay down your lives in their defense, and by your courage to keep them ever on the road to victory?[5]

"We swear!" the colonels cried out, lifting their eagle-topped flags and standards on high, as the bands of the Guard played, and the troops presented arms. What soldier could fail to be moved by such oratory and pageantry? Even the rain which drenched the parade following the ceremony did little to detract from the emotional impact of the occasion.

The two Guard cavalry regiments, dressed in their most magnificent uniforms, had played prominent roles in both of these grandiose spectacles. The new year was to see the Chasseurs performing a similar role in still another such ceremonial drama—the crowning of Napoleon as King of Italy. The incongruity of Napoleon's being at one and the same time the Emperor of the French and the President of the Italian Republic must certainly have been a factor in his decision to change that republic into a kingdom. At first he offered its throne to Joseph, who turned it down out of concern for losing his eventual rights in the Empire. Then Louis begged off having his young son given the title, since he would then be left with the inglorious role of acting as the boy's tutor. Finally Napoleon decided to crown himself—after all, he had some experience in performing that office—as king, with Eugène acting as his viceroy.

1805

In mid-January of 1805, Beauharnais, now *colonel-général* of the Chasseurs, received orders from his stepfather to proceed with his regiment to Italy within 24 hours. The following day, 16 January, after a review by Napoleon at Essone of 1,800 foot Grenadiers and Chasseurs

---

5 Lachouque, *The Anatomy of Glory*, p. 48.

and 1,000 mounted Grenadiers, Chasseurs, and Mamelukes, at noon Eugène set out at the head of a column composed of several squadrons each of the Grenadiers and Chasseurs, and the company of Mamelukes, some 900 men altogether. Although we do not know whether or not Daumesnil was among those selected for this occasion, our familiarity with his personality and ambitions suggests that, with his recently awarded cross of the Legion resplendent on his breast, he would have been among those so singled out.

At Roanne at five in the morning of 3 February, Captain Claude Guyot of the Chasseurs—later *général comte* Guyot—awakened Eugène with a message from the Emperor notifying him that he was now Prince Eugène, Arch-Chancellor of State, and Serene Highness. Furthermore, he was now a *général de brigade*, and still in command of the Chasseurs. The column pressed on in the face of blizzards, landslides, broken bridges, floods, fallen trees, rock falls, and drenching rains. The passage over the Mount Cenis pass was particularly painful and slow, but on 15 March the weather-worn troops, short 34 men and 36 horses, entered Milan through the Pavia gate. (Some of the missing men later turned up.)

The new prince went up to the old hunting lodge of Stupinigi, six miles out of Turin, to meet the Emperor and Empress, and escorted them back to Milan. On a beautiful clear day in May, Napoleon visited the battlefield of Marengo to observe a re-enactment of that victory. He wore the same hat and coat that he had worn on that famous day, and when he appeared on the reviewing stand, he was greeted by a thunderous roar from the assembled troops.

In the cathedral of Milan on the 26th, in a ceremony very similar to that which had taken place in Notre Dame five months previously, Napoleon crowned himself King of Italy with the Iron Crown of Lombardy. In a public appearance the following day, he announced the creation of the Order of the Iron Crown. On 7 June Napoleon informed the Legislative Assembly that he had appointed Prince Eugène Viceroy to rule in his absence, and Prince Eugène immediately took the oath of fidelity. On the 10th, Napoleon left for a tour of northern Italy.

Since Prince Eugène would now necessarily remain in Milan, he obviously could no longer actively exercise command of his regiment, although he would nominally retain the title of regimental commander until well into 1808. Consequently, by Imperial decree Colonel François Morland, *colonel commandant en second* under Beauharnais, became the effective commander of the Chasseurs, although that appointment was fated literally to be short-lived.

Evidently feeling no need to hasten back to Paris—and Boulogne—and possibly in order to afford some of his new subjects an opportunity to demonstrate their affection for their new monarch, the Emperor traveled with his Guard to Lodi, Piacenza, Parma, Reggio, Modena, and Bologna, before finally heading back to Paris. Perhaps Napoleon was also taking more than a little pleasure in the fact that, by doing so, he was rubbing the Emperor Francis's nose in the fact that he had driven the Austrians out of Italy.

Setting out on 13 July, *capitaine chef d'escadron* Guyot led 420 men of the regiment of Chasseurs back to Paris, arriving in the capital one month later.

Having, in effect, solidified his royal and imperial credentials on the world stage, now Napoleon once more directed his energies toward dealing with the unresolved "English problem." His strategy for luring the British fleet away from the Channel finally got underway in late March of 1805, when Admiral Villeneuve managed to slip past the British vessels blockading Toulon and set sail for the West Indies, with Nelson in pursuit. This particular "best laid plan" broke down, however, when Villeneuve, having returned to European waters from the West Indies, chose not to sail north to the Channel out of fear of being trapped there by the returning Nelson. Instead, after several days of indecision in mid-August, he sailed south, ending up in Cadiz where he was once more bottled up by the British fleet.

News of Villeneuve's action reached Napoleon on 25 August in his office in the small château of Pont-de-Briques, near Boulogne. One can easily imagine his furious reaction upon learning of this frustration of his grand design. "Jackass" is probably one of the politer terms that he applied to the hapless Villeneuve. Charged with cowardice by Napoleon, the admiral nevertheless retained his command long enough to challenge Nelson at Trafalgar, where he was roundly defeated and taken prisoner. Freed on parole, he returned to France, where he killed himself because of the disgrace.

Whether or not Napoleon was glad for an excuse to abandon the project for the invasion of England is an open question. He may well have begun to question its feasibility, even under the most favorable conditions, but it seems probable that concern over the growing military preparations by Austria and Russia and the formation of the Third Coalition, under the pressure of the English prime minister, Pitt, must have played a decisive role in his calculations. Whatever the truth of the matter, after scarcely an hour's reflection on the information he had just received, the Emperor dictated to Count Daru, in an unbroken stream and without any apparent consideration, the orders which would launch the massive force gathered in the north of France on seven different roads leading toward the heart of Europe. Bessières was instructed to put those squadrons of the two mounted Guard regiments in Paris, as well as those in Boulogne, on the road to Strasbourg on the 31st. The *Armée d'Angleterre* was about to become *La Grande Armée,* which would dominate European battlefields for the better part of the next decade.

Napoleon informed his army of the radical change in their future mission in these words:

Brave soldiers of the Boulogne Camp, you are not going to England.
The Emperor of Austria, bribed with English gold, has declared war
on us. His army has crossed prohibited frontiers. Bavaria is invaded!
Soldiers! New Laurels await you beyond the Rhine!

CHAPTER SEVEN
FROM ULM TO AUSTERLITZ TO WARSAW

1805

After four years of organization, training, maritime exercises, escort duties, inspections, parades, reviews, and role players in magnificent ceremonies, the *Chasseurs à cheval de la Garde Impériale* were now going to war for the first time as a full-strength regiment, which, for proud and ambitious young officers like Daumesnil, seemed to hold out promise for further opportunities for winning fame for themselves, their regiment, and their emperor.

The Austrian offensive, designed to strike through Bavaria toward Strasbourg and on into France, had begun on 2 September, with General Mack's army pushing rapidly westward as far as Ulm, in Württemberg. He was expecting Napoleon to follow the traditional invasion route into eastern Europe by coming through the Black Forest, and it was there that he planned to meet and defeat the French. Napoleon, however, had a very different concept of how he wished to see this conflict evolve. His grand strategy called for seven corps of the *Grande Armée* to enter Germany simultaneously along as many different routes, swinging north of and around the main Austrian army under the command of Archduke Ferdinand, finally converging in massive force between Ferdinand's army and Vienna.

Accordingly, on 30 September Marmont's 2nd Corps, Davout's 3rd Corps, Soult's 4th Corps, Ney's 6th Corps, and Lannes' 5th Corps, together with the Guard and Murat's cavalry reserve of 22,000 men, crossed the Rhine at different points, while Bernadotte's 1st Corps started down from the north through the Prussian territory of Ansbach. In order to foster Mack's illusion that the main French advance would be coming through the Black Forest, Murat was instructed to take part of his cavalry reserve and Lannes' corps and feint an advance through that area before swinging up to join the bulk of the army.

Out of concern that Ferdinand and his chief of staff, Mack, would awaken to the perilous reality of their situation before he was able to prevent their withdrawal by cutting off all possible escape routes, Napoleon went to great pains to cloak his strategy with all possible secrecy. It was essential for its success that Ferdinand and Mack remain in blissful ignorance of the fate being prepared for them until it was too late for them to escape it. It happened that an instrument for feeding on that ignorance was at hand.

As early as 1800, an Alsatian smuggler in Strasbourg named Karl Schulmeister had been employed by French forces on the German border as an intelligence agent. His career as a smuggler and his fluent German had permitted him to move easily back and forth across the border, and he had developed a considerable network of acquaintances among officials of the German states, and with Austrians in positions to facilitate his activities. A man of exceptional personal courage, with a flair and zest for covert activities, he had come to the attention of *général de division* Savary, the chief of Napoleon's planning staff and his chief of intelligence.

In September 1805 Schulmeister had been expelled from the department of Bas-Rhin by order of its prefect. It is not clear whether this action was taken because of Schulmeister's smuggling activities, or arranged by Savary as a way of permitting the agent to present himself in the camp of General Mack without difficulties. Whatever the truth of the matter, between them Savary and Schulmeister conceived a plan for planting critically important disinformation in the minds of Ferdinand and Mack, and on 1 October Savary presented Schulmeister to Napoleon, who listened to and approved the operation. With that, Schulmeister set out for Ulm.

Once there, he sought out a friend, Captain Wend, who was the chief of Mack's intelligence service. Wend presented Schulmeister to Mack as an Austrian spy, and very quickly the agent won Mack's complete confidence. As we shall presently see, Schulmeister had by now become "Baron Steinherr." He at once began to supply Mack with misleading information regarding the French, while at the same time he was reporting back to Savary what he was learning in the Austrian camp. He had yet to play his trump card however.

Throughout the first week of October the massive "swinging-door" made up of six corps and the cavalry reserve of the *Grande Armée* continued to grind on its hinge to the north of Ulm, and by the sixth its ponderous presence was northwest of Ferdinand and Mack, where they remained passively, still nursing delusions as to Napoleon's intentions. In fact, the emperor himself was not entirely clear as to his opponents' intentions. As the bulk of the French forces crossed to the south bank of the Danube in the vicinity of Donauwörth, Napoleon was under the impression that there were relatively few Austrian troops left in Ulm, and that he could expect to collide with Mack's force well east of that city, somewhere along the line of the Lech River. By the tenth, however, Ney's reporting from the vicinity of Ulm corrected that misapprehension. It was clear to the marshal that 40,000 to 50,000 Austrian troops were in or around Ulm.

On the 11th, Mack moved two of his divisions to the north bank of the Danube, where they encountered Dupont's division of Ney's corps in overwhelming numbers, inflicting heavy casualties on it and capturing some of Ney's orders, which revealed that the bulk of his corps was south of the river, thus leaving the north bank free for Mack to lead his army eastward for a rendezvous with the Russians – who were, in fact, still far off to the east. That same day, Steinherr/Schulmeister left Ulm for Stuttgart, whence he sent a dispatch to Mack conveying the "critical news" that the French army was pulling back to the Rhine: that a British force had landed on the French coast, and that an uprising had taken place in Paris. The situation was judged to be desperate for Napoleon.

In his monumental *The Campaigns of Napoleon* (p. 396), David Chandler has this to say about that extraordinary episode:

> In actual fact, at this particular time General Mack was indulging in an orgy of false optimism. An Austrian agent had reported that he had overheard a lunchtime conversation in a village on the French communications lines during which rumors of a British invasion at Boulogne were mentioned. This piece of unfounded gossip appealed to the Austrian general and appeared to throw the whole situation on the Danube into a more favorable light.

Chandler goes on to quote Mack as follows:

> The news brought to me by Baron Steinherr, a credible witness, of the conversation he had overheard, coincided so well with the opinions I had already formed on the facts before me, that I allowed myself to accept it as correct.

So much for generals acting as their own intelligence analysts. The operation conceived by Schulmeister and Savary had worked to perfection. Mack now gave up any idea of withdrawing eastward from Ulm along the north bank, and, instead, set about issuing orders to his army for the pursuit of the supposedly withdrawing French army. His illusions were rudely shattered on the 14th, however, when Ney's troops crossed the partially destroyed bridge at Elchingen and seized the heights looking down on Ulm, driving General Riesch back toward Ulm. The ring was almost closed.

The Archduke Ferdinand now decided that he would not risk giving Napoleon the satisfaction of capturing a Habsburg, and decided to take the cavalry and break out to the north. Mack refused to join him, but

Schwarzenburg and other officers deserted their troops to go with Ferdinand. Either on the night of the 14th or early on the 15th Ferdinand led 6,000 troopers out of Ulm, heading north to Herbrechtingen, hoping to rendezvous there with General Werneck's division, which had earlier escaped from Ulm. By the night of the 15th Ferdinand was even farther north, at Aalen.

During these days the Guard had remained with Napoleon, arriving with him in Augsburg on the 13th. By the evening of the 14th the Guard was at Albeck, some seven miles northeast of Ulm. The Guard cavalry spent a miserable night under a downpour, and within musket shot of the ramparts of Ulm. At dawn on the 15th, the sporadic fire from the city's walls, which had persisted during the night, intensified, and the famed La Tour dragoon regiment emerged at a fast trot from the main city gate, apparently under orders to attack the cavalry brigade attached to Ney's corps, while his infantry were working their way across the bridge at Elchingen to the north bank of the Danube, thus closing the ring around the city.

Seeing this threat to Ney's operations, Bessières ordered the Chasseurs, the Grenadiers, and the squadron of Mamelukes to drive the Austrian dragoons back into the city. Under abominable weather conditions and in semi-darkness, and in churned up mud and mire which made traction for the horses of both adversaries exceedingly difficult, there ensued what Krettly describes as a cavalry mêlée, with trooper against trooper in such close hand-to-hand combat that it was almost impossible for the Chasseurs to use the point of their sabers, so that some of them were clubbing their opponents' faces with the hilts of their blades. In that chaotic encounter the La Tour regiment gave proof that their reputation had not been exaggerated, but they had met their betters on that day, and after stiff resistance, they were forced back within the city walls.

That evening, drenched to the skin and exhausted by their day's work, the Chasseurs took possession of some structures which had been earmarked for the vehicles and personnel of the Imperial household, and were making themselves comfortable there when the men of the Emperor's *maison* arrived and tried to occupy the quarters. They were rudely ejected by the Chasseurs, however, and, as might well be imagined, the grievance of the emperor's staff promptly reached Imperial ears. In short order, the Chasseurs found themselves out in the damp and cold once more. The Emperor's "pet children" had become instead simply spoiled kids.

The escape northward of Ferdinand with a significant body of cavalry, combined with the fact that Werneck's division was still in a position to cut the French line of communications, gave Napoleon serious concern. Therefore, on the night of 14/15 October he instructed Murat to gather up whatever cavalry could be spared from operations against Ulm, and to pursue and drive back all Austrian forces on the Danube's north bank. As punishment for their misbehaviour, Napoleon specifically ordered Murat to put the Chasseurs in his advance guard for the remainder of the pursuit, and not to spare them. So for ten days the Chasseurs were deprived of the honor of serving as the Emperor's personal escort.

Having collected, in addition to the Chasseurs of the Guard, Fauconnet's brigade of horse chasseurs from Lannes' corps and the 1st *Hussards* attached to Dupont's division, Murat at once set out after the Austrians, with the Emperor's order "not to let any one escape" ringing in his ears. Somewhere along the way Murat had also picked up the six regiments of dragoons of Klein's division. On the road from Haslach to Brenz, he caught up with what was left of Dupont's division near Langenau, where Dupont was trying to talk General Werneck's greatly superior force into surrendering. When it became clear that the Austrian had no intention of doing so, Murat deployed Dupont's infantry, with his hussars and chasseurs on the right flank, and launched the infantry against the Austrian line. When the latter fought back stubbornly, Murat ordered the light cavalry forward, and very shortly the Austrians had broken, with 2,000 of them taken prisoner.

With scarcely a pause and leaving his hussars and chasseurs to follow, Murat took the Guard Chasseurs and the dragoons and continued the pursuit of the main Austrian body. Arriving before the village of Herbrechtingen late that afternoon, Murat halted to permit the infantry to catch up with him. When the 9th light infantry arrived, he ordered a bayonet attack on the village, while he personally led a charge of the Chasseurs and the dragoons. The fighting continued until midnight, and the Austrian rear guard was completely destroyed. Another 3,000 men, along with cannon, caissons, and baggage fell into French hands. All in all, a good day's work.

Starting at dawn on the 16th, by five that afternoon Murat had caught up with the Austrian rear guard at Neresheim. Despite the waning light, he ordered an attack by Klein's dragoons, which was at first repulsed by the Austrians. Successive charges broke them, however, and soon those who had not fallen prisoner to the French were once more fleeing, pursued by the Chasseurs and dragoons. The Archduke Ferdinand himself barely escaped on the horse of one of his aides de camp.

Murat's relentless pursuit once again ran down Werneck at Trochtelfingen on the 17th, and, after an attempt on the Austrian general's part to negotiate a truce under the cover of which he might slip away to the south, he recognized the hopelessness of his position, and on the 18th he surrendered the 8,000 infantry and officers, 50 cannon, and 18 flags of his command. At the same time Fauconnet's chasseurs scooped up the entire Austrian field park, consisting of 500 vehicles. Back at Ulm, on the 20th Mack finally accepted the inevitable, and 25,000 infantry and 2,000 cavalry of his garrison laid down their arms before Napoleon, standing amidst his staff on a rise at the foot of the Michelsberg Heights.

On the same day, Murat's hard-driven cavalry were again nipping at the heels of the Austrians, now at Echenau just outside Nuremberg. Leading a platoon of 30 Chasseurs of the Guard at the point of the advance guard, Lieutenant Desmichels attacked the Austrian rearguard of 300 light infantrymen, catching them unprepared to resist his attack, and they quickly surrendered. Desmichels pressed on, and another 400 Austrians and two flags fell into his hands.

Seeing the Austrian infantry being cut up and dispersed, the colonel of the La Tour dragoons spurred the 500 men of his regiment to their comrades' rescue, but in the narrow confines of the road on which the troops were engaged, he was unable to deploy his force so as to overwhelm the two dozen Chasseurs Desmichels still had in hand. Instead, the dauntless lieutenant attacked the head of the column of dragoons, driving them back on the following files. Then the rest of the Chasseurs, together with some carabiniers, came to Desmichels' support, completing the rout of the dragoons. 50 of the latter were killed and 150 captured, including the regiment's colonel. Once again, Prince Ferdinand got away by the skin of his teeth, with barely 1,000 of his men this time. That night the Chasseurs made camp on the outskirts of Nuremberg, while Murat established his headquarters in the city itself. In a letter to the Emperor on the 18th, Murat wrote, "I have much praise to give the Chasseurs of the Imperial Guard."

The booty collected by Murat's regiments, during five days of almost continuous fighting over a distance of more than 200 kilometers under execrable weather conditions, was extraordinary: 18 generals, 12,500 men captured, 11 flags, 120 cannon, and more than 1,500 caissons and wagons taken. Of the 22,000 Austrian soldiers who had broken out of Ulm, only 1,000 had survived and reached safety. In his report to Napoleon on the 21st, Murat wrote, "This evening, the debris of the army corps led by Prince Ferdinand has been completely beaten on the road from Nuremberg to Fürth. I owe the greatest praise to all of the cavalry, and, in particular, to the *Chasseurs à cheval* of your Guard, who began the attack and completely overwhelmed the enemy cavalry, although they were very inferior in number."

In a further report to the Emperor the next day, Murat described the Chasseurs' action in these words:

> I ordered the Chasseurs of Your Majesty's Guard to hasten, and to charge the enemy rear guard. Sire, your Chasseurs rushed forward with an unequaled impetuosity. A battalion of infantry, which was marching behind the Austrian cavalry, was broken into, dispersed, and taken prisoner without having had the time to reform and to fire a shot. 25 Chasseurs put to flight 300 cavalrymen. Sire, after that brilliant début, your Chasseurs overthrew all that were before them: canister didn't stop them, and they captured the cannon. All the Austrian infantry was scattered.

When the regiment rejoined Napoleon's headquarters at Mühldorf on the 29th, he showed his pleasure with its mens' performance. All was forgiven, and the regiment was back in their emperor's good graces. Desmichels was made a captain and given the star of the Legion,[1] and 30 Chasseurs received "silver eagles."

At this point the Archduke Ferdinand's army having been effectively destroyed, the target of the French pursuit became the army of Marshal Kutusov. Once the latter had realized that there was no chance of his coming to the aid of the besieged Mack, he had begun a slow withdrawal into Moravia, hoping to join forces with the army of Buxhövden coming down from Olmütz, to the northeast of Vienna. As he did so, he burned bridges behind him, and stripped the countryside of food.

Pressing forward with the advance guard, on the 13th of November Murat tricked the Austrian commanders at the main bridge leading into Vienna into believing that an armistice was about to be signed, and that therefore there was nothing to be gained by resisting the French entrance into the city. With scarcely a pause, Murat then led his regiments of light cavalry, Walther's dragoons, the heavy cavalry of Nansouty and d'Hautpoul, and the infantry of Lannes and Soult northward on the tracks of Kutusov. At Hollabrunn on the 15th Murat encountered 1500 Austrian cavalry, supported by Bagration's division of 6,000 men. After an inconclusive clash with the Austrians, Murat himself was now the victim of a tactical ruse played by Kutusov, permitting himself to be talked into signing a convention which would lead to an armistice. When he proudly reported this seeming "coup" to Napoleon, at midday on the 16th he received a blistering reprimand from the emperor for having signed the convention, and the order to attack the Austrian and Russian blocking force at once.

Bagration's orders had been to delay Murat as long as possible, while Kutusov withdrew the bulk of his force farther to the east, and Murat had been completely taken in by the flattery heaped on him by the Austrian and Russian intermediaries. Humiliated by Napoleon's harsh tongue-lashing, late that afternoon Murat threw his infantry against the Russian infantry in a bloody battle that went on until eleven that night. The 1800 prisoners and 12 cannon that fell into French hands were small consolation to Murat for his blunder. Bagration's remaining infantry had slipped away to join Kutusov.

At dawn on the 17th, Napoleon put himself at the head of the advance guard as it passed through Znaïm, en route to Brünn. Leading the advance guard were Walther's dragoons, led by Sébastiani's brigade, closely followed by d'Hautpoul's division of cuirassiers. Over the next several days the French continued to be in almost constant contact with the rear guard of the withdrawing Austrian and Russian troops. Then, having passed through Brünn on the 19th, on the following day Murat's

---

1 In 1811 he left the Guard, and became the colonel commanding the 3rd *Chasseurs à cheval*.

advance guard was stopped by a force of some 6,000 Russian cavalry, astride the Brünn-Olmütz road and giving no signs of withdrawing.

Successive attacks by Walter's three dragoon brigades, joined by d'Hautpoul's cuirassiers, failed to break the resolute barrier to the French advance. At that point Bessières arrived on the scene with the Guard cavalry. Following the Emperor's orders, he left the Mamelukes with Napoleon and formed the Chasseurs and the Grenadiers in two lines: in the first line, three squadrons of Grenadiers and two of Chasseurs, and in the second, the reverse. The second line was to attack only if the first line was repulsed. The charge of the first line drove the Russian cavalry from the field, leaving their light artillery in French hands. There was no need for the second line to attack. Five squadrons of the Guard had succeeded in doing in a few minutes what twelve regiments of dragoons and cuirassiers under Murat had been unable to accomplish in several hours.

On 23 November Napoleon, realizing that his soldiers were badly worn by the almost continuous fighting during the eight weeks of the offensive, called a halt to operations. He had learned that Kutusov had been able to join Buxhövden, and that the Tsar and the Emperor Francis had arrived at Olmütz. The next week saw little contact between the opposing forces, as Napoleon rested his troops, and maneuvered in such a way as to convey to the Russians and Austrians an impression of hesitancy and possible willingness to reach some sort of a peace agreement. At the same time, he was deploying his own force in a manner that made him confident of a victory in the decisive battle that he knew would take place in a very few days. As early as the 21st he had selected the field on which the battle of Austerlitz would occur.

There are too many excellent accounts of the Battle of the Three Emperors to warrant any effort on my part to retrace the ground covered in fine detail by numerous learned historians, so I shall instead confine my reporting of that epic engagement to those episodes in which the cavalry of the Guard, and particularly the Chasseurs, and hence Daumesnil, played key roles.

With all his troops positioned in accordance with his planned strategy, on the afternoon of 1 December, the eve of the anniversary of his coron-ation, Napoleon made a final examination of the French positions. In his *Mémoires*, one of the emperor's aides, Count Phillipe de Ségur, gives this account of an incident during that excursion:

> Napoleon, followed by several of us and twenty Chasseurs of his Guard, advanced between the two lines and rode the length of them, from right to left. He made this last general reconnaissance slowly, at a walk, and so close to the enemy that as we came near Pratzen, the captain of his Chasseur escort, Daumesnil, later famous for his defense of Vincennes, and I rashly provoked the enemy lines, a pistol shot away, for which we were sharply reprimanded. We had attracted

several shots, the balls of which whistled in the Emperor's ears.

I remember that, after having been reprimanded for that imprudence, we had arrived at the extreme left of our line, beyond the Santon, while Napoleon examined the approaches to it, and an argument had arisen between us regarding the distance that separated us at that point from the enemy. That same Daumesnil, an excellent shot, wanting to prove to me the proximity of the enemy, took a carbine from one of his men, and, placing its barrel on the chasseur's shoulder, with one shot he dismounted a Russian officer, who had made himself evident to us by the brilliant whiteness of his mount.[2]

In his *Austerlitz* (p. 43), Claude Manceron adds that Daumesnil then remounted his horse, observing, "That's one less for tomorrow, at any rate."

At 20:30 that evening Napoleon issued his orders, conferred with his marshals, and then stretched out in his hut and slept until 22:00. He then arose, mounted his horse, and headed toward the frozen ponds, escorted by 20 Chasseurs commanded by Daumesnil. It was in crossing a small stream that he escaped a Cossack patrol. He paused for a few moments at Vandamme's bivouac, and then resumed his course to the Imperial bivouac, cutting across the fields. It was a moonless night and there was a thick fog, and the Chasseurs lit torches of fir and straw to light the emperor's passage. Seeing in the light of their torches a group of mounted officers approaching them, the soldiers quickly recognized the Imperial party, and many lit torches as well. Soon the entire French line was ablaze, and repeated shouts of "*Vive l'Empereur!*" echoed across the Goldbach stream to the Russian lines. Regimental bands added their music to the exhilaration of the moment.

The battle began soon after daybreak on 2 December, with much of the battlefield still obscured by a heavy fog. As Napoleon had anticipated, the main attack was launched against the French right wing, driving down from the Allied positions atop the Pratzen plateau and directed toward the villages of Telnitz and Sokolnitz. Meanwhile, on the northern sector of the battlefield, Bagration and Lannes at first fenced indecisively, but as the day wore on, Lannes and Murat succeeded in almost completely sealing Bagration's force off from the rest of the Allied army.

When it was clear to Napoleon that the Allied troops dedicated to turning the French right flank had advanced far enough so that the Allied center had been significantly weakened, he ordered Soult's corps forward up the slope of the Pratzen plateau, setting in motion the attack which would split the Allied army in two. When Kutusov realized what was happening, he attempted to counter Soult's advance by ordering some of

---

2   Quoted by Clairval, *Daumesnil*, pp. 68–9.

his troops to counter-march and by sending his reserve, the guard infantry and cavalry, forward into the developing gap in the center of his line, in an effort to drive a wedge between Soult's and Bernadotte's corps.

By 11:00, a bayonet charge by Russian guard infantry had broken through the first line of Vandamme's division, but the fire of his second line drove them back to Krzenowitz to reform. At that point, in response to an order from Napoleon, Vandamme began to swing his division in echelons to the right, and, in doing so, he exposed the left flank and even the rear of its formation. The Grand Duke Constantine, in command of the Russian Imperial Guard, was quick to perceive the opportunity thus afforded to him, and he at once loosed the fifteen squadrons of Guard cuirassiers and hussars on Vandamme's infantry, as the reformed Russian grenadiers renewed their attack.

Vandamme attempted to fend off the Russian attack by ordering his 4th Line and 24th Light regiments to face quarter-left to confront the onrushing mass of cavalry, but two battalions of the 4th were overrun, one of them losing its eagle and most of its mens their weapons. The impetus of the Russian cavalry's charge had carried them through the ranks of Drouet d'Erlon's division, which had come up in support of Vandamme's men, and almost to the foot of the rise on which Napoleon and his staff were standing, in the midst of the Guard. Seeing his infantry being cut to pieces, Napoleon turned to Bessières and said, gesturing toward the mêlée in the near distance, said, "There's some disorder there. Set it straight!"[3]

At first Bessières ordered Morland, the colonel of the Chasseurs, to take two of his squadrons and go to the rescue of the survivors of the 4th Battalion, who were being hunted down by Russian grenadiers. The Russian cavalry had retired behind their infantry, in the center of which was a square formed by the Semyenovski Guard regiment. The charge in line of the two squadrons swept over the struggling infantry and crested like a wave on the Russian square, breaking into it briefly. The Chasseurs were almost immediately assailed by a heavy fusillade from the Preobrazhenski regiment, deployed in the nearby vineyards, however, and were forced to retire. Morland was mortally wounded, but, supported by a chasseur on each side of his horse, he was brought back to the French lines.

It was now obvious to Bessières that heavier weight needed to be brought to bear to repair the situation. Leaving one squadron each of the Chasseurs and the Grenadiers with the Emperor, he took matters in hand personally, deploying as a first line the other three squadrons of the Chasseurs, led by Morland's replacement, Colonel Dahlmann, and the company of Mamelukes, and in the second line, three squadrons of the Horse Grenadiers under General Ordener, supported by two batteries of Guard horse artillery. Napoleon's senior aide de camp, General Jean Rapp, placed himself at the head of the Mamelukes, alongside their

---

3 I have studied eight accounts, by as many authors—including an earlier one of my own—
   as to what happened at that point, and no two of them agree on all aspects of the actions

commander, Captain Delaître. This time, with Bessières in command, the charge of the Guard cavalry swept aside the Semenovski guardsmen, who were attempting to reform, and crashed into the squadrons of the Russian Guard cuirassiers and hussars. In the furious mêlée which ensued, the squadrons of Russian cavalrymen were broken apart and their troopers were cut down in the midst of their own infantry.

His blood up now and buoyed by the success of the charge, Rapp started forward again, his next target the Russian infantry and artillery. But a massive obstacle materialized before him and the men of the other squadrons, who had kept abreast of him: the eight squadrons of the Chevalier Guards and the Cossacks of the Guard, who had arrived on the scene in support of their comrades. The Grenadiers of the Guard had long been eager to meet in battle the famed Chevalier Guards, having heard of the latter's boasts directed at themselves, and now at last they had an opportunity to test one another's mettle.

The shock of the meeting of these two elite bodies of superb cavalry was a particularly violent one, and almost at once the collision evolved into a series of hand-to-hand encounters, spread across the plain in the shallow valley between the Pratzen Heights and Krzenowitz to the east. In his excitement, Rapp had outstripped his fellows, and suddenly found himself in the midst of a group of Russian cavalry, being called upon to surrender.

Already bleeding from two slight saber slashes, Rapp was prepared to sell his life as dearly as possible, when the tableau was suddenly disrupted by the arrival in its midst of a handful of saber-slashing, shouting Chasseurs, led by Daumesnil. Sabering right and left, his men cut down or drove off the startled Russians. Mameluke Lieutenant Chaïm helped Rapp onto his own horse, as Daumesnil led the little party back to the safety of his regiment. Embracing Rapp, Daumesnil said to him, "You've been carried away like a second lieutenant! Good lord, you're well decorated to go back to report to the Emperor, after having yourself dressed. Many would envy you those two 'button-holes'"![4]

In the midst of this action, Daumesnil, who had by this time been wounded himself, owed his safety to the courage of chief trumpet-major Krettly, who, in his *Souvenirs historiques*, provides this account of the action:

In the middle of the engagement, I glimpsed Colonel (*sic*)

---

resulting from Napoleon's order. In his own memoirs, Rapp has Napoleon giving him directly the order to take the Mamelukes, two squadrons of Guard Chasseurs, and one of Horse Grenadiers to reconnoiter the situation, which led to Rapp's initiating the first charge. Since I believe it is highly unlikely that Napoleon would have by-passed in that manner the commander of the Guard cavalry, Bessières, I have stayed with Lachouque's account. What follows, therefore, is my best distillation of the various versions of the events in question. In my view, the accounts of the heroic actions of the individuals concerned are more important than the exact sequence in which they occurred.

4 Manceron, *Austerlitz*, p. 278.

Daumesnil surrounded by a dozen Russians, against whom he was defending himself valiantly. He would certainly have succumbed if I had not seen him in the midst of this danger, selling dearly an honorable life that he did not wish to leave at the disposition of his enemies by becoming a captive—he who would much later be of service to his country.

Unexpectedly I fell upon his adversaries and cut down seven or eight of them while they were trying to take him prisoner. In short, I had the good luck to reach the colonel and to snatch him from their hands, after having killed the one who was holding him at bayonet-point, and sabering all those who opposed me.[5]

Finally the superior skill, courage, and determination of the French cavalry overpowered the Chevalier Guards. Their commander, the young Prince Repnine, along with 200 of his nobly-born troopers, was captured and presented to Napoleon by Rapp, along with some captured standards. It was a scene which would later be memorably depicted by the painter Gérard, who included in his portrayal of the scene the brave Horse Chasseur, who, though mortally wounded, managed to lay before Napoleon a standard which he had taken, before falling dead literally at his emperor's feet. Gazing on the crestfallen pride of the Tsar's personal escort, Napoleon commented to his staff, "Many fine ladies of St. Petersburg will lament this day!"

Later Napoleon would write:

That charge of the cavalry of the Imperial Guard, commanded by Marshal Bessières, is one of the finest ever to have taken place, and it does honor to the chief who commanded it as well as to the elite troops who executed it. Whatever the strength was of the enemy lines, whether infantry or cavalry, which found themselves in its path, none could resist its terrible shock: all was overthrown.[6]

The day's work was not over for the Chasseurs, however. Major Dahlmann took two of the regiment's squadrons to sweep the area above the Moenitz pond, where they collected 2,000 more prisoners, some flags, and eleven cannon. That evening, with the snow beginning to fall again, Dahlmann led two squadrons in a reconnaissance on the right wing of the retreating Russians, and picked up another 1,500 prisoners and 20 cannon.

The Chasseurs had lost their colonel, Morland, who had died at Brünn on the 3rd. His body, embalmed by the Guard's chief surgeon, Larrey, would be taken back to Paris by a Chasseur escort for entombment, and in February Napoleon would give Morland's name to a boulevard to honor his memory. A captain and eleven *sous-officiers* and troopers of the

---

5   Grandin, *Souvenirs historiques de Capitaine Krettly,* p. 181.
6   Quoted by Lachouque, *Napoléon à Austerlitz,* p. 322.

regiment had been killed, and 17 officers and 50 chasseurs wounded; 153 horses had been put out of action. The Grenadiers had only six officers wounded, but they had lost 99 horses.

Henri de Clairval comments that Rapp, who was always glad to present himself in the best possible light, failed to mention in his *Mémoires* that Daumesnil had saved his life that day. However, Bessières, who was very sensitive to anything having to do with the Guard, wrote in his report: "The aide de camp, Rapp, at the head of the Mamelukes, imparted (to the charge) an irresistible élan. Finding himself encircled by a group of the enemy, he only owes his safety to the intrepidity of Captain Daumesnil."[7]

The next day Napoleon issued this proclamation:

Soldiers! I am satisfied with you. On the day of Austerlitz you justified all that I expected of your bravery. You have decorated your eagles with an immortal glory. My people will see you once more with joy, and it will be enough for you to say "I was at the Battle of Austerlitz" for them to reply "There's a brave man."[8]

On 4 December the Guard marched with Napoleon to Ziaroschitz, a town on the road to Hungary. There, near the mill of Nasedlowitz, the Guard cleared an area where the regiments could be formed up in preparation for the meeting between the defeated Emperor Francis and Napoleon, and lit a large fire. When Francis appeared, escorted by Kienmayer's hussars and Schwarzenberg's lancers, he descended from his carriage, and Napoleon embraced him and then led him near the fire. Their interview lasted for two hours, and when the Austrian emperor had departed, Napoleon announced to his staff:

"Gentlemen, the peace is made. We shall return to Paris."

By the 12th, Napoleon was back at Schönbrunn, and the Guard was encamped nearby. On the 18th the Emperor distributed awards personally. Dahlmann succeeded Morland in command of the Chasseurs, and Daumesnil was promoted to the rank of *chef d'escadron*, the equivalent of lieutenant-colonel. One of his friends in the Chasseurs, Hercule Corbineau, was made a captain adjutant-major. We shall hear more of him in the future, since his future would be closely linked with Daumesnil's.

Krettly was made a second lieutenant in the Chasseurs. He would no longer have the occasion to sound the *trompette d'honneur* that he had been awarded after Marengo. On that occasion, as a *brigadier trompette* with the picket escort of Bonaparte, having been annoyed by the fire of an Austrian battery, he and several other *Guides* had attacked it, killed the gunners, and brought the two cannon to Bonaparte.

---

7 Quoted by Clairval, *Daumesnil*, pp 70–1.
8 Napoleon's *Proclamation* of 3 December 1805.

1806

The Guard left for Paris on 27 December, and en route they celebrated the New Year in Munich. Having attended Eugène's marriage to Princess Auguste-Amélie of Bavaria in Munich on 14 January, by the 26th the emperor was back in Paris. Finally, on 16 February the Guard made a triumphal into Paris by the Porte de la Villette, where they were greeted by the municipal authorities and a cheering populace. With the collapse of the Third Coalition compounded by the death of English Prime Minister Pitt in January of 1806, peace would once more settle, however briefly and uneasily, over the Continent.

For the Guard, it would be a time to replenish its regiments' ranks, train officers and men newly admitted to that "gilded phalanx" in its customs and traditions, perform ceremonial functions, and simply enjoy all that Paris had to offer to heroes returned from one of the Emperor's most brilliant victories.

On 14 March Daumesnil was made an officer of the *Légion d'Honneur*. It was at that time, and probably to "wash down" his new promotion, that Daumesnil gave a luncheon for the officers of his regiment. It was a sumptuous affair, which Dr. Veron describes in his *Mémoires d'un bourgeois de Paris* (vol. I, p. 120):

> General Daumesnil, who was the governor of Vincennes, gave a luncheon of oysters in the cellars of the *Frères-Provençaux* to all the officers of his regiment, although he was still only a *chef d'escadron* of the Chasseurs of the Guard. All the cellars were illuminated, and on each set of bottles was a card indicating the year and the vintage. All the vintages and years were drunk.

Daumesnil's free-spending tendencies were in later years to inflict hardships on his family.

∞

During this period of peace, the Chasseurs of the Guard performed guard and escort services at the Imperial residence. When on campaign, one of the regiment's squadrons was assigned to the personal guard of the Emperor, and the officer commanding it was constantly under his orders. Thus it was that for a long time Daumesnil was at the Emperor's side, part of his daily life and following his every step.

In his *Etudes sur Napoléon*, Baudus wrote:

> Napoleon had an affection for Daumesnil, which is easily explained. He probably believed that this man, who had saved his life twice, must bring him good luck, and could protect him in other circumstances. Furthermore, although all of the senior officers of the Chasseurs were men of intelligence and spirit, by the Emperor's

orders it was nonetheless Daumesnil who was chosen to command his escort when there were dangers to be encountered in those places that the prince was to traverse.

Bessières observed, "The Emperor is convinced that Daumesnil brings him luck."[9]

---

9 Both of these are quoted by Clairval, *Daumesnil*, p. 72.

CHAPTER EIGHT
JENA–AUERSTÄDT

I n the months leading up to Austerlitz, the Prussian government, most
especially King Frederick William himself and his notoriously belli-
cose queen, had been observing from the sidelines the developing
strategy of the powers of the Third Coalition designed to drive the
parvenu emperor back within France's pre-Revolutionary borders, with
confidence that the Austrian and Russian armies would be entirely
capable of performing that task. When that confidence proved to have
been badly misplaced, something like panic broke out in the Prussian
court. Panic was succeeded by shock, when Napoleon's vision for the role
to be played by Prussia in Europe's future was spelled out in the terms that
he dictated to Prussian Ambassador Haugwitz in Vienna, when the
Emperor finally consented to meet him on 15 December.

As the year wore on, growing resentment of a series of actions by
Napoleon, which were seen as seriously damaging to Prussian interests,
inflamed the sentiments of those in and around the Prussian court who
favored a military confrontation with France. When it was learned that
Napoleon had secretly offered to restore Hanover to George III, that at
last proved to be more than Prussia was prepared to stomach, and on 7
August 1806 the Prussian government secretly decided to throw down the
gauntlet at Napoleon's feet. Since they did not do so publicly, however, it
was not until September that the Emperor realized what was afoot.

Since the bulk of the *Grande Armée* had remained in southern Germany
after the conclusion of the campaign of 1805—some 160,000 men, plus
300 cannon and some small allied forces—this time there was no need for
a massive transfer of scores of thousands of soldiers across great distances.
Rather it was a question of designing a strategy best calculated to deal with
the threat of an imposing—on paper, at least—but untested Prussian
army. Napoleon's basic solution to this challenge was the concept of what
he termed *le bataillon carré*, which is to say, a massive square-shaped

formation made up of three enormous columns, each consisting of at least two corps, all of this proceeded by a formidable cavalry screen, with the cavalry reserve and the Guard bringing up the rear of the center column. A great advantage of this formation was its flexibility, which made it possible for its weight to be shifted, as a developing situation might require, to one or the other flank with a minimum of confusion.

From the parochial point of view of those of us interested primarily in following the career of Pierre Daumesnil, the most interesting thing about the campaign of 1806 is the fact that, with perhaps one exception, the cavalry of the Imperial Guard did not play an active role in its battles. It should be noted at this point that a third regiment was added to the ranks of the Guard cavalry during 1806. Napoleon had decided to honor the contributions made up until that time by the 30 dragoon regiments of the army by creating a Guard dragoon regiment. He gave the responsibility for organizing and commanding this new regiment to a cousin on his mother's side, Colonel Jean-Toussant Arrighi de Casanova. An Imperial decree of 15 April 1806, which reorganized the Guard, also created the Dragoons of the Imperial Guard. The new regiment soon acquired the unofficial but popular name, *les Dragons de l'Impératrice*, because at the time of its first public appearance, when it was presented to the Empress, she had agreed to be its "godmother." The organization of this regiment proceeded slowly, however, and it was only in the second half of November that the first 200 men of the regiment left Paris on foot, to be mounted with captured Prussian horses upon reaching Berlin. So, in common with their fellow Guard cavalry regiments, they took no part in the climactic twin battles of that campaign.

For whatever reason, none of the men of the Guard cavalry accompanied the Emperor when he left Paris on or about 25 September, at the start of the campaign. Instead, his escort was provided by the 1st *Hussards*.[1]

It should be noted that the decree reorganizing the Guard provided that, on campaign, the Chasseurs of the Guard would be divided into two *régiments de marche*, each consisting of two squadrons and each under the command of one of the regiment's two majors, under the overall command of the regiment's colonel. When on campaign or detached service, each squadron would be fleshed out to a strength of 250 men by the addition of 50 *vélites*[2], dispersed among the Old Guard troopers. As of the date of the Guard reorganization, the strength of the regiment of

---

1 Picard (*La Cavalrie dans les guerres*, p. 359) has this to say about the effect of escort duty on a cavalry regiment: "The 1st Hussars, who uniquely performed that service for the Emperor (during this campaign) and took no part in combat, was the regiment in all of the cavalry which had the greatest number of horses unfit for service. On 27 September 1806 this regiment had 524 combatants: on 31 October there were 213."

2 *Vélites* were physically fit young men of 18 years, selected from the conscripts of the reserve each year to serve at their parents' expense (300 francs a year for a cavalryman)

Chasseurs was 70 officers and 1,239 chasseurs.

On 18 December 1805, Claude-Etienne Guyot had been promoted to the Guard rank of major, and the following day the Emperor had given him the assignment of "organizing" the *vélites* for the Chasseurs of the Guard, a task which would occupy him until September of the following year. In all likelihood he commanded one of the two half-regiments of the Chasseurs when they crossed into Germany about the first of October, with Dahlmann having replaced Morland as regimental commander. It seems probable that the Grenadiers were with General Walther when he crossed the Rhine on 6 October, leading 1,300 men of the Guard cavalry and 300 Elite Gendarmes. .

There seems to have been some kind of an administrative missed connection with respect to the Guard Chasseurs, because when Napoleon was at Schleiz on 9 October he wrote: "I await my Horse Guard with impatience. Forty pieces of artillery and 3,000 cavalry like these are not to be sneezed at!"[3] But certainly none of them arrived at Jena in time to participate in that battle on the 14th. In his *Carnets*, Guyot notes that on that day the Chasseurs were at Lobenstein, 36 hours away from the battlefield. It's not clear to me where the Grenadiers were at that point, but they did not participate in either battle.

Following the movements of the Chasseurs, whether as the 1st or as the 2nd Chasseurs or as a whole, becomes more difficult after 14 October. The editor of Guyot's *Carnets* notes, with exasperating laconicism, that Guyot (presumably with at least the 1st *Chasseurs*, if not the entire regiment) rejoined the Emperor at Merseburg on the 19th, and from that point on commanded his escort, traveling via Halle, Dessau, and Wittemberg, and arriving at Potsdam on the 24th. Were the 1st *Hussards* relieved of escort duty at Merseburg, then? Lachouque says that when the Guard cavalry arrived in Potsdam on the 24th, they were exhausted, and therefore the 1st *Hussards* continued to serve as the Emperor's escorts.

Puzzling as that sounds, there is one more episode, which apparently occurred during the second half of October and which bears directly on Daumesnil personally, the circumstances of which are to this day unexplained. What follows is all that we know.

In a letter from Berlin on 30 October 1806 to Prince Eugène de Beauharnais, Viceroy of Italy and still Colonel General of the Chasseurs, the regiment's *commandant en seconde*, Dahlmann, wrote:

Mon Prince,
…In the letter that I had the honor to write you on the 19th of October, I reported that M. Daumesnil had been taken prisoner

---

as, in effect, cadets in the Guard regiments. After three years' service, these men were tested to determine whether they were qualified to serve as junior officers in Line regiments, or to be retained in the Guard as privates or corporals.

3 Lachouque, *The Anatomy of Glory*, p. 78.

with four chasseurs. It is with particular pleasure that I hasten to inform you of his return with the four men who accompanied him, and that no harm had befallen them.

Please accept, Prince, my assurance of the unlimited devotion of your corps of faithful subjects.

Dahlmann.[3]

Henri de Clairval doe not elaborate, because he himself has been unable to learn any details of the circumstances surrounding this event. I can find no record of the Chasseurs' having been in combat with any elements of the Prussian army during the period in question. Yet there can be no doubt as to the authenticity of Dahlmann's letter. We may ask ourselves whether the colonel would have written a similar letter to Beauharnais regarding the capture and safe release of any officer of the regiment of which the prince was still the nominal commander, or was it because he knew of a special interest on Beauharnais' part in Daumesnil? (At one point, the two of them had taken cooking lessons together.) We simply don't know.

In any event, the Guard was now in Potsdam, and on the 27th Napoleon entered Berlin in a splendid procession headed by the Mamelukes, the Foot Grenadiers and Chasseurs. Then the Horse Chasseurs followed, restored to their honorable role, preceding Napoleon and all of the marshals present on that day, with the Horse Grenadiers closing the glittering cavalcade. At the Brandenburger Gate, General Hulin, until recently commander of the Foot Grenadiers and now commander of the Berlin garrison, joined officials of the Berlin government in the ceremony of presenting the keys of the city to the Emperor.

In Potsdam the Horse Chasseurs and Grenadiers had occupied the luxurious stables of the Prussian *Garde du Corps*, some of whose gallants had, only a short while before, made a great show of sharpening their sabers on the steps of the French embassy. Now in Berlin, both regiments took over the no less splendid royal stables. They would remain in Berlin for almost a month. Napoleon frequently visited the various quarters in which his men were housed, accompanied by Murat, Berthier, and Duroc. Krettly recalls such a visit paid by the Emperor to the house in which he was quartered. "Well now, chasseurs," Napoleon addressed them with a pleasant air, "Are you glad to be in Berlin?" Almost with one voice, the men replied, "Yes, Sire, especially since we came here as conquerors!" There followed some comments from the soldiers on the hospitable character of the ladies of Berlin, which provoked roars of laughter from the illustrious party.[5]

By 7 November all of the Prussian army but General Lestocq's corps had surrendered. He would succeed in keeping his men out of French

---

4 Clairval collection.
5 Grandin, *Souvenirs historiques de Capitaine Krettly*, p. 203–4.

hands in the northeast of Prussia throughout November and December, joining forces with the Russians and continuing to be a secondary distraction to the French throughout that period. Quite apart from that minor annoyance, it was quite clear to Napoleon that the destruction of the Prussian army had by no means signaled another peaceful interlude in his struggle for the domination of the Continent. As early as late October he had begun to receive information regarding Russian moves and intentions, which made it seem probable that a head-on collision with a Russian army could not be indefinitely postponed. That realization made it essential in the Emperor's mind that the *Grande Armée* be placed as early as possible in the best possible strategic posture for such a confrontation. It was no less essential that Austria be convinced that its best interests lay in maintaining its neutrality.

On 5 November Napoleon ordered Davout to push a large cavalry reconnaissance as far east as Posen, while on the army's southern flank Jerome Bonaparte was instructed to occupy Glogau with his Ninth Corps. Four days later, further intelligence reached the Emperor regarding the movement of an army of some 56,000 men under General Bennigsen west from Grodny, suggesting a possible Russian intention to advance at least to the Vistula, if not beyond. Accordingly, he ordered an advance of five corps on a broad front, extending from Thorn in the north to Kalisch in the south. He and the Guard would for the moment remain in Berlin. By the 24th of November, however, the first regiments of the Horse Chasseurs and the Horse Grenadiers were already in Posen, and from there General Watier wrote to Murat to tell him that those regiments, plus the Guard artillery, would be leaving Posen on the 25th to join him.

On 24 November the Emperor left Berlin, arriving in Posen on the 27th and remaining there until 15 December. On the 28th of November Murat had occupied Warsaw on the heels of the withdrawing Russians, and on 19 December Napoleon arrived in Warsaw on horseback, accompanied only by a picket of Chasseurs of the Guard, his carriage and the remainder of his party having been unable to keep up with him because of the execrable traveling conditions. He still was hoping to be able to inflict a decisive defeat on Bennigsen's army before it could be further reinforced, and at the same time eliminate Lestocq's Prussians from the equation. In light of the apparent Russian withdrawal from the area northeast of Warsaw, the tactical situation seemed to invite a *manoeuvre sur les derrières* of Bennigsen's army. (Actually, that army was briefly under the overall command of the elderly Marshal Kamenskoi before the latter faced up to the fact that the responsibility was too much for him, and relinquished command to Bennigsen in January of 1807.)

In the event, it became uncomfortably evident that, far from abandoning to the French the area of the confluence of the Bug, the Narew, the Ukra, and the Vistula, the Russians were moving southwest from Pultusk. As a consequence, when the renewed French offensive got underway on 22 December, Davout had to fight his way across the Narew at Tscharnovo, at a cost of 1,400 casualties. On the morning of the 23rd, Napoleon left Warsaw, accompanied by the Chasseurs of the Guard, and soon joined Lannes' Fifth Corps as it was preparing to cross the Narew and drive towards Pultusk on the right flank of Davout's Third Corps. Together they pushed north through Nasielsk, where there was a sharp action with the Russian rearguard on the 24th.

At Lopaczyn on the 25th, two squadrons of the Horse Chasseurs and the Mameluke company, under Murat's command, cut up and dispersed a Russian hussar regiment, capturing three cannon. In his report to the Emperor from Sousk, behind Golaczyna, Murat wrote:

The enemy was encountered at Lopaczyn by the advance guard of the Chasseurs of Your Majesty's Horse Guard, where they were vigorously charged at the bridge by the Chasseurs. Then, at Golaczyna the enemy was vigorously charged from all sides. Colonel Dahlmann, who was then leading the attack, hit them so hard that he captured two cannon and killed a great many of the enemy. He will report the results of this brilliant charge to Your Majesty personally. Your Majesty's Guard has been ordered to return to your General Headquarters. I owe the greatest praise to the *chef d'escadron* of Your Guard who charged so vigorously at Lopaczyn: the Chasseurs and the Mameluks [*sic*] conducted themselves with the greatest intrepidity.[6]

In that affair, Daumesnil's close friend, Hercule Corbineau, received seven saber wounds, which left him with a large vertical scar on his left cheek and another on his right temple. All in a day's work! At Golymin on the following day, Murat's and Augereau's forces clashed with Dokhturov, although it's not clear whether or not the Chasseurs took part in that action. After dark, the Russian general was able to extract his troops from an attempt by Davout's leading division to encircle them, and to retreat northward.

On the French right flank, by the 26th Lannes had reached Pultusk, where he found Bennigsen strongly entrenched and with superior forces. Nonetheless, Lannes attacked, but darkness ended the indecisive struggle for possession of the town. Soon thereafter, however, Bennigsen withdrew his army northward along the Narew to Ostrolenka.

On 26 December Berthier instructed Murat to send the Horse Chasseurs of the Guard to the Emperor's headquarters.

These actions at Golymin and Pultusk marked a temporary cessation of hostilities. Napoleon now had to face the fact that his army was badly worn down by almost incessant campaigning since October, often under

---

6   Murat, *Lettres et documents*, vol. V, p. 78.

weather conditions that tested the stoutest hearts and in countrysides almost stripped bare of food supplies. Morale was low, regimental strengths were depleted to an alarming degree by men who had fallen out as marauders, and the entire infrastructure of the army needed refurbishing. So he sent the army back to the vicinity of Warsaw to catch its collective breath. His headquarters and the Guard went into winter quarters in Warsaw itself.

Under those circumstances, it seems paradoxical for Picard to write of that moment in the campaigns of the Empire:

> Never was the military spirit in the French army more exalted than at that time. It was no longer the soil of the fatherland that the soldiers were going to defend, 500 leagues from its frontiers, but it was glory that they were seeking, marching in the footsteps of the man who fascinated and dazzled them. One began to make war not out of necessity, or out of duty, but to do so for the pleasure of doing it.[7]

That may well have been true of the officers, but one has to wonder whether the common soldier felt such exaltation at the prospects that lay before him.

---

7   Picard, *La Cavalrie dans les guerres*, p. 363.

CHAPTER NINE
THE BLOODY SNOWS OF EYLAU

1807

The pause in hostilities at the end of 1806 was to be of short duration. On 18 January, a detachment of Ney's cavalry had been on a reconnaissance well to the north of the Sixth Corps' assigned winter quarters area, in part to forage for rations and fodder and in part simply because Ney wanted to know what Lestocq and the Russians were doing in the region south of Königstein. It was set upon by a superior Russian force, and its commander only managed to extricate his men from a difficult situation after painful losses. During the following days, reports of other Russian movements reaching Napoleon made it clear that Bennigsen was launching an offensive designed to drive the French army back across the Oder. A steady outpouring of the Emperor's orders brought each corps of the army out of its cantonments and bivouacs and set them on the march. By the end of January the realigned front of the army extended in an enormous arc from Strasburg on the left flank through Hohenstein and Ortelsburg, then south to Ostrolenka on the Narew, and thence down to Pultusk and Warsaw. On the 30th, preceded by the Guard, Napoleon left Warsaw to join his advance guard at Przasnysz.

When the Emperor had arrived in Warsaw from Posen in mid-December, he had been greeted by a Polish guard of honor, whose patriotism and martial spirit had made a very favorable impression on him. Now, before rejoining the army, he gave orders that a regiment of light horse, composed of young Polish noblemen able to supply their own mounts, be formed for addition to the cavalry of the Guard. A decree of 2 March 1807 provided for the formation of such a regiment, and on 16 April it was formally established as the *Chevau-légers Polonais de la Garde* (Polish Light Horse of the Guard).

Napoleon's operational plan for the resumption of the offensive called for the formation of three columns composed of the roughly 100,000 men available. On the left would be Ney, on the right, Davout, and in the center Soult, Augereau, Murat with the cavalry reserve, and the Guard. In the days leading up to the climactic battle at Eylau on the 7th and 8th of February, there was a succession of clashes between the advancing French and the withdrawing Russians. Napoleon was anxious to bring Bennigsen to battle as soon as possible to prevent his withdrawing beyond practicable reach, and very nearly succeeded in doing so on 3 February at Yonkowo, but, after a sharp, indecisive engagement which was brought to a close by darkness, during the bitterly cold night Bennigsen had slipped away again.

On the 6th, Murat and Soult caught up with the Russian rear guard at Hoff, and a fierce exchange left several thousand Russians and five guns in French hands, at a cost of 2,200 French casualties. That evening Bennigsen's men reached Eylau, and bivouacked as best they could in strong defensive positions.

On the afternoon of the 7th, the head of the French center column, consisting of Murat's cavalry and Soult's corps, had reached the outskirts of Eylau, although Ney's corps was at some distance off to the west attempting to prevent Lestocq's Prussians from joining Bennigsen, and on the French right Davout was still working his way north from Bartenstein. Soon thereafter, Augureau and the Guard arrived on the heights west of Eylau and in the late afternoon, more by accident than intention, fighting broke out between Russian pickets on the western edge of the town and men of the Emperor's baggage carriages, who had brought the Emperor's effects to the spot chosen for his headquarters and were beginning to set up his headquarters. Guardsmen rushed to their rescue, and, as commanders on both sides committed more and more men to the struggle, it took on serious dimensions. The town cemetery, in the center of the fighting, changed hands several times, and it was not until late evening that the fighting finally died town. By then the French had taken possession of the battered town, but this impromptu preview of the next day's violent and bloody collision had cost both sides some 4,000 casualties.

As the battle began at dawn on the 8th, Bennigsen's force had a slight numerical advantage of troops, and a great superiority in guns—450 to the 200 that the French had been able to drag to the scene. However, as Davout's divisions began to arrive on the scene in succession and closed on the Russian left flank, the manpower scales became more evenly balanced. Ney's corps, still a considerable distance off to the northwest, would reach Eylau too late to affect the immediate outcome of the battle. (Inexplicably, Napoleon had failed to summon Ney until 08:00 the morning of the 8th.) The impact of Davout's steady pressure on Bennigsen's left was significantly blunted by the arrival on the scene late in the day of Lestocq, who had managed to slip away from Ney, and to cross north and in the rear of the main battle, through Schloditten, bent on coming to the support of the faltering Russian left wing. His corps, reinforced by Russian units he had gathered up as he hastened to reinforce Bennigsen's battered divisions, temporarily drove back some of Davout's infantry and cavalry, who had occupied Kutschnitten.

Napoleon had been delaying his planned attack by Augereau's corps and Murat's cavalry in the center of the French line in the hope that both Davout and Ney would arrive in time to support that attack. While the Emperor was thus hesitating, at 08:00 Bennigsen took the initiative by opening the battle with an intensive bombardment, which immediately drew an equivalent French response. This thunderous exchange of roundshot and canister cost the Russians more heavily than the French, because the smaller numbers of the latter meant that they were more widely spread across their front, whereas the Russian infantry were arrayed in densely packed masses. Furthermore, a number of the French soldiers were able to benefit from the shelter afforded by the buildings in Eylau, although they would soon be set ablaze by the Russian bombardment.

In order to draw Bennigsen's attention toward his own right flank and therefore away from the planned axis of the French attack, Napoleon ordered Soult's divisions to make a feint attack on the Russian right as a means of delaying an attack by the massed Russian infantry and cavalry. At first this went well, but General Tutchkov responded by sending forward several of his divisions, and, after a ferocious hand-to-hand struggle, Soult's men were sent reeling back into Eylau. At the same time Friant's division, leading Davout's Third corps, was coming up on the right, but was encountering masses of Tolstoi's cavalry, significantly delaying their advance.

Even though his entire strength was not yet been gathered under his hand, Napoleon decided that it was time to set in motion his effort to divide Bennigsen's force, and ordered forward Augereau's divisions. In the blinding snow that had by now enveloped the battlefield, the marshal's two divisions became disoriented, and instead of proceeding straight ahead toward their designated target, Tolstoi's infantry, they veered to the left, placing themselves almost at the mouths of the massed cannon arrayed before the infantry of Sacken and Essen, and losing contact with St. Hilaire's division of Soult's corps on their right. Almost at once they came under a devastating hail of metal from those guns, which was rendered even more horrific by shells of French counter-battery fire falling among their ranks. Their desperate situation was worsened when Bennigsen ordered his reserve cavalry, supported by an infantry division, to drive the shattered remnants of Augereau's divisions back towards Eylau. In the brief space of time that their attack had taken, the divisions of the Seventh Corps had lost over 900 killed and more than 4,000 wounded. Augereau, although suffering badly from rheumatism and with a burning fever, had had himself tied in his saddle so that he might participate in the attack, and now he was being brought back with a bullet wound in his thigh. One of his division commanders had been killed and the other severely wounded. His corps had practically ceased to exist.

As the survivors of that disastrous attack fought their way back to the French lines, Napoleon made out massed ranks of Russian infantry advancing steadily across the body-strewn wreckage of the battlefield. With Soult's corps still collecting itself after its bloody repulse, and Gudin's division of the Third Corps not yet come in line, a yawning gap in the French line had opened up. Seeing a column of some 15,000 Russian infantry with fixed bayonets advancing into that gap, Napoleon exclaimed to those near him, "What courage! What courage!" Berthier responded, "Yes, but doesn't Your Majesty perceive that because of that courage, he is within 100 meters of their bullets?"

Turning to Murat, the Emperor said, "Well, are you going to let those people devour us? Take what cavalry you have in hand and crush that column!" The Grand Duke of Berg was not slow—and most certainly not reluctant—to grasp what was expected of him. He at once spun his horse around, and spurred it across the 500 yards separating the Imperial staff from the ranks of the dragoons, cuirassiers, and chasseurs of the cavalry reserve, and then, in a spray of snow, wrenched his mount to a skidding halt before their steadfast ranks.

Deployed in the first line were Grouchy's, Klein's, and Milhaud's dragoon divisions of six regiments apiece, and, behind them, the two brigades of d'Hautpoul's cuirassiers, four regiments in all. Normal practice would have called for the heavy cavalry to lead such a charge, but time was of the essence, so there was no time to maneuver the regiments into such a formation. Instead, rising to his full height in his stirrups and withdrawing his Turkish scimitar from its scabbard, Murat held it high above his head and shouted in his best parade-ground voice, "Follow me!"

Without as much as a backward glance to see whether his command was being obeyed, Murat hauled his horse around and pointed its head toward the advancing mass of gray-clad infantry, the steel of their bayonets gleaming in the pale sun which had by now broken through the snow-laden clouds. He had launched what has gone down in history as the greatest cavalry charge of all time, carried out by some 80 squadrons[1] of more than 10,000 battle-hardened cavalrymen, eager to come to grips with the enemy, after having had to endure the fire of Russian guns during much of the morning.

Murat led his cavalry off in a column of squadrons, with Grouchy's dragoons leading, their task being to sweep aside the Russian cavalry that was pursuing the retreating survivors of Augereau's corps. They succeeded in driving the Russian light cavalry off to the northwest, but Grouchy's horse had been killed, and the general was pinned under its body. In the confusion of the collision of the two bodies of cavalry, Grouchy's troopers had not seen their general go down. His aide-de-camp had, however, managed to break free from the foaming torrent of riders to

---

1   While this number is most often cited, there may actually have been no more than 52 squadrons.

turn back, dismount, pull his general from beneath the dying animal, and help Grouchy onto his own horse. With the aide clutching the horse's tail, the two men managed to catch up with the 3rd brigade of the division, and were able to rejoin the combat.

Following close behind Grouchy's squadrons, the cuirassiers smashed through the first line of Russian infantry, with the other two dragoon divisions widening the breach their comrades had opened in the Russian ranks. Although a great many of the men of the first Russian line had been killed or wounded by that battering ram of heavy cavalry, many had instead fallen to the ground and let the surging wave of cavalry pass over them. They now picked themselves up and began firing into the backs of the dragoons and cuirassiers, just as the latter were coming down on the second Russian line. Those men had not had time to form into squares, but nonetheless they were able to pour a heavy fire on the French cavalry-men. Nonetheless, the cuirassiers tore that line apart, driving many of its men back into a woods south of Anklappen, where they took shelter under the 24 guns of a reserve artillery brigade. The guns of those batteries at once opened fire on the mass of French cavalry and Russian infantry locked in a desperate hand-to-hand struggle, killing friend and foe alike.

By this time the cohesion of the French regiments, and even of their individual squadrons, had been broken, as countless hand-to-hand combats swirled across the nightmarish landscape, strewn with bodies of dead and dying men and horses trodden into the mud and snow, amid the discarded debris of combat. General d'Hautpoul had been mortally wounded, and there were many casualties in all of the regiments. It was clear to Murat that, with the threat of the massive Russian column having been eliminated, he must now rally his regiments and lead them back within French lines. As he attempted by sweeping gestures to convey his intentions to his commanders, they began to collect their men in loose formations, and to follow Murat as he led them in a large circle intended to take them back over the path they had previously hacked through Russian lines. As they did so, a daunting scene developed before their eyes.

Of the 15,000 Russian grenadiers originally making up that enormous attack column, the French cavalry had probably killed or wounded something like one-third of them. Of the others, some had simply survived, huddled in creases in the terrain as the horsemen swept over them, or had only been badly shaken or unnerved. Now their officers got those men back into rough formations facing the disordered French cavalry, and opened a heavy musket fire on them. What had been the second Russian line now became the first line facing Murat's cavalry. With the latter now in a considerable state of disorganization, with some officers having no more than a platoon under their control, and with the mens' horses having been pushed to their limits by their exertions, it appeared to be beyond the capacity of the surviving officers to form, from this incoherent mass, a spearhead strong enough to break through the bristling barrier now confronting them.

The first slashing passage of Murat and the regiments of the cavalry reserve though the ranks of the Russian column had been followed intently by all the officers of the Imperial headquarters with great admiration, mixed with anxiety for the fate of the brave men of those scores of squadrons. Their relief at seeing the ponderous Russian attack at first blunted and then completely disrupted soon gave way to dismay, however, when it began to look as though the horsemen, who had so fearlessly dashed into the mouths of Russian cannon and against the bayonets and musketry of the Russian grenadiers, might not be able to regain the French lines. It was unthinkable to permit their loss.

On the left, Soult's divisions were struggling to hold their own in the face of continuing pressure by Tutchkov. To the right of the gap through which Murat had led the charge, St. Hilaire's division had been forced back, exposing the flank of Morand's division of Davout's corps as it advanced toward Serpallen. The three regiments of the Guard cavalry—the Guard dragoons had by now joined that elite body—had been standing in ranks slightly to the rear of Imperial headquarters since the start of the battle, the Horse Grenadiers in the first line, then the Chasseurs and the Mamelukes, and in the rear, the as yet untested Dragoons. The Emperor's service squadron was being supplied by Daumesnil's Chasseurs.

It must have seemed obvious to the Emperor that he had immediately at hand, in the form of the Guard cavalry, the means with which to deal with this crisis. He now ordered Bessières to take the Horse Grenadiers, the Chasseurs, and the Mamelukes—altogether no more than some 2,000 sabers—with which to free Murat's entrapped cavalrymen. But it would prove to be enough. Dahlmann, who had succeeded Morland as commander of the Chasseurs after the latter's death at Austerlitz, had been promoted to the rank of general on 29 December, and was now attached to the Imperial staff. Hearing that the Chasseurs were now to go into action at a critical point in the battle, Dahlmann asked the Empereur for the honor of leading his old regiment. Permission was granted, and Dahlmann placed himself at the head of the 1st *Chasseurs*: Guyot would lead the 2nd *Chasseurs*.

Throughout the morning all three regiments had been exposed to hostile fire of various types. A few moments before he and his men were called upon to go to the rescue of their entrapped comrades, the commander of the Horse Guards, Colonel-major Lepic, had been irritated by what he apparently felt was the craven behaviour of some of his troopers, whom he had detected crouching down behind their horses' necks. So he shouted to them, "Heads up, Goddammit! Those are bullets, not turds!"[2] Now he led them off down the slope in front of the cemetery in which the Emperor's headquarters was installed. In his memoirs, Jean-

---

2   Lachouque, *The Anatomy of Glory*, p. 88.

Marie Merme, who had been a trooper in Daumesnil's squadron on that occasion, has this to say about those few critical moments.

As General Dahlmann started the Chasseurs and Mamelukes off behind the Grenadiers, Napoleon called Daumesnil to him, ordering him to charge with his regiment, and to overwhelm whatever opposed him. Merme continues, "Leading us across in front of the Emperor, Daumesnil commanded, 'Soldiers, draw sabers!' and off we went at a gallop, with a shout of '*Vive l'Empereur!*'" Falling in with the other squadrons of the regiment, Daumesnil's troopers extended its line as they rode hard on the heels of the Grenadiers.

Crossing the intervening space at a flat-out gallop, both regiments and the company of Mamelukes smashed into the Russian infantry, now formed in defensive squares, some of them still absorbed in an attempt to capture or annihilate Murat's men. Krettly's account of those critical moments reads:

> We broke into a Russian square, but that square concealed another, and momentarily, at least, we were forced to pull back. But then we found ourselves before eighteen artillery pieces, arrayed in a battery and set to sweep us away. The danger was immediate. General (*sic*) Daumesnil rushed up, and, seeing me, he shouted, "With me, Krettly! Come on, to the guns!"
>
> I had heard his voice and understood his thought, and I rode there almost as quickly as he did, with the rest of our squadron following us, and we seized the guns, after having cut down the cannoneers. This capture was very important, because our artillery could in turn fire canister on the squares, and help us stop the enemy battalions.[3]

General Dahlmann had been mortally wounded, and Chasseur Brice, his nephew, managed to get to his uncle, pick him up, and place the dying man on his horse. As he did so, he was attacked and his shoulder dislocated, but Chasseur Dufour cut down his attackers, and he was able to regain the French lines. Dahlmann was able to die amidst his own on the following day. But the Russian lines had been torn asunder, and Murat's cavalry was pouring back through the breach opened by the Guard cavalry. Guyot rallied the Chasseurs and brought them back to the French lines, with the help of some cuirassiers, who drove off some Russian cavalry attempting to pursue the Chasseurs.

Lepic, commanding the Horse Grenadiers, had also cut through the Russian lines with some of his men, but the enemy had closed in behind him and he and his troopers were now cut off. Carried on by his momentum, he had penetrated too deeply within the Russian lines.

---

3   Grandin, *Souvenirs historiques de Capitaine Krettly,* pp 223–4.

Disoriented in the swirling snow and wounded, with only a handful of Grenadiers near him, he was surrounded. "Surrender, general!" a Russian officer called out to him in French. "Your courage has carried you too far. You are within our lines!"

"Look at those faces and see if they look as though they want to surrender," Lepic replied, gesturing to his men. He then shouted to his men, "Grenadiers, follow me!" and, forming his men in a column of platoons, he succeeded in leading them back through the first Russian line, losing an officer and five Grenadiers as he did so. Finally, they succeeded in cutting their way through the second and third Russian lines, although, as they approached the French lines, some confused French infantry fired on them, killing two Grenadiers and several horses. When Lepic, bleeding from six wounds, had led his men up the slope and behind the cemetery to where the Chasseurs were reforming, he rode forward to the Emperor to report. Napoleon, greeting him with the new grade that he was simultaneously conferring on him, said to Lepic, "I thought that you had been made prisoner, General, and I was deeply distressed."

"You will only hear of my death, Sire," was Lepic's reply. Napoleon gave him 50,000 francs, which he distributed among the Grenadiers.

The Chasseurs had paid heavily for that brilliantly successful action. In addition to the loss of Dahlmann, Daumesnil's friend, Corbineau, had been wounded again, this time by a bullet in his right thigh. 21 officers and 224 men had been killed or wounded, and 235 horses killed or put out of action. Lt. Rabusson had been wounded fourteen times, but had survived. Three lieutenants of the Horse Grenadiers had been killed and thirteen other officers wounded, including Lepic. Captain Auzony of the first squadron had been mortally wounded, but, at his request, his men had left him in the snow on the battlefield. 143 of their horses had been killed.

As the cavalry engagement was gradually dying down, a column of some 4,000 Russian infantry appeared through the heavy snow, marching steadily up the slope leading to the northwest edge of the cemetery, their muskets in their arms, and seemingly heading for Imperial headquarters. Alerted to this threat, the Emperor calmly ordered General Dorsenne to take some of the Guard infantry to deal with this imminent danger.

Murat, who had by now rejoined the Emperor's staff, immediately saw the necessity for reinforcing the Foot Guard's attack on the column with a strong body of cavalry. As he swept his gaze over the regiments of the cavalry reserve, just now in the process of reforming, his eyes lit on General Bruyères' still fresh brigade of light cavalry. He called out to their commander, "Take your brigade and follow me!" With scarcely a moment's hesitation, Bruyères drew his saber, and shouted to his regimental commanders, "*1e Hussards et 13e Chasseurs, à moi!*" As their colonels ordered "*Le sabre à la main!*" 800 sabers rasped from their scabbards in almost a single motion, and the two regiments swung in line of squadrons behind the marshal and the general, who were already galloping toward the advancing enemy. As they drew near the enemy column, Murat gestured toward them and commanded Bruyères and his two colonels, Juniac of the Hussars and Demangeot of the Chasseurs, "Charge that for me!"[4]

As the brigade swept down on the flank of the column, the grenadiers facing the onrushing cavalry raised their muskets, and in a crashing volley sent a hail of lead scything toward the riders. Bruyères and Demangeot both went down, grievously wounded, but their hussars and chasseurs would avenge them. Breaking into the ranks of the grenadiers, cutting and thrusting, they tore apart the column. At the same time, Dorsenne had brought forward the 2nd Grenadiers and the 2nd *Chasseurs*, and they were now smashing into the head of the column. An officer had suggested to Dorsenne that their men fire on the Russians, but the general replied, "The Old Guard only fights with the bayonet!" With that, the Grenadiers split asunder the leading ranks of the Russian infantry and sent them stumbling backwards, leaving many of their comrades prostrate and bleeding in the trampled snow. Before long, those men who had survived the double onslaught of the cavalry brigade and the Guard infantry fled down the slope toward their own lines.

Picard[5] says that the Chasseur duty squadron, presumably still under Daumesnil's command, was also ordered by Napoleon to assist in driving off that menacing Russian column. Lachouque[6] says "the service squadrons attacked (the Russians') flanks," thus implying the participation of a squadron of Horse Grenadiers as well in that action. If both sources are correct, it means that, soon after having participated in that enormous effort to disengage the trapped cavalry reserve, and having regained the French lines, both Daumesnil and the commander of the Grenadier's service squadron had been able to collect the men of their squadrons—at least, those who had not been left in the muddy chaos of the plain between the enemy armies—and had been able to sort out and dress them up and then lead them back into the duty squadrons' proper positioning in the immediate vicinity of the Emperor. If that is so, it affords striking evidence of the limitless dedication of those soldiers to their responsibility for the Emperor's security.

That day the cavalry had saved the army from a potentially disastrous defeat, heavy though the cost to its regiments had been. The Chasseurs had lost one quarter of their strength, and the Emperor made a particular point of expressing to them individually his gratitude for the role they had played in the day's success, slim though the margin of victory had been. He went among their ranks, calling those he knew by name, taking their arms, grasping their shoulders, and calling them his companions, his Invincibles, and expressing his sorrow over those who were no longer

---

4 These exchanges are all recorded by Dupont, *Cavaliers d'epopée*, pp. 98–9.
5 Picard, *La Cavalrie dans les guerres*, p. 389.
6 Lachouque, *The Anatomy of Glory*, p. 89.

among them. "For a long time I've known that the French infantry is the best in the world. Now I see that my cavalry has no equal," the Emperor declared. Eight senior *sous-officiers* of the regiment were awarded the silver stars of the Legion, and eight more were promoted to the rank of captains in Line regiments.

A little later, the renowned light cavalry leader, General Lasalle, to whom the Emperor had just given command of a division of cavalry, was heard expressing his great regret at not having been given command of the Horse Chasseurs of the Guard. While thanking Napoleon for his new command, it was clearly evident to the Emperor that the brilliant young cavalryman was not satisfied.

"What's the matter?" Napoleon said to him. "You don't seem satisfied."

"I am happy because of your kindness, Sire," replied Lasalle, "but I am still not satisfied. I had hoped that Your Majesty would have chosen me to command the first regiment in the world. In a word, I had hoped to replace General Dahlmann at the head of your Chasseurs."

"When General Lasalle no longer drinks, no longer swears, and no longer smokes," the Emperor replied, "not only will I put him at the head of a regiment of cavalry of my Guard, but I will make him one of my chamberlains."

Not to be completely put out of countenance, Lasalle bowed and replied, "Sire, since I have all the attributes of a sailor, I ought to ask Your Majesty for the command of a frigate."

"Oh, no!" responded the Emperor with a laugh. "That would not be my wish. You shall command the twenty cavalry regiments in the absence of Prince Murat, who is returning to his duchy."[7]

It is noteworthy that Napoleon said "… at the head of a regiment of cavalry of my Guard …" After all, there were now three such regiments and would soon be a fourth. It seems to me that, for all of Lasalle's extraordinary qualities as a fearless and skilled cavalry leader, Napoleon did not consider that his character had the requisite steadiness to command the elite of the elite. The question would be rendered moot a little more than a year later by a bullet between Lasalle's eyes on the field of Wagram.

Be that as it may, for a divisional general—and a very special one, at that—to ask for the command of the Horse Chasseurs of the Guard demonstrates the prestige that this regiment enjoyed throughout the army. In his *Cavaliers de Napoléon*, Frédéric Masson writes:

---

7   Quotations from Clairval, *Daumesnil*, p. 79.

For an officer to be admitted to the Chasseurs of the Guard, even though it meant losing a hard-earned grade, is the highest recompense to be wished for as a reward for ten campaigns and twenty glorious deeds. It is to enter into a class apart, the highest there can be in the army.

The Battle of Eylau itself was by no means over yet, however, and the arrival at seven o'clock that evening of Ney's corps at Altof, at the extreme left of the French line, reignited serious fighting, as the marshal's troops seized the village of Schloditten from Tutchkov's troops, and then withdrew to align themselves with the left of Soult's corps. As the fighting finally died down and the night wore on, after conferring with his generals, Bennigsen decided to withdraw entirely from the battlefield, and by morning the Russian army was gone. Both armies were exhausted by the extraordinary effort and sacrifices that this campaign had cost them, and undoubtedly they were equally glad to leave behind the charnel house that Eylau had become.

To screen his preparations for moving the army into winter quarters centered on Osterode, Napoleon had sent Ney a few miles north of Eylau, Bernadotte to Kreuzburg, Davout to Friedland, and Soult to Schloditten. Murat took a position centered on Wittenberg. On the evening of the 9th, Guyot says in his *Carnets de Campagnes* (p. 67), the Chasseurs bivouacked in the hamlet of Rottenheim, slightly to the north of the blood-soaked Eylau battlefield, and presumably in the company of the rest of the Guard and the Imperial staff. He notes that five to six hundred French wounded had been collected there, most of whom underwent amputations. The regiment would remain there until 16 February.

On 17 February the entire army began a gradual withdrawal, and the Chasseurs moved to the village of Petersvaldt, again presumably in the vicinity of the Emperor's headquarters. On 12 April Imperial Headquarters were moved back to Finkenstein. On the same date Napoleon had made Guyot a colonel of the Guard, and, as a major colonel, not as *"colonel des Chasseurs à cheval"* as Morland and Dahlmann had been, he took command of the regiment. It was a subtle distinction, perhaps signifying that the Emperor wanted to see how Guyot handled the command before removing that slight implied qualifier. (It will be recalled that Beauharnais was still the regiment's nominal commander.)

Sporadic fighting in isolated sectors erupted periodically during the following weeks, until finally Bennigsen, too, went into winter quarters early in March. In the north, Lefebvre had begun the siege of Danzig early in March, and on 27 April its commander, Marshal Kalkreuth, had accepted the generous terms of surrender offered to him by Napoleon. The Guard remained with the Emperor throughout this period, and certainly some elements of it entered Danzig with Napoleon on 1 June.

Baudus tells of an experience he had during this brief interval in campaigning, which well illustrates the spirit of comradeship which animated Daumesnil, senior officer of this most elite of regiments though he was:

I shall never forget that, arriving late in February of 1807, still very young and assigned to the staff of Marshal Bessières, who had his general headquarters at Osterode, I was showered with kindness by Daumesnil, the value of which was further raised in my eyes by the senior grade and the brilliant reputation of the person who was extending them to me. An infantry officer, who had never in my life learned a single principle of riding, and now, thanks to the generosity of the marshal, one of his aides de camp, without Daumesnil I would have been as embarrassed to play that role as those conscripts who, scarcely out of their family's womb, were set on a horse and immediately left for the army. Daumesnil was very glad to take the trouble to give me the first lessons, having me ride every day with him.[8]

By coincidence, both Napoleon and Alexander, the latter in coordination with King Frederick William, had planned to initiate offensives during the first week of June. Bennigsen had intended to launch his on 5 June, but it was triggered prematurely by Lestocq on the 4th, as a result of a breakdown in communications between the two. Three-pronged Russian attacks against Bernadotte at the north of the French line of defense, and then successively on Ney and Soult, not only failed to achieve break-throughs, but were driven back at the cost of considerable losses. Bennigsen concluded that the better part of valor would be to withdraw to previously prepared defensive positions, and proceeded to do so, having first paused briefly at Güttstadt before continuing to Heilsburg.

On 10 June an ill-advised attack by the army's advance guard under Murat's command led to a major engagement at Heilsburg, which cost the French well over 10,000 casualties, without any clear resultant advantage, although, as at Eylau, Napoleon was left in possession of the field. Having evacuated the fortifications on Heilsburg Heights, Bennigsen continued to lead his army to the northeast, in what Napoleon believed was an attempt to reach the Russian's major operational base at Königsberg. The Emperor was determined to prevent his opponent's achievement of that objective, but he was still having difficulty in determining exactly how and where to come to grips with Bennigsen. In the event, the opposing armies would finally confront one another before the town of Friedland at dawn on 14 June. The ensuing battle would prove to be one of Napoleon's greatest victories, resulting in the almost complete destruction of the Russian army, and leading to a request by Emperor Alexander for an armistice.

---

8   Quoted by Clairval, *Daumesnil*, p. 80.

Since our focus is on the actions of Daumesnil and his regiment, there is no need to recapitulate the well-known events of that momentous day, since, in fact, the Guard played almost no role in its actions. With one exception, the Emperor refrained from calling on the Guard cavalry on that day, partly out of consideration for the severe losses they had incurred at Eylau, but also because there was no need for their services.

That one exception was to send off the squadrons of the newest of those regiments, the Dragoons, together with Lannes' Saxon cavalry, in pursuit of some Russian troops, who were retreating down the west bank of the Alle. It was late in the evening, after the battle had ended, and when the Dragoons and the Saxons ran into a stubborn Russian rear guard, they pulled back, causing some confusion, and no doubt irritation, among the infantry who had been following along behind them. Perhaps this was the Emperor's way of seeing how that ingénue regiment would perform in combat. If so, the manner in which they met that test was hardly impressive. Still, it was the Dragoons' first action as a regiment, so one shouldn't be too hard on them. They would in due course earn and deserve a place in that extraordinary, highly select company.[9]

Napoleon agreed to an armistice, and on the 19th the Emperor and the Guard entered Tilsit. The armistice was signed on 21 June and ratified on the 23rd. In the famous meeting on a raft in the middle of the Niemen, Napoleon and Alexander agreed on the establishment of a Franco-Russian defensive alliance. On successive days, the Guard infantry, Davout's corps, the Guard artillery, and, finally, the Guard cavalry paraded for the benefit of the Tsar and Frederick William and his queen. Treaties of peace were signed with the Tsar on 9 July, and with Frederick William on the 12th. The Emperor had left on the 9th for Königsberg, arriving on the next day. On the 13th he left for Dresden, with the Chasseurs escorting him until that stage of his journey. He finally returned to Paris on 27 July, after an absence of ten months.

In his *Souvenirs*, Chasseur Merme[10] writes that, before leaving Tilsit, Napoleon had told Bessières that he wanted to have the best mounted squadron of the Chasseurs on hand for the celebration of his birthday on 15 August. Since there was a distance of more than 300 leagues (about 1,500 kilometers, or 930 miles) between Tilsit and Paris, this requirement placed on the regiment gave rise to a bet between Bessières and Duroc as to whether or not a horseman, however well mounted he might be, could cover that distance in time to be in Paris for the Emperor's anniversary. There were now 36 days in which to accomplish that journey, which meant averaging 42 kilometers, or 26 miles, per day. That was equivalent

---

9 In *The Campaigns of Napoleon* (p. 579), Chandler says that Napoleon briefly employed the Horse Chasseurs and the Polish Light Horse, together with the Fusiliers of the Guard, to threaten troops commanded by General Gortschakoff, but almost immediately withdrew them, when that purpose had been served.

10 Merme, *Des pyramids á Moscou*, p. 39.

of three of the normal stages per day for a regiment on the move. To cover that distance in a day, or even for a few days in succession, would scarcely pose a challenge for an experienced cavalryman, but for five weeks without a break—well, that was quite another matter!

Merme was one of the Chasseurs chosen to perform this mission, and Daumesnil had the honor of being given the responsibility for its successful execution. Bessières instructed Daumesnil to have all his men's equipment sent on to Paris by post wagon, retaining for the journey only their saddles and sabers. The squadron reached Paris on the eve of the Emperor's birthday, although it cost them ten horses, which had died en route. Napoleon had each member of the squadron given 100 francs as a reward. We don't know how much Bessières collected from Duroc. As we shall shortly see, Daumesnil's role in that spectacular performance, as well as his recent conduct on the battlefield, did not go unrewarded.

After the festivities surrounding the Emperor's birthday, Daumesnil's squadron accompanied Napoleon to Fontainebleau, a château that he only occupied when he wanted to hunt. Merme recollects that the Emperor always had meals for himself and his suite brought out into the forest, and that the table for the Chasseurs was always close by that of the Emperor. Before sitting down at table himself, Napoleon would come to the Chasseurs' table with a glass in hand to taste their wine, and to assure himself that they were being given the same food that his party was receiving. When he was satisfied on both scores, he would then partake of his own meal.

After these hunting parties the Emperor would normally return to Paris. On this occasion, when he did so the squadron was ordered to proceed to Bordeaux, where it was to remain for a month. For whatever reason, Daumesnil remained in Paris, rather than accompanying the squadron, which he would join later, as we shall see.

In the meanwhile, the other squadrons of the regiment made their way back to Paris in a leisurely manner, via Berlin, Magdeburg, Hanover, Cassel, Frankfort, and Meaux, finally entering Paris with the rest of the Guard at *la barrière St. Martin* on 25 November.

The Emperor had issued the following instructions for the manner in which the Guard was to make its triumphal return to the capital:

> There will be no distribution of uniforms to the Guard before its entrance; it will enter in its campaign uniforms.
>
> It will march in the following order: the *Chasseurs à cheval*, the *Fusiliers*, the *Chasseurs à pied*, the *Grenadiers à pied*, the *Dragons*, and the *Grenadiers à cheval*.[11]

Napoleon had decided to absent himself from that joyous occasion so

---

11 Guyot, *Carnets de campagnes*, p. 150.

that the Paris population's tribute would be paid to the army itself, through the Guard. The impression made on the public would be more powerful because the uniforms of the soldiers would be those in which they had achieved their victories.

So it was Bessières, at the head of his staff, who led the procession of campaign-worn soldiers as they passed under a triumphal arch erected for the occasion. Immediately following were the eagles of the regiments, each of which was crowned by the prefect of Seine with a golden wreath of laurel leaves, as a gift from the City of Paris. The Chasseurs were led by their trumpeters, while immediately behind them was drawn a wagon bearing the body of their former commander, Colonel Dahlmann, accompanied on each side by Chasseurs, a star of the Legion glistening on the left breast of each of them. Then the regiment followed, led by its new commander, Major-Colonel Guyot.

In the shower of honors and gold that rained down on the Guard, reflecting Napoleon's appreciation for their services during the recently concluded campaign, Daumesnil was not ignored. On 7 September he was granted an annual pension of 3,000 francs drawn on the Emperor's privy purse, as well as a bonus of 6,000 francs. On the first of February of 1808, he was awarded an emolument of 2,000 francs on the Monte Napoleone fund, in Milan. But by that time he was already off on another campaign.

CHAPTER TEN
ONCE AGAIN, SPAIN

1808

On 6 December 1807 Bessières signed an order instructing Daumesnil to leave Paris immediately by post carriage, to take command of the detachment of the Chasseurs already present in Bordeaux. There is no need to dwell here on the complex maneuvers by which Napoleon created an excuse for the invasion of Portugal, by signing the Treaty of Fontainebleau with Spain, under the terms of which half of Portugal would be given to Spain, while the other half came under French control. He then climaxed his intrigues by deposing both Charles IV and his son, bundling them off to France, and then installing his brother, Joseph, on the Spanish throne. I shall instead limit our focus to the events immediately involving *chef d'escadron* Daumesnil.

Under the terms of the treaty with Spain, on 19 October 1807 General Junot had led what was grandiloquently termed the *1er Corps d'Observation de la Gironde,* consisting of 23,000 men, through northern Spain and on into Portugal, although he had barely 1,500 men still with him when he finally occupied Lisbon late in November. The agreement with the Spanish provided for the stationing of French troops along Junot's lines of communication. However, the presence in Spain of French troops would soon be increased well beyond any such requirement by the successive dispatch of three corps under Dupont, Moncey, and Duhesme respectively. The gradual infusion of those formidable forces into Spain had little to do with Portugal, instead constituting the initial step toward the eventual French occupation of all of Spain.

Daumesnil probably arrived in Bordeaux in mid-December 1807, where he took command of the 150 Chasseurs and the squadron of Mamelukes, commanded by Captain Renno, who were already there. Also present were a squadron of the Horse Grenadiers of the Guard, a squadron of the Guard Dragoons under Major Jolivet, a squadron of Elite

Gendarmes, and the entire newest regiment of the Guard cavalry, the Polish Light Horse, led by their colonel, Vincent Corvin Krasinski. Overall Guard commander was General Lepic. Napoleon had designated Murat as his Lieutenant for operations in Spain, until such time as the Emperor himself might decide to enter upon the scene.

In January the army moved to Bayonne, which was to be the base for its Spanish operations. On 2 March 1808, Murat wrote to Napoleon, "The Chasseurs, the Mamelukes, and the Light Horse arrived today in Bayonne. Between the 10th and the 12th the entire Guard will move to Vitoria."[1] On the following day he reviewed the Guard infantry, the Chasseurs and Mamelukes, the Polish Light Horse, and the artillery, and designated the Chasseurs as his personal escort. It was at that time that Napoleon gave command of the Chasseurs of the Guard to *général de brigade* Charles Lefebvre-Desnoëttes, finally ending the anomaly of Prince Eugène's being the regiment's commander. It would be some time, however, before its new commander would lead the rest of the regiment into Spain.

Starting early in February 1808, the French had seized a number of Spanish frontier fortresses bloodlessly by employing a variety of ruses, but those actions made Napoleon's ultimate intentions with respect to Spain unmistakably clear to its people. It was actually on 9 March that Murat led Marshal Moncey's *Corps d'Observation des Côtes de l'Océan* and the Guard detachments across the Spanish border at Irun, and on to Vitoria. Together with Dupont's and Duhesme's corps, backed up by Bessières' reserve, there were now 118,000 French troops on Spanish soil. After pausing briefly in Burgos, Murat pressed on to Madrid, which he entered on 23 March. By 15 April, the troops in and around Madrid included 2,800 men of the Guard, under General Lepic's command. The detachment consisted of Fusiliers, Foot and Horse Grenadiers, Horse Chasseurs, Dragoons, and Polish Light Horse, all subject only to the direct command of the Emperor.

In the meanwhile, the populace had become increasingly concerned about the trend of events, and when Charles IV seemed to be on the point of fleeing to Latin America, on 17 March the people of Madrid arose in protest, venting their anger particularly on Emmanuel Godoy, the so-called Prince of Peace and the Queen's favorite, who had been the virtual ruler of Spain. After rooting him out of the attic of the palace at Aranjuez, where he had been hiding for 36 hours, the furious *madrileños* would have strung him up on the spot, if it were not for the intervention of the king's son, Ferdinand, who was a popular figure. Instead, the former prime minister and generalissimo was imprisoned in the château of Villaviciosa, about six miles from Madrid.

Since Godoy was an essential pawn in the complex game that Napoleon was playing with Charles and his son Ferdinand, it was necessary to

1   Rossetti, *Journal inédit*, vol. V, p. 303.

remove Godoy from Villaviciosa in order that he could be brought to Bayonne in mid-April so that he might be present at the "family council" that Napoleon was convening. Its purpose was ostensibly to sort out the tangled affairs of the Spanish monarchy, but in reality its purpose was to have done with that Bourbon monarchy, for once and for all. Accordingly, on the night of 19/20 April Murat sent General Exelmans, accompanied by *chef d'escadron* Rossetti, one of Murat's aides de camp, with Daumesnil and his squadron as their escort, to effect the release of Godoy, who was then sent off to Bayonne, together with the King and Queen.

When at the end of April the people of Madrid learned that the Infante Don Francisco, the only member of the royal family still in Madrid, was also to leave for Bayonne, that proved to be the spark which set off an explosion. On the morning of 2 May, when the carriage carrying the Infante attempted to set out, the grooms, assisted by the mob, unhitched its horses. A French officer of Murat's staff, who had come to see the prince off, was seized and beaten before he could be rescued by a patrol of the Guard. At the same time, an unarmed ration party of French soldiers were set upon and massacred.

The greater part of the French army occupied three camps, each several miles from the center of the city (see map overleaf). The only troops immediately at Murat's disposal were Daumesnil's squadron, including the attached company of Mamelukes, a half-battalion of Seamen of the Guard, and a company of Basques. Murat had established his headquarters near the Puerta de San Vincente (48), in an extension of the royal palace. When word of the riot reached him, he ordered the drummers of the Seamen of the Guard to beat the General Alarm, and sent off aides to the units encamped outside the city, ordering that reinforcements to the units at his disposal be sent into the city on the double. By noon, four columns of troops began to enter the city by the gates to its north and east, converging on the Puerta del Sol (35), and sweeping before them all that they encountered. At 12:30, a column of infantry led by General Grouchy entered through the Puerta de Fuencarral (14), and joined, via the Plaza de San Domingo (39), the troops defending the approaches to the royal palace.

The Chasseurs were quartered in the convent of Saint Francis, in the Buen Retiro quarter (F), on the opposite side of the city from the royal palace. Daumesnil ordered the squadron of Chasseurs into their saddles, and set out at once to cross the city to join Murat. As the men made their way through the city, they were assailed by musket fire from windows, boiling water and oil poured down on them, paving stones hurled at them, and wooden barricades thrust in their path. It was only with great difficulty that they reached Murat at his headquarters. Reporting to Murat, Daumesnil asked permission to avenge the treatment to which his troops had been subjected. The indignation of the French was further inflamed by the news, which had just reached Murat, of the massacre by

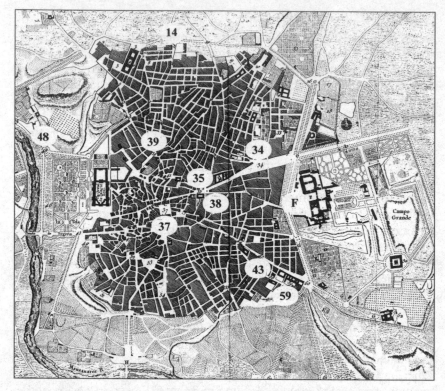

Plan of Madrid, 1813. The large numbers superimposed on the map locate the following gates, streets, plazas, and other points mentioned in the text:

14	Puerta de Fuencarral
34	Calle de Alcala
35	Puerta del Sol
37	Plaza Mayor
38	Calle de San Geronimo
39	Plaza de San Domingo
43	Calle de Atocha
48	Murat's headquarters, Puerta de San Vicente
59	General hospital
F	Buen Retiro, where Daumesnil's squadron was positioned.

their Spanish attendants of French patients in the military hospital (59).

Daumesnil had his Chasseurs and Mamelukes in a combat formation, awaiting approval to exact revenge, but Murat was awaiting the arrival of the reinforcements that had been summoned from the encampments on all sides of the city. Towards one in the afternoon, however, he was ready to launch an attack on the rioters. In order to coordinate the attack with that of Gobert's division at the Retiro, on the far side of the city, he ordered Rossetti to carry his instructions to General Gobert, at the same time ordering Daumesnil to cut a path through the mob for his aide.

In his *Guides de Bonaparte et chasseurs à cheval de la Garde* (p. 75), Marcel Dupont says:

It would have been impossible to have made a better choice. Daumesnil was the type of *sabreur*, a powerful light cavalryman, absolutely fearless and capable of cutting off a head with a single blow of his terrible saber, a Damascene blade brought back from Egypt.

At the head of his 300 Chasseurs and Mamelukes, Daumesnil set out at a gallop. The bells of all Madrid churches were ringing out the tocsin, calling the people of Madrid to revolt. As the troops rode into the Puerta del Sol, they collided with a mob of armed insurgents. Shouts of "Death to the French!" mingled with the crackling of musket fire. Daumesnil dashed unhesitatingly toward the dense mass of bodies. As heads began falling to the scimitar-like blades of the Mamelukes, the hatred of the *madrileños* of these "pagans" knew no bounds. Women jumped on the cruppers of their horses, attempting to stab and unsaddle their riders. The Mamelukes and Chasseurs continued to clear a path for Rossetti with their sabers.

Suddenly Daumesnil's horse went down, killed by a shot, and he himself was wounded in the thigh by a bullet. With his right leg caught beneath his mount, he was at once surrounded by rioters bent on cutting his throat. He was on the point of being overcome when Lieutenant Chaïm of the Mamelukes, wounded himself and almost blinded by his own blood, succeeded in clearing a space with his scimitar around his commander and dragging him up onto his saddle. Daumesnil at once managed to seize the reins of the horse of a Chasseur who had been killed, and to vault into its saddle, but he had scarcely gathered the horse under him and reached the Calle de Alcala (34) when it, too, was felled by a shot. Somehow he managed to catch a third horse, and put himself back at the head of his embattled men.

As the troop rode past the residence of the Duke of Hijar on the Calle de San Geronimo (38), two Mamelukes were shot down by musket fire from the building's windows. There was no time to avenge them: it was urgent to press on. When the squadron arrived at the Retiro, Rossetti delivered Murat's orders to General Gobert, instructing him to march on the Puerta del Sol, the arsenal, and the hospital. Daumesnil took the head of the column as they headed back to that square. When they came to the residence of the Duke of Hijar, the Mamelukes dismounted to look for the bodies of their comrades. Chasseur Merme, who was in Daumesnil's squadron, has provided this account of what ensued:

Following a trail of blood, the Mamelukes entered the house of the Duke, where they found one of their fellows, his head crushed by stones and his body mutilated, and it was that sight which set off their orgy of killing. They cut off the heads of the residents, men and women alike, and threw their bodies out the windows. They then smashed all the furniture, even the richest and finest. Then they discovered a chest full of Spanish silver coins, which they divided amongst themselves. But a few moments later they happened on another chest, this one filled with Spanish gold coins four times as valuable as the silver, and in a great quantity, so they threw the silver coins out the windows and down the stairs, keeping instead the gold. The only person who survived the killing was the Duke himself, who escaped over the roof. His wife, his children, and his servants had all been killed.[2]

While the Chasseurs were maintaining control over the tumultuous scene in the square, Daumesnil, hearing the extraordinary uproar in the duke's residence, sent an officer with five Chasseurs, including Merme, to investigate the matter. As they went up the stairs, the men began to pick up the silver coins, but the officer told them to drop them and not touch the others. Then, seeing the havoc that the Mamelukes had wrought, the Chasseurs were outraged. They arrested the Mamelukes and returned them to the ranks.

There was one more such incident as the troops reached the crossing where the monastery of Santa Maria de Atocha stood. Several monks lying in wait there killed a Mameluke and wounded two Chasseurs. According to Rossetti, furious Mamelukes entered the monastery and "extracted a terrible vengeance." By five that afternoon, the insurrection had been crushed.

At seven that evening Murat wrote two letters. The first, to the Emperor, read:

Sire,

There were a lot of people killed. The Chasseurs of your Guard lost a few men. Colonel Daumesnil conducted himself in his usual manner, bravely: twice he crossed through the mob with his Chasseurs and Mamelukes. He had twenty men put out of action and two horses shot out from under him. He was wounded lightly in the knee.

This evening I will report more exactly to Your Majesty regarding this event, when I have received all the detailed reports of the different commanding generals. This event, however unfortunate, ensures for us permanently the tranquility of the capital and, I hope, of the kingdom.[3]

The obtuseness of that final sentence leaves one stunned.

The second letter, to Bessières, read:

Monsieur le Maréchal,

Today we had our turn. We have just given a good lesson to the

---

2 Merme, *Des pyramids à Moscou*, p. 42.
3 Rossetti, *Journal inédit*, vol. VI, p. 38.

rabble of Madrid. At least one thousand men died. The Chasseurs and the Mamelukes conducted themselves marvelously. Daumesnil fought in his usual fashion, and was lightly wounded. Order has been restored.

Je vous embrasse,
Joachim[4]

When order had been re-established in the city a few days later, the Duke of Hijar went to Murat to complain of the losses that he had suffered at the hands of the Mamelukes, principally the chests of coins, saying that the fact that the soldiers had found their comrade slain in his residence did not prove that it was his people who were responsible for the man's death. For that reason, he argued, he should not have had to suffer such losses, and therefore he had come to Prince Murat to ask for justice or repayment. Murat agreed with the justice of the duke's complaint and dismissed him. He then sent for Lepic, explained to him the basis for the duke's complaint, and told him to take appropriate action. On 11 May General Lepic wrote to Daumesnil, "This is to notify you, Colonel, that His Highness Prince Murat has decided that the funds which were found on your Mamelukes should be deposited in your chest in replacement for those which were in it at the time that it was looted."[5] Presumably by "your" chest, Lepic meant the chest that was being held by Daumesnil for returning to the Duke of Hijar.

Daumesnil assembled the squadron under arms and with their baggage, went through all of it, and collected all of the Spanish money that he found. All of it was then returned to the duke, who expressed himself as satisfied, although it clearly was not all that had been lost, not to mention the murdered members of his household. Merme comments that the news of this restoration of the money spread though the city and contributed significantly to calming the spirits of the population.

On 4 May Murat again wrote to the Emperor, at four in the morning (he must have *really* been worried!), saying:

Yesterday (*sic*) I reported in haste to Your Majesty the events of the day. Today I provide you an account of our losses. If I ordered the Chasseurs and the Mamelukes to charge, it was because the situation demanded it. I absolutely had to establish my communications with General Grouchy. The Mamelukes alone cut off at least a hundred heads.[6]

---

4   *Ibid.*
5   Copy of letter in Clairval collection.
6   Rossetti, *Journal inédit*, vol. VI, p. 47. Grouchy had been made military governor of Madrid. It's not clear why Murat told the Emperor that it was Grouchy with whom he wanted to coordinate his actions, when, in fact, he had sent his aide to Gobert.

Murat was attempting to justify his employment of the Emperor's "dear children," knowing the affection that Napoleon had for his Chasseurs. He considered the eldest in service of them—those who had been his *Guides* in Italy and Egypt—as his companions in arms from his first hour, and he never exposed them unnecessarily, only committing them at the critical moment to gain a decision in a battle. The Chasseurs of the Guard, as well as the Mamelukes, only took their orders from the Emperor. He, and he alone, ordered and approved nominations to those corps. This being so, Daumesnil inadvertently put himself in an awkward position vis à vis Napoleon in just such a matter.

On 30 April, Daumesnil had written the following letter to Murat:

I have the honor to inform your Imperial Highness that, according to a decree of his Majesty, the corps of Mameluks should be raised to the number of 160 men. The impossibility of being able to attain that number in France has resulted in the corps' being reduced to 86 men, including the depot. I ask your Imperial Highness's authorization to take into the corps some *vallone* guards, a dozen former Mamelukes, and forty Greeks or Albanians, all of whom have relatives in the company of Mamelukes.

I have the honor, etc.[7]

When Napoleon, then in Bayonne, opened his mail of 4 May from Murat and saw the letter from Daumesnil, evidently passed along without comment by the prince, he reacted sharply, and immediately dictated the following letter to Bessières, the Guard commander, at Burgos:

Mon cousin,

In the mail from the Grand Duke of Berg I find the attached letter from an officer of my Guard. I am surprised that this officer dares to address any one other than myself to request recruitment for my Guard. I don't want in my Guard any man coming from the Walloon Guard or other Spanish troops; if there are any, remove them immediately. The corps of Mamelukes stands at 86 men; let it remain there. I created this corps to reward those men who served me in Egypt, and not to make a collection of adventurers. I'm surprised that Daumesnil would dare to come up with such an idea.[8]

Napoleon's comments regarding Daumesnil are rather severe, but, nonetheless, categorical. Nothing escaped him; his word was law.

Murat reassured the Emperor without delay. Writing on the 8th at 3:00 in the morning (now he was *really* worried!) from Madrid, he assured

---

7 *Vallones* were Walloons in the service of Spain.
8 *Archives Nationales*, Bessières collection, 32 AP 1.

Napoleon that, "No foreign Mameluke will enter into the Mamelukes of your Guard."

That little contretemps notwithstanding, Daumesnil received the following letter from the new commander of his regiment, Lefebvre-Desnoëttes:

> I had not received your letter of 3 May, dear Colonel, but I have just received your report on the affair of the second. I am well aware of the role that you played in that affair, and I extend my sincere compliments. You continue to justify the good reputation that you have long since earned. I have suggested to the Marshal the cross of the *Couronne de fer*[9] for you, but he thought you already had it. He is, however, disposed to do whatever is necessary to arrange for that. I hope that the Grand Duke will pay you for your horses; I'll make that my affair. In any case, I don't want you lose in any respect from this affair.
>
> I said in my last letter that I don't want the Chasseurs and Mamelukes to want for anything; at present you should be all right with boots. If you need trousers, I authorize you to have 50 pair made if necessary, and if you find some good material.
>
> Finally, ask me for what you need for expenses.
>
> I do want the *maréchal des logis chef* to join me. Do whatever suits you. I rely completely on you to take care of our interests and to keep your squadron in the best condition.

Having signed the letter, Lefebvre-Desnoëttes then added this note:

> The officers who are here, not having their effects, are in a great state of destitution. Therefore I would like it if you would send them by a caisson, which would remain here until the reunion of the detachments of the corps.[10]

Getting separated from one's kit must have been a common problem for officers in the field. Considering the cost of uniforms of officers of the Guard, one can well imagine the concern that officers felt about their possible loss.

This warmly phrased letter demonstrates not only the practical administrative difficulties of keeping one's troops properly attired under

---

9   This order was created by Napoleon on 5 June 1805, several days after his crowning in Milan as King of Italy. The title of the order derives from the presence within the crown of the kings of Lombardy of a ring of iron, said to have been forged from a nail of Christ's cross. With the fall of the Empire, the order was taken over by the Austrian emperor, who gave previous holders of that decoration the right to wear it, as a "replacement." On 24 December 1818, the High Chancelry of the Legion of Honor authorized Daumesnil to wear the decoration of a Chevalier of the Cross of Iron of Austria.

10 Desclozeaux archives.

difficult field conditions, but, more importantly, the high level of confidence that the new regimental commander had in Daumesnil's ability to handle a key element of the regiment on his own.

In General Lepic's official account of the officers, *sous-officiers*, and soldiers of the Chasseurs and Mamelukes killed or wounded in the affair of 2 May, Daumesnil is noted as having been wounded in the thigh by a bullet, and having suffered contusions in his chest and right leg as a result of his horse's fall. Two Mamelukes and two Chasseurs had been killed, and 51 of all ranks wounded.

As the Spanish population awakened to the reality of the cynical take-over of their country by Napoleon, the confirmation by the puppet regency junta of Joseph Bonaparte as their king on 24 May removed whatever vestiges of uncertainty may have lingered in their minds. By late May, provincial juntas throughout the country were raising armies of patriots, and by the end of the month major revolts had spread to Valencia, the Asturias, and Seville.

At the head of one of the regional armies was General José Palafox, an officer of the Royal Guard, who had accompanied Crown Prince Ferdinand to Bayonne that spring, but who had escaped and returned to Aragon to raise an army. In Bayonne, as he received reports of the gathering Spanish forces, Napoleon dispatched various of his generals to the multiple flash-points. Lefebvre-Desnouëttes was sent off with 5,000 men from Pamplona to deal with the threat posed by Palafox, and, passing through Tudela, he succeeded in driving the Spanish general into Saragossa, which was placed under siege. By 10 June, every province was arming, or in open revolt.

At the same time, Murat's disappointment at not having been given the Spanish throne by Napoleon was complicated by the onset of what was said to be a serious illness, apparently a fever, with intestinal complications. In any case, Murat decided he had had enough of Spain. Napoleon had given him, in lieu of the Spanish throne, a choice of the throne of Portugal or of Naples, demanding an immediate decision. Murat promptly replied that he chose the crown of Naples. On 31 May he asked the Emperor to send a replacement for him to Madrid, and on 15 June General Savary arrived in Madrid to serve as a temporary replacement for the Grand Duke of Berg, pending Joseph's arrival on the scene. On 18 June Savary assumed command, and on the 29th, Murat, still so ill that he had to be carried in a litter, departed, doubtless with an enormous sense of relief.

After the almost complete absence of central direction of military operations because of Murat's illness and his unwillingness to attempt to deal with the urgent problems arising on every hand, Savary proved to be an able executor of Napoleon's steady stream of instructions for coping with the threats to French control posed by the insurgent armies. On 14 July, at Medina del Rio Seco, Bessières was confronted by the local patriot armies of Castille and Galicia, under Generals La Cuesta and Blake respectively. Bessières had at his disposal a Guard detachment consisting of four battalions of infantry, a squadron of Horse Grenadiers, Daumesnil's Chasseurs, and ten cannon. At one point the enthusiastic fervor of La Cuesta's grenadiers and the volunteers of Santiago carried them to the muzzles of the French cannon, four of which were temporarily silenced, but a charge by the Horse Grenadiers and Chasseurs drove off the insurgents. By two in the afternoon the battle was over, and the Spanish troops were in flight. Lasalle started off in pursuit of the enemy with the two Guard squadrons, but, judging that their strength was insufficient for the task, Bessières recalled them, rather than see them compromised needlessly.

Daumesnil's Chasseurs and the Mamelukes were soon called on to serve as the escort for the new king of Spain, Joseph having by now been instructed by the Emperor to proceed to his new capital. He had scarcely arrived in Madrid on 20 July, however, when the news of Dupont's surrender at Bailen on 21 July reached the capital. Joseph soon concluded that it was not safe for him to remain in the center of the country, and he forthwith demanded a retreat northward. Savary was persuaded that the sooner Joseph was removed from a position of command, the better, so on 30 July the evacuation of the royal party began. The next day the Guard cavalry joined the jittery king in Chamartin, where he had spent the night. Two weeks later its caravan halted at Vitoria, north of the Ebro. In a state of agitated anxiety, Joseph wrote to his brother: "Philip V had only one competitor to conquer: I have an entire nation. I won't reign over a people who don't want me."[11]

Between 1 and 5 August, far away on the Portuguese coast at Mondego Bay, 14,000 British troops, under the temporary command of Sir Arthur Wellesley, came ashore. After dispersing French detachments at Obidos and Roliça, on 21 August the British defeated Junot himself at Vimiero. With the British evacuation by sea of Junot's force, in accordance with the terms of the Convention of Cintra, the French foothold in Portugal was for the moment lost.

Before leaving Madrid, Joseph had ordered General Verdier to abandon the siege of Saragossa, which Palafox had been stubbornly defending since early June. By early September, the French presence in Spain had been reduced to those forces north of the Ebro, including the French garrison under Duhesme in Barcelona. There ensued a pause in operations on the part of both adversaries. While the Spanish regional juntas struggled to reconcile their differences, Napoleon took the opportunity to give orders to his generals to dispose their commands in defensive postures to afford him breathing space in which to develop a strategy, which would serve to reverse his armies' fortunes in the Peninsula.

---

11 Pigeard, *Les Campagnes Napoléoniennes,* vol. 1, p. 338.

The indispensable first phase of such a strategy was to ensure, insofar as possible, that the present political stability in central, eastern, and southern Europe remain undisturbed. Ensuring the continued cooperation of Tsar Alexander was an essential element in that strategy. Consequently, at Napoleon's initiative a conference between the two monarchs for a review of their existing alliance was agreed upon. Their meeting in Erfurt in early October concluded with the signing of a Convention, which gave Napoleon the confidence that he could now draw down significantly his veteran forces in Germany in order to shift the bulk of them to the Spanish frontier. The *Grande Armée* was disbanded, and the new Army of Spain, composed of six corps totaling some 100,000 men, plus half of the Guard, was put on the roads to the Pyrenees, under the personal command of the Emperor.

In anticipation of a satisfactory outcome of the Erfurt conference, a number of units had already started south. On 8 October *colonel major* Guyot set out for Bordeaux with those squadrons of the Guard Chasseurs, which were not already in Spain under Daumesnil's command. By 30 October the Army of Spain, poised on the Spanish border, included all four regiments of the Guard cavalry, plus the company of Mamelukes and the *Gendarmes d'Elite*. On 4 November Napoleon crossed the Bidassoa, escorted by Lefebvre-Desnouëttes and the Chasseurs. Detachments of Horse Grenadiers had been posted at intervals along the route for security purposes. The following day it would be the turn of Daumesnil's Chasseurs and Major Jolivet's Dragoons to provide that service. On the evening of the 5th, the Chasseurs led the Emperor into Vitoria, where King Joseph awaited him.

After a pause of three days to permit rear echelon units to catch up, on 9 November Napoleon set out for Burgos, with Soult, Bessières, and the Guard. Bessières had been replaced by Soult and given command of the cavalry reserve. After brushing aside General Belveder's small corps on the road to Burgos, the army marched on Burgos, which was entered after a brisk skirmish and a fine charge by Bessières, leading the Guard cavalry. The unrestrained pillaging of the city which followed, despite an order that any soldier caught looting would be shot, was an ominous prelude to the bitter form of warfare that the French soldiers were soon to experience. They quickly learned that to stray away even briefly from one's comrades was to invite a quick and unpleasant death.

For the next two weeks the Emperor remained in Burgos, directing operations of the corps of Moncy, Ney, Lefebvre and Soult against the armies of Blake, Palafox, Belveder, and Castaños, in an effort to encircle and destroy them. When his strategy failed to achieve that objective, he decided that it was essential to get on with re-installing Joseph on his throne in Madrid. Therefore, on 23 November the Emperor set out for the capital with the Guard, Victor's corps, and those cavalry regiments which were still on hand. The route to Madrid would take the army south through Sepulveda and over the pass of Somo-Sierra, and then on through Buitrago to the capital.

By the 29th, Napoleon and the army had arrived at the village of Boceguillas, a short distance from a larger town, Sepulveda, which was situated slightly north of the pass of Somo-Sierra. That pass, some 1,500 meters in altitude, provided the most direct means of passage through the Guadarrama range to the plain leading to Madrid. The Supreme Junta in Madrid had given General Benito San Juan 13,000 troops—six regular, two militia, and seven levy battalions, plus sixteen cannon—with which to bar Napoleon's path through the mountains. San Juan had placed 3,500 of his men in Sepulveda, and then deployed the other 9,000 men and the cannon along the 3-kilometer long narrow road leading through the Somo-Sierra pass itself.

Late on the 29th, General Savary launched an attack with a brigade of Guard infantry against the Spanish troops in Sepulveda, but it was sharply repulsed, and at some considerable expense to the French. However, as San Juan's troops became increasingly aware of the mass of French troops that continued to accumulate north of the town, a considerable number of the Spanish troops quietly slipped away to Segovia. Since they didn't bother to notify San Juan of their intentions, one might well say that they were taking "French leave."

Early on the 30th, the Emperor left his headquarters at Boceguillas for the passage over the Guadarrama and on to Madrid. At dawn that morning, a heavy mist obscured the entrance to the pass of Somo-Sierra, as the French advance guard drew up near a stone pillar marking its entrance. That day Napoleon was escorted by the third squadron of the Guard cavalry's newest regiment, the Polish Light Horse. A prisoner, brought by a picket of the squadron to the spot where the Emperor and his staff were gathered, was questioned, and responded that the pass was guarded by many thousands of Spanish infantry and gunners, with batteries placed at each of the four bends in the road as it wound up to the summit of the pass. General Ruffin, a divisional commander of Victor's corps, ordered three of his regiments to start working their way up the pass: the 9th Light on the precipitous rocky slope on the right, the 24th Line on the left slope, and the 96th Line on the narrow path itself, with six artillery pieces in support. Soon gunfire could be heard, muffled by the fog, as the defenders, scattered over both hillsides looming over the pass, took the advancing French infantry under fire.

Now I beg the reader's indulgence, while I pause briefly before continuing my narrative. Any one attempting to write military history is bound, sooner or later, to be confronted with the necessity for reconciling, as best he can, varying and often contradictory accounts of the actions he wishes to describe, in an effort to arrive at what is termed these days "ground truth." Well, good luck to him, say I. Sentiments of national pride and prestige almost inevitably color the accounts of various sources, eyewitnesses or otherwise, thereby complicating the problem for the perplexed author. Memoirs written many years after the event in question, setting down oft-told tales in which the teller is the central figure, are often of undependable reliability. The taking of the pass of Somo-Sierra by the 3rd squadron of the Polish Light Horse of the Imperial Guard is a striking case in point. What follows immediately hereafter represents my best judgment as to what actually happened on that occasion. Since I have chosen to discard other versions of this affair as in some respects inaccurate, it would be pointless to pause over them. It should be said, however, that, regardless of the disparities in the various accounts of the manner in which this action transpired, what a handful of young, unblooded Polish cavalrymen did at a pass in Spain's Guadaramma mountains on 30 November 1808 justifiably won for this fledgling regiment everlasting fame. Now, on with the story!

When it became evident to the waiting Emperor and his staff that Ruffin's men were being held up by the combination of the lingering dense fog and the fusillades being poured down on them from both hillsides, Napoleon became increasingly impatient and irritated by the thought that his advance on Madrid was being delayed "by peasants, mere armed brigands," as he put it. When, late in the morning the sun at last broke through, in an effort to gauge the feasibility of a direct cavalry attack straight up the narrow, winding road, and with Spanish cannon balls and bullets already falling in the vicinity of Napoleon and his staff, Colonel Piré, commander of the cavalry of the advance guard, went forward with several of his staff to examine the situation at first-hand. Almost at once he returned to the increasingly agitated Emperor, exclaiming, "Sire, it's impossible!"

Predictably, Napoleon's angry response was, "Impossible? I don't know the meaning of that word!"[12] He then called for the duty squadron's commander, Major Jean Kozietulski. When that young officer advanced to the Emperor's side and saluted, Napoleon said to him, "Here's an opportunity for you to earn your spurs. Take that pass for me—at a gallop!" Doubtless Kozietulski understood that he and his men were being given what amounted to a "forlorn hope" kind of mission, but if that meant sacrificing his own and his men's lives for this man, who was destined—or so a great many Poles thought—to liberate Poland, then this represented a golden chance to demonstrate his devotion to that cause. So, elated at the prospect of shining in the eyes of the Emperor, he placed himself at the head of his squadron, raised his saber, and set his men in motion with the command, "Trot!" Then, ordering them into a gallop, he led them past Napoleon to the accompaniment of shouts of "*Vivat Caesarz!*" The narrowness of the road meant that the troopers were compelled to ride four abreast, and Kozietulski's inexperience—this affair

---

12 Tranié & Carmigniani, *Les Polonais de Napoléon,* p.36.

was literally the regiment's "blooding"—resulted in his forming the 150 men of the two companies of the squadron in a compact body, thus rendering them an easier target for the waiting Spanish musketeers and gunners than if there had been intervals between the companies and platoons.

A painting by Lejeune in the Musée de Versailles, *The Battle of Somo-Sierra*, presumably based on his own visit at some point to the terrain where the engagement took place, as well as a modern photograph taken from the summit of the pass, make it evident that it would not have been possible for Napoleon, even with his long-glass, to follow the course of the action, once the galloping squadron had rounded the shoulder of the nearest rocky slope overhanging the road. But the intensified crackle of musketry and repeated thunder of cannon fire made it clear to the army waiting at the foot of the pass that the squadron was riding through a hail of lead and iron. Clearly Ruffin's infantry had not succeeded in completely clearing the slopes of Spanish "brigands."

Undaunted by the fiery reception accorded them, Kozietulski and his men had taken in their stride a ditch cut across the road, and overrun the first of the four gun emplacements, sabering the pieces' cannoneers, and then pressing on to the next battery. Holes in the squadron's ranks began appearing, and Kozietulski's horse went down, mortally stricken, leaving its rider with a badly bruised left leg, unable to continue up the road with his men (Given the number of wounds he accumulated on that occasion, however, he may have caught a loose horse and managed to fight his way farther up the road before falling again.) Next Captain Pierre Krasinski—presumably the son of the regiment's commanding officer—fell wounded. Then it was Captain Dziewanowski who managed to sustain the impetus of the attack, leading the surviving troopers up to and over the third battery before he, too, was mortally struck down. The sole surviving officer, Lieutenant Niegolewski, together with the handful of troopers still in their saddles, finally reached the last of the batteries, at the summit of the pass, and there two balls tore into the young man's body, knocking him from his saddle. He was instantly set upon by the battery's gunners, who added seven bayonet wounds to his injuries.

The sheer audacity and intensity of this seemingly mad attack, coming in combination with the continuing three-pronged advance by Ruffin's infantry and the knowledge that a large army was gathered and waiting at the foot of pass, sowed the seeds of panic among the surviving defenders of the pass, and, first a few at a time, they began to abandon their positions and retreat toward the summit, in spite of General San Juan's efforts to hold them in their emplacements.

Although, as noted above, the character of the terrain between the foot of the pass and its summit would have prevented Napoleon and his staff from following visually the entire course of this memorable charge, which had scarcely occupied seven minutes, the officers and men of Ruffin's three regiments would have had a grandstand view of the entire drama, and certainly must have sent back word as to its outcome.

When the results of the charge were reported to Napoleon, his reaction was to exclaim, "Those are greenhorns! They don't know how to fight!" Berthier advised awaiting the arrival of additional infantry, with which a more effective attack could be mounted, but Napoleon wouldn't hear of it. Instead, he went to the spot where the other three squadrons of the regiment were waiting in anxious suspense. He complimented them on the bravery of their comrades, and told them that their losses were caused by their inexperience, but that now he was going to put one of his cavalry generals at their head, and that they should follow his instructions explicitly. Then, he said, they would be worthy of the honor he had paid them by making them part of his Guard.

Having said that, Napoleon turned over in his mind possible candidates for the role he had in mind. Seeing his hesitation, Berthier suggested General Montbrun, along with Lasalle one of the most brilliant cavalry leaders of the Empire. For reasons we need not detail here, this famous *sabreur* was in the Emperor's bad books at this point, and had been lingering on the outskirts of the general staff in the hope that an opportunity for regaining Napoleon's favor would present itself. Accepting Berthier's suggestion, the Emperor had Montbrun brought to him. Napoleon said to him,

"I wish to give you the opportunity to rehabilitate yourself in my eyes. Take command of my *chevaux-légers*, open the road to Madrid, and all will be forgiven."

"Sire," Montbrun replied, "in a quarter of an hour either I shall be dead or Your Majesty will be able to be on your way!"[13]

With that, Montbrun swung into his saddle and placed himself at the head of the waiting Poles. Calling the regiment's remaining officers around him, he explained how he proposed to conduct the attack. "Keep a distance of 300 meters between each squadron so that, if the first is stopped, there will be time for it to reform before it slows the impetus of the following squadron. In each platoon, leave space between the troopers, so as not to offer easy targets. " And to their commander, he added, "Keep your eyes on me, and do exactly what I do! Now, comrades, let's go! Vive l'Empereur!"

In a hail of bullets, Montbrun passed through the entrance to the gorge at the head of the three squadrons, and in a few minutes the riders were approaching the crest of the pass, where the road straightened out. A cannon of the fourth battery, still manned by its crew, fired, but at too great a distance for its shot to be effective. Seeing the palisade before him, Montbrun reined in his horse, leapt to the ground and started to tear its planks away with his bare hands. In a moment the Polish troopers were

---

13 Dupont, *Cavaliers d'epopée*, p. 118.

following his example. The astonished Spanish gunners and riflemen scarcely managed to get off a few shots at the Poles before the latter were among them with slashing sabers. In a few minutes the entire defense had crumbled, and, seeing that the passage had been forced, those Spanish infantry who were still on the slopes bordering the road took flight. In the course of their retreat they only paused briefly to tie San Juan to a tree and execute him.

Leaving two squadrons of the Light Horse to mop up the few remaining gunners and take possession of their pieces, Montbrun remounted and led the rest of the regiment on a headlong dash for Buitrago. The Horse Chasseurs of the Guard had been ordered forward in support of the Poles, and now they joined Montbrun and his men in sweeping up the fleeing Spaniards, finally drawing up that evening at La Cabrera.

Of the 150 officers and men of the 3rd squadron, who had set out in an ardently enthusiastic response to Napoleon's challenge, 83 of them, including all seven officers, had been killed or wounded. One of Napoleon's aides-de-camp, young Philippe de Ségur, who had galloped off with the 3rd squadron, evidently in the hope of winning a bit of glory for himself, paid for that impetuosity by being severely wounded.

Wounded eleven times in the first charge, Kozietulski lived to fight another day. During the Russian campaign, it was he who commanded the duty squadron at Malo-Yaroslavetz, when he just barely managed to save Napoleon from capture by a swarm of Cossacks, who suddenly appeared while the Emperor was visiting the site of the previous day's battle. Kozietulski was also wounded on that occasion.

As Napoleon passed the scene of the fiercest engagement, he saw the wounded Lieutenant Niegolewski being tended by the side of the road. Dismounting and bending over the prostrate young man, the Emperor removed his own cross of the Legion of Honor and pinned it on the wounded man's tunic. The lieutenant would live to a ripe old age, doubtless telling and retelling the story of that memorable day countless times. 47 years later he would write, "May many other young people have such a memory!"[14]

The following day, with the Polish Light Horse drawn up before him, a number of the men in first-aid dressings or supported by comrades, Napoleon presented sixteen stars of the Legion to its men—eight to its officers and eight to its *sous-officiers* and troopers. Taking his hat off, he declared to them, "You are worthy of my Old Guard! Honor to the bravest of the Brave!" With that acclamation, the regiment had won advancement from the Young Guard to the Old Guard, passing over the Middle Guard, an exceptional honor.

In the 13th *Bulletin* of the Army, published on 2 December, Napoleon declared, "A charge made by the Polish Light Horse of the Guard, led by

---

14 Pigeard, *Les Campagnes Napoléoniennes, vol. 1*, p.348.

General Montbrun, decided the affair; this charge was brilliant, and the regiment covered itself with glory and showed its worthiness of a place in the Imperial Guard ... Eight Polish Light Horsemen were killed in the midst of the guns, and sixteen more were wounded." This was not the first or the last time that Napoleon chose to make light of casualties. Montbrun had indeed rehabilitated himself in the Emperor's eyes, and would go on to higher commands and greater distinctions, until a shell fragment tore into his stomach on the field of Borodino. He died that evening.

It's not clear what role—if any—Colonel Krasinski, the commanding officer of the regiment, played in this affair, although presumably he went up the pass with the three as yet uncommitted squadrons of the regiment. In his *Les Etoiles de Napoléon* (p. 424), Pigeard says that Krasinski was wounded at Somo-Sierra, but this is probably a case of confusion with the Captain Krasinski, who was, as noted, wounded on that occasion. A painting by H. Vernet portrays Kozietulski and Krasinski together at the summit of the pass, while the former recounts for his colonel the manner in which the action occurred. (That seems remarkably inconsistent with Kozietulski's allegedly having received eleven wounds that day, but, nevertheless, it makes for a dramatic painting.)

On the morning of 2 December, the French advance guard reached Madrid's suburbs, and by evening the bulk of the army was encamped on the city's outskirts. Sent to the city to demand its capitulation, Bessières was defiantly rebuffed by the Junta, to the accompaniment of shouts from the crowd of "Long live Fernando VI and damn the tyrant Emperor!"

Napoleon was in no mood to tolerate Spanish intransigence, and at nine on the morning of the 3rd, French artillery commenced fire on the city's walls in order to open breaches through which the troops could penetrate into the city. To afford the city's defenders one more chance to avoid an all-out assault on the capital, the Emperor sent General Bigarré, an aide de camp of Joseph's, to deliver to General Mora, the commander of the city's defenders, a demand for the city's capitulation. To ensure that his passage would not be blocked, Bigarré took with him a battery of field artillery, and, as his escort, *chef d'escadron* Daumesnil. Passing through one of the shattered gates to the city, Bigarré led his party to the fountain on the Rua de Alcala, and from there he ordered his cannoneers to fire a salvo on the Puerta del Sol, which was, as it had been on the *Dos de Mayo*, a center of resistance.

In his *Mémoires* (p. 71), Bigarré describes his experience on that occasion in these words:

Proceeding along the houses of the Rua de Alcala with *chef d'escadron* Daumesnil, who was accompanied by a trumpeter of his regiment, I succeeded in reaching an entrenchment at the Plaza del Sol, and having myself accepted as a *parlementaire*. The Spanish General Mora emerged from that redoubt, and approached me with

176

a downcast air. Before I could say a word, he said to me that the people were in a rage, and didn't want to hear any talk about capitulation. He went on to say that if he were to go back into the redoubt from which he had come to speak to me, he could be cut to pieces, as had happened to General Peralès one time. He entreated me to tell the Emperor that that the people had complete control of the city, and that the civil and military authorities were no longer recognized.

Chef d'escadron Daumesnil and I returned by the same route by which we had reached the redoubt. Once at the fountain from which I had departed, I immediately went to the Emperor's tent to report what I had learned. The Emperor exploded with anger at Mora, saying, "Imagine this General Mora! He helped put arms in the hands of the people, and now he doesn't have the courage to take them away from them. Go tell him for me that if he doesn't bring me the keys of the city within two hours, I'll set fire to the entire city and put to the sword every one within at the time a forced entry is made."[15]

General Bigarré left to convey this ultimatum to Mora, but the latter had already decided to lay down arms. That night the capitulation was signed in the Emperor's tent, and the following day the army entered Madrid. It was an almost deserted city that awaited the army. Windows in houses lining the boulevards were shuttered, and the few individuals on the streets for the most part turned their backs on the marching troops. With the glaring exception of Moscow, other European capitals occupied by the French generally took the experience in stride, more as a temporary inconvenience rather than as a plague visited on them by the devil. The ladies of Berlin, for example, rather than seeking an opportunity to slip a dagger between the ribs of a Gallic lover, apparently found the gay, young French visitors an agreeable change from their regular fare, and the Viennese grew quite accustomed to the sight of blue uniforms and tricolor flags. But the *madrileños,* far from displaying any such disposition, made it their business to render their occupiers' lives as threatened and perilous as possible.

King Joseph, who had a much more realistic view than his brother's of the long-term prospects for a peaceful incorporation of Spain in the Empire, observed, once he had been re-installed on his throne, "It would take 100,000 permanent scaffolds to maintain a prince condemned to reign over the Spaniards." How he longed to be back in Naples, but his was not to reason why.

Only the Guard artillery participated in the army's entrance into the city, the other regiments remaining near the Emperor's encampment at

---

15 Napoleon had a particular reason for despising Mora, since it was he who was primarily responsible for dishonoring the terms of Dupont's capitulation at Bailen.

Chamartin. During the next two weeks, while Napoleon busied himself with reforming the Spanish government —including abolishing the Inquisition—and reordering the dispositions of the Army of Spain, the army's soldiers had a welcome respite in which to restore themselves, and to repair worn uniforms and equipment. They also learned never to wander about the city by themselves.

A review of the Guard was in progress at Chamartin on the 19th, when a courier brought the Emperor a dispatch from Marshal Soult. Its contents informed him that on 14 December British cavalry and infantry had overrun Soult's posts at Rueda and Tordesillas, and that the people of Vallalodid were in a state of insurrection. It came as a considerable surprise to Napoleon that General Moore was not on his way back to Portugal to re-embark his troops for England, but instead was posing a serious threat to Soult's corps, and even to the French line of communications back through Burgos to Bayonne. He immediately set about shifting the troop dispositions he had just effected, with the new objective of attempting to interpose French forces between Moore and the coast, and thereby entrap and destroy his army.

Ney was ordered to put his corps on the road to the Guadarramas, with Lefebvre-Desnoëttes and the Guard cavalry close behind, their departure set for the 21st. When the Guard cavalry passed through Escorial, snow was already falling, and the weather would continue to deteriorate sharply as the column reached the foothills of the mountain range. Ney's troops had already managed, with great difficulty, to get across the summit of the pass, but now the Guard cavalry was finding it almost impossible to make any progress. The Chasseurs walked on the lee side of their horses, which gave them some protection from the icy gales, and the trampling of their horses' hooves to some degree broke a path for the following infantry. Marbot speaks of the snow, driven by violent winds, blinding men and their horses alike, and sweeping some of the troopers and their mounts over precipices. Savary adds these details of that appallingly difficult passage:

> The Emperor passed through the ranks of infantry with the regiment of the Guard Chasseurs. He then made the regiment form a tight column occupying the entire width of the road. Then, having made the men dismount, he placed himself on foot behind the first platoon, and ordered the march to begin, with each trooper leading his horse by the bridle. Arriving at the summit and starting down the opposite slope, Napoleon slipped and slid, exclaiming as he did, "Damned profession!"[16]

At last the exhausted soldiers were led by their Emperor into the village of Villacastin, where camp had already been set up. Those who had

---

16 Savary, *Mémoires du Duc de Rovigo*, quoted in Clairval's notes.

crossed the St. Bernard pass eight years before thought that getting over the Guadarramas was a more painful experience. The effort required to surmount that icy barrier had cost the army two days' march on the British, however, so now it was imperative to drive ahead as quickly as possible, if Moore's force was to be cut off and destroyed.

By Christmas Day, the Guard was at Tordesillas, from which Soult's men had been driven by Moore ten days previously, but there was no time for thoughts of peace on earth. At 5:30 that afternoon, the Guard foot and cavalry were again on the move, following Ney's troops, headed for Medina del Rio Seco, since the Emperor's latest reports had placed the British in the Leon-Sahagun area. But Moore was proving to be an elusive quarry, and by the 27th his whereabouts were still not clear. Then Ney's cavalry scouts found the British at Mayorga, and once again Napoleon shifted the direction of Ney's advance toward Valderas, in order to swing behind and around Moore. Then, learning that the British were in Benavente, Napoleon wrote to Lefebvre-Desnoëttes, telling him to press ahead with the Chasseurs to make contact with the enemy, and to attempt by harassing actions to fix them until the rest of the army could come up. Finally, he sent the Polish Light Horse to support Lefebvre-Desnoëttes.

In his *Carnets,* Guyot provides a baldly factual account of the ill-advised and disastrous action into which Lefèbvre-Desnoëttes impetuously plunged the Chasseurs. Arriving in Castro Gonsalvo on the late afternoon of the 28th, well in advance of the General Headquarters, Lefebvre-Desnoëttes sent an advance guard of Chasseurs to scout out British activity in the vicinity of Benavente, on the opposite side of the Esla, a small river flowing southwest and emptying into the Duoro. The Chasseurs observed some British troops engaging in demolishing the wooden bridge leading across the Esla to Benavente, and a brief exchange of musket fire took place, resulting in the fatal wounding of one of the Mameluke officers, Azaria.

At 6:00 the next morning, the young general had his regiment in the saddle, and was looking for a means of crossing the river in order to continue the reconnaissance to Benavente and beyond. By that time, the bridge had been rendered impassable, and any effort to repair it in the face of the enemy, who could be seen on the far bank observing the French movements, was out of the question. As it happened, at virtually the same time Napoleon was writing to Lefebvre-Desnoëttes, telling him not to compromise the Guard cavalry and not to push the matter, if the bridge was guarded by infantry.

Apparently without having received the Emperor's instructions, and having located a ford opposite Castro Gonsalvo, Lefebvre-Desnoëttes led his 400 Chasseurs through the rapid-flowing, powerful currents of the Esla, swollen by snow and rain, and the regiment's advance guard galloped off in pursuit of the forty British cavalry, who had been posted near the bridgehead. Having pursued the enemy for several kilometers, right up to the gates to Benavente, the Chasseurs were driven back by the British main guard. Lefebvre then sent forward the first and fifth companies to support the advance guard, but those men were immediately set upon by three British squadrons coming out of Benavente.

Guyot was then ordered to take the second and sixth companies to disengage the men of the regiment from their assailants so that they might withdraw, but the continuing increase in the numbers of British cavalry being fed into the fray was making the regiment's position increasingly perilous. At the head of the second and sixth companies, Guyot charged a dense column of cavalry approaching his line of battle, breaking up several of its squadrons. In a few moments, he had 30 to 40 prisoners to deal with, and a number of wounded on the field of battle. Some 60 riderless British horses were running loose through the regiment's ranks.

Guyot managed to amalgamate his two companies with the first and fifth and to get them in a line of battle, but by now there were 19 British squadrons facing him, and he was forced to retreat. At that point Lefebvre-Desnoëttes sent Major Thiry, with the last 150 men of the final companies, to Guyot's aid, but that weak reinforcement could only fire on the mass of British cavalry, without having an appreciable effect. Lord Paget, commanding the British cavalry, ordered his men to charge the French, and they succeeded in pushing the Chasseurs back to the ford across from Castro Gonsalvo, despite a stubborn resistance on the latter's part. The colonel of the 7th Light Dragoons and a major were killed, and some 200 British troopers wounded, of whom 27 died either on the field of battle or in Benavente the next day.

In their precipitate retreat, the Chasseurs had lost two officers and six troopers killed, and another 35 men, whose horses were too worn and exhausted to go on, had been captured. It was at the ford, through which the regiment had passed just one hour previously, that Lefebvre-Desnoëttes was captured, as he vainly attempted to keep the men of the regiment from returning to the left bank of the river. Guyot comments that it was a very good thing that he was unable to do so, because if the Chasseurs had retreated down that bank of the Esla, they would have fallen into the hands of another eight squadrons of British cavalry, who were covering the right flank of the retreating British column.

Guyot concludes his account by saying that, once he had regained the left bank with the surviving 300 Chasseurs, they remained there, and the British made no attempt to pursue them through the ford. He sent a report of the affair to the Emperor, who was still at Valderas, and by three that afternoon Napoleon had arrived at Castro Gonsalvo. Guyot's resentment over Lefebvre-Desnoëtte's having been given command of the regiment in preference to himself was undoubtedly heightened by the rash and disastrous conduct of his commander on this occasion. Guyot commented that Lefebvre-Desnoëttes was made a prisoner, together with three other officers, because he abandoned the regiment at the height of the retreat.

The losses to the regiment were severe: two lieutenants and six Chasseurs killed, and six officers and 62 Chasseurs wounded. When Napoleon learned how roughly his favorite regiment had been handled, he was furious, but he ended up by seemingly approving their commander's conduct. Dupont comments that, in order to make it clear to every one that he did not harbor any resentment against the young general for his ill-considered action, Napoleon declared that the position of regimental commander would remain vacant until Lefebvre-Desnoëttes' return. One can imagine the effect that that decision had on Guyot, who would, by reason of that decision, remain as the acting regimental commander until Lefebvre's return in 1812.[17] Although he never realized his ambition to command the regiment in which he had played such an important role, Guyot became a *général de division* in December 1811, and was given command of the Horse Grenadiers in November of 1813.

In a letter to Josephine on 31 December, Napoleon told her of Lefebvre-Desnoëttes' capture:

Lefebvre has been captured. He has had a skirmish with 300 Chasseurs. These gallants swam a river, and ended up in the middle of the English cavalry. They killed a number of them, but Lefebvre's horse was wounded, and when he was swimming back, the current carried him to the opposite bank, where he was taken. Console his wife.[18]

In her *Sir John Moore*, Carola Oman provides a few details regarding the reception that Lefebvre-Desnoëttes was accorded by Sir John Moore, when the bedraggled Frenchman was brought to the former's headquarters. Here is her account of that episode.

[Lefebvre-Desnoëttes] had given up his sword, and blood was streaming from his brow. The British commander-in-chief, speaking the French of the *ancien régime*, received [him] with every courtesy. Sir John called for water and washed the prisoner's wound with his own hands. It was superficial. He next observed that his guest was very wet, and the Imperial Hussar (*sic*), who had been captured when his wounded horse refused to swim the Esla a second time, withdrew to be provided with some of General Moore's body-linen. A flag of truce was sent across the river to request that the prisoner's baggage might be forwarded, and this arrived in good time for

---

17 The British refused a French request to exchange one of their prisoners of an equivalent grade for Lefebvre-Desnoëttes. When later there were negotiations for an exchange, the French turned over a suitable prisoner, but the British reneged on the deal. Learning of this, Lefebvre-Desnoëttes considered himself no longer bound by his parole, and managed to escape to France in 1812.

18 Balagny, *Campagnes de l'Empereur Napoléon en Espagne*, vol. IV, p. 172.

General Lefebvre-Desnoëttes to appear for supper in a fresh and even more splendid toilette. French generals always had a remarkable proportion of baggage, and several horses and servants came in for this one that night. Sir John, looking thoughtful, asked his secretary if he thought it would be right to ask the General for a written promise not to escape, and Colborne, quite sure, and a little shocked, advised not. He remembered a French officer in Sicily to have been much affronted by such a request. When the French general appeared to sup, his host hoped that he now had everything he needed, upon which the captive cast a stricken look at his empty side. Sir John Moore, without another word, unbuckled the fine saber of East-India workmanship, which he himself was wearing.

That's all very chivalrous, but one is left wondering whether Lefebvre-Desnoëttes had as much concern for his captured comrades—a number of them no doubt wounded—whom he had so rashly led into a trap, as he did for his toilette.

There is no evidence that Daumesnil was present during that unfortunate engagement. Since Lefebvre and Guyot had only two squadrons with them at the time, the likelihood is that the other squadrons of the regiment were with the general headquarters of the army, and that Daumesnil was in command of the Emperor's escort squadron. It will be recalled that Napoleon always wanted Daumesnil to perform that function when he, Napoleon, was in a war zone in which he might be put at risk. In fact, on the previous day the Emperor, accompanied only by a single squadron of Chasseurs, had been well ahead of the main body of the army, and had arrived in Valderas a scant two hours after the British had left that town.

1809

By now it was becoming increasingly apparent to Napoleon that Moore was likely to be able to avoid French efforts to entrap his force, and would therefore succeed in saving his army by evacuating it via La Coruña. Moreover, reports reaching the Emperor from Paris regarding Austrian rearmament, as well as rumors of conspiratorial behaviour on the part of Talleyrand, Fouché, and even Murat, combined to convince him that his return to Paris was essential. Therefore, even though he was reluctant to acknowledge that, in a sense, Moore had gotten the better of him, the Emperor turned responsibility for the further pursuit of Moore over to Soult, and on 3 January 1809 he left Astorga for Valladolid, escorted by elements of the Guard. Arriving on the afternoon of the 6th, he entered that city on horseback, escorted by Guard Dragoons and Chasseurs, galloping by platoons.

On 11 January the Emperor wrote to Bessières, "The *Chasseurs à cheval* and the *Chevau-légers Polonais* of our Guard will leave Valladolid tomorrow, 12 January, for Vitoria, where they will remain until further orders." He himself left Valladolid that day, proceeding via Burgos, Miranda, and Vitoria to Bayonne, where he arrived on the 19th. In accordance with the Emperor's instructions, Daumesnil had also left Valladolid on the 11th, at the head of 100 Chasseurs and an equal number of Polish Light Horse under the command of *chef d'escadron* Lubienski, with orders to proceed to Bayonne by forced marches. In fact, Daumesnil took his squadron to Mont de Marsan, some 55 miles northeast of Bayonne, perhaps because Bayonne was already overflowing with troops. On the 18th, Lubienski and his squadron joined them there.

At that moment Napoleon's intention was to leave a substantial portion of the Guard in Spain, although he had ordered that all of the Guard's depots be removed from Madrid to Vitoria. On 15 January he had written to Bessières, "My Guard remains here under your orders." One indication that the Emperor was of two minds about that decision is the fact that he ordered Guyot to take the rest of the regiment of Chasseurs to Tolosa, just south of the French border, to await further orders. They would remain there until 27 February, when orders for the regiment to proceed to Paris arrived.

Scarcely pausing in Bayonne, Napoleon pressed on, traveling day and night, and arrived in Paris in the middle of the night of the 22nd. On 6 February he wrote to Berthier:

> *Mon Cousin,*
> Send orders by courier this evening to *chef d'escadron* Daumesnil and to *chef d'escadron* Lubienski to leave Bayonne with the 200 Chasseurs and Poles of my Guard who are there, to proceed to Paris.[19]

On the 11th the Emperor apparently reminded himself that he ought to notify Bessières, under whose command Daumesnil had been, of the action that he had taken, since on that date he sent the marshal a note saying that Daumesnil's squadron "which was at Mont de Marsan, has been ordered to go to Paris." A further order to Bessières on 15 February instructed the latter to send the *Chevau-légers Polonais* back to France, as well as the *Grenadiers à cheval*, the *Dragons*, and the *Chasseurs à cheval*, each of those regiments, however, leaving one squadron and a *chef d'escadron* in Tolosa, all three squadrons under the command of Major Chastel. This did not apply to Daumesnil's squadron, which was directed to proceed directly to Mont de Marsan. This illustrates the manner in which the squadrons of these regiments frequently operated as widely separated units.

Daumesnil proceeded to carry out his orders by forced marches. His

---

19 *Correspondance inédite de Napoléon Ier conservées aux Archives de la Guerre.*

route took him through Périgueux, where he was able to visit briefly with his parents, after an interval of fifteen years since the day when he had run off to join the army because of his fatal duel with the artilleryman. It was the last time that his mother would see her celebrated son, resplendent in his regimentals, since she was to die two months later.

Thus ended Daumesnil's second, and final, experience of warfare in Spain. In the intervening fifteen years he had progressed from being an unknown, inexperienced trooper in a half-starved cavalry regiment, lacking almost everything but the barest necessities, to filling the role of one of the senior officers in the most prestigious regiment of the Imperial armies, and a favorite of his emperor's. On 17 November 1808 he received another mark of distinction, when he was named a knight of the Order of the Iron Crown. Perhaps Lefebvre-Desnoëttes had followed up on his promise, before being captured and carted off to England.

CHAPTER ELEVEN
THE TURNING POINT

1809

There had never been any doubt in Napoleon's mind that at some point the Austrians would seek revenge for the humiliating defeats that he had inflicted on their empire in 1796–1797, 1800, and 1805, not only for the sake of regaining the territories that had been lost to France as a result of those defeats, but also in order to restore Austria's status as a first-class world power, left more than somewhat tattered by Austria's previous collisions with the Emperor. It was only a question of when the Austrians would decide to try their luck again against the parvenu emperor. In a quite direct sense, Napoleon himself supplied the answer to that question by the self-inflicted wound that his ill-advised effort to incorporate Spain in his empire represented.

Napoleon's brutal theft of the Spanish throne from the hapless King Charles, the fierce, unremitting resistance of the Spanish populace to the French occupation, the deep involvement in Spain of the majority of the veterans of the French army, including the greater part of the Imperial Guard, and—most tellingly—the capitulation of General Dupont at Bailen, which dealt a serious blow to the myth of Napoleonic invincibility —all of these factors had combined in the minds of the war party in Vienna to convince them that the time to strike back at Napoleon was at hand.

During the three years since the disaster of Austerlitz, the Archduke Charles, Austria's most capable military thinker and leader, had devoted himself, to great good effect, to the reform and modernization of the Austrian army. By early 1809 the regular army had been built up to strength of some 340,000 men, including an artillery furnished with almost 800 cannon. As a support force, Charles had established a home guard, the *Landwehr*, suitable for garrison and replacement service, which would eventually total 230,000 men. Profiting by Napoleon's example, he had organized this new Austrian army along the lines of the *Grande Armée*, creating nine line corps and two reserve corps. All in all, it was a considerably more capable force than that of 1805.

These developments certainly did not catch Napoleon unawares, since storm signals had been flying as early as June of 1808, when the ordinance creating the *Landwehr* was issued. The French government had protested this action and asked what it signified with respect to Austrian intentions, only to be assured that they were peaceful. By mid-January of 1809, however, increasing evidence of Austrian military preparations had persuaded the Emperor, as noted above, that his presence in Paris was vital. Once there, he set about redeploying his own scattered forces. At the turn of the year, three-fifths of the most capable regiments and officers of the French army were in corps and detachments spread across a Spain which was momentarily subdued, but simmering menacingly. Now, however, he urgently needed the greater part of those troops to be brought back into France and sent on into Germany as soon as possible. Consequently, the complex orders directing this massive shift of manpower went out as fast as the Emperor's harried secretaries could transcribe them.

Napoleon's calculations as to the time available to him in which to complete this enormously complicated transfer of his forces proved to be overly optimistic, when on 10 April Metternich, the Austrian ambassador to France, demanded his passport. One day earlier the Archduke Charles had delivered to the French minister in Munich and to Marshal Lefebvre, commander of the Bavarian troops, brief notes informing them that his troops would be advancing into Bavaria. On the following day, at Braunau, Scharding, and Mulheim, the Austrian army began crossing the river Inn into Bavaria.

As elements of the Guard had arrived in Paris from Spain, they had been given very brief respite before being sent on their way to Strasbourg. On 7 March the Emperor instructed Minister of War Clarke to have 300 *Chasseurs à cheval,* 150 *Dragons,* 150 *Grenadiers à cheval, and* 150 *Gendarmes d'élite* ready to leave Paris on the 15th. Clarke relayed that order to General Walther. Accordingly, before he himself left Paris on 2 April, Walther had sent off to Strasbourg, under the command of General Roguet, several columns made up of Guard infantry, an artillery detachment, 300 men of the Polish *Chevau-légers*, Daumesnil's squadron, and a second group of Guard Chasseurs, who had been remounted at the Paris depot. Another of the Emperor's orders on 2 April dispatched to Strasbourg 150 of the *Chevau-légers Polonais*, together with several battalions of Guard infantry. Other Polish *Chevau-légers* detachments left their depot at Chantilly on 10 April, 7 May, and 13 June.[1]

A young friend of Daumesnil's and one of his first biographers, Emile

---

1   Rembowski, *Sources documentaires*, p. 45

Deschamps, states that the Emperor had given Daumesnil some important missions at that time, which, he writes, "were accomplished promptly and intelligently," although we are left in the dark as to what these missions may have involved.[2]

Some of what we know regarding the role played by Daumesnil and his squadron during the following weeks is derived from the *Souvenirs du Lieutenant Chevalier*. Jean-Michel Chevalier had joined the army in 1795 as an artilleryman, and had been transferred to the 9th *Chasseurs à cheval* five years later. By 1806 he was a *sous-officier* in that regiment, and in November of 1808 he was taken into the *Chasseurs à cheval* as a chasseur, the customary down-grading of any soldier entering the Guard from a Line regiment. He would eventually rise to the grade of *sous-lieutenant*.

Chevalier states that Daumesnil's men left Paris on 26 March, which is consistent with Lachouque's statement. Their intended assignment was to provide the Emperor's escort, once he had arrived in the field. Chevalier commented that many of the Chasseurs in the squadron were, like himself, newly admitted to the Guard. Nonetheless, the fact that they passed the high requirements for admission to the Guard testifies to their excellent military records and personal qualifications. Noting that the greater part of the Guard cavalry had not yet returned from Spain, Chevalier says that the constant escort service was painful for his comrades, since there were no other squadrons to relieve his squadron periodically. As "newly admitted" Guard Chasseurs, some of them obviously had not yet become accustomed to the rigors of that service.

Since Lachouque[3] says a total of 450 "Polish *Chevau-légers*"—presumably members of the Guard regiment—had left Paris for Strasbourg by 7 April, Chevalier's comment that the escort service was painful, because other units of the Guard cavalry had not yet arrived from Spain, is puzzling. The explanation may lie in the fact that Napoleon always wanted to have Daumesnil in command of his escort squadron when he was in a combat area, which he was continuously during the second half of April, although Daumesnil's presence certainly did nothing to prevent the Emperor's slight wounding at Ratisbon.

Between the time of Napoleon's departure from Paris on 13 April and his arrival at Donauwörth on the 17th, General Berthier, who had been entrusted by the Emperor with the command of all French forces in Germany, had been doing his best to keep the Archduke's four army corps, positioned both north and south of the Danube, from attacking and defeating separately the widely dispersed corps of Masséna, Oudinot, and Davout, as well as Lefebvre's three Bavarian divisions. However, confusion caused by apparently contradictory orders, or orders from Napoleon arriving late because fog delayed the transmission of telegraphic orders to Berthier's headquarters, or orders simply being lost, was

---

2 Deschamps, *Biographie du Général Daumesnil*, p. 5.
3 Lachouque, *The Anatomy of Glory*, pp 149–50.

compounded by a lack of reliable information on Austrian movements and intentions. The result was some wasteful marching and counter-marching by Davout's troops, and the absence of a coordinated effort to cope with what seemed potentially to be a disastrous situation. The harried Berthier had finally appealed in blunt terms for Napoleon to hasten to the scene of action, and when the Emperor arrived at Donauwörth on the 17th, his chief of staff lost no time in briefing his master on the tactical situation, and reverting to the staff role at which he so excelled.

The measures which Napoleon immediately took to assert his control over the disarray existing in the French camp quickly brought order out of the previously disjointed tactical situation, arresting what had until then seemed to be a serious Austrian threat to the entire French strategic position in central Europe and Italy. On the 16th, Austrian forces at Landshut had pushed Lefebvre's Bavarians back across the Isar, and were in a position to threaten the French center in the Eckmühl-Ratisbon area.

Having paused in Donauwörth only long enough to size up the tactical situation and to commence issuing orders for the realignment of his forces, by the 19th Napoleon had passed through Ingolstadt, and would spend the night at Vohburg. By now Daumesnil and his squadron had taken over the role of the service squadron, which they would retain all the way to Vienna.[4]

The next few days would see an almost complete reversal of fortunes for both opponents, as Davout's corps, moving westward from Ratisbon, combined with Lefebvre's troops to break through the Austrian Fifth Corps at Abensburg on the 20th, while to the south Oudinot inflicted a defeat on Hiller's Sixth Corps. Having delivered an exhortation to the German contingent under Lefebvre's command before the battle at Abensberg, Napoleon was soon on the move again, and arrived at Landshut in time to take a hand in the attack on that city by the greater part of Masséna's forces on the 21st. To carry the city more quickly, Napoleon formed a column of grenadiers, with his aide de camp, General Mouton, in command, and sent them across a burning bridge into the city. The capture of the city yielded a large quantity of munitions, and 10,000 prisoners.

At six the following morning, the Emperor set off again, this time for Eckmühl, and by early afternoon that town had fallen to the on-rushing French divisions. A chaotic cavalry action some distance north of the city finally ended at ten that evening, with the Archduke Charles himself barely escaping capture.[5] Chevalier says that in the course of the battle a regiment of cuirassiers executed a brilliant charge, and the infantry broke

---

4 In *The Anatomy of Glory* (p. 151), Lachouque says that, for several days prior to and at Eckmühl on 22 April, the escort responsibility was assumed by the 1st *Chasseurs à cheval* of the Line, because the Guard Chasseurs had been worn down by their incessant duties.

5 It must have been in this action that Daumesnil received a lance wound. Chevalier says that on 21 April the Guard Chasseurs carried out several charges against the Austrian cavalry, which included the uhlan regiment No. 2 of Schwarzenberg. This is confirmed by

off from their combat long enough to applaud enthusiastically and shout, "*Vive les cuirassiers!*" That victory won for Davout the title *Prince d'Eckmühl*. That night the Emperor slept in the Alteglofsheim Castle, a dozen kilometers south of Ratisbon. No wonder Chevalier and his comrades were feeling a bit harried!

On the 20th, Kollowrat's Second Corps had captured Ratisbon, forcing the commander of its small garrison, Colonel Coutard, to capitulate before his men had been able to destroy its stone bridge across the Danube. Whatever hopes the Archduke Charles may have had for utilizing Ratisbon as a base for further operations were dashed, however, by the defeats suffered by his forces at Landshut and Eckmühl. By the morning of the 23rd, Austrian troops began crossing the bridge to the northern bank of the Danube, in apparent retreat toward Bohemia.

When this news reached Napoleon, it intensified his concern that Charles would be able to escape the entrapment and destruction of the Austrian forces that he had hoped to accomplish. It was therefore urgent that Ratisbon be retaken as quickly as possible so that the pursuit of Charles could go forward. The army's advance guard soon determined, however, that a rear guard of 6,000 men had been left in Ratisbon, and the first approaches of the French to the city's fortifications were met with lively musket and cannon fire, making it evident that an assault on the city would be necessary. There could be no question of by-passing Ratisbon, leaving it in the rear of the French as they marched toward Vienna, thereby permitting Archduke Charles to recross the Danube and cut across the French lines of communications. There was no alternative: Ratisbon had to be assaulted.

The attack upon and capture of Ratisbon by the French are especially noteworthy in the annals of the First Empire for two exceptional incidents: Napoleon's wounding, for the second and last time in his career (he had received a bayonet thrust in the thigh while leading an infantry assault at Toulon); and a theatrical, though no less genuine, dispute between Marshal Lannes and his aides de camp over the honor of leading an assault on the city's high walls Having decided that the importance of getting on with the pursuit of the Austrians would not permit any further delay, the Emperor had given the responsibility for its capture to Marshal Lannes. We are indebted to General Marbot for the following account of how this was accomplished.

Hippolyte Larrey, the son of the famous surgeon of the Imperial Guard. In his *Notice historique sur le général Daumesnil*, which he read on 26 May 1873 on the occasion of the inauguration of the statue of Daumesnil in Vincennes, he stated: "It was in 1809, in the German campaign, and more precisely, at the Battle of Eckmühl, that he (Daumesnil) was wounded by a lance." In the course of that address, the surgeon's son related this anecdote. "During his retirement, Daumesnil often suffered from very severe and long-lasting sciatica in his good leg, which prompted him to say to my father, 'My dear Larrey, the leg that you took off is better than the other, and gives me better service. I think of you, in leaning on it.'"

Although Ratisbon's ancient fortifications would not have stood up for long in the face of a serious siege, there was no time for the elaborate preparations for such an operation. Nonetheless, the city's high walls, before which a deep ditch prevented ready access to the base of the fortifications, presented a formidable obstacle to an infantry assault. At Napoleon's direction, French gunners had reduced to rubble a stone house imprudently built into one section of the wall, thereby partially filling the defensive ditch in that area, and it was at that point that the scaling of the walls was to be attempted. Lannes had assembled grenadiers from Morand's division in the shelter of a large stone storehouse adjoining a promenade, which encircled the city. Ladders collected from surrounding villages had been brought to the vicinity of that structure.

While Napoleon was preoccupied with issuing the orders for that operation, a spent bullet from the city's ramparts struck him in the right ankle, wounding it slightly. The Emperor is said to have remarked, "That could only have been a Tiroler!" The Guard's surgeon-in-chief, Dominique Larrey, was immediately summoned, and, upon examining the injured member, declared the wound to be a minor one. The news of Napoleon's wounding had spread in a flash throughout the army, however, prompting masses of soldiers to flock to the scene out of concern for the Emperor's safety. In order to reassure his troops, and at the same time permit the planned assault to go forward without further delay, Napoleon mounted and rode down the front of the whole line, being greeted by loud cheers as he did so.

When all was ready for launching the assault, Lannes called for 50 volunteers to lead the attack, which would require their placing ladders on which to descend into the ditch, and then a second set atop the rubble of the stone house to permit them to scale the dozen or so feet to the top of the wall. A large number of men stepped forward, and Lannes reduced them to the required number. Then, led by volunteer officers, the men picked up the ladders and ran toward the ditch. Almost immediately, they were met by a storm of lead, winnowing their ranks, so that only a few of them reached and descended into the ditch, where they suffered further losses. Those who had survived the fusillade staggered back to the shelter of the storehouse, almost all bleeding profusely.

After a momentary pause, Lannes and Morand again called for volunteers, and another 50 grenadiers stepped forward, and dashed toward the enemy's defenses with ladders. This time the fire from atop the walls was even hotter, with similar painful consequences.

Unwilling to order soldiers into such a perilous action—an order which they would certainly have obeyed—Lannes once more called for volunteers, but his summons was met with a grim silence. Despite his appeals to their honor, and the reminder that the Emperor was watching them, not a man moved. Finally, in anger and frustration, Lannes picked up a ladder lying at his feet, and shouldering it, called out to the silent

190

soldiers, "Well, I will let you see that I was a grenadier before I was a marshal, and still am one!"

He would have started toward the ditch alone if his aides had not attempted to stop him. There ensued a tug-of-war between the marshal and Marbot, who exclaimed to the angry Lannes, "*Monsieur le Maréchal*, you would not wish us to be disgraced, and that we should be, if you were to receive the slightest wound in carrying that ladder to the ramparts as long as one of your aides de camp was left alive."

Finally wresting the ladder away from the marshal, Marbot and one of his comrades each took an end of it, as others of the aides followed their example. The spectacle of the marshal disputing with his aides for the honor of leading the assault galvanized the troops, who rushed forward and attempted to seize the ladders. Before permitting the assault to go forward, however, Marbot organized the men in a loose formation, which would render them less vulnerable to the enemy's fire.

When the attack was launched, the tactics Marbot had devised proved to be eminently successful, and he was one of the first over the wall. This bold action led to the fall of the city later that day. Although the *mise en scène* and the players were, of course, different in this instance, there is a striking parallel between this successful action under Marbot's leadership, after two bloody failed attempts, and Montbrun's tactical reorganization of three squadrons of the Polish *Chevau-légers* before leading them in a hell-bent-for-leather charge up and over the pass at Somo-Sierra, after Spanish fusillades and cannon fire had killed or wounded half of the men of the first of the regiment's squadrons to gallop up that fateful pass.

With the re-capture of Ratisbon, its garrison of 6,000 men fell into French hands, and the 2,000 men of Colonel Coutard's 65th Regiment, who had surrendered after Davout had left them in the city as its garrison, were freed. In the six days since his arrival in Donauwörth, Napoleon had succeeded, by his masterful maneuvering of the French forces he had found widely dispersed upon arrival, in effecting an almost complete reversal of the strategic situation. He had done so despite the fact that many of the regiments were largely made up of raw conscripts, and that very few units of the Guard had yet arrived from Spain. The major defeat inflicted on the Archduke Charles's troops at Eckmühl had prompted Charles to send the Emperor Francis a message saying, "If we have another engagement such as this, I shall have no army left. I am awaiting negotiations." Yet, despite the defeats that Austrian forces had suffered, which had cost them some 30,000 casualties, there was still a good deal of fight left in the Austrian army, and its final defeat would only come two months later, after the bitterly fierce and bloody battles of Aspern-Essling and Wagram.

There now ensued a race to Vienna between Napoleon and Charles, the former advancing along the Danube's south bank, while Charles withdrew on its north bank. Davout had taken his Third Corps across to the north bank to conduct the pursuit of Charles's force, while Lefebvre's Seventh Corps was given the responsibility for leading operations on the right flank of the advancing army and for reestablishing direct contact with Eugène's army, coming up from Italy. After several days, Napoleon concluded that attempting to pursue Charles into the mountains of Bohemia would not be a fruitful enterprise, so on 29 April he brought Davout's corps back to the south bank of the Danube in order to concentrate his forces for the drive on Vienna.

During this time, General Hiller was skillfully conducting a fighting retreat, which precipitated a series of battles, first at Wels on 2 May, and then a bloodier engagement at Ebelsberg the following day, where Masséna launched a large-scale frontal attack on the town's fortifications, which cost his corps 3,000 casualties. Chevalier, in his *Souvenirs des guerres Napoléoniennes* (p. 97), paints a grim picture of the condition of that town in the wake of the struggle for its capture:

> Entering the town, the artillery marched in the center, while we, the cavalry of the Guard, marched slowly on each side, which was horrible and would have made the most intrepid shudder. There were to be seen parts of men and horses ground up under the wheels and the feet of the horses. We marched amidst the bloody debris of cadavers, fire and smoke. Burning houses collapsed on us, carrying down the bodies of unfortunate wounded, who had sought shelter in the houses, which became their tombs.

Hiller had retreated to Krems, and then crossed to the north bank of the river, still attempting to reach Vienna before the French. By 8 May the Emperor was at St. Pölten, with 300 Guard Chasseurs and 90 Polish Light Horse, the rest of the Guard cavalry having been sent to Neumarkt and Ips.

On 10 May, Lannes was ordered to march on Vienna, and later that day Napoleon was at Schönnbrunn. When it appeared that Vienna's garrison of 12,000 men, commanded by the young Archduke Maximilian, was going to offer resistance to the occupation of the city, Napoleon ordered that it be bombarded. In the space of a few hours, some 1,800 shells poured down on the hapless city. When it became evident that any resistance was out of the question, on 12 May Maximilian withdrew his men to the suburb of Florisdorf on the north bank of the Danube, destroying the four bridges connecting it with the city as he did so, and on the same day the French entered Vienna for the second time.

By 16 May Charles had brought his troops together with Hiller's north of, and within striking distance of Vienna. Although Napoleon now occupied the capital of the Hapsburgs, that was small satisfaction to him, when a powerful and undefeated Austrian army was still in the field across a now bridgeless river in full flood, and while Archduke John's three corps in the Styrian Alps and Carinthia posed a threat from the south to French forces strung out between Ratisbon and Vienna. Napoleon's initial judgment that bridging the Danube in order to bring Charles to battle on its north bank would not be an excessively difficult challenge proved to be a serious miscalculation.

The story of the bridging of the Danube by French engineers, and the subsequent severing and re-building of the bridges, needs no re-telling here, extraordinary story though it is. Let us rather fix on the roles played by the Guard cavalry—and in particular, the Chasseurs—in the twin battles of Aspern and Essling, on 21 and 22 May.

The strength of the Guard cavalry present on 18 May in Schönn-brunn, Ebersdorf, and neighboring villages was as follows:

Chevau-légers Polonais – 26 officers, 484 *sous-officiers* and troopers
Chasseurs à cheval – 16 officers, 402 *sous-officiers* and troopers
Grenadiers à cheval – 8 officers, 228 *sous-officiers* and troopers
Dragons – 11 officers, 266 *sous-officiers* and troopers.[6]

For information regarding the Guard cavalry's role in the two-day battle of Aspern-Essling, we have eye-witness accounts of Lieutenant Chevalier, of the Chasseurs, and Captain Dezydery Chlapowski, an aide de camp on Napoleon's staff. During the night of 20/21 May, the first contingents of the French army had crossed from the Isle of Lobau to the north bank of the Danube, and were being deployed between Aspern on the left, and Essling on the right flank. Chlapowski says that the initial disposition of the Chasseurs and the two squadrons of the Polish Light Horse on the morning of 21 May placed them in reserve behind four battalions of the Guard *Chasseurs à pied* and two of the *Grenadiers à pied*, on the right wing. (The *Dragons*, *Grenadiers à cheval*, and *Gendarmes d'Elite* had remained on the river's south bank.) Chevalier (pp 104–5) gives this account of the participation of his squadron of the Chasseurs at Essling on the 21st:

The enemy's charge having forced our gunners to abandon their pieces, Marshal Bessières ordered us to charge the Austrian cavalry, and we threw ourselves like lions on them, slashing our way through the first two lines and reaching the third line. (I believe there were five lines of cavalry.) But, satisfied with having overwhelmed them, created disorder in their ranks, and blunted their attacks, we returned to the vicinity of the Emperor with fourteen cannon that we had taken. We had only lost a few men because of the rapidity of our attack.

Despite the vastly superior strength of the Austrian forces, the first day

---

6 Saski, *Campagne de 1809 en Allemagne et en Autriche.*

of the battle ended inconclusively, with the French clinging to their precarious holds in both Aspern and Essling. Fighting resumed on the 22nd, and again two squadrons of the Polish Light Horse and two of the Chasseurs stood in reserve behind four battalions of Foot Chasseurs and two of Grenadiers of the Old Guard. Throughout the morning and early afternoon, the two armies were locked in a furious struggle. At four in the afternoon, while he was resting briefly from his intense efforts to beat back the continuing Austrian onslaughts, Lannes was badly wounded by a ricocheting cannonball, which smashed his left leg and right knee.

After consultation with several other senior surgeons, the Guard's surgeon-in-chief, Dominique Larrey, decided to amputate the left leg and did so rapidly. Lannes was evacuated to Ebersdorf, where he lingered until he died on the 31st, during those days allegedly calling for or cursing the Emperor. It was toward the end when Napoleon, who had come to Lannes' side immediately after the surgery, visited him for the last time. The dying, well-loved young marshal had some somber words of counsel for the Emperor.

There are probably as many versions of Lannes' words on that occasion as there were witnesses to that touching scene, and the passage of years has doubtless given rise to further variations, but it seems clear that approaching death inspired an exceptional frankness on the part of the young marshal and dear friend of the Emperor. The following version seems most likely to be a reasonably accurate record of those fateful words:

> Your mistakes have cost you your best friend, but I don't think it makes any difference to you. You sacrifice those who've served you best, and when they die, I don't think you're even sorry. You've surrounded yourself with flunkies, who tell you what you want to hear, but they'll betray you in the end. I'm not like that, never have been, and I'm saying this because I care about you.[7]

That can hardly have been the kind of farewell that Napoleon would

---

7 Perhaps somewhere in the vast Napoleonic literature there is a record of Napoleon's inner reactions to Lannes' ominously prophetic words, which must have had some impact on him, even if only momentarily. It may be that the dying marshal's words inspired the many visits the Emperor subsequently paid to the Guard hospital that Larrey had established in Ebersdorf, during which he distributed *écus* from his privy purse, gave 60 francs to each man, and awarded crosses and pensions. Officers received from 150 to 1,500 francs, according to their rank. If he was affected by Lannes' starkly honest counsel, he was not above misrepresenting the dying man's words. In Johnston's *In the Words of Napoleon*, p. 220, this quote from a letter to Josephine appears:

> With his remnant of life he clung to me; he wanted only me, thought only of me. A sort of instinct! For surely he loved his young wife and his children more than he did me; yet he never spoke of them, which was because he expected no help from them. But I was his protector; for him I was some vague and superior power; I was his Providence, and he was imploring …

Yes, imploring Napoleon to face up to the reality of the course he had embarked on, but, tragically, that wise counsel went unheeded.

have wished to hear from that brilliant young warrior, upon whom he had heaped great honors. It is one of Europe's great tragedies that Napoleon was, at that point, beyond grasping the wisdom of those words, and being guided by them. It is worth noting that Marbot, who at that time was an aide to Lannes, denies that the marshal made such a statement. He writes: "Some evil-disposed persons have written that Marshal Lannes addressed the Emperor reproachfully, and implored him to make war no longer; but I was at that moment supporting the marshal's shoulders and heard everything he said, and I can assert that this was not the case." It may well be that Marbot's loyalty to the much-loved young idol of the army—and to Napoleon, for that matter—caused him to wish to efface the memory of that bitter farewell, in whatever words it may actually have been phrased.

By the end of the battle on the second day, it was clear to the Emperor that the periodic rupture of the bridges from the south bank of the river to the Isle of Lobau and thence to the north bank would make it impossible to maintain a bridgehead there, so he ordered a general withdrawal to Lobau, and retired himself to Ebersdorf, where he established his general headquarters. After the Guard cavalry had been withdrawn from the Isle of Lobau, the Chasseurs went into cantonment in Penzing, near Schönnbrunn. On the 23rd, Guyot arrived with those squadrons which had been left in Spain, exhausted from the forced march they had made. Consequently, for the first time in months, the regiment was collected in one place. Chevalier says the squadrons totaled 1,000 to 1,200 men, including the Mamelukes.

The hard-fought, two-day battle had cost both sides more than 20,000 casualties, and those French corps and divisions which had participated were badly in need of reorganization, rehabilitation, and reinforcement. The ensuing pause of more than a month in the campaign afforded Napoleon the essential time in which to carry out those necessary measures, plan for the resumption of hostilities, and dispose his forces in a manner to provide for all conceivable contingencies, once the guns started firing again.

On 5 June Guyot was promoted to *colonel en second* of the Chasseurs, as its *de facto* commander, and on the 13th both Daumesnil and Hercule Corbineau were promoted to the rank of major, which is to say, lieutenant-colonel. When campaigning, the regiment was divided into two operational units, called *régiments de marche,* each commanded by a major. Now Daumesnil was given command of the 1st regiment, and Corbineau, of the 2nd. The Chasseurs and the Polish Light Horse together formed the Light Brigade of the Guard cavalry, while the Dragoons, the Horse Grenadiers, and the Elite Gendarmes made up the Guard cavalry's Heavy Brigade. At the age of 32, in command of one of the two regiments making up the Corps of Chasseurs of the Guard, the most prestigious formation of the Napoleonic armies, and with a reputation as one of the most brilliant of its cavalry leaders, Daumesnil had reached the apogee of his career in the field.

General Ambert wrote of Daumesnil:

Riddled with wounds, admired by the entire army, a magnificent horseman, Daumesnil possessed the confidence and the affection of the Emperor, who said one day, gesturing to Daumesnil, "It's with such men that one wins battles." Napoleon had a strange feeling for Daumesnil, which was more than affection,and more than confidence in him. He thought that, at Daumesnil's side, death could not touch him. For that reason, he always wanted Daumesnil as his escort in perilous circumstances.[8]

After the sanguinary repulse he had suffered at the hands of the Archduke Charles in late May, Napoleon was determined to ensure that the next attempt to come to grips with the Austrians north of the Danube would not be frustrated by insufficient planning and preparations, or inadequate forces. During the five weeks of the effective ceasefire, the Isle of Lobau was turned into a massive fortress and operational base, with great quantities of stores and ammunition. Exploration of possible river crossing points farther downstream revealed a series of small islands in the river on the eastern edge of Lobau, which were christened in sequence *Isle Masséna, Isle Bessières, Isle Espagne, Isle Pouzel, Isle Lannes,* and *Isle Alexandre* (in honor of Berthier). These islands were captured and fortified without any interference by the Austrians.

During this time, Charles had remained relatively inactive, confining himself to regrouping his own forces and fortifying a line running, on the west, from the bank of the river through Aspern and Essling to slightly beyond Gross-Enzersdorf on the east. This defensive line would be—and was—by-passed by the crossings planned from the southeastern corner of Lobau. By 1 July, Napoleon had gathered a force of some 160,000 men in the vicinity of Vienna, with more en route.

Action was initiated on 30 June, when, as a feint, Legrand's division crossed unopposed from Lobau over the restored bridge into the Mühlau salient on the north bank, short of the Austrian defensive line between Aspern and Essling. During the next several days the continuous movement of French troops on to Lobau was intended to persuade Austrian observers that Napoleon was going to try once more to attack through the gap between Aspern and Essling. What happened, instead, was an extraordinary example of Napoleonic planning and execution at its best, which befuddled the Archduke Charles completely, and gave the Emperor an initial advantage over his opponent which he never lost, resulting finally in one of his greatest victories.

Further measures designed to sow confusion in the minds of the

---

8   Ambert, *Trois hommes de coeur*, pp 75–6.

Austrian commander and his staff were a diversionary attack on 2 July on the town of Stadlau, a mile or so west of Aspern on the north bank, while batteries arrayed along the north shore of Lobau heavily shelled the Austrian Aspern-Essling defense line. On the night of 3/4 July, the main attack force began to move onto the Isle of Lobau. By an extraordinary effort on the part of the French *pontonniers*, during the next 24 hours four more bridges were built parallel to the existing one leading to the Mühlau salient, and another ten were thrown from the eastern shore of Lobau across the series of small islands now bearing French generals' names. On the evening of the 4th, the massive force started moving across the eastern bridges, continuing throughout the night, and by nine on the morning of the fifth, Masséna's, Oudinot's, and Davout's corps were well across the river, and beginning to move into their assigned positions on an extended line of battle across the broad expanse of the Marchfeld. What little resistance had been offered by the small garrisons in Ufer Haus, Mühlleuten, Sachsengang, and Wittau was quickly overcome. The entire complex operation had been carried out flawlessly, and the Archduke Charles had been completely misled as to Napoleon's intentions.

Chevalier says that the four Guard cavalry regiments were ceaselessly on the move across the French front during the entire day, first from right to left, and then from left to right, engaging in twenty clashes with the enemy, commencing engagements that were never quite finished.

By six that evening, the French army was arrayed on a 5-mile front, extending from Leopoldau and Süssenbrünn on the left flank to Glitzendorf and Leopoldsdorf on the right, with the Russbach effectively marking the boundary between the opposing forces. Hoping to disrupt the Austrians before they had had an opportunity to consolidate their positions, Napoleon ordered an attack along the line at seven that evening. After some initial successes, the French were thrown back, and by 10:00 both exhausted armies settled down on their weapons for the night. Chevalier says that his squadron—which is to say, Daumesnil's men of the First Regiment—made camp as best they could near the Emperor's tents, without fires, food, or drink for men or horses, only to be awakened after a few hours by the recommencement of gunfire at dawn on the 6th.

Contrary to Napoleon's expectations and intentions, the day's battle had been initiated by the Austrians, when at 04:00 Prince Rosenburg launched his Fourth Corps against Davout's position on the French right flank, below Markgrafneusiedl. The Emperor at once headed for the sound of the guns, taking with him Nansouty's and Arrighi's cuirassiers and carabiniers, and shifting the Guard slightly eastward. By 06:00, with the support of Nansouty's horse artillery, Davout had blunted the Austrian attack and driven Rosenburg's troops back behind the Russbach. Ordering Davout to take Markgrafneusiedl, Napoleon rode back toward the center of the line, where Oudinot's corps was deployed. As he did so, a shell burst not far from him. "Sire, be careful," Marshal Oudinot observed, "they're firing on your staff." Unruffled, the Emperor replied, "In war, all accidents are possible." He then returned with the Guard to the vicinity of his tents, on the road from Raschdorf to Grosshofen, behind the center of the French line.[9]

At 09:00 word was brought to the Emperor that the French left flank had been endangered by the uncoordinated withdrawal of Bernadotte's Ninth Corps from Aderklaa, which Bellegarde was moving to occupy. Bernadotte's Saxon infantry, which had been the victims of "friendly fire" on the previous evening, when French infantry had mistaken their white uniforms for those of Austrian troops, had now broken and were in flight. From his position on the left wing of the army, Masséna hurried to the scene, arriving almost simultaneously with Napoleon, and between them they restored the situation. Bernadotte, who had been trying to rally his panicking Saxons, had the misfortune to encounter Napoleon while he seemed to be heading away from the action.

The previous evening some of Bernadotte's criticism of the manner in which Napoleon had handled that day's action had been reported to the latter, and this episode brought to the surface the Emperor's increasing dissatisfaction with Bernadotte's performance in general. He at once relieved the marshal from his command, and ordered him to leave his presence immediately, and the *Grande Armée* within 24 hours. Bernadotte's treasonable behaviour had finally caught up with him.

It was now clear that Charles' intent was to swing around the French left flank, cutting the army off from the bridges to the south bank, and then attempt an encirclement by bringing his own left flank forward to cut through Davout's corps. The advance guard of Klenau's Third Corps was already in Essling, and the continuing movement of the rest of its divisions was threatening the envelopment of the French left. It was clear that it was essential to take the pressure off Masséna's men, who were being hard pressed by masses of Austrian infantry between Aderklaa and Süssenbrünn, so that three of his divisions could be marched south to where Boudet's division, having lost its artillery, was struggling to hold the bridgehead in the Mühlau salient.

To deal with this emergency, the Emperor formed a battery of 112 guns under General Lauriston, drawing 72 pieces from the Guard artillery, to which he added 40 from Eugène's Army of Italy. When the cannonade from this enormous battery, extended along a mile of front, was directed against Klenau's corps, it was brought to a standstill, while Reynier's batteries on Lobau poured fire onto his columns from the south. Lauriston's cannoneers themselves were sustaining heavy counter-battery fire, and when some of the gun crews were reduced to several men, Napoleon called for volunteers from the Guard foot regiments to go to the aid of the gunners. Scores of men stepped forward, and ran to their

---

9   Clairval, *Daumesnil*, p. 98.

comrades' assistance.

The bombardment of the Austrian lines was intended to pave the way for an advance by Macdonald's corps of the Army of Italy toward Süssenbrünn. To support Macdonald's attack, the Emperor ordered Bessières to charge with the cavalry reserve and the light cavalry brigade of the Guard. The marshal had at his disposition Nansouty's division of cuirassiers and carabiniers, and the Chasseurs and the Polish Light horse. At this point of the battle, the Emperor and his staff occupied a hillock some 2,000 yards southeast of Aderklaa, well within range of Austrian guns. As Bessières was engaged in deploying the regiments of Nansouty's division, not far from the Emperor's position, a cannonball struck his horse dead, at the same time grazing Bessières' thigh and hurling him to the ground. As the word of his mishap spread through the army, there was great distress over the presumed loss of this greatly admired officer, who was, however, merely stunned. Nonetheless, his temporary removal from the battlefield was to have unfortunate consequences. However much Bessières' accident may have distressed the Emperor, he did not permit it to distract him from his concentration on the critical situation, merely ordering Nansouty to lead the cavalry charge in Bessières' stead.

As was usual in such circumstances, Daumesnil was at the head of the service squadron, some paces to the left and to the rear of the Emperor and his staff, in a position to respond instantly to whatever instructions Napoleon might give him. Scarcely a few minutes after Bessières was thrown from his horse, a ball stuck Daumesnil in the left leg, badly wounding his left foot and ankle. He was immediately carried to the nearby forward Guard dressing station, where the Guard surgeon-in-chief, Larrey, and his assistants were dealing with the steady flood of wounded being brought to their open air surgery. Although a common assumption has been that Daumesnil's wounding occurred while he was leading his regiment in the charge which took place on that occasion, we have the above account of the circumstances from Lieutenant-Colonel Baudus, who was an aide de camp of Bessières, and an eye-witness of that incident.

By an extraordinary coincidence, almost simultaneously Daumesnil's friend and comrade-in-arms, Hercule Corbineau, who in all likelihood was nearby at the head of the 2nd *Chasseur* regiment, was struck by a bullet in his right knee, and he, too, had to be borne from the battlefield. Meanwhile, Macdonald was deploying his men in a large, oblong formation and starting them forward, expecting Nansouty to be supporting his attack. In his *Souvenirs*, Macdonald provides the following account of what happened at that point:

My square was formed in part by a portion of the division of Nansouty, who had been put under my orders that morning. I ordered Nansouty to charge, at the same time asking the commandant of the cavalry that I saw behind me to do the same. Unfortunately, the latter was not under my orders, and the Emperor was not there to give the order.

I was in desperation over Nansouty's slowness, but finally he got underway, but too late to take advantage of the hole that I had just made in the center of the Austrian army. Nansouty's cavalry was repulsed, but not followed up. The results would have been enormous if he had charged immediately, supported by the cavalry which was in my rear.

While I was awaiting reinforcements, a general in full dress approached me. It was General Walther, of the Guard. "Is it you," I said to him, "who commands that splendid and numerous cavalry that I see in the rear?" "Yes, it is," he replied. "Well, then, why didn't you charge the enemy in that decisive moment when they were in the disorder in which I have put them, and when I had several times invited you to do so? The Emperor should be, and will be, very dissatisfied with the immobility of the cavalry of the Guard." "In the Guard," he replied, "direct orders from the Emperor or our commander, Marshal Bessières, are necessary, and since the latter was wounded, there was only the Emperor, and he hasn't sent us any word." I understood later that the Emperor had treated him, as well as other generals of his Guard, very badly.

The reinforcement that I had asked for finally arrived. It consisted of the Bavarian Division of General Wrede and the brigade of light cavalry of the Guard, commanded by General Guyot. The enemy had continued his withdrawal, and I began to follow him. Toward the evening, I reached Süssenbrünn. I drew my force together, and warned General Guyot to be ready to charge. He replied that the Guard was quite ready, a reply which he justified an instant later.

Chevalier at that time a *maréchal-des-logis en chef* of the Chasseurs, provides this account in his *Souvenirs* (pp 118, 119) of the regiment's action, once the order to charge had been given:

We set out at a gallop, heads down, as a frightful hail of artillery struck us. Our brave light artillery was almost destroyed—men, horses, caissons, all was overthrown. There were only us Chasseurs and the Poles. For a moment, we had to stop our charge, because the bullets, the shells, and the cannister were riddling us. My file leader was killed, and as I replaced him, the man who took my place was killed. My two neighbors on the right and left also went down. My captain, Muzy, had a beautiful dog, which was chasing the cannonballs rolling on the plain. Just when he was running after one, another killed him. The captain turned his head, and cried out, "Ah,

1 *Maison Daumesnil*, Daumesnil's birthplace, Périgueux. Clairval collection.

2 *Les Uniformes du 1ᵉʳ Empire. Les Guides de Bonaparte, Cdt Bucquoy. Left: no.5, Trompette et Guide – 1797. Right: no.6, Capitaine Bessières, Commandant les Guides, 1797 – Grande tenue.* See Notes on Illustrations, p. 397, no. 5.

3 Top: *Siège de St Jean d'Acre, (Bonaparte et Daumesnil)*, by Steuber. Below: The caption reads *Le Boulet qui me tuera n'est pas encoure fondu* (The bullet that will kill me has not yet been cast). By V. Adam, 1833. Clairval collection.

Le Gal Daumesnil, Gouverneur de Vincennes.

A AUSTERLITZ.

Kretly effrayée le Colonel Daumesnil environné d'une douzaine de Russes, contre lequel il se défendait, il vole au secours tué de soldats qui voulaient l'arrêter.

1833-65.

4 *Le Gal Daumesnil, Gouverneur de Vincennes. A Austerlitz.* Kretly, seeing Colonel Daumesnil surrounded by a dozen Russians, against whom he is defending himself, flies to him and frees him, after having killed the soldiers who wanted to stop him. Lithograph by B. Victor (1833), Bibliothèque Nationale de France, Prints.

204

Le G.ªl Daumesnil, Gouverneur de Vincennes.

A LA BATAILLE D'EYLAU.

5 *Le G.ªl Daumesnil, Gouverneur de Vincennes. A La Bataille d'Eylau.* Breaking out of the Russian battalion square Daumesnil and Krettly, with the rest of their squadron, capture eighteen cannon after having cut down all the gunners. By B. Victor (1833), Bibliothèque Nationale de France, Prints.

6 *Lepic at Eylau.* 'Look at those faces and see if they look as though they want to surrender!' By V. Huen (1908). Author's collection.

7 Top: Miniature of Daumesnil, as a *maréchal des logis des Chasseurs à cheval de la Garde des Consuls*. Clairval collection. Below: Daumesnil's coat of arms (see page 227 below).

Du 2 Février 1812

Mariage,

Mr. le Baron Daumesnil
Et Mademoiselle Garat

8 Top left: *Léonie Garat (Baronne Daumesnil)*, at the time of her marriage. Mme. Mésséan collection. Below left: *Baronne Daumesnil, née Léonie Garat*. Aquarelle. Clairval collection. Right: The title page of the Daumesnil–Garat marriage contract and its fourteenth page, on which appear the signatures of Napoleon, Marie Louise, Alexandre (Berthier), Le Prince de Benavente (Talleyrand), and Le Maréchal duc d'Istrie (Bessières) and Cambacérès. Clairval collection.

9 *Vue générale de Vincennes, prise côté du bois.* (General View of Vincennes, seen from the forest side.) Thekund, Bibliothèque Nationale de France, Prints. See *Notes on Illustrations*, p. 397, no. 6.

10 *Vue intérieure du Château de Vincennes.* (Interior View of the Château of Vincennes.) Hugot, Bibliothèque Nationale de France. See *Notes on Illustrations*, p. 397, no. 7.

11 *Donjon du Château de Vincennes* (Keep of the Château of Vincennes), by J. Nash. Robert Jennings & William Chaplin, Cheapside, London, 1830. Bibliothèque Nationale de France, Prints.

12 *G! Daumesnil. Lorsque l'on me rendra la jambe que j'ai perdu à Wagram, je rendrai ce fort* (When I'm given back the leg that I lost at Wagram, I'll surrender this fort), by Bernard. Bibliothèque Nationale de France.

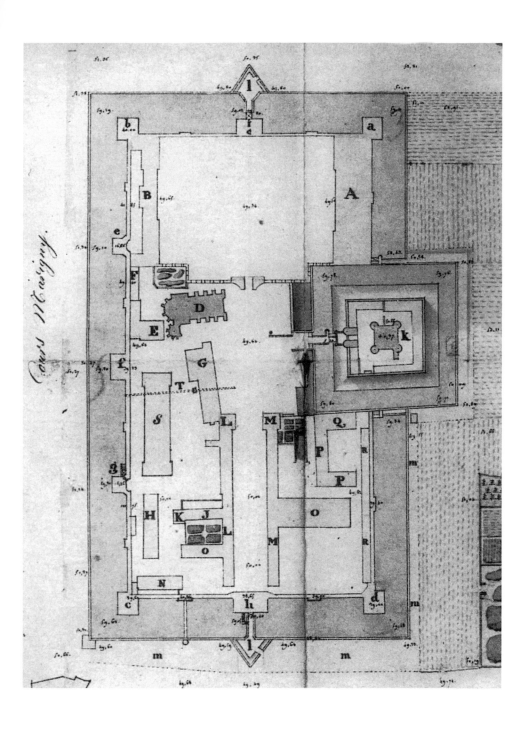

13 *Plan du Château de Vincennes Relatif aux projets de 1818.* (Plan of the Chateau of Vincennes in relation to the projects of 1818. See *Notes on Illustrations*, p. 397, no. 8, for a key to this plan.). S.H.A.T., Vincennes.

DÉTAILS SUR LE GÉNÉRAL DAUMESNIL,
(*La Jambe de Bois de Vincennes*), *mort du choléra.*

Brillant discours prononcé sur sa tombe. — Réponse qu'il fit aux Cosaques, en refusant de rendre le fort de Vincennes dont il était gouverneur. — Autres détails intéressans relatifs à ce brave Général. — Le Tombeau de Daumesnil; les Émigrés.

LE TOMBEAU DE DAUMESNIL.

LES ÉMIGRÉS.

FIN.

Sans peur, sans reproche, ô! moderne Bayard!
De l'or de l'étranger tu refusas ta part.
Fidélité, constance à ton noble drapeau;
Ta probité sans tache te suit jusqu'au tombeau.

Paris, chez Garson, Fabricant d'Images, rue de la Huchette, n. 25.

---

14 *DÉTAILS SUR LE GÉNÉRAL DAUMESNIL, (La Jambe de Bois de Vincennes), mort du choléra.* (Details about General Daumesnil, *La Jambe de Bois* of Vincennes, dead of cholera.) Paris, chez Garson, Fabricant d'Images. See *Notes on Illustrations*, p. 397, no. 9. Bibliothèque Nationale de France, Prints.

15 *L'Histoire de France en Images. Le Général Daumesnil 1777–1832*, (The History of France in Pictures.) Marcel Vagné, Imprimeur-Editeur, Pont-à-Mousson. Daumesnil loses his leg at Wagram; Daumesnil resists the Cossacks in 1814; Daumesnil resists the Prussians in 1815; Daumesnil resists the Parisians in 1830; the death of Daumesnil; the statue of Daumesnil at Vincennes. Clairval collection.

215

16 Left: Daumesnil family tomb, Vincennes municipal cemetery. Top right: Daumesnil's name inscribed on the north wall of the Arc de Triomphe. Below right: Statue of Daumesnil in front of the Vincennes town hall.

my poor do..." He couldn't finish: a bullet struck him in the chest, and another killed his horse. At the same moment, my horse and two others fell, struck by the same bullet. I struggled to pull myself out from under the bodies of men and horses, and was lucky enough to catch the horse of a man who had been killed. The officer who had replaced the captain gave an order to a *maréchal-des-logis chef*, and as he did so, a bullet sent his head flying, and it killed the *maréchal-des-logis chef*. In an hour we lost nearly three hundred horses, our two majors, Daumesnil and Corbineau, two *chefs d'escadron*, several captains, a great number of officers, 150 men wounded, and 25 killed.

To add to the horror of that battlefield, the ripe grain had caught fire, and the plain was ablaze, with the wounded lying in its midst suffering terribly. Disregarding the shot and shell, we dismounted and tried to cut the grain around the unfortunate wounded. The place was no longer tenable: our horses were dancing among the flames, which were singeing their feet.

He goes on to paint further battlefield horrors, amidst which the Chasseurs and the Poles pursue the withdrawing Austrians, reaching a small village through which they drive the enemy. Finally, in a *belle et brilliante charge*, the men of the Light Cavalry Brigade who are still in their saddles slice through a regiment of uhlans, disperse four battalion squares of infantry, and capture several cannon.[10]

A complementary account of that action may be found in the notes by General Delâitre, supplementing the manuscript of General Dautancourt, both of whom had been senior officers of the Polish Light Horse.[11] Here is that account:

The morning of the 6th, the regiment was together with all the cavalry of the Guard, which the Emperor held in reserve until 10:00, when the movements of the enemy decided him to effect a change of the front of the entire Guard—infantry, cavalry, and artillery—so as to bring it into line opposite the enemy corps, which was threatening to pierce our lines. In this movement, which was carried out under the enemy's fire, the regiment suffered considerable losses.

As a result of this manoeuvre, which halted the Austrian advance, the regiment was placed in a position to support several batteries of

---

10 See also Guyot's account of this action in the following text
11 S.H.A.T. MR 2331. As a lieutenant-colonel of the *Gendarmerie d'Elite*, Dautancourt had been assigned to the *Chevau-légers Polonais* when that regiment was formed in 1807. As the regiment's *major en second*, he served as the regiment's organizer and instructor. He won the affection of the entire regiment, and when in 1814 the regiment returned to Poland, its commander, General Krasinski, begged Dautancourt to accompany it. Dautancourt explained his unwillingness to do so very simply: "*Prince, je suis français.*"

the Guard, which was exchanging a terrible fire with the enemy. In that position, where it remained for a long time, and where its presence was necessary to contain a large corps of Austrian cavalry which was threatening our batteries, it lost a rather large number of men and horses killed or wounded by enemy fire.

After the retreat of the Austrians began, the regiment was ordered to follow the movements of Marshal Macdonald, responsible for hurrying them along. Towards four or five o'clock of the evening, the marshal, finally yielding to the urgings of Colonel Krasinsky to put his regiment into action, thought he saw a favorable moment in which to charge a strong Austrian division, which was withdrawing in good order towards a defile, protected by 20 cannon and two regiments of cavalry on its left flank. Such a charge presented little chance of success for five squadrons.

From the moment that I foresaw the outcome of this affair, and recognized that I would have no support, I had no doubt as to its consequences. I sent *adjutant major* Duvivier at top speed to Colonel Guyot, who was at some distance with the Chasseurs of the Guard, and was about to carry out the order that he had received to rejoin the Emperor's general headquarters. Guyot at once saw the danger of my position, and, as a good and loyal comrade, took it on himself to defer his own movement and to come to my support. He came to place himself behind my squadrons at a distance suitable for supporting me.

I had continued to advance, finding at each step new obstacles of terrain and being compelled to shorten the front of my line to a single squadron, when cannon fire began to reach us, and several shells which burst in our ranks killed or wounded a rather large number of horses at the very moment when I gave the order to charge. However, the disorder caused by the enemy's fire was such that I was only obeyed by some twenty men, and the rest, with several officers, turned around and abandoned us. I had at my sides *chef d'escadron* Lubiensky, *adjutant major* Duvivier, *lieutenant* Zaluski, and another officer, whose name I don't recall. It was then that I had to congratulate myself on the precaution that I had taken in asking for the support of Colonel Guyot and his regiment, for, from the moment the retreat of my squadrons was perceived by the enemy, they themselves prepared to charge us. Fortunately, the slowness of their manoeuvre and the arrival of the Chasseurs of the Guard gave us the time to rally and to face the enemy in good shape.

A kind of mêlée then ensued, in which we killed or took some sixty men, including the young Prince d'Auersperg, the son of the colonel of the regiment of that name. We lost 35 or 40 men: *chef d'escadron* Kossiatutsky, and three other officers received lance wounds. The second regiment that we encountered was made up of the uhlans of Prince Charles, composed almost entirely of Poles from Galicia, and the animosity of ours against them manifested itself violently because of that circumstance.

Such was the result of that ill-conceived charge, which might have resulted in the loss of the regiment. The marshal who had ordered it felt obliged to pay us a number of compliments, and Krasinski, who that evening wept about it like a child, three days afterward talked about it everywhere. He pretended to have received several lance wounds, and each day his recital of that glorious affair was embellished with more completely false details and the most ridiculous bragging.

In his own notes on that affair, referring to Dautancourt's manuscript (S.H.A.T. MR 2331) the then General Duvivier offers quite a different account regarding the manner in which that episode unfolded, which presents the role played by the Polish regiment in a considerably more favorable light than Delaître's version:

Between five and six in the evening, an aide of the Emperor [Captain Dezyderi Chlapowski] had directed the regiment to attack the enemy (directly in front of us). At their head were the uhlans of the Schwarzenberg regiment, some light dragoons, infantry in a square, and some artillery, which was already firing on us. I was at the head of the regiment beside Major Delaître. General Krasinski followed with two other squadrons, and, as we struck the Schwarzenberg uhlans obliquely, some shells landing in our ranks sowed some disorder. Major Delaître drew his saber, saying, "Let's get this charge under way, Duvivier!" At the moment of that command, Marshal Macdonald passed in front of us, and said to Major Delaître and me, "Gentlemen of the Guard, here's the moment to win some glory. Show yourselves worthy of the fine name that you bear!" I confess that I felt inspired with a sense of the duty that I had to fulfill. Then Major Delaître said to me, "Let's go, Duvivier!" and the charge set off bravely.

Although I remained at the side of Major Delaître, when we struck the infantry square, I became separated, and my horse was killed. Making my way back painfully on foot, I found General Guyot, who charged with the Chasseurs, and finished what we had happily started. Their artillery was captured, and many of their men killed. General Krasinski charged immediately after us, and before the arrival of the Chasseurs, with the two other squadrons. As for General Krasinski, I certify that he was in the second charge.

Still another version of the comportment of the Polish *Chevau-légers* on that occasion is provided by the testimony of the same Captain

Chlapowski, who was in a position, as an aide carrying the Emperor's orders to Krasinski, to observe the incident. What is most interesting about his account is that it seems to provide an explanation for the apparent about-face of the Polish troopers, just as the charge was launched. This is Chlapowski's account (*Memoirs*, pp 84–5):

I didn't participate in that charge, but I learned later that it had succeeded perfectly. During the charge there occurred an incident, which could have had an unfavorable result without the presence of mind of *chef d'escadron* Kozietulski. The two first squadrons were commanded by Major Delaître, the other two by Kozietulski. Delaître was short-sighted and wore glasses. Seeing the Austrian uhlans ready to attack us, and overestimating their strength, as they seemed to be deploying to fall on the Guard Chasseurs behind us, he commanded, "Face about on the right!" As the longest serving officer of the regiment, Kozietulski perceived the danger of this movement, which would have permitted the Austrians to fall on the rear of the Poles. He at once gave the same command, and, as he had a stentorian voice and held the confidence of the regiment, our troopers made a second about-face immediately, and again presented a front of one line to the enemy. As soon as they had done so, Kozietulski shouted "Attention! Point (sabers)! Trot!" The charge succeeded, and Delaître thanked Kozietulski cordially. They took 150 uhlans prisoner, including several officers, among them the Prince d'Auersperg, colonel of the regiment.

Or was it the son of the colonel who was captured, as Delaître says? As is obvious, memories as to exactly what happened on that occasion differ as to details, but what matters is that the combined charges of the two regiments of the Guard Light Cavalry Brigade bested some of the finest of the Austrian regiments. With Wrede's support, Macdonald, whose total force by that time was reduced to 1,500 infantry, finally succeeded in breaking through the Austrian line at Süssenbrünn, and entered that village, supported by the Guard Chasseurs. The Austrians withdrew, attempting to retain possession of Gerarsdorf, but a charge of the Chasseurs and the Poles forced them to evacuate the town. In a letter to Daumesnil from Wolkersdorf on 9 July, Guyot described for his wounded friend the remarkable action carried out by the Chasseurs that evening. (See below.)

Before we go back in time to the middle of that day, when Bessières' wounding forced his withdrawal from the battlefield, and when both Daumesnil and Corbineau were almost simultaneously struck down with far more serious injuries and also had to be carried off the field, some thoughts regarding this pivotal battle in the Napoleonic epic may be in order.

While it was a victory for Napoleon, its cost was a heavy one, and the outcome something less than the Emperor had hoped for. Although the Archduke Charles had been driven from the field, the exhaustion of the French the evening of the 6th made any pursuit of the enemy out of the question. The physical cost to the French was 34,000 casualties, some twenty-five per cent of the effective total, of whom 1,862 were officers. Among the latter were 40 generals, five of whom—including that remarkable cavalry leader, Lasalle—were killed. That bloody toll must have lent added weight in the minds of the army's officers to the stark words of the dying Lannes. Yet the majority of them would continue for another six years to risk their lives for fame and glory in the eyes of the Emperor. Lasalle's famous remark—that a hussar who was not dead by the age of 30 was a jackass—may well have represented the attitude of many of the fearless, young officers of the Napoleonic armies, although Lasalle beat his own odds: he was 33—one year older than Daumesnil— when an Austrian bullet in his forehead put an end to his brilliant career.

The imaginative planning and the meticulous execution of the initial phase of the battle were masterful. When full-scale combat began on the 6th, as the enemy's moves required him to adapt his own plans and intentions to changing circumstances, Napoleon reacted quickly and decisively, and to good effect. Constantly exposing himself to danger and almost continuously moving from one part of the battlefield to another, he encouraged and inspired his officers and men to surpass themselves in the face of a stubborn, skilled and resourceful enemy. He personally involved himself in the formation of Macdonald's attack formation and in the deployment of Lauriston's massive battery, as well as its reinforcement by volunteers from infantry of the Guard, when the ranks of the gunners were thinned by Austrian fire. It was a virtuoso performance on the Emperor's part, and, for the most part, the supporting players excelled themselves.

Now let us return to the scene of Daumesnil's wounding, some time between 11:00 and noon, in the vicinity of the hillock from which the Emperor was directing the battle's progress. When the seriousness of Daumesnil's wound was realized, he was immediately borne to the principal Guard field dressing station, where Larrey and his assistants were working at top speed in an effort to keep abreast of the steady flow of casualties being brought to them. (By that evening they had treated 500 wounded.) Scarcely had Daumesnil been laid among the other wounded when his dear friend and fellow major, Corbineau, was deposited nearby. While he had borne his own pain without complaint, the sight of his badly injured companion-in-arms brought tears to Daumesnil's eyes. By that time he had been informed of the death of his oldest friend in the regiment, Captain Muzy, a comrade who had campaigned with him in Egypt, in Italy, and had fought beside him in all the great battles since. A few months younger than Daumesnil, Muzy's rise in rank had not been as rapid, but their friendship had endured.

Writing in his *Mémoires* (p. 380) of the losses incurred during the Battle of Wagram, General Marbot says: "Among the twelve colonels wounded were three for whom the Emperor had the greatest affection—Daumesnil, Corbineau, and Sainte-Croix. The first two, who belonged to the *Chasseurs à cheval*, each lost a leg. The Emperor heaped rewards on them."

When Larrey saw that one of his patients was Daumesnil, he observed to the wounded man, "You're a terrible customer!" (He had in the past cared for almost all of Daumesnil's previous nineteen wounds.) The projectile had badly mutilated the left foot and the tibial-tarsal joint. Corbineau's wound was somewhat worse, since his right knee had been smashed altogether. It was clear to Larrey that immediate amputation was necessary in both cases. Daumesnil's leg would be taken off just below the knee, while the amputation of Corbineau's leg would have to be above the knee.[12]

While the prospect of the end of his galloping across battlefields at the head of his magnificent regiment, and of serving at the Emperor's side in peace and war, must have dealt a crushing blow to the young officer, Daumesnil was able to mask his mental anguish with a jest. "You're a pitiless man, to deprive me of all hope of getting my two dozen scars," he said to Larrey. "Go ahead, I'd rather live with three limbs than die with four." Without delay, Larrey, assisted by Surgeon-major of the Guard Lachôme, proceeded to remove Daumesnil's left leg just below the knee, and Corbineau's above the mangled right knee. Larrey's experience had persuaded him that, once amputation was clearly necessary, the sooner the operation was performed, the better the chance was for the patient's survival.

When Bessières had been thrown from his horse and lightly wounded, he had been transported to the Esterhazy palace in Vienna, and now he gave instructions that Daumesnil be brought there as well, so that he could be cared for under his own supervision. But when Daumesnil wouldn't consent to be separated from Corbineau, they were both placed in the same room in the Esterhazy palace, despite the conviction, Lieutenant-colonel Baudus wrote, that if one of them were to die, the other would also succumb.

A few days later, Daumesnil received the following letter from his regiment's commander, General Guyot:

Wolkersdorf, 9 July 1809
I was so dismayed by the blow which struck you, my dear Daumesnil, that I didn't have the courage to ask at once what danger it might have put you in, but I have since learned that you courageously stood up under the operation which it necessitated.

---

12 Larrey, *Mémoires de chirurgie*, vol. III, p. 379.

You have my every wish to encourage you, and for your recovery. Those are the feelings of all who know you. I know that in such circumstances one's dire imaginings can be harmful, but we all hope that you and your friend Corbineau will overcome these first painful sentiments.

For a long time the regiment endured other similar misfortunes, of which I'll give you the details, but at seven in the evening I went with the Poles to Gerarsdorf, where we had occasion to charge two regiments of dragoons and one of uhlans, who were making their way up the hill, which leads to the road from Brünn to Vienna, and four masses of infantry, which we estimated at 5,000 men, and three cannon, all marching together on the same point. We didn't hesitate at all to charge the cavalry, which we put to rout, killing some 60 men. The 1st regiment was recalled once, because that infantry formed a square and killed a dozen of our men and as many horses, but I sent them the 2nd regiment, which convinced them that we were the stronger.

Of the three cannon which had been used against us, one was taken from them. They only kept the other two for want of horses to draw them away. That was about the end of our day, my dear friend.

Yesterday I saw His Majesty, who asked about the state of your health and that of Corbineau. I am sending you Thomas[13], to whom I hope you will give some news of the health of the Marshal. Please tell him that the entire regiment shares in his misfortune.

I'm not writing to Corbineau, since he is in the room with you. Thomas will see him. I'll send you your effects and those of M. Corbineau. Yesterday I gave instructions for one of the two surgeon-majors to remain near you.

Guyot

P.S. The Austrian army was beaten completely and driven off at every point on the sixth, and on the same evening it retreated toward several locations in the direction of Brünn and Bohemia. Already we're finding thousands of deserters:it seems that they're in the greatest disorder.[14]

Guyot's letter serves to demonstrate the affection with which Daumesnil was regarded—and admired—by all who knew him. Despite his physical pain and the psychological stress that he must have been enduring, Daumesnil did his best to keep up his own spirits, as well as those of Corbineau. Scarcely 29 years old, the latter was in despair at the thought of his military career's coming to an end.

The flap of skin over the stump of Daumesnil's left leg was healing

---

13 Hippolyte Thomas, a lieutenant in the *Chasseurs*.
14 Clairval, *Daumesnil*, p. 107.

nicely, and one day, in between having it dressed, he put a nightcap over the stump, and drew the face of an infant on the bandages. Then he began to rock it, as a child would a doll in a cradle. At just that time, Marshal Berthier arrived to ask, in behalf of the Emperor, how the two of them were getting along. "Tell His Majesty," Daumesnil said, "that, as far as I'm concerned, mother and child are just fine."[15]

On the occasion of the Emperor's birthday, 15 August, great celebrations took place in Vienna. That evening, the illuminations drew the entire population out into the streets and parks. On the second floor of the Esterhazy palace, Daumesnil and Corbineau were alone, having given the servants who were attending them permission to go watch the fireworks. Corbineau seemed to be sleeping. Suddenly Daumesnil heard what sounded like water dripping on the floor. He called to his friend, but got no reply. He called a second time, but again elicited no response. Slipping out of his own bed, he dragged himself over to his friend's bed and saw that his comrade was unconscious, and barely breathing. The stitches of Corbineau's wound had parted, and he was losing a great deal of blood.

Daumesnil called for help, but no one heard him. Then he no longer hesitated. At the risk of causing the same accident to himself, he dragged himself across the floor, and managed to open the door. Raising himself on his wrists and sliding on his back, he made his way through two large rooms, and in that way succeeded in reaching the landing of the staircase. Then, hanging on to the banister, and step by step, he finally reached the ground floor. With a stentorian voice, he then repeated his call for assistance and, exhausted by the effort, he then fainted.

He had been heard, and people ran to get a surgeon, and soon both men were being revived and cared for. When they both had regained consciousness, Daumesnil asked Corbineau, "Did you know, I've been to see the fireworks?" When Larrey asked how he was getting along, Daumesnil wrote to him on the 30th:

> Everything's going well, my dear Larrey. My wound will soon be healed, and there will only remain as a souvenir of my accident one less leg of flesh and bone and one more of wood. I haven't gotten off too badly. Please accept my thanks in writing, since I don't know when I'll be able to give them to you in person.[16]

Ironically, given the probable casualty rate among officers of his regiment during the next six years, Daumesnil's wounding may well have saved his life. What is certain, however, is that it led to his earning for himself a place in the history of his country far greater than he might otherwise have done, whatever other honors he might have won on the battlefield.

---

15 Clairval, *Daumesnil*, p. 108.
16 *Ibid.*, p. 109.

One of Daumesnil's fellow countrymen, Jean-Baptiste Poumiès, a *vélite* in the Foot Chasseurs of the Guard, expressed to him his great distress upon learning of his friend's wounding. "Good heavens," Daumesnil cheerfully replied, "it's not as great a misfortune as one imagines. For more than ten years I had a wound in that leg that caused me horrible suffering. Now I'm cured, and don't feel a thing!"[17] When his orderly expressed his great regret over such a sad accident, Daumesnil began to laugh, saying, "What are you complaining about? From now on you'll have only one boot to polish."

It was said that the Emperor came to see Daumesnil, and said to him, "Well now, will you no longer be able to serve me?" "If I have a leg of wood, Sire," was said to be Daumesnil's reply, "I have an arm of iron." There is no record of such a meeting's having taken place, but it would only be a few years before Napoleon would devise a means of employing, if not that arm, then at least that will of iron in his service, not just once more, but twice.

---

17 He was probably referring to his first wound, incurred in the Roussillon in 1794, when a surgeon very nearly amputated the same leg, thus depriving history of the remarkable story of this exceptional individual. Clairval, *Daumesnil*, p. 109.

CHAPTER TWELVE
NEW HONORS, NEW DISTRACTIONS

1810

W hile Daumesnil was still recovering from his injury in Vienna, the Emperor conferred on him the title of baron, and two days later granted him an endowment of 8,000 francs annually to be derived from property in Hanover, which was the increase in pay conveyed by the awarding of the baronetcy. Letters patent of 9 March 1810 established his coat of arms. The vert in the dexter-chief quarter recalls the predominant color of the uniform of the *Chasseurs à cheval*, and the or (golden) hunter's horn is the traditional symbol of a chasseur. The gules sinister-chief quarter symbolizes blood shed, in reference to Daumesnil's twenty wounds. The upright argent sword is the symbol of a military baron, and the trophy in the azure base commemorates flags, muskets, and cannon captured by Daumesnil from the enemy. Below the shield depend his *Légion d'honneur* and the Order of the *Couronne de fer*.

In the sixteen years since he had run through that insulting artilleryman in a Périgueux side street and run off from the family hearth to be a soldier, Daumesnil had seen and done enough to fill a long lifetime, yet there were greater, more momentous events still to come in the life of this illustrious thirty-three year old. Starting his extraordinary career as a raw trooper in a skeletal, undernourished cavalry regiment mounted on half-starved horses, he had begun to learn the trade of soldiering under harsh conditions, and against a formidable foe, of whose fiery mettle he would have further proof one day in Madrid, fourteen years later. Driven by a relentless determination to win recognition and consequent advancement and fame, he constantly sought out opportunities to excel in the eyes of his superiors, and before long he had begun to be singled out for his fearlessness and headlong recklessness in combat. In that first campaign, he had the good fortune to be noticed by the then Captain Bessières, and in due course there developed between them a friendship, which would later help Daumesnil make the psychological transition from the character of a daring, relatively untutored and brash cavalry trooper to that of a young officer and rising star in the most prestigious regiment of the French army, frequently under the eyes of the commander-in-chief of the Army of Italy, and then his Emperor.

At Arcola, he had helped drag Bonaparte from the sucking swamp at the foot of the bridge, and then at both Saint-Jean d'Acre in Syria, and during the Battle of Aboukir, he had saved his commander-in-chief from enemy fire, prompting some to refer to him as "Bonaparte's guardian angel." Paradoxically, it was to Bonaparte that Daumesnil owed his own life, in a sense, since the former had reprieved him from the firing squad that had taken the lives of several of his companions. His subsequent feats of arms in Egypt and during Bonaparte's second Italian campaign earned him his first promotions and entry into the select body of the *Guides*/Chasseurs, in which he would thenceforth earn his battlefield laurels, accumulating nineteen wounds along the way as he did so.

Now, at the peak of his career, his prospects for winning further fame and glory seemed to have been dashed by an Austrian cannonball. Fortunately, Daumesnil's resilience of spirit determined him to make the best of his situation, rather than permitting him to brood over it. On 9 August, Napoleon had promoted Guyot to the rank of *général de brigade*, while leaving him in command of the Chasseurs. (Lefebvre-Desnöettes did not manage to escape from England until 1811, when he resumed command of the regiment, as Napoleon had promised he would.) The Emperor retained both Daumesnil and Corbineau on the regiment's rolls, however, while naming a third major, Jean Dieudonné Lion. The Emperor was unable to restrain himself from commenting—to the accompaniment of appreciative chuckles all around, no doubt—that he needed a lion for a major in that regiment.

On 14 October 1809, peace was signed at Schönbrunn. Two days later the regiment set out for Paris, arriving there late in the month under the command of its new major, Jean Lion. By that time, Daumesnil and Corbineau were fit enough to travel, and went with the regiment. Soon both were able to resume their peacetime duties in the regiment, and Daumesnil, at least, taught himself how to ride well enough with a wooden left leg. But no doubt the question of his future role, in the army or out of it, weighed heavily on his mind. On 4 December, Bessières wrote him from Goës, in the Netherlands:

I've received your letter, my dear Daumesnil, which has given me great pleasure. I hope that you'll be entirely rehabilitated. You will agree, my dear friend, that with a wooden leg, it will be difficult to perform a service as active as a that of a major of the *Chasseurs à cheval*. I therefore encourage you to take your retirement, unless the Emperor wishes to give you command of the depot of the *Chasseurs*.

But if you'll take my advice, you'll request retirement, and ask that you be as well provided for as possible. Then, ask for a position that you can fulfill, and ask directly to the Emperor, leaving the choice to him: he'll give you a better prize than you could get by yourself.

Then be sensible, and marry well. You should give it some thought, without any haste. I suggest you marry in your own part of the country.

Adieu, mille amitiés,
Le Maréchal duc d'Istrie.[1]

It seems highly probable that the gallant, widely known[2], and respected young major of the Chasseurs had, as Trumpet-major Krettly expressed it, "made more peaceful conquests than those of the battlefield," but perhaps, up until now, he had simply had the good sense not to form any lasting attachments, as long as he knew his life was at risk every time the regiment took to the field. Now, however, Bessières' counsel seems to have struck home. At the same time, it was no doubt difficult for Daumesnil to contemplate giving up the profession, which had been his entire life for those sixteen years, in exchange for some less fulfilling occupation. For his part, however, Corbineau had already crossed that bridge. Early in 1810, he went one morning to the Tuileries and asked the Emperor to appoint him to the tax collector's office of Rouen, which had been vacant for some time. One of the most remunerative of such offices in France, its chief would have to provide a very large surety bond. "So who is going to furnish the bond?" Napoleon asked. "My leg, Sire," was Corbineau's prompt response. "And myself, as well!" answered the Emperor, laughing. On 14 March an Imperial decree made Corbineau the tax collector for the Department of Lower Seine. Five days earlier, he had received letters of patent granting him a baronetcy.[3]

The following month, Corbineau married. His courtship of the lady in question, Rose de Kermarec de Traurout, very nearly broke up the friendship of the two young men, however, since Daumesnil had also been smitten by her charms. The object of their affections was 21, the daughter of a former counselor of the parliament of Brittany, and quite a lovely young lady. Both young gallants assiduously courted her, and their rivalry reached the point at which there was talk about meeting "on the ground." Then Corbineau exclaimed, "No, I can't duel with some one who saved

---

1 Clairval collection.
2 Marbot, *Memoirs*, p. 246, refers to him as "the renowned Daumesnil."
3 Clairval, *Daumesnil*, p. 115. At the time of the First Restoration, the Bourbon government transferred Corbineau to the less important tax office of Châlons-sur-Marne. That demotion didn't sit well with Corbineau, so when Napoleon returned from Elba, the former Chasseur didn't hesitate, and turned over all the money in his cash box to General Rigau, commandant of the Department of the Marne, to permit himself to join the Emperor in support of his plans. Arrested for that action during the Second Restoration, Corbineau was acquitted.

my life at the peril of his own. She will have to choose between us."

Rose de Kermarec was in love with Corbineau, and that settled the question. Daumesnil was too warm-hearted to harbor any bitterness against his comrade-in-arms, and they never ceased to be friends.

Now, for the first time in his life, Daumesnil was in a position financially to live in the style customary for a senior officer of the Guard, to whom honors and generous allowances had been granted, and he was determined to make the most of his situation. For all of his remarkable qualities, money management was not one of them. But, in all fairness, leading cavalry charges through shot and shell across battlefields strewn with the bodies of your fellows is hardly calculated to instill in one an instinct for long-range financial planning. But this insouciance in such matters would eventually create some disagreeable problems for him, and his family-to-be.

In any case, Daumesnil now set out to fashion a suitable life style for himself. He took a handsome apartment at number 76, rue Saint-Lazare, near the Tivoli Gardens, and sought out the services of a popular portrait painter, Henri-François Riesener, for whom he sat in the full-dress uniform of a colonel-major of the *Chasseurs à cheval de la Garde*. If that was an extravagance, we can be glad that he did not stint himself in that instance, since it has provided us with the best idea of his appearance at the peak of his career as a cavalry leader. Pinned to his *pelisse*, trimmed with the white fur of the throat of Canadian fox, can be seen his two decorations, Officer of the *Légion d'honneur* and Chevalier of the *Couronne de fer*.

In December of 1811, Daumesnil acquired, at a cost of 5,500 francs, an elaborately furnished and equipped coach, with his coat of arms painted on the doors, as was no doubt the fashion for the new nobility, which at least had won its honors, rather than simply inheriting them. As a colonel of the Guard, he was invited everywhere. His cheerful liveliness and what we call today charisma made him a popular invitee at the frequent receptions and famous salons. Despite his handicap, he was still an excellent dancer. Indeed, it may well have been the fact that he did not permit his injury to inhibit him or dampen his spirits that particularly appealed to the ladies and made him something of a celebrity in the gilded Napoleonic society.

Except for one squadron, which was sent off to join the army in Spain, the Chasseurs remained in Paris throughout 1810 and 1811. Late in 1811, as the Emperor began preparations for his Russian campaign, he chose another new major for the regiment, a friend of Daumesnil's, *général de brigade* Rémy-Joseph-Isidore Exelmans, of whom we shall hear more later. That Napoleon would appoint an officer of that rank and experience as a major in the regiment is a clear indication of the high regard that he had for it. For the present, Daumesnil retained his position as a *major à la suite*, which is to say, attached to the regiment without a specific position.

A report of 16 December 1811 to the Emperor from his aide de camp, General Mouton, included Daumesnil as one of the three majors of the Chasseurs "for subsistence."

That the Emperor had not forgotten his "guardian angel" is attested to by the fact that, on 18 August 1811, he granted Daumesnil shares in the *Petites Affiches* (the government's income from payments for notices) worth 16,000 francs annually, and a new allowance of 4,000 francs annual income on property in Ilyria. All the while, Daumesnil was turning over in his mind Bessières' advice: "think about marrying well."

CHAPTER THIRTEEN
THE BEST OF TIMES

1812

It would not be long before Daumesnil would put behind him his disappointment over his failed suit of Rose de Kermarec, since his continuing attendance at social affairs of one sort or another constantly brought him in contact with new members of the circle of eligible young ladies of that brilliant society. In January of 1812 he met a young girl of sixteen and a half, Léonie Garat, who was the daughter of Baron Martin Garat, Director General of the *Banque de France*. Anne-Fortunée-Léonie Garat had been born in Chesnay, near Versailles, on 29 June 1795. She had deeply impressed Daumesnil with her intelligence, her unaffected manner, and her general air of distinction. Her mother, Catherine-Charlotte Gebaüer baronne Garat, was the sister of three composers, one of whom, Michel-Joseph Gebaüer, had composed a good many military marches.[1]

At the age of 22 Martin Garat had started his career as a banker in the most important business establishment in Bayonne. Moving to Paris, he entered the Royal Treasury, in which he advanced rapidly to a senior position. After running afoul of the Revolutionary government, he retired. During the Terror, he was imprisoned for almost a year in the notorious prison, *La Force*. However, his services at the Treasury were so essential that every morning a carriage came to the prison to take him there, and returned him to *La Force* that evening. The fall of Robespierre proved to be his salvation. Under the Consulate, Garat was made Director General of the Fund of Current Accounts, and when the Bank of France was created in 1800, he was made its Director General. The Emperor had made him a baron.

Daumesnil had fallen madly in love with Léonie, and he learned from

---

1 His *March of the Grenadiers, or ... of the Old Guard*, was played for the last time under the Empire at Waterloo. He had died during the retreat from Russia.

a young lady friend of his that his sentiments were reciprocated. However, his consciousness of his semi-invalid condition made him hesitate to confess his true feelings to Léonie. She, however, had anticipated the possibility of a proposal from her dashing, bemedaled suitor, and said to her mother, "Heaven forbid that I should refuse him. He would believe that I was refusing him because of his misfortune, and it's just that which attracts me to him."

Perhaps having had a hint that a proposal would receive a positive response, Daumesnil did finally make a formal declaration of his feelings and intentions, which was accepted with equal formality, and he was welcomed as a visitor to the family's spacious apartments in the residence of the Banque de France, on the rue Vrillière.

The salons of the Garats were frequented by the most prominent personages of the day. Among them was a niece of the arch-chancellor, Cambacérès, Mme. Lavollée, whose husband, a wealthy financier, was Léonie's godfather. Mme. Lavollée often helped her uncle "do the honors" at the brilliant affairs that he gave for the Emperor. In her *Mémoires,* Léonie describes an eventful evening, when their father took her older sister, Saubade, and her to one of those receptions. She was then just thirteen. It was a costume ball, and Saubade was dressed as a sultan's favorite, while Léonie was in the costume of a Swiss peasant. As a way of escaping from the formality of official affairs, Napoleon often enjoyed attending such masked balls wearing a black domino, or hood, and presumably civilian clothing.

This is Léonie's account of that remarkable evening:

I had no sooner entered the immense salons of the Chancellery than I felt something like an electric shock, like a blow to my heart. However, it didn't seem to be anything other than a black domino, only a man who had passed close by me. But that man had a glance so powerful and so fascinating that the slight brush with him so shook me that I said to myself in a low voice, "It's he, it's the master of the world!" And I became terribly frightened when he came and sat down next to me. I had never seen the Emperor, and had no idea of the sound of his voice. How gently it now reached my ears, that voice!

"It seems that you have taken off your mask out of flirtatiousness," he said to me.

In a trembling voice I replied, "Why should I be flirtatious? My sister is older than me, and I'm not even 14."

"Don't you think about making yourself attractive and marrying?"

"I just think about dancing."

"Because of those pretty feet, I suspect."

Then that voice added, in an almost imperative tone, "Your name!"

"Léonie," I replied, after a long silence.

"Léonie," he responded with a gesture of surprise. "Léonie! Are you Italian, then?"

At that exclamation my fear intensified, because this was he who made peoples and kings tremble. I thought I was going to die. Finally I had to reply that I was not Italian, but that didn't satisfy him.

"Well, who are you, then," he asked, "if Léonie is not your family name?"

"I'm, I'm the daughter of M. Garat."

"Of Garat, the senator?"

"No, sire, my father is director of the Bank of France."

"Is he a relative of the senator?" he resumed in a more affable manner, still pursuing his thought.

"Yes, from the same part of the country, and a second cousin, I believe."

"Child," he continued, "you don't go to masked balls often?"

"Oh," I hastened to reply, as if to excuse myself for my stupidity, "it's the first time."

"I wouldn't doubt it. I wouldn't doubt it."

And getting up, he made a gesture of regret, which seemed to me to say: "What a shame, you pretty little girl, that you're so silly. What a shame!" His gesture said a great deal more, and, before leaving me completely, he retraced his steps several times.

Perhaps the Emperor abhorred all the intoxicating coquetries, all the pretences of the beautiful ladies of the court, who had gradually gathered around him, and who were beginning to fight over their conqueror. The Emperor turned toward me a last time, as if to take away with him a memory of that young girl of thirteen years, fresh and naïve, which could somehow refresh his own heart a bit.[2]

It would be another three years before Léonie and Daumesnil met. In the meanwhile, her sister, Saubade, had married the colonel commanding the 6th *Hussards*, Baron Louis Vallin, who would go on to have a distinguished career under the Empire, and then under the Bourbons. By now Daumesnil had met Léonie and fallen in love. In her diary, Léonie wrote this about her first impressions of her suitor:

He had his left leg carried off at Wagram, while charging at the head of his squadron.[3] He was covered with other wounds, but those were scarcely apparent, and moreover, the more the young major had

---

2   Léonie's recollections here and subsequently are from her *Journal de mes souvenirs* in the Clairval collection.

3   The "charging at the head of his squadron" was obviously a misunderstanding on Léonie's part.

been badly treated by the enemy, the more I felt myself disposed in his favor. It was, in fact, to that severed leg that we owed our being brought together, for, from the time that Daumesnil was presented to me, my heart was filled with a tender interest and sweet compassion for a soldier, so handsome and with such a martial air, being put out of action so soon.

She goes on to say,

> In fact, having just barely had my 17th birthday,[4] and being so happy to be with my loving parents, I had not yet developed an interest in marriage, although I had already had several proposals, and, among others, by a young and charming general ... but he hadn't happened to have been wounded at Wagram!
>
> For me, it was therefore a supreme happiness to imagine serving as the guide and support for this poor disabled person, to be for my husband the dog that follows the steps of his master, the child who leads Belisarius. One may laugh at my dream, but one should remember that the man, for whom I wanted to be everything, both dog and child, both lover and friend, was young and handsome, who had a great and strong soul, which showed itself in a regard reflecting strength. Remember, I say, that this man was Daumesnil, and you will not be surprised that I wanted to love him with all my heart, that my only ambition was to serve him, and that to become indispensable to him would be my greatest happiness.

As their lives turned out, marrying this remarkable young lady would turn out to be one of the most fortunate happenings in Daumesnil's life.

---

4   In fact, she was in her 17th year and would not be 17 until 29 June 1812.

CHAPTER FOURTEEN
"I NEED A MAN ON WHOM I CAN COUNT"

A mid his innumerable other concerns, the Emperor still managed to find time to consider how best to put to use the exceptional qualities of the young officer, for whom he had developed a soldierly affection. On 27 January 1812 he wrote the following note to Bessières, commander of the Imperial Guard: *Mon cousin,* Give me a report on the general staff of the Guard. I'll start with the *Chevau-légers Polonais...*"

Then he goes on as follows:

> General Guyot commands the *Chasseurs à cheval*; Colonel Lion is one of the majors; I've named Exelmans a major in that regiment. Daumesnil, being a major, cannot remain as a major. I need a report on that officer, whom I intend to employ militarily. Couldn't we give him command of Vincennes, with a higher grade and a good allowance? Vincennes' being a state prison and one of the quarters of my Guard, I need a sure man there.[1]

Napoleon was not devoting his attention to this matter entirely out of concern for Daumesnil's welfare and future, however. At that time his plans for the invasion of Russia had begun to take form in his head, and he wanted to ensure that the supply of weapons and munitions of every type would be on hand in sufficient quantities when that enterprise was launched. To that end, he had decided that Vincennes would become the primary arsenal for the French army.

On 30 January, Bessières replied. In the context of his report on all of the Guard regiments, he included this statement: "I propose that Your Majesty name Major Daumesnil governor of Vincennes, with the grade of

---

1   Archives Nationales, Bessières collection, 32 AP1.

général de brigade. He is a staunch officer, on whom Your Majesty can count." Coming from the Duc d'Istrie, that recommendation and judgment not only reflected the high esteem in which the marshal held his old comrade-in-arms, but in coming years would be shown to have been infallibly correct.

Having summoned Daumesnil, the Emperor said to him, "I need a man on whom I can count, and I thought of you. The materiel and munitions necessary for my army must be sent from Vincennes."[2] In the Palace of the Tuileries on 2 February 1812, Napoleon signed the decree nominating Daumesnil as a *général de brigade*. In his own hand, he appended to that text "*Commandant de Vincennes*."

It was a momentous day for Daumesnil, since it was in the residence of the Banque de France on that same day that the marriage contract between Baron Pierre Daumesnil and Léonie Garat was signed. The contract provided that the fiancée's dowry was to be 100,000 francs. In addition to the signatures of the Garat family on that contract, those of the other individuals represented a "Who's Who" of the military and governmental hierarchy of the day: Talleyrand, Cambacérès, Marshals Berthier, Bessières, and Lefebvre, Minister of Police Savary, Grand Marshal of the Palace Duroc, and Minister-secretary of State Daru. Many of Daumesnil's brothers-in-arms added their signatures, as well: Generals Guyot, Exelmans, Lion, Morand, and many others, among them some who would soon be setting out on a campaign from which they would not return.

An Imperial decree of 16 June 1808 required that marriages of officers of the Guard be approved by the Minister of War. On 3 February Bessières had written to the Minister requesting his approval for this marriage, and on 5 February the Minister replied that it was suitable "in all respects," and that it was therefore approved. On 10 February, the marriage contract was signed in the Tuileries by Napoleon, and in the Elysée on the same day by the Empress Marie-Louise. The former Empress Josephine signed it in her residence, the Château of Malmaison.

Meanwhile, Daumesnil was almost frenetically engaged in last-minute shopping for expensive presents of all sorts for Léonie, and in ordering for himself, among other things, seventeen wooden legs. (Two months later, he needed nine more! What can he have been doing to wear them out so fast?) The extravagance of his purchases—four dozen pairs of white gloves, for example—reflects not only his extraordinary excitement about the new phase of his life that was about to begin and his desire to shower gifts on his beloved, but also his free-spending tendencies, which would eventually create difficulties for his family. Among his purchases was a *corbeille de mariage*, a basket in which gifts for the bride and groom might be placed.

---

2   Clairval, *Daumesnil*, p. 130.

On 11 February the civil marriage ceremony took place in the office of the mayor of the 3rd arrondissement, followed by the religious ceremony in the church of Notre-Dame-des-Victoires, appropriately enough. Daumesnil's witnesses were General Guyot and the new colonel-major of the Chasseurs, Baron Jean Lion, while Léonie's were her brother-in-law, Colonel Vallin, and a M. Luce, a stockbroker. Napoleon placed in the *corbeille de mariage* a pair of *général de brigade's* epaulets for the bridegroom. The splendor of the young couple's wedding and reception must have made it one of the highlights of the Paris social season.

For a young lady who had yet to reach her 17th birthday, the suddenness with which this had all happened seemed almost overwhelming, and the rush of events left her with conflicting emotions, as the following passage from her *Journal* reveals:

> The day of my marriage was rather sad. I had only known my husband for a month, and it was as if I had scarcely spoken to him. Everything about him deeply impressed me—his splendid stature and countenance, his richness and glory, his manner of walking, the uniform, and the prestige that he enjoyed. Yet for him I was leaving everything that had made me, up until then, the happiest of young girls.

As luck would have it, before the newly-weds could take up their quarters in Vincennes, Léonie came down with the measles, but as soon as she had recovered, they went to the château, where they moved into the Pavillon de la Reine.

The origin of the Château of Vincennes goes back to the 13th century, when the then manor house became second only to the palace on the Ile de la Cité as the favorite residence of sovereigns and their families. By the end of the 14th century, continuing construction by successive kings had created the basic structure as it existed at the start of the 19th century, and still does today. A high, moated wall, 228 by 326 meters, is dominated by a keep (*donjon*) in the middle of its west side. The keep itself, a square, nine-story tall structure with round towers at each corner, is surrounded by a 50-meter-square moated wall. Nine towers were built into the curtain wall, three of which—on the north, east, and south sides of the rectangle—loomed over gates equipped with drawbridges.

The construction of the Palace of Versailles, far across Paris to the west, signaled the end of Vincennes as a royal residence, and from 1670 onwards, the king and his court deserted it for the new palace. In September of 1715, in accordance with a last wish of his father, Louis XV and his court returned to Vincennes, where they remained until the end of the year. Their departure marked its last use as a royal residence. The king permitted the use of the buildings within the outer walls for a variety of purposes, and it was there that the famous porcelain factory of Sèvres had its origin in 1740. Finally, in 1784 the king decreed that the keep was no longer to be used as a state prison, and that the château was to be removed from the list of royal residences. In 1787 an attempt to sell the domain found no buyers.

Since the 16th century, the keep had been used periodically as a State prison for small numbers of individuals, including the Marquis de Sade and Louis the XIV's finance minister, Nicolas Fouquet, who made the egregiously unwise error of entertaining the king too opulently at his magnificent château, Vaux-le-Vicomte. During the Revolution the keep was briefly returned to its role as a prison, but in February of 1791, in protest the Paris population began to tear it down. It was saved from destruction, however, by Lafayette, who happened to be passing by as its demolition was in progress. Then, in 1796 the Directory decided to transfer the Paris arsenal to Vincennes.

By the beginning of the 19th century, the château had fallen into a semi-ruin, but in 1808 Napoleon decided to convert it into a principal arsenal, at the same time restoring and modifying its structural defenses so that it could serve as an essential element in the chain of forts defending Paris. After inspecting the château on 16 March of that year, he issued a decree directing that, among other things, the towers flanking the curtain walls be provided with cannon, except for those in poor condition, which would be razed to the height of the curtain walls, and provided with platforms for artillery.[3]

One tower would become a magazine for munitions, and another a powder magazine. The tower over the postern on the east side of the fortress would be designated for the delivery of salutes and salvos, and furnished with a dozen cannon of heavy caliber selected from those taken in Vienna or Rome. A continuous fire-step would encircle the outer walls and those of the keep. The latter would be returned to the police as a prison, and the chapel would become a storehouse for the artillery and other arms. Since the fort belonged to the Guard, a colonel of the Guard would be its governor. Its garrison would consist of 600 mounted troops and 1,000 infantry and their officers. A bakery of three or four ovens would be established to care for the needs of the garrison. The Pavillion of the Queen would be restored so that it could serve as the governor's residence, while the facing Pavillion of the King would become a barracks.

In 1810, all of the bays and arcades which existed in the outer walls were blocked, and all the houses which had been built against the walls on their exteriors were destroyed, after compensation had been paid to their owners. It is important to note that at that time, the village of Vincennes was quite small, and clustered close by the north front of the château.

It might be said that all of these works, which were undertaken immediately, were of an administrative character, rather than representing an effort to render the fortress capable of withstanding a serious assault.

---

3   At that time, only two of the towers — the Queen's, in the southeast corner of the outer walls, and the Paris tower, in the northwest corner — were trimmed down in that way.

The director of fortifications, General Montfort, observed in October of that year: "The artillery in a fort of this value is intended to make an impression, rather than contributing seriously to its defense."[4] Certainly the Emperor, who had stinted on the reconstruction costs, was well aware of that, yet, in the event, this fortress would prove to be of great service to France.

In 1812 Napoleon expanded further on the concept for the design and employment of Vincennes, declaring that the château was to be the most important arsenal for the army. Consequently, he wanted all further work done there to be of a permanent nature, and designed to ensure that the fortress not only be handsome, but of such a character that it could guarantee the security of the depots established within it. He further required that the interior of the fortress be laid out in such a way that, in case of need, it could serve as a point of evacuation for a large amount of artillery from a frontier, which might be threatened.

In an order of 12 March 1812 to General Clarke, Minister of War, the Emperor directed that there should be a company of artillery of the Guard at Vincennes at all times, with a sufficient number of cannoneers. There was also to be a barracks for a thousand men and a *salle d'armes* for 10,000 muskets, magazines for 100,000 pounds of powder, as well as for a great number of munitions. Sheds for several thousand spare wagons and carriages were to be erected, as well as forges and workshops for woodworkers. There was to be a fine lodging for the governor, with quarters large enough so that, in certain circumstances, one could place there a personage such as a prince or foreigner of high rank to be held there safely, but whom one wouldn't wish to imprison.

This, then, was the "work-in-progress" entrusted to Daumesnil by the Emperor, who had correctly gauged that the former Chasseur major, now a newly minted *général de brigade*, was a man on whom he could count to fulfill his wishes exactly. His service record reflected his participation in 22 campaigns, eight enemy flags captured, four generals made prisoner, one of the first *sabres d'honneur* awarded in the French army, a second given to him by the King of Spain, and his 20 wounds. At a time when heroism was common currency, Daumesnil's bravery was proverbial. The loss of a leg had not affected his physical energy, or in any degree lessened the determination of his character.

Very demanding of himself, Daumesnil expected a great deal of his subordinates, and received as much, for the reason that he led by example. At the same time, he leavened his seeming inflexibility by an extreme kindness and courtesy, and an even temper—well, *most* of the time! His general sense of cheerfulness and good humor won people to him, even before they had come to appreciate the depth of his moral qualities.

By now Daumesnil was well off, by any standard. His allowance as

---

4 Fossa, *Le château historique de Vincennes*, p. 224.

governor of Vincennes was 24,000 francs. This was, of course, on top of the allowances and annuities that the Emperor had previously granted him: a pension of 3,000 francs on the purse of the Emperor, one of 600 francs on the Cisalpine Republic, endowments of 2,000 francs on the Monte Napoleone in Milan, 8,000 francs on property in Hanover (replaced in 1813 by an endowment of 8,000 francs on property in the Department of Rome), and 4,000 francs on property in Illyria, and stock worth 16,000 francs on the *petites affiches*.[5]

Periodically during his active service, Daumesnil frequently received cash bonuses for especially outstanding actions: on one occasion, such an award amounted to 6,000 francs. He was additionally compensated for the loss of his leg, perhaps in the amount of 2,000 francs.[6]

The importance that Napoleon attached to the functioning and security of this critically important establishment is attested to by his order of 10 March 1812, which stated that the governor was required to live in the fortress without ever sleeping elsewhere, or even leaving it without orders permitting him to do so. On the twentieth of March, Daumesnil was formally invested with the title of Governor of Vincennes, a title that had been especially created for him.

With the young couple still living in Daumesnil's apartment on the Rue Saint-Lazare, on 30 March Daumesnil wrote this letter to the Minister of War:

> The Emperor has asked me several times, including yesterday, whether I was now installed in Vincennes. In replying negatively, I didn't think that I should inform His Majesty that the place wasn't fit for habitation. It requires furnishing that my fortune doesn't permit me to afford. I ask Your Excellency to give me the order to have it examined, having a strong desire to report to my post and fulfill His Majesty's desire.

There was to have been a sum of 400,000 francs set aside for the rehabilitation and furnishing of the governor's apartments in the Pavilion of the Queen, but in order to be able to move into them, Daumesnil had drawn on Léonie's dowry, and had then sought reimbursement for that expense.

On 19 April Daumesnil again wrote to the Minister of War, this time asking whether his promotion to *général de brigade* required him to take a new oath of fidelity. He was informed that it would, and on 26 April, in the

---

5 Public notices were taxed by the government.
6 In an Imperial decree of 8 April 1810, the Emperor specified that an amount of revenue totaling 8,000 francs and 26 centimes should be allocated to Daumesnil, the funds to be drawn from "the property reserved to us in the province of Hanover," which at that time had produced for Napoleon an annual revenue of 786,264 francs 45 centimes. (Archives Nationales)

Palace of St. Cloud, Daumesnil swore "obedience to the Constitution and fidelity to the Emperor." In his *Mémoires* (p. 252), General Louis Lejeune provides a description of the manner in which that ceremony transpired on an earlier occasion:

> This ceremony was given a great deal of splendor in order to link the officers of the army more closely with the chief of the vast empire, which they had helped to found. The newly promoted were called, each in turn, into the Throne Room, where the great officers of the crown were grouped around the Emperor. When entering, we bowed three times, as we had been taught to do by M. Gardel, ballet master of the *Opéra*. That instruction greatly amused us, although it taught most of us very little of the gracefulness of the men of the court, since we had remained rather rough soldiers, and still republicans. Finally, when we had learned to withdraw the right foot gracefully while respectfully inclining the head and shoulders, we arrived at the Tuileries, where we proudly moved on into the Throne Room, toward the noble and gracious gathering, where we would take an oath before the Emperor to be faithful to him. The awkwardness of some of us in making the unaccustomed bow put the dignified audience in the embarrassing situation of having to smother gales of laughter, which would have detracted from the dignity of the occasion.

Poor Daumesnil must have had some difficulty in "withdrawing his right foot," while maintaining his balance with his *jambe de bois*, but no doubt he was equal to the occasion.

Daumesnil's inexperience—one might say, naïveté—in financial matters would prove to be a problem for his new family in the coming years. A serious indication of that was his ill-considered purchase of a country house in his native province, for which he retained an emotional attachment. In April he bought the château of Nanthiat, in the Dordogne, the property of which consisted of ten small farms, a mill, and a lake. Well and fine, except for the fact that the Emperor's orders to remain constantly in Vincennes made the ownership of that domain completely impractical. A year later, Daumesnil sold the property, at a slight loss. His trusting nature made him prey to the unscrupulous manipulations of the notary, *Maître* Fournier-Verneuil, to whom he had entrusted the business. It seems clear that the latter made out well on the affair, at his client's expense.

CHAPTER FIFTEEN
THE GATHERING STORM

For a happy young lady not quite 17, the forbidding character of the château/fortress of Vincennes was less romantic than it was depressing. Once the young couple had moved into their apartments in the Pavilion of the Queen, Léonie wrote in her diary:

> Vincennes was not at all a pleasant place, far from it. Its aspect was instead horribly sad. Nonetheless, I had a magnificent apartment, elegant carriages, several fine horses in my stable, and a fine table — in a word, a splendid establishment, for which my husband gave me his salary as governor.

Although it was eight years since the young Duc d'Enghien had been shot in the moat of the château, the memory of that unhappy act of vengeance on the Emperor's part clung to the walls of the fortress, made more vivid for Léonie by the presence of the *commandant d'armes de la place*,[1] Jacques Harel, who had served in Vincennes since 1801 as its *de facto* jailer, and was still fulfilling that role when the Daumesnils arrived in Vincennes. She noted in her diary that Harel's stern countenance must have been hardened, like his heart, by the air of the prison, since his yellowish skin was like parchment. In fact, there were still a few State prisoners held in Vincennes,[2] under the jurisdiction of Captain Lelarge, but he was directly answerable to the police, so Daumesnil had no

---

1 The word *place* is a general term covering a range of military installations, from forts, to camps, to fortified towns, or to military jurisdictions, as, for example, *la place de Paris*.

2 One of those prisoners was *général de brigade* Victor Lahorie, who had been a friend of Moreau's. He had left France after Moreau's trial, and had then come back to France in 1808. He was then arrested and imprisoned in La Force. Released by Malet during the latter's conspiracy, he had been re-arrested and imprisoned in Vincennes. He was shot in October 1812.

responsibility for that aspect of the activity within the fortress. As it happened, on 9 January 1813 the Emperor sent a note to the Minister of War noting that, with Daumesnil's becoming governor of Vincennes, Harel's role had become redundant, and instructing the minister to find other employment for him. His departure on 5 February 1813 served in some measure to lift the shadow of the execution of the last of the Condés, which had been hanging over the establishment.

While Daumesnil plunged into the task of carrying out Napoleon's instructions for bringing the fortress into an improved state of readiness for the role which the Emperor had assigned it, Léonie began to play the traditional role of the *châtelaine*, visiting the poor in the village of Vincennes in their modest houses, clustered outside the fortress's gates, and distributing assistance in various forms to the needy. It wasn't long before she had won the hearts of the villagers. At the same time, the increased tempo of work within the fortress brought a mild prosperity to the Vincennes townspeople.

The new governor's task was a formidable one. All the military establishments of the Empire had been instructed to send to Vincennes all the materiel which was not strictly necessary for their own defense, so that it could be reconditioned, and then sent to those armies for which it was needed. In his *Gens de Guerre* , General Ambert states that, at the time of the Russian campaign, 500 fully equipped artillery pieces left the fortress's workshops every month.[3] Between 1812 and 1815, on an average 350,000 cartridges and 40,000 cannon cartridges were produced daily. It was not unusual to see as many as 150 wagons of powder arrive in a single day.

1813

The enormous losses of materiel in Russia, and the necessity for rebuilding the army in early 1813, intensified the pressure on the workshops and forges of Vincennes to increase their production. Whether or not Daumesnil missed the comradeship of his fellow officers in the field, he may well have been grateful for having missed the Russian campaign. Now, however, he could take satisfaction in the vital role that he was playing in helping to re-equip the Emperor's new armies.

This year would see what David Chandler calls "one of the longest, most expensive and ultimately decisive of all the struggles of the Napoleonic Wars." Russia was now joined by Prussia in her determination to eject the French from central Europe, while Sweden and a number of the German princelings had allied themselves with the effort to liberate Germany from Napoleon's domination. For the moment, Austria was awaiting the turn of events. With some 250,000 of his troops and a number of his ablest commanders mired down in the doomed attempt to subdue the irreconcilable Spanish, his ports blockaded by the British, and even a

---

3   Cited by Fossa, *Le château historique de Vincennes*, p. 231.

number of his generals wondering where this seemingly endless bleeding of their nation's manhood would all end, it was the greatest challenge of the Emperor's career. But he seems not to have entertained seriously the idea of withdrawing within France's natural boundaries, and attempting to arrive at a satisfactory peace with his increasingly powerful adversaries.

The first three months of the year had seen the steady advance of the Russians and Prussians into the heart of Europe, in the face of weak resistance by Eugène's skeletal forces. Napoleon's strategy was to take the initiative with his re-built army in the spring, and to defeat the coalition partners successively. By a display of almost superhuman energy, by mid-April Napoleon had managed to concentrate in central Germany a force of some 150,000 men, and on 2 May at Lützen, he defeated the combined Russian and Prussian armies. The day before the battle, however, one of the best of the marshals—and the longtime friend and patron of Daumesnil's—was fatally wounded, when a cannon ball struck Bessières, while he was conducting a reconnaissance on the heights above the Rippach.

Again, on 20 and 21 May, in a furious and hard-fought battle at Bautzen, the Emperor decisively defeated the combined Russian-Prussian armies, leaving the latter much the worse for wear, although the casualties on both sides had been roughly equal. When Austria, acting as a mediator, proposed an armistice, both antagonists agreed to accept the proposal, and on 2 June it took effect, to run until 20 July.

During these momentous events, back in the bustling and noisy interior of the fortress of Vincennes Léonie was discovering that her girlish vision of tenderly caring for the wounded hero, and being the faithful dog following in its master's traces, wasn't working out quite as she had expected. Far from being in need of such attentions, Daumesnil remained a vigorous individual, impelled by his sense of duty to involve himself directly in the work of the vast arsenal over which he presided, while continuing to indulge, when his duties permitted, in what had been for years his passion for hunting. In an effort to introduce his young wife to hunting so that they might share this passion of his, Daumesnil took Léonie hunting with him on several occasions, each of which ended unhappily, when, in the first instance, she shot a rabbit coming out of its burrow, and shortly thereafter, when she successfully brought down "a poor, little bird." That was enough for the young bride, and she declared that it was a cruel sport.

In her diary Léonie wrote:

I only saw him at the end of the day, and then very late! It is true, however, that he happily returned to me, and showered me with a thousand caresses, but these transient pleasures were not enough for my loving soul. The isolation was killing me, and my husband's absences were sapping my strength and health. Despite my 17 years, I no longer laughed or sang.

Daumesnil's father-in-law gave him long sermons, suggesting that too much marital affection was the cause of Léonie's ill health, and poor Daumesnil found himself at his wit's end to know how to deal with a feminine psychological problem, which was for him an unfamiliar challenge. An unanticipated event brought a happy solution to the matter, however, when in August of 1813 Léonie gave birth to a son, Léon. Both parents were ecstatic. "From that moment," Léonie wrote, "everything changed the color of my life for me. In tears I had begged God to send me a child. My husband adores them, and in my heart I felt sure that he would be a good father." Once more Léonie sat down at her piano, and the apartment was filled with flowers. Daumesnil was joyous.

In light of this happy event, Léonie now felt able to take more pleasure in, and to preside over with good grace, what she termed the "large and ruinous receptions" that her hospitable husband was so fond of giving for his many friends, one of whom was his old companion-in-arms, Hercule Corbineau, who had not been as successful as Daumesnil in recovering from his injury, but who often made his painful way to Vincennes. [4]

At this time circumstances brought a friend of another period of Daumesnil's career to Vincennes in an official capacity. *Lieutenant de vaisseau* Grivel, of the Seamen of the Guard, had made Daumesnil's acquaintance in 1804, when he was attached to the *Armée des côtes de l'Océan* (Army of the Ocean Coasts), when Daumesnil had participated aboard Grivel's gunboat in exercises intended to prepare for the planned invasion of England. In his *Mémoires* (Clairval collection), the then Vice Admiral Baron Grivel wrote:

> I had been sent to Vincennes with my men as part of the garrison, and spent some time there, near my former comrade Daumesnil, of the *Chasseurs à cheval*. The Emperor had put him there as a man on whom he could count in matters of life or death, and certainly he could not have made a better choice. Furthermore, he had married a Garat daughter, and in that way this brave young man had practically settled his fortunes. Daumesnil treated me just as he did when he was embarked on my gunboat, and where we were both on equal terms. His honors had not changed him at all, and the loss of his leg hadn't altered his good spirits. As might be imagined, I didn't take advantage of our former acquaintanceship, keeping my place, but I greatly enjoyed the society of the governor. In any case, that association only lasted a few months, and one fine morning I received orders to leave for the army.

Daumesnil greatly enjoyed receiving his friends in Vincennes, and they invariably found him to be a warm and cheerful companion. One day he

---

4 Corbineau died in 1823, at the age of 43, as a result of his wound's failure ever to heal properly.

made a wager with some of them that he alone could prepare a dinner for fifteen. As it happened, many years previously he and Prince Eugène had taken cooking and carving lessons together from the famous chef, Méaux. Daumesnil set to work at four o'clock, and the dinner was served at six. Léonie noted afterwards, "He won his bet, to the general satisfaction of all, since the dinner was excellent, and the Parisians were far from losing, I can assure you."

It was probably inevitable that, sooner rather than later, there would be a clash between the proud, battle-scarred governor and the *petit-bourgeois* mayor of Vincennes, a jumped-up notary. It came about in a curious way. On 8 August, on his handsome official stationery headed *Le Baron de l'Empire, Général de Brigade, Officier de la Légion d'Honneur, Chevalier de la Couronne de Fer, Gouverneur de Vincennes,* Daumesnil wrote the mayor the following letter:

Hunting is only permitted from 1 September in your commune, as in all others. Last Sunday you hunted in the small Park with Messieurs Grimpsel and others. Since you remained at the distance from the fortress prescribed by the law, I thought that I should remain silent. Today some residents allowed themselves to hunt in front of my sentries. You will find enclosed their names. I ask that you kindly forward my complaint to the Prefect.

With each man determined to assert his prerogatives, real or imagined, the mayor fired the next salvo, in this letter to the governor on the 12th:

Monsieur,
I have the honour to inform you that next Sunday, the day of the Assumption and the festival of Saint Napoleon, the patron of His Majesty, at the end of the high mass, that is, towards noon, there will be sung in the church of Vincennes a thanksgiving *Te deum.* I hope that you will be kind enough to increase the solemnity of this celebration by your presence. The authorities will gather at my home; they would like to form with you just the one procession to move to the church.
Accept, Monsieur, the assurance of my high esteem,
Champfort

When he read this barely courteous letter, Daumesnil's blood pressure went off the scale. The idea that a mere *pékin* (military slang; a "civvy"), who divided his time between being a notary public and a mayor, should dare to give him such instructions was simply too much to be tolerated. The only people he, Daumesnil, took orders from were the highest dignitaries of the Empire, or the Emperor himself. Seizing another sheet of his fine letter-head stationary, Daumesnil wrote the following reply:

Vincennes, 13 August
Monsieur le Maire,
The local authorities will come here next Sunday in conformance with the Imperial decree dated at Saint-Cloud *le 24 messidor an douze* [13 July 1804]. I invite you to be here, and ask that you kindly note that governors always are in command, even over prefects, within their own government.
Since the question of rank has not been prescribed in your commune, I shall send your two letters to the Prefect of your Department; perhaps he will not find the first of them very honest.
I have the honor to be, *Monsieur le Maire*, your very humble servant, Daumesnil.

The governor was at least going to teach that *pékin* something about the proper form of official correspondence. Daumesnil mentions two letters, while we have only the one. We may assume that the missing letter was in reply to Daumesnil's complaint about hunting out of season. But the mayor was not willing to let Daumesnil have the last word. The following day he sent this uncompromising letter to Daumesnil:

I could not be more pleased that you have asked for an interpretation of the last line of paragraph [?] of the Imperial decree of *24 messidor An XII.* For my part, I have also asked the Prefect about this matter, but, since we should in no way prejudge the matter, I believe that it is appropriate that, until then, matters should proceed as in the past. When that regulation has been made in accordance with your wishes, you will see from my willingness to execute it how much I desire that the duties of my position coincide with what is agreeable to you.

It would be October before the Prefect of Seine et Oise weighed in on this rather childish case of one-upmanship, perhaps because by this time he had more urgent matters on his mind, since events in the world outside the confines of Vincennes had been taking a turn for the worse. After Austria had declared war on France on 12 August, and the armistice had been broken by Blücher on the 13th, the campaigning began again, and, at Dresden on the 26th and 27th, Napoleon again defeated the three Allied main armies, although stinging drubbings administered separately to his lieutenants, Macdonald and Vandamme, each of whom lost thousands of their men as prisoners, rendered the Emperor's victory at Dresden a hollow one. But worse was yet to come.

That second campaign of 1813 ended with the "Battle of the Nations" at Leipzig, during the four days from 16 to 19 October. It was an unmitigated disaster for Napoleon. While Allied casualties probably amounted to some 54,000 killed and wounded, there must be added to

250

French battle casualties of more than 38,000 men another 30,000 taken prisoner. Among the latter were General Lauriston and General Reynier, and 36 other generals. Twelve hours after having been made a marshal, the wounded Poniatowski drowned trying to swim the Elster. This defeat not only dealt a serious blow to Napoleon's reputation as a supreme strategist and combat commander, but it also signaled the end of the French Empire east of the Rhine.

Although the Emperor skillfully managed the withdrawal of his spent forces from Germany after Leipzig—in the course of so doing, he had administered a crushing defeat to the incautious Bavarian General Wrede at Hanau, when that defector from the French cause attempted to intercept and destroy the retreating French columns—there were at the most 120,000 men in the army which crossed the Rhine into France late in the year. Typhus had swept through the retreating army, and many of the soldiers stricken by it brought it back into France with them. In Metz alone, starting on 11 November more than 5,000 sick and dying soldiers were brought into the city, and all institutions of charity, as well as churches, were instructed to take in those unfortunates. Despite the risks of contagion, the inhabitants did their best to care for these victims of an attack, against which no cuirass could shield them. In December, 1600 soldiers died in Metz, and the disease had begun to spread among the civil population. In the following three months, another 5,000 soldiers and 1300 civilians would die.

∞

A pause in hostilities at the end of November resulted, in part, from the mutual exhaustion and disorganization of both antagonists, and, in part, from disagreement among the Allies as to whether or not to attempt at once to pursue Napoleon into France. During this interval in hostilities, ideas and proposals for a peace agreement, some genuine and some simply psychological warfare on Metternich's part, were bruited, but it was clear to Napoleon that none of them would meet his own views as to what would be acceptable to France.

Brushing aside Switzerland's neutrality, in December an Austrian division began to occupy that country. Then, on 21 December Wrede led his Bavarians out of Basel across the Rhine, and laid siege to Huningue, a small town and fortress slightly north of Basel on the French side of the river. Its garrison of 300 mixed *chasseurs à cheval*, line infantry, and light infantry, under the command of Colonel Chancel, successfully resisted all Austrian attempts to take the town until 16 April 1814, when it was clear that further resistance was pointless. Then Allied troops entered the town, with at their head the Russian princes, Nicholas and Mikhail, brothers of the Tsar. (Huningue would undergo a second siege in 1815, as we shall see in due course.). On 29 December Blücher's troops began crossing the Rhine at Mainz, while General Schwarzenberg was moving on Colmar by New Year's Day of 1814. To borrow a phrase that Sir Arthur Conan Doyle would make memorable some 70 years later, it would be fair to say that now, truly, "the game was afoot."

1814

Since his return to Paris in mid-November, Napoleon had been intensely engaged in planning for the defense of France's frontiers, in the face of many seemingly intractable problems: a war-weary population, a number of his marshals longing for an opportunity to enjoy in peace their hard-won honors, conscripts deserting en masse, Wellington pressing Soult and Suchet back into the Pyrenees, Holland in a state of rebellion and Belgium teetering on the brink of following suit, and Eugène in Italy under heavy Austrian pressure. On 11 January Murat deserted Napoleon's cause, freeing 30,000 Neapolitan troops for employment by the Allies. As the Emperor undoubtedly knew, Talleyrand was in touch with the Bourbons, ensuring that, when the end came, as it inevitably must, he would be on the winning side. But the spirit of the Emperor was still unquenchable.

Somehow, Napoleon managed to marshal his greatly diminished forces in thinly spread dispositions best calculated to meet the steady advance of the Allies into northeastern France. Yet, during this perilous and daunting hour, the Emperor found time to visit Vincennes before leaving on 25 January for the opening of the Campaign of France. But it was a practical, rather than a social call that he paid to the château, since he was clear-sighted enough at that point to understand that, before long, he might find himself fighting on the outskirts of his capital, and he was depending on that fortress to play a key role in the defense of Paris.

In her journal on that occasion, Léonie wrote:

Young mother as I was, I was almost as nervous as I had been as a girl, and at first, just as foolish, when Napoleon asked me some questions about my happiness, my husband, whether I was satisfied, etc., etc. I replied naïvely that he was charming, which made him smile.

Léonie then collected herself, however, and when the Emperor asked her, after having kissed her son, what she wished for him, "Nothing more, Sire," she replied.

Napoleon then proceeded with Daumesnil to inspect the fortress minutely, telling the governor to raze or cut down unhesitatingly any impediments to the line of fire of the fortress's batteries, in the event of a possible attack. He pointed out in particular a house built close up under the outer wall of the fortress, which, he said, should be demolished. As it happened, that house and its little garden belonged to a Monsieur Segond. Daumesnil had had his eye on that property for his own use, since the residence of the fortress had no garden of its own, and he had sounded out its owner as to its availability. But M. Segond made it clear that he had no desire to sell As a consequence, relations between the two of them had become very frosty.

Some months later, circumstances would seem to require that the house be destroyed, and a few shells from one of the fortress's heavy caliber cannon would have sufficed to do the job. But when preparations for the demolition of the house had been made, Daumesnil decided against doing so, commenting that M. Segond enjoyed being his enemy, and would claim that the governor was avenging himself because he, Segond, had refused to sell the house it to him. In fact, the house was never destroyed, and later the two men became fast friends.

CHAPTER SIXTEEN
THE DELUGE

1814

The story of the remarkable Campaign of France, when Napoleon ceased to be an emperor and became once more simply a general, as he put it, need not delay us here. Suffice it to say that neither the last-ditch devotion of those men like Daumesnil, for whom Napoleon was still and would always be their Emperor, nor the extraordinary performance of the Marie-Louise conscripts, nor his own extraordinary skill in employing his skeletal regiments in a manner calculated to baffle his ponderous adversaries, would prevent the inevitable and final collapse of the Empire. His string of victories at Brienne, Champaubert, Montmirail, Vauchamps, Laon, and Arcis-sur-Aube, brilliantly fought as they were, in the end failed to stem the flood of Russian, Prussian, and Austrian columns converging on the capital.

On 28 March, the Empress left the capital for Rambouillet, accompanied by the King of Rome, Madame Mère, King Jerome and Queen Catherine of Westphalia, the ministers and their staffs, and the Council of State. King Joseph remained to organize the defense of Paris, with Marshals Moncey, Mortier, and Marmont as his commanders. Moncey had 30,000 National Guards, half of them without muskets. There were in addition some 20,000 Line conscripts manning fortress guns in fixed positions, Marmont's corps, and roughly 12,000 Guardsmen, mostly from their regiments' Paris depots.

At four in the morning on the 30th, the Allied assault on the capital began, with a shot from one of Marshal Mortier's cannon, positioned in a redoubt before La Villette. When the marshal had spied a band of Cossacks approaching along the road to Le Bourget, he called out to his men, "Gunners, let us see if your big piece caught cold last night!"

Joseph had established his command post up on Montmartre. As heavy fighting broke out and grew in intensity throughout the morning, in the early afternoon Joseph sent word to the marshals, telling them "to surrender if they could no longer hold their positions," and left for Rambouillet. The marshals were left to fend for themselves, which is what they had already been doing, in any case. As the day wore on, numerous disparate French units on the perimeter of Paris fought heroically against impossible odds, gradually being forced to give way at all points. At the *barrière de Clichy,* Moncey's National Guardsmen and 400 men of the Old Guard were down to their last cartridges and forced to withdraw.

Finally Marmont and Mortier, who had been driven back to the heights of Montmartre, accepted the inevitable, and at 02:00 on the 31st, Marmont agreed to an armistice, and withdrew his troops south of the city. Mortier ordered the Guard to leave Paris by the Fontainebleau Gate.

The right flank of the line of defense on the northern outskirts of Paris, which Joseph and the marshals had at first attempted to establish, had been hinged on Vincennes. The garrison of the fortress at that critical time was made up of 300 *invalides,* retired old soldiers of unquestionable loyalty, and 1,000 National Guards, whose dependability was less certain. As the Allies closed in on Paris, Daumesnil had sent Léonie and their little Léon to his father-in-law's apartment in the Banque de France, while he intensified his men's efforts to prepare the château's fortifications to withstand an attack. 700 cannon of various calibers were in position on the towers of the outer wall and the platform atop the keep, or otherwise disposed within the fortress. The armories and magazines were crammed with weapons, ammunition, and powder. Still, it was not a fortress which could long resist an assault by heavy artillery and storming infantry, commanded by a skilled and determined general.

Léonie did not wish to leave her husband:

I was determined to remain closed up in Vincennes and to share the fate of my husband. It had been completely agreed between us. However, one morning I was awakened by the sound of a cannon. I jumped out of my bed, and roused my child and his nurse. I started to write to my mother, confiding this dear child to her care, because I knew what Daumesnil's determination was, and I expected nothing less than to die with him. However, big tears, betraying my emotion as a mother, were flowing from my eyes, when Daumesnil, who felt no less than me the importance of this last moment, came into my room, took me in his arms, picked me up like a feather, and placed me in a waiting carriage. Then, handing me his son, he entrusted him to my loving care, assuring me that his own affection, no less than his duty, would not permit him to keep us by him.

"I thought I would be stronger in the face of the danger threatening you," he said.

"Who knows whether my courage would fail, seeing you suffer."

I wanted to reply, but couldn't finish, because I was already far away. I don't know whether the horses sensed the enemy, who were marching down from the heights of Montreuil and the neighboring villages, and if they feared having to enter in the service of the Russians or Cossacks, but we went like the wind. That speed served us well, because the gates of Paris were being closed just as we reached them, and I had to identify myself so that we could enter.

While the men within the fortress waited tensely for the tide of combat to lap at their walls, another dramatic attempt to hold back those onrushing waters was enacted not far from those walls. Three companies of artillery, made up of students of the Ecole Polytechnique under the command of Major Evain, second in command at the school, their cannon drawn by barge and hack horses, had been deployed at the junction of the Charonne and Saint-Mandé roads, in the face of Russian troops coming from Montreuil. At first the Russian commander, Count Pahlen, believed that he had run up against an entire division, and paused, but when he learned of the fragility of the obstacle presented, he ordered General Kamenev to press forward, supported by a battery of light artillery.

Daumesnil was able to observe the development of this confrontation, but it was taking place beyond the range of his cannon. He had hoped, nonetheless, to be able to prevent the junction of Russian forces, coming from Fontenay and Montreuil, and attacking the *polytechniens* from behind. However, a squadron of Cossacks, sheltering behind the houses of the town of Vincennes, emerged on the Highway of the Throne, and delivered three unsuccessful charges against the young artillerymen. The gunners were given a temporary respite when Colonel Ordener, at the head of a squadron of Polish Light Horse Lancers of the Guard, drove into the right flank of Kamenev's men, forcing the Russians to abandon the two cannon which the had captured. But the students' sacrifice was in vain, as were so many others on that fatal day, that had only served to delay by a few hours the capitulation of the French army.

By evening the struggle had ceased, and the French capital, with all its materiel of war, was turned over to France's enemies. A relative calm had settled over the city, which was broken only by sporadic cannon fire from the fortress of Vincennes. Then, as night fell, even those cannon were stilled.

The terms of the capitulation required that all arsenals, workshops, military establishments, equipment, and stores be left just as they were before the signing of the surrender. But Daumesnil, who had been able to remain abreast of these events, took a different view of the matter. When the night's darkness had settled over Paris, the drawbridge of the Tour du Village was quietly lowered and *la Jambe de Bois*, astride a dray horse— this was not a time for mettlesome chargers!—rode through the portal at the head of 250 horsemen, drawing behind them a variety of carts and wagons. Without awakening any of the slumbering troops of the victorious Allied armies, this cortège made its way up onto the heights on the northern outskirts of the city, as they went gathering up and piling into the wagons and carts as they went all the abandoned muskets and ammunition they found, and hitching up those caissons and cannon left behind by Mortier's and Marmont's withdrawing troops. When men and beasts could carry no more, the procession retraced its steps, and the drawbridge was raised once more as the last cart passed through the gate.

With the arrival of daybreak, Allied commanders gradually became aware of the daring feat that had been carried out by the Vincennes governor and his men. The Russian commander-in-chief, Field Marshal Barclay de Tolly, had not intended to assault Vincennes, knowing that it was the French army's most important arsenal and wishing to preserve its valuable munitions for the Allies' use. He had counted on being able to take possession of the fort without encountering any serious resistance. Now, having learned of coup performed by the fortress's commander, he sent a colonel as a *parlementaire* to the gate of the fortress to demand its surrender.

The Russian colonel appeared at the edge of the moat before the Tour du Village, and called out to the watching sentries that he had come in the name of the commander-in-chief of the Russian forces to demand the surrender of the fortress. Daumesnil was informed, and came to the gate with members of his staff. When the drawbridge had been lowered and the Russian had walked across it to the gate itself and courteously saluted the governor, he repeated that, in the name of Field Marshal Barclay de Tolly, he had come to demand the surrender of the fortress to the Allies.

Daumesnil replied, "I will only surrender this fort on the orders of His Majesty, the Emperor."

The Russian was not satisfied with that reply, and insisted that the fortress must be turned over to de Barclay's troops without further delay. Losing his patience in the face of this obstinate insistence, Daumesnil replied, "The Austrians took one of my legs. Let them return it, or come take the other. In the meanwhile, I advise you to stay clear of my guns, if you do not wish to feel their effect."[1]

The Russian officer responded, "You're completely surrounded. You'll be starved out!"

"Try it," was Daumesnil's laconic reply.

"Well, if that's the way it is," said the Russian, "we'll blow you up."

Gesturing to the buildings, in which some 180,000 pounds of powder were stored, Daumesnil said to him, "Go ahead, and we'll all go up in the air together, and if we should pass one another in mid-air, I won't promise not to give you a scratch."

Seeing that he had no prospect of receiving the response he had been

---

1   There are a number of versions of the wording of this defiant reply, but I believe that this one, which is Parquin's (Jones, *Napoleon's Army*, p. 104), comes closest to what Daumesnil probably said. Some of the other versions, which have Daumesnil referring to the Russians' having taken his leg, automatically disqualify themselves, since he was unlikely to have forgotten that it was to the Austrians that he owed his disability

sent to obtain, the baffled emissary returned to de Tolly's headquarters. The latter immediately ordered the establishment of a blockade of the fortress.

It should be noted that Daumesnil's statement that he would only surrender Vincennes in response to a direct order from the Emperor was not a frivolous one. He must have been well aware of the fact that, although the army had withdrawn from Paris, it still constituted a considerable force, and a significant portion of it was still available to Napoleon near Fontainebleau. The establishment of the blockade may well have cut Daumesnil off from news of the Emperor's last-minute efforts to salvage something from the collapse of his empire, but the Russian intermediary had evidently not attempted to argue that the Emperor's writ no longer extended to Vincennes.

Although by 2 April Talleyrand had presented the keys to Paris to the Tsar, French troops in the provinces still constituted a force to be reckoned with. The Emperor still had an army of 60,000 men, including much of the Guard, in and around Fontainebleau, and a number of fortresses were still under siege.

In Fontainebleau at noon on 3 April, Napoleon was reviewing and inspecting the Guard in the court of *Le Cheval Blanc*, still nursing the belief that, somehow, he could reverse his foundering fortunes once more. But the marshals would no longer march to his orders, and on 4 April Napoleon signed a conditional abdication. Nonetheless, on the 5th he was still thinking of taking the troops at Fontainebleau and retiring to the south in order to effect a junction with the numerous formations in the Midi, Lyons, and the Pyrenees, and had written out orders for the first day's march. But by the 5th, Marmont had defected, with the 6th Corps, and this event made it evident to the Tsar that Napoleon no longer could count on the army's support. Accordingly, Alexander sent word to Fontainebleau that the conditional abdication would not do; it had to be an unconditional act.

Napoleon finally realized the impossibility of any other outcome to this nightmarish situation, and on the 6th he signed the unconditional abdication document and gave it to the French commissioners, Caulaincourt, Ney, and Macdonald.

At Vincennes, Daumesnil was resolved to resist to the utmost any attempt to seize the fortress, since he was determined not to permit the enormously valuable munitions of every description, for the safety of which he was responsible, to fall into the hands of the Allies. Whether or not Napoleon or Louis XVIII sat on the throne, that treasure belonged to France, and when conditions permitted him to place it intact under French control, he would unhesitatingly do so.

At 11:00 on the morning of the 31st, the Allies began to enter Paris by the Pantin gate. The Cossacks of the Guard rode at the head of the seemingly endless procession, followed by Alexander, with Prince Schwarzenberg, representing Austria, on his right, and King Frederick

William of Prussia on his left. For the most part the scant crowds lining the Boulevard St. Denis, down which the procession was passing, watched silently, with a mixture of curiosity, apprehension, and certainly some sense of humiliation, but, as the cavalcade reached the more middle-class parts of the city, a sprinkling of royalists, sporting the white cockade of the Bourbons on their hats or clothing, began calling out, "*Vive les Bourbons!*" What disturbances occurred were caused by the resentment of the Parisians against the noisy pro-Bourbon demonstrators, who that evening made an unsuccessful attempt to topple the column in the Place Vendôme commemorating Napoleon's victories, rather than against the foreign armies flooding into their city.

In a meeting that he had early that morning in his headquarters at Bondy with a delegation from Paris, led by the Prefect of Police, Etienne-Denis Pasquier, the Tsar expressed his hatred for Napoleon, "who has deceived me in the most unworthy manner, abused my confidence, betrayed every oath he made to me, and involved my country in the most iniquitous and hateful war."[2] He then went on to say that, apart from Napoleon, he was well disposed toward all Frenchmen, and that he was not entering Paris as an enemy, but that it was up to the city's people whether he was to be their friend. There can be little doubt that the French welcomed the idea of a peace, even one bestowed on them by foreign rulers, after all the *gloire*, Imperial drama, conquests—and sacrifices, human and material—of the past twenty years, but still, Cossacks making camp under the trees along the Champs Elysées—well, that was another matter entirely! Who could have imagined it? *We're* the ones who are expected to occupy foreign capitals, and cart home their treasures!

On 1 April, a provisional French government was formed, under the leadership of Talleyrand, and on the third, both the Senate and the Legislature voted for the deposition of Napoleon. While the three Allied leaders debated among themselves, and with the members of the provisional government, as to the best manner in which to achieve a peaceful transition from Napoleon's empire to a successor government satisfactory to themselves and acceptable to the French people, the matter of the stand-off between the governor of the fortress of Vincennes and the encircling Russian force did not occupy their immediate attention. Consequently, the siege continued, punctuated by a sort of low-scale duel, which continued to sputter inconclusively outside the fortress's walls.

Sorties from the fortress, led by Daumesnil at the head of a handful of the garrison's veterans, were intended to harass the Russian besiegers in order to hold them at a respectful distance from the Vincennes domain, which included the town itself. On one of these occasions, his men had managed to seize and draw back to the fortress several cannon, which the Russians had indiscreetly left inadequately protected. As he stood watching

---

2   Pasquier, *Mémoires*, p. 160.

his men file back through the fortress gate, the fact that a number were equipped, like himself, with wooden legs caught his eye, and Daumesnil burst out laughing, remarking, "The enemy has shown his respect for our game of ten pins, since he hasn't dared to bowl any of his iron balls at it."

On 5 April, the new Minister of War, General Pierre Dupont de l'Etang— the Dupont of the capitulation of Bailen, who had been imprisoned, stripped of his rank and decorations, his name expunged from the role of the *Légion d'honneur* by Napoleon, and who had now been rehabilitated by the provisional government—wrote to Daumesnil the following:

Monsieur le Commandant,
By an act of the *Senat-Conservateur* on the date of 3 April current, Napoleon Bonaparte has been declared deposed from the throne, and the hereditary right established within his family has been abolished. By a declaration dated the same day, the legislative corps has adhered to the act of the *Senat-Conservateur.*

The Senate has ordered the establishment of a provisional Commission of Government, and that Commission, by a subsequent decree, has invested me with the functions of Minister of War, for the Ministry and the Administration of War combined.

I have the honor to send you, *Monsieur le Commandant,* all the acts on this subject emanating from the *Senat-Conservateur,* the legislative Corps, and the provisional government of France. I do not doubt that, after having become acquainted with them, you will respond to the appeal made, in these circumstances, to all true Frenchmen, especially those who are affected by the words honor and country, (and that) you will consequently adhere to all of the acts emanating from the national authority, and that you will immediately make them known to all the French troops under your orders.

I request that you, *Monsieur le Commandant,* send me as quickly as possible your personal act of adhesion, as well as those of the troops under your command, to the changes made in the Constitution of the state, and to put me in a position , as soon as I shall have presented that act to the provisional Government of France, to send you Instructions appropriate to your present situation.

From the moment your act of adhesion is known, all hostilities between the troops under your orders and those of the Allied Powers will cease.
Receive, etc[3]

It requires little imagination to envision Daumesnil's reaction to this peremptory summons, especially coming as it did from a man for whom he doubtless felt contempt.

---

3   Desclozeaux archives.

When it became known that Napoleon had signed an unconditional act of abdication on 6 April, the Senate lost no time in proclaiming Louis XVIII king. That action formally released the army from its collective oath of allegiance to the deposed Emperor. For the most part, the marshals and generals were off the mark just as quickly, in order to bargain with the new government for posts and positions—in most cases, successfully. In a letter to his sister, Marshal Mortier wrote: "Every one is trying to feather his own nest. I only desire to preserve my honor and merit the esteem of my friends and foes alike. All my colleagues have been pushing themselves forward." Nansouty seems to have been at the head of the pack, with a letter of 2 April, but Sébastiani, Colbert, Ornano, Lion, and dozens of others were not far behind, presenting not only their personal allegiance to the new government, but that of the officers and men in their own commands as well.

To the extent that Daumesnil was aware of this "rallying" to the Bourbons, he was undoubtedly repelled by it, since he saw matters in a very different light. His oath of fidelity to his emperor would remain unbroken. Whenever Russian troops approached the walls of Vincennes too closely for his taste, Daumesnil ordered that a few warning shots be fired off at them, causing their withdrawal to a more discreet distance.

At this time the garrison consisted of 300 veterans of unquestionable reliability, and 1,000 National Guards of less proven quality, and it was among the latter that signs of dissension now made their appearance. Word of the governor's threat to blow up the fortress in the event of a Russian attack had quickly spread among the men of the garrison, and they knew that Daumesnil was perfectly capable of carrying out his threat, if he deemed it to be the only way of denying a vast booty to the Allies. On the 7th, a number of the men of the garrison had gathered in the courtyard of the fort, some among them openly debating the risks they were being expected to face. In their view their commander was being unreasonably stubborn in resisting the Russian demand, since Napoleon had by now abdicated, and the possibility of their being buried alive under tons of the château's stone and brick walls, simply for a matter of principle, had little appeal for them.

Having been informed of this unease among the troops, Daumesnil went to talk to them. As he approached them, one of the Guardsmen took aim at him and let off a shot. Fortunately the *cantinière*, Madame Obriot, happened to be standing next to the man and struck up his musket, so that the shot went wild. Daumesnil simply ignored it, and, ordering the rebellious soldiers to put down their arms, exclaimed, "I've never seen any place that needed timid men. Let all the cowards get out of here!" Seizing one of the men by the arm, he asked, "Are you one of them? Do you want to abandon me, too?"[4]

---

4   Clairval, *Daumesnil*, p. 155.

The governor's vigorous and determined attitude revived the spirits of most of the men, who did not wish to be accused of cowardice, and they vehemently denied any intention of deserting their commander. A few of the Guardsmen, however, maintained their desire to be permitted to leave for their homes, so Daumesnil had them stripped of their uniforms and ejected from the fortress, whence they fled to the accompaniment of their comrades' insults and their enemies' bullets, as the drawbridge was wound up behind them.

Feelings against the provisional government were running high among the Paris working class, who blamed its members for selling France to foreigners. They contrasted the new government's behaviour with that of the brave governor of Vincennes, *la Jambe de Bois*. "If Marmont had acted as *he* did," they exclaimed, "we wouldn't be in this fix!"

In fact, Daumesnil's failure to respond promptly and obediently to Dupont's summons was creating a dilemma for the provisional government. It may be assumed that Barclay de Tolly had informed the Tsar of the difficulty he had encountered in taking possession of Vincennes, and that the Tsar had, in turn, expressed his concern over this untoward development to his friend, Talleyrand. While the latter and his fellow members of the provisional government may have been pleased that the valuable contents of the fortress of Vincennes had not yet become war booty for the Allies, they certainly felt considerable concern over the fact that Daumesnil had not yet dutifully submitted to their authority. Indeed, they wondered if he would ever consider himself freed from his oath of fidelity to Napoleon, and hoist the white flag of the Bourbons over the château. It was now a question as to whether the obstinate governor would surrender Vincennes to either the Allies *or* to the new government.

With characteristic, if flawed, ingenuity, Talleyrand then hit upon a solution to this vexing problem: make Daumesnil a member of the provisional government. That way the risk of conflict would be avoided, while the government would at the same time gain a valuable supporter. But how could one put this proposition to the prickly governor in a manner calculated to win his agreement? Whatever Daumesnil's opinion of the Minister of War, General Dupont, may have been, it happened that the man and his brother, General Dupont-Chaumont, were friends of the Garat family. During these days Dupont-Chaumont frequently stopped by the Banque de France to see if he could get any idea of the situation within Vincennes, but Léonie was in complete ignorance of the situation there, and consumed with anxiety over her husband's fate, so she was of no help.

In trying to think of an emissary acceptable to Daumesnil to whom they could safely entrust this delicate mission, Talleyrand and the Minister hit upon the chief of the general staff of the National Guard, *adjutant-commandant* Tourton, who was known to be a good friend of Daumesnil's, going back to the latter's bachelor days. Talleyrand won Tourton's agreement to take on this task, emphasizing to him that it was critically important to convince Daumesnil that he must surrender the fortress, but that he would be able to set the conditions for so doing. In any case, Talleyrand said, it was essential that the governor hoist the white flag of the Bourbons over the fortress.

At the same time, Talleyrand had General Sacken, the Russian commander on the scene at Vincennes, and Prince Schwarzenberg informed of the prospective negotiations, so that the necessary *laissez-passez* for Tourton could be issued, Vincennes now being in a state of siege. The requisite passes for Talleyrand's messenger were quickly forthcoming, since there was a common desire on the part of all to arrive at a solution to this awkward situation, which, it was recognized, would not be easily achieved with a man of Daumesnil's stamp.

In addition to Talleyrand's briefing, Tourton was given a letter, signed by all members of the provisional government, specifying the purpose of his mission. Despite his warm friendship with Daumesnil, the thought of trying to convince this strong-willed man to do something that he was obviously not prepared to do aroused in Tourton considerable trepidation. Then he thought of a means of facilitating his task: he would ask Léonie to accompany him, bringing little Léon with her. Surely, he thought, she would prove to be a staunch ally, when he sought to bring Daumesnil around. He forthwith repaired to the Banque de France and explained his mission to Léonie. She was far from convinced that her presence would affect her husband's sense of where his duty lay, and was, moreover, fearful that, no matter how this all turned out, her husband would come off badly. On top of that, she was very reluctant to expose her seven-months-old son to the risks of a quasi-battlefield, but Tourton finally won her over. The visit to Vincennes was set for the following day, 8 April.

Since Tourton was anxious to give himself every possible advantage in carrying out this daunting mission, he bethought himself of some of the fine occasions that he and Daumesnil had enjoyed together. He had the good fortune to be the owner of the Clos-Vougeot vineyard, so a hastily prepared basket included several bottles of his best vintage, some *pâté de fois gras* from Madame Chevet in the Palais Royal, some *terrines* from Nérac, and a variety of other tasty comestibles. But this was all window-dressing for the envelope which Tourton would be carrying, which contained the following letter, addressed simply to "*Monsieur Daumesnil, Commandant militaire du Château de Vincennes:*"

> *Monsieur,*
> The provisional government is sending you the most accurate account of the developments which have taken place for several days, since now truth is the only language which authority has reason to employ. You will see, *Monsieur,* how many men of consequence in the army have dedicated their efforts and their

services to the pure and glorious cause to which we are devoting ourselves: Marshals Marmont, Ney Macdonald, Oudinot, Generals Legrand, Dupont, Dessoles, Nansouty, etc., who, closer to events, came ahead of all the others. But your honor, *Monsieur*, your love for the country, your generous ardor inform us of your sentiments.

We do not come to commit you to surrender the château that you command to the Allied troops, but rather to recognize the provisional government and to submit to the orders that General Dupont, chief administrator in the Department of War, will send you in his name.

Your resistance, praiseworthy until now, would become culpable if it were prolonged, and could only have a regrettable result for yourself and the small number of brave men whom you command.

The letter had originally ended at that point, with the "*Recevez, Monsieur...*" formal ending, but one of its drafters had an afterthought, and had scratched out the formal ending and added the following sentence. "The Emperor Napoleon having renounced for himself and his family the thrones of France and Italy, you no longer have any orders to receive from him," and had scrawled below that added sentence, "*Recevez, etc.*"

Referring to the Minister of War as "the Chief Administrator" in the Department of War is curious, especially since Dupont himself had already written to Daumesnil as Minister of War. Perhaps this choice of terms was inspired by a concern that calling this once reviled man "Minister" would have unnecessarily gotten Daumesnil's back up, before he even read the letter.

For this account of how the mission transpired, we are indebted to the *Mémoires* of the Duchess d'Abrantès,[5] supplemented by Tourton's own recollection of his meeting with Daumesnil.

Having arrived just beyond the range of the cannon on the fortress's walls, M. Tourton stopped the carriage and helped *la baronne* Daumesnil and her infant down from it. Offering one arm to the young mother, her son in her arms, Tourton held a bottle of his Clos-Vougeot and a white handkerchief in his other hand. Behind them walked two servants, whose livery should have been visible from a distance, both of them carrying the *pâtés*. At that location there was a wall behind which an Austrian post had been established. The

---

5   Laure Permon, the widow of General Junot, the Duc d'Abrantès. She had incurred the enmity of Napoleon's mother and sister, Pauline, and the Emperor would not allow her within 50 leagues of Paris. She was a notorious embroiderer of facts, but if one is able to sort out fact from fiction in her accounts, they can often prove to be illuminating. This account is reproduced in Fossa, *Le château historique de Vincennes* and Clairval, *Daumesnil*, pp. 161–163.

soldiers didn't dare make a fire, because the unfortunate Daumesnil would shoot in the direction of the fire, on the assumption that there would be some one around a fire in the open field.

M. Tourton stopped his little party behind this wall, and, taking a long glass, focused it on the keep. At first he saw nothing, but a shot was fired from the fortress. Since they were out of its range, Tourton laughed, and signaled to the carriage to move forward. Then he saw some movement on the ramparts of the keep, and soon he was able to make out Daumesnil, who was examining through his long glass the unusual party approaching the château.

"Now we can walk ahead," exclaimed M. Tourton, "he's seen us, and he would be a real devil to fire on his wife and son, quite apart from our friendship."

In fact, General Daumesnil had just barely recognized the individuals who were coming toward the château before he hastened to met them. They met him at the first postern gate. Daumesnil embraced Léonie lovingly. 'What have you come looking for here?' he asked sadly. With a laugh, Tourton replied, "We came to have lunch with you!"

"What do you think a poor besieged man, who hasn't enough for himself and his companions, can offer you?"
"Oh," exclaimed Tourton, "I didn't take a chance on having a poor luncheon. Here's enough to treat the whole garrison. Come on, let's sit down at the table, and afterwards we'll talk."

They had their luncheon, and when they were alone, Tourton asked Daumesnil,

"What is it that you want to do?"
"My duty," was the governor's simple reply.
"I know that," replied Tourton, "and I haven't come here to advise you otherwise. But the enemy is in our capital, our armies have been dispersed. What can we do in the face of such great misfortunes? I'm instructed to tell you, on behalf of the provisional government, that you will always have command of Vincennes, that nothing will be taken away from it."

As he spoke, Tourton handed Daumesnil the letter from the provisional government. The governor had been listening without comment to his friend's words. He now read the letter, and at once wrote a reply. As he handed it to Tourton, he said, "I will only turn Vincennes over to the hands of Frenchmen. That is my final intention. I will not put a single cartridge

266

in the hands of enemics."

"And I approve of you with all my heart," Tourton chimed in, not wanting to appear less imbued with patriotic sentiments. "The country before all else! It's for her that we'll always fight! The country! Our native soil! Those are our masters, my friend! Let us be faithful to them always!"

Then, having clasped Tourton's hand and embraced his wife and son, Daumesnil withdrew to the isolation of the fortress.

In fact, Daumesnil had accompanied his family and Tourton as far as the Austrian outposts before bidding them farewell. Although he had been happy to see Léonie and his son, he had been saddened by the thought that an effort had been made to use them as a means of weakening his determination.

Daumesnil's reply to the provisional government, which Tourton took away with him, read as follows:

Vincennes 8 April 1814
Messieurs,
I have received the letter that you have done me the honor of sending to me. It seems to me that my duty is to preserve for France the immense quantity of artillery and munitions of all kinds which the fort of Vincennes contains. Without taking any position with respect to the request that you make for my joining the provisional government, a question that merits serious consideration, I will tell you that what would enormously affect my opinion and my determination would be to receive the certitude that these precious stores would be saved for France, and that no Allied force would enter the fort to take possession of them.

I request the provisional government to give me a positive response to that effect, which *adjutant-commandant* Tourton could bring back to me tomorrow.

There are in the fort two companies of Dutch artillery that I wish to send home. I ask for the authorization of the government to do so, and the assurance that they will in no way be inconvenienced.

I have the honor to be, *Messieurs,* with the highest respect,
Le général gouverneur de Vincennes
Baron Daumesnil.[6]

Having received this letter, Talleyrand at once wrote as follows to Prince Schwarzenberg, the commander-in-chief of the Allied armies:

---

6   Author's translation of a copy in the Clairval collection of a letter in the archives of the *Service Historique de l'Armée, Campagne de France Correspondance, C 187.*

Paris, 9 April 1814
Monseigneur,
The governor of Vincennes appears to be disposed to submit to the
orders of the provisional government. He has attached a condition
that the fort not be occupied by Allied troops and that the military
supplies be preserved for France. The principles expressed by the
Powers leave us in no doubt that Your Serene Highness, in his
capacity as commander-in-chief of the Allied armies, will agree to
these requests, and permit us to speed up the surrender of this fort.
If Your Serene Highness agrees, the commandant will remain there
with two hundred men, and the others will be at the disposition of
the Minister of War.
Accept, etc.[7]

In the midst of these negotiations, there occurred an incident that very
nearly caused them to break down. It happened that Schwarzenberg's
carriage was being driven along the slopes of Montreuil, north of the
fortress. Seeing the Austrian cavalry accompanying the carriage,
Daumesnil took this movement for an attempt to outflank him, while at
the same time negotiating with him, and ordered his gunners to fire on
them. As luck would have it, two of the prince's finest horses were killed by
the shot. As might be imagined, the Allied commander-in-chief was
extremely irritated, and one can as easily picture Talleyrand's dismay at
this untoward event. Tourton was with him when news of this incident was
reported to him, and Talleyrand turned to that officer for a suggestion as
to how to repair the damage.

"There's only one thing to do," Tourton replied. "Take two horses from
the Emperor's stables, and send them to the prince. I'll take care of
explaining to Daumesnil that he's blundered."[8]

Talleyrand gave the order to do as Tourton had suggested, while the
latter returned to Vincennes, where he explained to Daumesnil how the
coaches of Prince Schwarzenberg were required to be escorted.

In his reply to Talleyrand that same day, Schwarzenberg's attitude
toward Daumesnil was clearly unfavorable:

Monseigneur,
I don't attach great importance, from a military point of view, to
accelerating the surrender of the fort of Vincennes. Nonetheless,
since that surrender could offer some advantages to the government,
I would agree with pleasure, and in conformance with your desires,
to enter into such arrangements.
I would only observe, *Monseigneur,* that it is indispensable, before

---

7   Author's translation of a copy in the Clairval collection of a letter in the *Archives
    Nationales.*
8   Clairval, *Daumesnil,* p. 168.

the blockade is raised, that the garrison be replaced by troops of the National Guard, and that the commandant be replaced by an officer of your choice.

That measure, while offering the Allied Powers a sufficient guarantee, will satisfy fully my own views, and will put at the disposition of the government the considerable resources that the fort of Vincennes offers.

Accept, etc.

Schwarzenberg.[9]

The prince's acceptance of Daumesnil's two conditions certainly represented progress, thought the government, and changing the composition of the garrison was probably workable, but they recognized at the same time that withdrawing Daumesnil from his command would be a clear signal to him that the place was to be turned over to the Allies, so Talleyrand resumed negotiations. Perhaps Schwarzenberg was tired of the whole business, for he finally agreed that Daumesnil might remain as commander of Vincennes.

On 9 April the provisional government addressed this letter to *M. le Gal. Baron Daumesnil, Commandant le fort de Vincennes*:

Paris, 9 April 1814
The provisional Government has made all the necessary arrangements in order that the convention, by which it was promised that no troops of the Allied armies will occupy the fort of Vincennes and that no munitions of any character whatsoever will be taken away, may be executed with the utmost fidelity. It had at first been a question of placing in the fort, as a garrison, the National Guard of Paris, of which *Monsieur* Daumesnil would have retained the command, because it had been the intention to employ Line troops of the army. A fresh agreement will be reached with the commanding general of the Allied armies, Prince Schwarzenberg, so that the plan for the occupation of the fort of Vincennes by the National Guard may be changed, and that there will remain two hundred men of the present garrison under the command of *Monsieur* Daumesnil.

Le Prince de Bénévent
Le Duc de Dalberg
Le Gal. Comte De Beurnonville
L'abbé De Montesquiou
For the Provisional Government
DuPont (de Nemours) Lte. Gal.[10]

Such was the provisional government that Talleyrand, the Prince of

---

9   Clairval, *Daumesnil*, p. 168.
10 Desclozeaux archives.

Bénévent (Benavente) and master intriguer, had cobbled together.

The contrast in tone between Dupont's direct, almost harshly phrased orders to Daumesnil in his letter of 5 April and the tactfully couched language of the government's letter of the 9th reflects Talleyrand's appreciation of the fact that kid gloves were an essential requirement when dealing with this unpredictable and strong-willed general, whose nerves as a gambler were no less remarkable than his courage on the battlefield. When you've cheerfully risked your life on scores of battlefields for the sake of shining in the eyes of a man you idolize, and come away with nothing worse than a missing leg, having to negotiate single-handedly with powerful opponents, however lofty, would not be apt to shake a battle-tested temperament.

Just what, then, had happened? This mere brigadier general with one wooden leg had stated his determination, in the face of heavy pressure by representatives of the Tsar of Russia, the King of Prussia, and the Emperor of Austria, and demands and cajoling by the of the government of France—such as it was—all backed by the threat of the employment of overwhelming military force, to stand his ground, and he had won both of his demands. We have no record of his reaction to the receipt of that letter, but it must have been a mixture of quiet exultation, heartfelt relief, and cautious concern as to whether or not those conciliatory phrases would prove to be true or false. His conditions having been met, he would now accept the white flag of the Bourbons. He seems never to have responded to Talleyrand's suggestion that he become a member of the provisional government, since he recognized what lay behind it, and had no intention of being taken in by it. As for Talleyrand, if he had ever meant the proposal seriously, he was obviously glad to drop it, when it was clear that it was no longer a useful idea.

On 12 April the blockade was raised. The occupation of Paris would last until June. During those months the people of Paris coined a new phrase: rather than saying, "Let's go to Vincennes!" they would say, "Let's go to France!" The foundation for Daumesnil's emerging as a national hero had been laid.

It should not be thought, however, that Daumesnil's resistance to an attempt by the invading Allied forces to take over the fortress under his command was unique. It seems fair to say that there was not a fortress, or fortified town, on the frontiers of France that, when summoned to surrender, did so without firing one shot. A few of the more noteworthy examples of refusal to accept such demands will serve to demonstrate that few commanders, finding themselves faced with such summonses, were prepared to accede readily to them.

In Soissons, Major Gérard, with an assortment of some 1,500 *voltigeurs, tirailleurs,* scout-lancers, National Guards, and 150 gunners, had been besieged since 20 March by 20,000 Prussians, with 60 guns. Despite bombardment and repeated attacks, Gérard refused to surrender, and even ordered a successful sortie on 28 March. When Prussian General von Borstell led his brigade from Holland to Soissons and posted it in the vicinity of the city's gates, on 3 April Major Braun, of the Young Guard, took 500 of his men out the gates and drove the Prussian outposts back on their main body. Repeated efforts to persuade Gérard to surrender the city were summarily rejected, and it was not until 15 April that an armistice was concluded. Finally, on 4 May Gérard notified the city council that the siege had been lifted.

In Compiègne, Major Lecomte, an old grenadier of the Consular Guard, who had been sent there with 500 *voltigeurs* and 24 gunners of the Guard to help the town's garrison resist attacks by von Bülow's corps, replied in the same manner that Daumesnil had, when called upon to surrender, saying that the town would capitulate "when the Emperor so ordered." When he learned on 3 April of the fall of Paris, he capitulated.

In Belfort, the siege would drag on until 16 April, and on the same day Huningue, which had been under siege since 21 December, opened its gates to the invaders. It would be 21 April before General Marulaz, commanding in Besançon, agreed to an armistice with the Austrian commander, the Prince of Lichtenstein, and the siege was finally lifted on 2 May. In the north, at the end of March the border fortresses were still held by their garrisons, and on the 31st General Maison, with Barrois' Young Guard division, Castex's 900 Horse Grenadiers, a Line division, and the garrison of Antwerp, which had fought its way out of that city, defeated the two Prussian corps of Thielmann and the Prince of Saxe-Weimar near Courtrai.

Davout had been blockaded in Hamburg since January of 1814, defending it with 30,000 men against three times as many Russians, commanded by General Bennigsen. When on 15 April a Danish officer brought a letter from Bennigsen telling Davout that Louis XVIII had been recognized by the French senate as the sovereign of France, and asking the marshal what "his dispositions" would be, Davout replied, "I am unable to respond to this letter other than a simple statement of reception; a man of honor does not regard himself as released from his oaths of fidelity, because his sovereign may have suffered reverses." Negotiations for the surrender of Hamburg dragged in for another month, and it was only on a direct order from Louis XVIII that Davout finally led his men out of Hamburg on 27 May, and back to France.[11]

Bayonne had been under siege by a combined British-Spanish-Portuguese army under Wellington's command since 27 February. After the entry of the Allies into Paris and Napoleon's abdication had become known in Bayonne on 11 April, the British siege commander, General Hope, informed the governor of Bayonne, *général de division* Pierre Thouvenot, that war between France and England had ceased. The

---

11 Full details of these events may be found in Gallaher's *The Iron Marshal*, from which this information is drawn.

governor refused to take that communication into account, stating that he only took orders from his own commander, Marshal Soult. On12 April Hope sent to Thouvenot as an emissary a French officer, who had arrived from Paris announcing the return of the Bourbons, but he had no better luck than Hope's first parliamentary, although the governor hinted to him that the British "would hear from him before long."

It evidently didn't occur to the British that that remark was an indication of forthcoming action on the part of the garrison, so they simply settled down to maintain a passive blockade until the situation could be sorted out at a higher level. When Thouvenot launched a three-pronged attack on British positions at three o'clock on the morning of the 14th, the British were caught completely off guard. In the ensuing fierce fighting, General Hope was wounded and captured. By the time the French withdrew into the Bayonne citadel at seven o'clock, the Allied army had lost 1,173 men, including 900 killed or wounded, and 273 prisoners. French killed and wounded were identical with those of the Allies.

Firing from the citadel on Allied positions continued until 21 April, when an officer sent by Soult informed the garrison of a truce concluded between Soult and Wellington. In a ceremony on the 28th, the splendid tricolor flying above the fortress was replaced by a very small and rather dirty white flag of the Bourbons. Witnesses reported that the cannon firing a salute at that moment were charged with sand and mud, as a final expression of the garrison's contempt for the authority to which circumstances had forced them to submit.[12] It was the fourteenth siege in Bayonne's history.

What is one to make of such a seemingly purposeless and futile action, costing hundreds of lives on both sides? Pride must have played an important role in it—a desire to demonstrate that, despite circumstances beyond their control, they were every bit as good soldiers as their British opponents, against whom they had been pitted for long years. Perhaps a hope-against-hope that, somehow, Napoleon would manage to put things right again was part of it. In fact, during the One Hundred Days, Thouvenot once again was made governor in Bayonne. His defense of Bayonne in 1814 won for him the honor of having his name carved on the south face of the Arc de Triomphe.

Citing these instances of resistance on the part of commanders of fortresses guarding France's frontiers in 1814 in no way detracts from the significance of Daumesnil's successful defiance of the Allies in both 1814 and 1815, because critically important factors differentiated the case of Vincennes from all the others:

* Daumesnil's motivation was to ensure that what was, in essence,

---

12 *Carnet de la Sabretache, Nouvelle Série No. 71, 1er Trimestre 1984.*

national treasure would not fall into foreign hands, and he achieved that goal,

* he never did capitulate, though all the others eventually did,
* Vincennes was on the outskirts of the nation's capital, where its resistance inspired the Parisians, and served as a constant reminder to the Allied leaders that there were limits to their power,
* and, in both instances, the summons to surrender Vincennes came not from field commanders of the Allied armies, but directly from the heads of the Allied powers and the French government.

In both 1814 and 1815, only Daumesnil would not surrender, and in both cases his antagonists were forced to yield to his unshakable determination and superior psychological skills. As we shall see, there would be still a third instance in which, by sheer power of character and personality, he successfully faced down a challenge to his authority and responsibilities.

CHAPTER SEVENTEEN
THE TIGHTROPE

Despite the favorable outcome of the confrontation between Daumesnil and the provisional government, backed by the Allies, it must have been clear to him that all would not be smooth sailing from that point on. If he had any illusions on that score, they must have been dispelled by this letter from the 3rd Division of the Ministry of War, dated12 April:

General,
The intention of the provisional Government is that the garrison of the fort of Vincennes be reduced to 200 men, not including the detachments of the 7th and 15th companies of artillery workmen, who will continue to be part of it. The choice of the officers and troops who will make up the garrison is yours. The battalion of National Guards of the Department of Seine et Oise will deposit their arms in the fort, and will be sent to Versailles, where they will be discharged. The same will be done with the detachment of National Guards of Deux-Sèvres, which will be sent to Niort, where they will also be discharged.

As for the surplus of troops of all arms, who will no longer be part of the garrison of of Vincennes, you will send them to the 6th army corps, commanded by Marshal Marmont, at Meulan. I ask, General, that you report to me the execution of this arrangement, and send me as soon as possible the list of officers, and the number of troops who will definitely make up the garrison of the Fort of Vincennes, and the strength of those that you deduct from it.
For the minister and by his order,
The secretary general of the Department of War."[1]

---

1 Desclozeaux archives.

"Just in case you're wondering who's in charge now, General," the tone of that letter, signed by an underling at the ministry, seemed to say. At least, Daumesnil's little family was re-united, and Léonie's fears set to rest for the moment, although uncertainty as to what lay in their future over-shadowed the lives of the young couple.

On 30 May the Treaty of Paris had been signed, by Talleyrand for France, Castlereagh for England, Nesselrode for Russia, Metternich for Austria, and Hardenberg for Prussia. With some minor exceptions, France now returned to its frontiers of 1 January 1792, and the Allied forces began their withdrawal. Blücher went off to England, where he was received by cheering crowds, and, in his General Orders of 14 June, Wellington stated his intention of returning to England.

Although Daumesnil had successfully faced down the Allied Powers and the provisional government by an act of courage for which the latter should have been grateful, there seems to have been a feeling among France's new leaders that the legitimacy and prestige of the restored monarchy had somehow been diminished by this instance of an independent-minded individual's apparent defiance of their authority. The popular approval of Daumesnil's principled actions no doubt fed this concern. As a consequence, those authorities began to employ tactics calculated to weaken, and even to undermine, his position.

Meanwhile, Daumesnil's prickly relations with the Vincennes mayor, Champfort, continued to have their ups and downs. In mid-May it happened that 25 Russian military musicians were passing through Vincennes and apparently in need of lodging, so the mayor and the secretary of the fortress took it on themselves to billet the men with some residents of Vincennes. When Daumesnil heard about this he was furious, and had his *adjutant major* fire off a letter to the mayor telling him that the commune of Vincennes should never give lodging to foreign troops without being authorized by the French government, the commandant of the First military division, or the governor of Vincennes. Champfort wrote to the Minister of War, saying "He insulted me, and said that he was going to have me arrested. But I was surprised to see him beat the secretary of the fort with his cane."

Several weeks later the Duc de Berry[2] came to Vincennes to review the garrison, and, on the instructions of the king, presented to the mayor, his deputy, and six officers of the National Guard the Order of the Lily (*Lys*). This, in fact, had been done on Daumesnil's recommendation, perhaps as a fence-mending gesture. In any case, on 1 June the mayor wrote as follows to the governor:

I could not be more appreciative of the interest that you were been kind enough to to take with respect to His Highness the Duke of

---

2   The younger son of the *Comte d'Artois*, the brother of Louis XVI, whom the *Comte* succeeded as Charles X.

Berry as concerns the officers of the National Guard of Vincennes, my assistant and myself. I thank you in the name of all for the favor that you have done them. In my own case, I assure you that such a gesture will never be effaced from my memory.[3]

Nonetheless, when three months later Daumesnil and a few friends went hunting in the forest of Vincennes the day before the hunting season opened, Champfort wrote to the King's prosecutor of the magistrate's court of the Department complaining about it, and enclosing a statement of Daumesnil's apparently justifying his action. In early October that official wrote a mollifying letter back to both, apparently having no desire to get in between these two disputants and hoping to put this trivial matter to rest. For all we know, that was the end of the matter. Perhaps the matter was simply evidence of Daumesnil's increasing sensitivities about his prerogatives, the more he saw them being gnawed away at by a hostile administration.

One measure adopted by the Ministry of War that greatly disturbed Daumesnil was the rotation on a monthly basis of the composition of the garrison, employing for that purpose troops under the direct command of different staffs headquartered in Paris. He expressed his concern for the effect which he considered that practice had on the security of the fortress in this letter to the minister:

Monseigneur,
By a decree of 16 March 1808 the château of Vincennes was in-cluded in the number of fortified places, and created by the same decree an Imperial barracks. I was named governor of that place on 2 February 1812. My letters patent provided that I would only correspond with the Minister of War and the Colonel General of the Guard. Since that time I have received no other instructions.

In a fort as important as Vincennes, which is a depot for arms and munitions, I believe, Monseigneur, that a permanent garrison is essential. The present garrison is relieved every month, and receives its orders directly from different chiefs and generals in Paris, which is contrary to the law, in conformance with Title 34 of the law of 1 March 1768.

I beg Your Excellence to kindly provide new instructions, and to be certain that I shall not fail to execute those orders.
With the greatest respect ...[4]

This appeal, not surprisingly, seems to have been ignored, or, at least, gone unanswered, since there was no change in the practice in question. Whatever other questions he raised with the ministry were either

3 This is from a copy of a letter in the Clairval collection, the original being in Vincennes town hall.
4 S.H.A.T., Daumesnil files.

disregarded, or met with ill will on the part of the authorities. When the Allies had been closing in on Paris, the directors of the state prison in the château's keep had released the few prisoners there, destroyed the police records, locked up the entire keep, and departed. The then Minister of War, Clarke, had ordered that the keep be turned over to the artillery. Daumesnil had asked for the keys to the keep, but his request had been ignored, so when the Duc de Berry had asked to visit the keep, Daumesnil had been unable to show it to him. A considerable number of officers without assignments had been sent to Vincennes, but there were no apartments in which to lodge them, and many of the people in the village of Vincennes has closed their homes and moved away, so billeting these surplus officers in their homes was not possible.

Throughout the summer, the initial euphoria with which the French population had greeted the return of peace to their lives had begun to dissipate, as it became increasingly clear that, in Talleyrand's famous phrase, the returned émigrés had forgotten nothing, and learned nothing. It seemed that the split between the old and the new France, which the Revolution had created, was now re-emerging, and in a more virulent form. Ultraloyalists, led by the Comte d'Artois, were plotting the abrogation of the Charter—which Louis XVIII had "granted" the people—rather than accepting it, and the restoration of royal absolutism. There were rumors of conspiracies among the serving military.

By autumn, Louis XVIII had become dissatisfied with the performance of Dupont as Minister of War, on the grounds that he was insufficiently authoritative, so in the beginning of December he replaced him with Soult. A man of a hard temperament and almost brutal character, Soult had earned for himself among the soldiers the nickname, *Bras-de-Fer* (Arm of Iron), and it was that quality which had recommended him to the king, who felt the need to reestablish discipline in the army. At a review at Fontainebleau on 25 July the Duc de Berry's rather clownish attempts to ingratiate himself with the re-christened Grenadiers and Chasseurs of the Old Guard—now the Grenadiers and Chasseurs of France—by aping Napoleon's gestures of familiarity with the soldiers had been received frostily, despite a wholesale distribution of Orders of the Lily, and the Duke had come away from the scene fuming.

Jean-de-Dieu Soult, who had been quick to demonstrate his royalist zeal after Napoleon's abdication, was equally prompt in taking actions designed to quell any perceived disloyal tendencies among the officers and men of the army. The arrival in Vincennes of large numbers of officers without assignments, noted above, was doubtless a result of a measure issued by Soult banning all unemployed officers from Paris. He placed an additional 700 officers on half-pay. All of his promotions to the ranks of generals went to émigrés and *chouans*.[5] General Exelmans had been

---

5   French counter-revolutionaries in the Vendée.

appointed Inspector General of Cavalry, but when a letter that he had written to Murat was intercepted, he was arrested and imprisoned, but then acquitted after a trial.

Discontent within the army had become so palpable by this time that there was serious concern within the government and around the king that a revolt might erupt within the military. The continuing popularity of *la Jambe de Bois* among the Parisian population, as well as within the army, made him appear to be a possible rallying point for the growing unrest. In such an event, control of the arsenal that Vincennes constituted, crammed full of arms and munitions as it was, would be absolutely vital. While scrupulously accepting and executing the orders emanating from the ministry, Daumesnil made no secret of his continuing attachment to the deposed emperor. Consequently, the members of the government felt themselves unable to rely on his willingness to follow orders, which might be contrary to his personal inclinations, in the event of a revolt. The circumstances seemed to demand that a royalist of complete dependability be installed in Vincennes. However, the removal of the present governor had to be accomplished in a manner which would not risk provoking a strong public reaction.

It's not clear whether it was on his own initiative, or in response to instructions from the government, but, in any case, at the end of December Soult eliminated the position of governor of Vincennes, thereby technically removing the justification for Daumesnil's remaining as the Vincennes commander. Nominated on 24 December to replace him, but simply as *commandant de la place*—commander of the fort—was the Marquis de Puivert,[6] who had been promoted only three days previously to the rank of *maréchal de camp*, the royalist rank equivalent to *général de brigade*, which was also by now Daumesnil's proper title. Vincennes was not unfamiliar to the marquis, a former émigré, who had been compromised in the Cadoudal plot,[7] and had spent ten years in state prisons, including the keep of the Vincennes château. So there was considerable irony in his appointment. At the same time, it was a stunning act of royal ingratitude to the man who had prevented an immensely valuable national asset from falling into foreign hands. In her diary, Léonie

---

6   Bernard Emmanuel Jacques de Roux Marquis de Puivert (Puyvert),1755–1832. In 1788, commissioned as a *major en second* in the Guyenne infantry regiment. Emigrated in 1790, upon his return to France, was arrested in 1804, and held in various prisons until April 1814. In December 1814, reinstated in the army with rank of *maréchal de camp*. On 24 December 1814, named commandant of the fort of Vincennes. 20 March 1815, relieved of command. 9 December 1815, re-appointed governor of Vincennes. 5 August 1830, relieved of functions as governor of Vincennes and retired.

7   George Cadoudal, a Chouan chief, who repeatedly refused overtures from Bonaparte after the repression of the Vendée. In 1800 his first attempt to kill the First Consul with "an infernal machine" (i.e., a bomb) failed, and he fled abroad. In 1803 he returned to France, and continued plotting against Bonaparte. Finally, in 1804 he was arrested, tried, and executed.

describes the manner in which the news of his replacement was made known to Daumesnil.

> That day my father was dining with us. Just as we were about to sit down at the table, General Despinois, commander of the 1st division, and the Marquis de Puivert were announced.
>
> The former was a big officer, with an air as haughty as it was severe; the latter appeared to me completely ridiculous. As soon as the customary greetings had been exchanged, M. Despinois gave Daumesnil a dispatch from the Ministry of War and, although in similar circumstances my husband would not easily have let his emotions show, hearing him give the duty officer the order to assemble the garrison under arms, I realized that it had to do with a very serious matter. What's more, Daumesnil didn't leave my father and me in doubt for very long, since, turning to us, he informed us that the purpose of this measure was simply to make the Marquis de Puivert known as his replacement.
>
> "But, my dear Ninette," he added, "since this could take rather long, I'm concerned about our stomachs, and especially your father's. So ask these gentlemen to share our meal.
>
> Then he repeated more quietly, squeezing my hand, "I beg of you."
>
> I will confess that it required a great effort on my part to extend that invitation. After dinner, M. Despinois and M. de Puivert went to the great court of the château to have the last governor of Vincennes acknowledged, in the name of His Majesty Louis XVIII.
>
> At first silence and consternation greeted this order of the day, like a death sentence for each soldier of the garrison, then, from time to time, a confused murmer of voices, muffled by fear.
>
> This scene took place beneath the windows of our apartment: I could see and hear everything. Daumesnil was careful not to show himself: he was too prudent, and knew that his presence would spoil everything. He realized that he must leave his fortress as soon as possible.

Daumesnil immediately left the château with his father-in-law, and ended up at the apartments of the Banque de France, rue de la Vrillière, without any idea of what was in store for him. He wondered whether he was going to be put on half-pay, like so many of his comrades-in-arms. Léonie had remained in Vincennes to manage moving the family out of the château. When one day she wanted to take little Léon out in the small garden that Daumesnil had created for him, she found the gate guarded by a sentry, who turned her and her son away.

Daumesnil had never received compensation for the expenses that he had incurred in taking up his position as governor in Vincennes and in fulfilling his duties there, and now he determined to make another effort to be appropriately reimbursed. To that end he began his letter to the Minister of War by recalling in unvarnished language his services to France:

Monseigneur,

I made 22 campaigns, captured eight flags, more than twenty cannon, and four generals. At Aboukir I took one of the horse-tail standards of the Captain Pacha, who commanded the Ottoman army. I participated in all the combats and all the battles fought by the French army until the Battle of Wagram, where I lost a leg.

These facts are recorded in the rolls of the regiment of guides or *chasseurs à cheval* of the Guard and in the War offices. In compensation for my services I have received a pension of 600 francs from the Cisalpine Republic for having been one of the first across the bridge at Arcola; I have had one of the first sabers of honor given in France,[8] and a second saber of honor given by the King of Spain,[9] 2,000 francs on Mont-Napoleon, 3,000 francs on the Emperor's privy purse, 8,000 francs in Illyria, 8,000 francs in Hanover, 7,000 francs on the Little Advertisements. On 2 March 1812 I was named governor for life of the château of Vincennes, with an allowance of 25,000 francs. At that time I had married the daughter of Baron Garat, director of the Banque de France. In order to establish and furnish in an appropriate manner the residence which had been assigned to me, I had to expend her dowry and the modest funds available to me.

In accordance with the Emperor's orders given to the Duke of Feltre[10] by Count Daru, there was to have been established an account of 400,000 francs for the governor's residence. The Duke of Frioul[11] and the Duke of Feltre promised me to make advances from it, with which I would be reimbursed. I hope that Your Excellency will be so good as to have a report made on that matter and see that justice is done to me. I rely entirely on the kindness with which (Your Excellency) has already been deigned to honor me, up until the present time.

I am, with profound respect, Monseigneur, the very humble and obedient servant of Your Excellency,

Baron Daumesnil[12]

---

8 Awarded to Daumesnil for his actions at Saint-Jean-d'Acre.

9 This second *sabre d'honneur* was presented to Daumesnil by the then King Joseph in 1808, as a reward for his conduct during the campaign in Spain.

10 General Clarke.

11 Duroc.

12 This is from a copy of a letter in the Clairval collection. The original is in the Daumesnil files, S.H.A.T. archives.

This cannot have been an easy letter for the proud officer to write, and yet his own habitually off-hand attitude toward financial matters was to some degree responsible for the family's now straitened circumstances. With Napoleon's deposition, it seems most probable that the various pensions that Daumesnil identifies in his letter would have been cut off. Mention of the Emperor's privy purse among them must have prompted a few sardonic smiles among the minister's staff. It should be noted that the allowance of 400,000 francs had not been intended for Daumesnil's personal benefit, but had been designated by the Emperor for the preparation of quarters suitable for the accommodation of prominent or distinguished individuals, by which he presumably meant such individuals as deposed monarchs, whose continued presence in their countries was deemed undesirable.

The cloud of uncertainty hanging over the family was lifted when a proposal by Marshal Soult to appoint Daumesnil to the position of senior commandant of the *arrondissement* of Condé was approved by the king on 31 December. Condé sur l'Escaut, a small fortified town on the Belgian border at the confluence of the Escaut and Hainaut rivers and midway between Valenciennes and Mons, had passed into the possession of François de Bourbon late in the 15th century, and its name had been associated with that branch of the Bourbon family ever since. It is mildly ironic that, when he was living in Turin in 1790 as an émigré, Puivert was offered a position on the general staff of his army by the Prince of Condé, leader of the loyalist émigrés.

From the government's point of view, this appointment had two particular advantages: it moved the popular *Jambe de Bois* well away from the Paris scene, while leaving him in a location where surveillance of his activities would be relatively easy; and it placed him in an assignment which, on the face of it, could be seen as appropriate to his rank as a *maréchal de camp*, rather than risking a strong public reaction which might be triggered by putting him on half-pay. Daumesnil's reaction to this action must have been a combination of relief that he had, at least, been retained on active service, and resentment and humiliation at being shipped off to the provinces, while a nonentity moved into Vincennes, still glowing in the aura of its successful defense by Daumesnil.

1815

It is not clear when Puivert actually took up his post at Vincennes. On 4 January 1815 he received formal confirmation of that assignment in a letter dated 31 December 1814, naming him commandant of the fortress of Vincennes. It seems reasonable to assume that he waited until Léonie had finished "packing out" of the Daumesnil's quarters. What is certain is that Daumesnil himself did not return to the château after that fateful dinner.

On 10 January Daumesnil received a reply to his claim for reimbursement for expenses that he had incurred during his service as governor at Vincennes. Couched in the characteristically bureaucratic language of all finance officers from time immemorial, it read as follows:

General,
His Excellency the Minister of War has received your undated letter relating to a claim which seems to concern expenses that you incurred in the lodgings that you occupy in the château of Vincennes.

In order that His Excellency may rule on this claim as you wish, it is necessary that you kindly inform him of its nature in a more precise manner, all the more so because, at the time of your installation in the government of Vincennes, the Minister having granted you an allowance of an initial 4,000 francs, and an annual sum of 1,000 francs, it may not be presumed that your claim relates to that subject. His Excellency asks that you give him detailed information, after which he will be able to judge with respect to your request,
Receive, etc.

That response was so far from what Daumesnil had asked for that he may well have thrown up his hands and decided that his attempt to be reimbursed was a lost cause.

Daumesnil was hurried along to Condé by the receipt of this letter, dated 12 January 1815, from the chief of the general staff of the 1st Military Division:

General,
His Excellency the Minister of War wishes to advise *M. le Gouverneur* that the king having named you commandant of the *arrondissement* of Condé, you should make your arrangements to go to your destination at the soonest possible time.

In order that this order of the Minister may be carried out without delay, *M. le Gouverneur,* (he) authorizes you to turn over the command of the château of Vincennes provisionally to Colonel Maurin, if M. de Puivert has not already taken possession of it. At the same time His Excellency asks that you let him know the day of your departure for Condé in order that he may report it to the Minister as His Excellency wishes.
Receive, General … etc.[13]

The awkward bureaucratic wording of this letter—there seems to be a superfluity of "His Excellencies"—doesn't mask its harshness. It was

---

13 Desclozeaux archives.

signed by *Le Comte* Gentil-Saint-Alphonse, *Maréchal de camp* and chief of the general staff.

In a gesture evidently designed to disguise the shabby treatment which been accorded to Daumesnil, on 17 January he was awarded the cross of a *chevalier* of the Order of Saint-Louis. However, he never wore that decoration. Léonie explains that her husband refused to do so, when he realized that, for him to sign his name at the bottom of the document accepting the decoration, he would have to swear an oath of fidelity to the king, which he was unwilling to do.

CHAPTER EIGHTEEN
THE ONE HUNDRED DAYS

Although the north of France was at that time permeated by royalist sympathies, one particular event sparked an outburst of Bonapartism. As noted above, General Exelmans had been arrested on grounds of being in touch with Murat, still King of Naples at that time. His trial in Lille before a council of war had ended with his acquittal, and he had been borne away from the court in triumph by some of the city's citizens.

Anti-royalist pamphlets being distributed by peddlers gave evidence of growing discontent and disillusionment throughout France with the re-stored House of Bourbon. A striking example of such subversive literature is a lampoon entitled "*La Jambe de Bois de Vincennes,* or the Commandant firmly at his post." In exalting Daumesnil's heroism, its author even goes so far as to add to his injuries the loss of an eye. He writes:

> It is at a time when greed and weakness dictate and accept laws that a simple individual raises such a monument to the nation's honor. Oh, traitors! When you have been led astray by hypocrisy, there remains that fortress of Vincennes to accuse you. It constitutes an irrevocable judgment, which has endowed the governor of Vincennes with an immortality, which, one feels, has redoubled one's patriotic confidence in the outcome of the present struggle, when one knows that the warrior with the wooden leg and one eye missing still occupies an important position in our outposts.[1]

However high-flown that language, it is nonetheless an accurate gauge of the popularity which Daumesnil enjoyed among the French people.

As fate would have it, Daumesnil had scarcely had time to settle into his

---

1 Clairval, *Daumesnil*, p. 181.

new post[2] when startling news reached Condé and the commandant of the *arrondissement*. On the first of March, the once-and-future emperor, having sailed from Elba on 26 February aboard the *Inconstant*, had appeared in the Golfe-Juan, and had gone ashore with his veterans near the Gabelle[3] tower in Antibes. At midnight, with General Cambronne leading 50 grenadiers, Napoleon's little column set out for Paris. As officers and men from the Antibes garrison, and half-pay officers who had been drawn to the scene, joined the column, they formed what would soon become known as the "Sacred Battalions." Soon copies of the proclamation that Napoleon had issued before departing from Antibes were being picked up and distributed by travelers and couriers north-bound on the highways, and copied and re-copied as quickly as they were seized by officials and the merely curious. Its language recalled the ringing cadences of Imperial Bulletins:

> Soldiers! In my exile I have heard your voices. Your general, called to the throne by the voice of the people and raised on your shields, has been restored to you—come join him. Reclaim those eagles that you had at Ulm, at Austerlitz, at Jéna, at Eylau, at Friedland, at Tudella, at Eckmühl, at Essling, at Wagram, at Smolensk, at the Moskowa. Victory will march at the pace of a charge. The eagle, with the national colors, will fly from steeple to steeple to the very towers of Notre Dame.[4]

The progression of the steadily swelling column was by no means an uninterrupted triumphal procession, as generals who had risen to glory under Napoleon and then rallied to the Bourbons, perplexed local garrison commanders, uncertain colonels of regiments encountered along the way, and white-haired grenadiers with tears streaming down their cheeks, struggled to reconcile their emotional attachment to the Empire with their oaths of loyalty to the king, and their sense of duty to France. But that progress had the same inevitability as that of a mountain stream racing toward the sea, gathering in its path first pebbles, then stones and rocks, and finally boulders, carrying its burden around or over obstacles until at last its torrential rush deposits its spoil at its eagerly sought goal.

This particular stream, grown to a torrent after twenty drama-filled days of hard marching, deposited its human burden on the steps of the Tuileries at nine in the evening of 20 March, whence that individual was borne on the shoulders of a cheering crowd into the palace. He then made his way, seemingly almost in a hypnotic spell, up the grand staircase to the throne room, where, earlier in the evening, ladies had busied themselves tearing off the white lilies, which had been sewn over the golden bees on the carpet.

---

2   Léonie had remained in her parents' apartments in Paris, with little Léon.

3   The salt tax tower.

4   Johnston, *In the Words of Napoleon*, p. 308.

The previous evening, Louis XVIII had left Paris for Belgium, escorted by his personal guard, but without informing his ministers. Apparently it was a question of *sauve qui peut*. By the 22nd, he had arrived in Lille.

Word of this world-shaking event was slow in reaching Condé, and the first reports reflected the pro-royalist sympathies of northern newspaper editors, whose accounts may well have been deliberately misleading in nature. Napoleon was said to be in flight, abandoned by his soldiers. Soon, however, Daumesnil learned that the seemingly impossible was true: the Emperor had re-taken his throne! He lost no time in hoisting the tricolor above the fortress of Condé. When he learned that other towns in the north were still flying the white flag of the Bourbons, he declared Condé to be in a state of siege, and on the 24th he had this letter sent to the mayor of Condé:

> *Monsieur Le Maire,*
> By virtue of the orders of *M. Le Général de Brigade* Daumesnil *Baron de l'Empire* and commandant at Condé, now placed in a state of siege, the tricolor Flag will be hoisted at once on all towers, steeples, and bell towers.
>   The civil, administrative, and judicial authorities, and the clergy will be brought together in the town hall, where the orders of the existing government contained in the two *Moniteurs* which arrived today will be read, and the tricolor cockade put on. The mayor will see to the execution of all of these measures, for which he will be personally responsible, and will have all of these above-mentioned orders published in the official journal.[5]

This unequivocal document was signed by *Le chevalier* Hochet de la Terrie, *chef de batallion* and *commandant d'armes* of the fort at Condé.

Daumesnil's built-up resentment over the shabby treatment that he had received at the hands of the provisional government and the king burst forth in the wording of that imperative directive, undoubtedly written at his dictation. On the same day, he wrote to the new Minister of War, Marshal Davout, informing him that, since the tricolor was not being flown in the cities neighboring Condé, he had felt it necessary to declare Condé in a state of siege, and to refuse to obey any orders from General de Jumilhac, commandant of the 16th military division, in Lille. He reported further on events in Belgium, informing Davout that the king had been in Tournai on the 23rd.

Daumesnil had been galvanized into spirited action by this extraordinary turn of events. Now he wanted to profit by his strategic location to keep like-minded commanders in the north, as well as the minister in Paris, informed with respect to developments in his vicinity.

---

5 Desclozeaux archives.

On 25 March he sent this report to *Maréchal de camp baron* Lahure, commander of the *arrondissements* of Douai and Cambrai, who re-transmitted it to the minister:

> 25 March Hollain was occupied by two English squadrons, Bruielle is occupied by a larger force, believed to be about 5,000 men.
>
> The enemy has established a camp before Tournai, on the Condé side.
>
> A proclamation published in Tournai asked for 2,000 laborers, to be paid 20 *sols* a day. The engineer colonel is an Englishman named Spieldauer.
>
> The commanding general in Tournai is General Count Dietz, of Brussels. 500 men and 900 artillery horses arrived in Tournai on 22 March.
>
> The enemy is pushing his reconnaissance as far as Bon Secours, and at Peruwel there are 400 men, including 100 Belgian *gendarmes*. Between Peruwel and Kievrin the country was occupied on the 23rd by 15,000 English.
>
> The city of Mons is commanded by Colonel Duvivier, a Belgian by birth and the former commander of the 3rd dragoons. The governor of Mons is an English general. The English have six companies of light artillery and 22,000 men, both infantry and cavalry, at Mons, most of them Belgians and Hanoverians. They have set up an entrenched camp at Mont Pariselle, before Mons, between Lyon and Symphorien.
>
> In all Belgium feelings are running high. The day when the Prince of Nassau was proclaimed king, all the countryside rang with cries of "*Vive l'Empereur.*[6]

Two things are obvious about that report: first, that Daumesnil had quickly organized a useful network of informants; and second, that he was demonstrating to Davout that he was ready to take up once more an active role in the service of the Emperor. Moreover, it seems likely that he realized that the reaction of the Allies to Napoleon's return was very likely to be swift and strong, and that the sooner the Emperor was informed as to the probable character and location of that reaction, the better his chances would be for meeting it successfully.

Let us now return to Vincennes to see what the impact of this extraordinary turn of events has had on the affairs of its new commandant, the Marquis de Puivert.

When the news of Napoleon's landing at Antibes reached Vincennes, Puivert was just beginning to reorganize the garrison. He at once sent to Paris for instructions, but by that time the government had been thrown

---

6 S.H.A.T.,.*Correspondence Générale*, C 16 2.

into complete disarray by Napoleon's rapid march on the capital. At first, the ministry sent Puivert a battalion of the regiment of the Queen, and then a battalion of volunteers made up of medical students. Then, by some inexplicable quirk, he was sent 30 half-pay officers, who could only be a hindrance to him, since their anti-royalist sentiments were well known. On the 17th, he received 250 cannoneers, who had refused to follow General Lallemand, because he had spoken out for the Emperor.

The following day the battalion from the Queen's regiment was ordered to rejoin its regiment, and was replaced by several companies of veterans collected from various places, all of them ill-disposed toward the government. Finally, at midnight on the 19th, a general came to the château with an order from the king, ordering Puivert to take their arms away from the royal volunteers, to relieve them of their cartridges, and to send them to Charenton. The general confided to Puivert that the king had left Paris, and that he didn't want these young men to compromise themselves, so they were to be discharged.

On the morning of the 20th, there only remained in the fortress 400 veterans and a crowd of officers without troops, giving the marquis good cause for concern. The garrison was without bread, food of any other kind, money, or direction. In the rush of events, it had been completely forgotten. Puivert's Wheel of Fortune had taken a sudden downward lurch.

Without any news from Paris, on the morning of the 21st the marquis brought back into the château the 250 artillerymen, who had been lodged in the town of Vincennes, in the hope that, as a consequence of their earlier behaviour, they might afford him some support. In the course of the day, the two battalions of royal volunteers returned from Charenton, and stacked their arms on the glacis of the fort, on either side of the main entrance.

Back in Paris, General Antoine-Eugène Merlin emerged from his residence to see what was happening, and discovered that General Exelmans had seized the Tuileries. Mounting his horse and thinking he might make himself useful, Merlin galloped to the palace, where he found Exelmans in the courtyard. Telling Merlin that Paris was already in their hands, Exelmans added that it was essential, however, to take over Vincennes, where, he said, there were a number of troops who might prove to be troublesome. He urged Merlin to go there in order to seize control of the fortress before Napoleon arrived in Paris. At Merlin's request, Exelmans gave him a written order, reading:

In the name of His Majesty the Emperor, General Baron Merlin is ordered to proceed immediately to the château of Vincennes. He will take command of it and direct the officer now commanding there to leave. The garrison of the château will at once carry out all the orders given to them by General Merlin.

289

Interim Commanding General,
Count Exelmans.[7]

Merlin collected four officers and two gendarmes who happened to be passing by, and with his aide de camp he set out for Vincennes. He knew that Puivert could be counted on to resist his demand, and he had no reliable information about the attitude of the men of the garrison. If the commandant withdrew within the château, Merlin knew he would be unable to execute his mission. Obviously, boldness and bluff would be key ingredients in the tactics he would need to employ.

As Merlin rode through the narrow streets of Vincennes adjacent to the château, some of the town's inhabitants, seeing the riders' tricolor cockades, greeted the men with cries of *"Vive l'Empereur!"* The two battalions of volunteers, who were arrayed before the main gate of the fortress, one to its right, the other to its left, had now taken up their muskets, although those on the left seemed to share some of the enthusiasm of the citizenry.

Galloping up in front of that battalion, Merlin called out, "Who's in charge here?"

"I am," replied a colonel, identifying himself as the Marquis d'Etang.

"Very well, Monsieur le Marquis d'Etang," responded Merlin. "In the name of the Emperor, who has just entered Paris, I order you to stack arms, and to withdraw, with your troops."

The colonel did not refuse to obey Merlin's command, but instead asked for a written order to the same effect. Merlin got down from his horse, took a piece of paper and a pencil, and resting the paper on his hat, wrote out the order and handed it to d'Etang. With that, the battalion dispersed. The second battalion, initially more hostile, soon stood aside, and, after some parleying with other officers who emerged from the fort, Merlin was escorted into the main courtyard, where Puivert, surrounded by his staff, met him.

Merlin stated that, the Emperor having been re-established on the throne, he had come in the Emperor's name to take possession of the keys to the fortress. Puivert replied that, as a man of honor, he could not yield up a fort entrusted to him without resistance, or even firing a shot. Merlin laughed scornfully, saying, "That's something! The Emperor's come from Cannes to Paris without lighting a primer, and you talk about firing a cannon! I hold you responsible for any calamities that may arise from your stubbornness. Besides, you must realize that any resistance would be useless."

As they were speaking, more cries of *"Vive l'Empereur!"* were heard from artillerymen gathered outside the guardroom in which they were meeting, and several of them could be seen tearing up the flag of the Bourbons as others hoisted the tricolor over the keep. Puivert asked for a

---

7   Fossa, *Le château historique de Vincennes*, p. 244–7.

few moments to consult with his staff, and soon found that they were, almost to a man, supporters of Napoleon. He therefore told Merlin that he was prepared to turn over to him the keys and the archives of the château, only asking that he, and whichever officers wished to accompany him, be given passports to cross to the other side of the Loire.

The terms of the capitulation were then drawn up and signed, and, when the garrison had been assembled in the courtyard, Merlin had them swear an oath of fidelity to the Emperor. Only the second battalion of volunteers, made up mostly of law students, refused to be won over. Finally, seeing that they were isolated, the young men departed in the direction of Paris. Towards midnight, Puivert left the château, accompanied by only two officers, one a squadron commander, the other the young Count de Monticot, a junior lieutenant. The next day, in the Emperor's name General Bertrand wrote a letter of congratulations to Merlin.[8]

On 23 March Louis XVIII had recognized the futility—and the personal danger—of remaining any longer on French soil, and had crossed into Belgium. In bidding him farewell, Marshal Macdonald, who had accompanied the king to the frontier, said, "Sire, I shall see you in three months!" Not too far off the mark!

The new Minister of War, Marshal Davout, had sent an aide de camp, *chef d'escadron* Laloy, on a quick tour of the north to gather information regarding conditions in general there, and the military situation in particular. On 27 March Laloy wrote this report to Davout:

Monseigneur,
Everywhere I found the same spirit, the same enthusiasm for the person of His Majesty.

On the 22nd, *M. le général* Daumesnil, governor of Condé, full of enthusiasm for His Majesty, announced to his garrison that henceforth the fort would be defended in the name of the Emperor. He was the first to swear to die, if necessary, for such a splendid cause, and to refuse any demand contrary to the commitment that he had just taken. In the face of this noble fervor on the part of a general, with a limb lost in the defense of the State, soldiers of the 42nd couldn't contain their emotion and broke ranks, surrounding their general, and promising to support him in this noble enterprise. They swore to do so in the name of the Emperor, and at once donned the tricolor cockade.

From that day, Condé was declared to be in a state of siege, and that fort was for the Emperor, even before knowing that France, faithful to His Majesty, had brought him in triumph back to his capital.

---

8   Fossa, *Le château historique de Vincennes, passim.*

Your Excellency will recognize, in this noble devotion, this brave soldier, who, since the first Italian campaign, never left the Emperor, and never ceased to be faithful to him.[9]

Several days later, Daumesnil received the following letter from Marshal Davout:

Paris, 28 March 1815
Monsieur le Général,
The Emperor has been informed that, as of the 22nd, you had announced that the fort would be defended in the name of the Emperor: that you had communicated your enthusiasm and your devotion to the entire garrison of Condé, and that that fort was already for the Emperor, even before knowing that France, faithful to His Majesty, had brought him back in triumph to his capital.

The Emperor has recognized in your conduct a man whom he had honored in Italy, and who, in Vincennes, had attested to his faithfulness to the Emperor by resisting both the arms and the seductions of the enemy, and preserving for our country many cannon and munitions.

The Emperor will have great pleasure in seeing you.[10]

That same day, Davout signed the official document placing Daumesnil in command of the fortress of Vincennes. The text reads: "[The Emperor] having to name a *Maréchal de Camp* to be employed in that capacity in command of the Fort of Vincennes (First military Division) has chosen *M. le Maréchal de Camp* Daumesnil.

That slightly ambiguous wording, "in command of", would be made unambiguous ten days later in the Emperor's decree of 8 April, appointing Daumesnil to his former position of *governor* of Vincennes. It may seem like a distinction without a difference, but it seems to have mattered not only to Daumesnil, but as well to the men who would rule on his position during the Second Restoration, as we shall see.

Still in Condé on the 31st, Daumesnil wrote this letter to the editor of the *Moniteur* in Paris:

I must ask you to correct an error in your issue of the 29th: it is not the 12th regiment which is at Condé, but rather the 42nd of the Line, which I can only praise by citing the quality which characterizes the spirit of this brave regiment.

Sixty brave soldiers, who had the right to retire to their homes because of wounds or length of service, refused to be included

---

9 S.H.A.T, *Correspondance Générale*, C16 2. This report appeared, in almost identical terms, in *Le Moniteur* of 29 March 1815.
10 Mazade, *Correspondance du Maréchal Davout, 1801–1815*, vol 4, p. 376.

among those being mustered out as soon as they learned of the happy arrival in France of His Majesty the Emperor, protesting that they wanted always to remain in his service.

He added to that letter a copy of an "address" to the Emperor, which had been written on the 23rd in behalf of the officers and men of the 42nd regiment, couched in the loftiest terms and most emotional sentiments, swearing to defend "a frontier fort of the greatest importance," and to preserve it for France.[11] However one may view the grandiose language of that letter, there can be little doubt that the emotion which inspired it was genuine. The psychological enthrallment in which "the Little Corporal" held fast those men who had served him, officers and men alike, is a puzzle for the ages.

Although Daumesnil has left no record of his reactions to this sudden reversal of his fortunes, it is not difficult to imagine what they must have been: certainly elation, at the prospect of being able once again to serve the individual for whom his admiration knew no bounds, and no doubt a sense of satisfaction at seeing put down those vindictive officers, who had bedeviled his existence for the final six months of his stay in Vincennes. But he was not a vengeful man, and a desire or intent to revenge himself on those who had humiliated him does not seem to have animated him, with one possible exception, which we shall examine in due course. Nor was he naïve with respects to the long-term prospects for Napoleon's retaining his grasp on the governance of France, in the face of Allied determination to prevent his doing so. Nonetheless, Daumesnil's ingrained determination to do his duty to the fullest extent of his capabilities was, in all probability, strengthened by this extraordinary political convulsion.

Léonie's diary does not reveal her sentiments at this point in their lives, but they may well have echoed that laconic phrase of Napoleon's mother at the time of his coronation, when some one gushed to her about how marvelous it must be to see her son crowned emperor. "*Pourvu que ça dure!*" (Provided it lasts!) was her response. No doubt Léonie was glad to see her husband once again raised in the eyes of the world to the position of eminence that he had won for himself, but she, too, must have had some misgivings about its permanence. Whatever the case, she now had to occupy herself with the practical problems of packing up whatever of their household effects they had brought from Vincennes to the apartment of her parents in Paris, and re-installing the little family in the château there. (She and Léon had not gone to Condé.) She was no longer the shy 17-year-old who had married a wounded hero, however, but a mature young mother, who had endured uncomplainingly the buffetings of political adversity. So, resignedly she set about her humble tasks, while her

---

11 The text of the address is shown at Annex E below.

husband came down to Paris to pay his respects to the Emperor.

It seems probable that, at that time, the Emperor expressed to Daumesnil his intention of strengthening the fortress of Vincennes, so that it might serve as a formidable point of defense on the eastern approaches to Paris, since in the middle of May he ordered General Sylvain Valée, commander-in-chief of the artillery reserve in Paris, to furnish Daumesnil with the means of increasing the armament of the fortress. The ramparts were to be provided with all the cannon deemed necessary for its defense, and carriages were to be constructed for the naval guns on hand.

Daumesnil lost no time in resuming the rigorous pace of activity that had marked his previous tenure in Vincennes. Now there was even greater urgency than there had been the previous year for ensuring that the fortress was as prepared as possible to sustain an attack, including possible sabotage by dissident plotters. On 19 May he issued an "Order of the Day" containing, in eleven articles, very precise language specifying in great detail those persons who might, and might not, be admitted to the fortress, and under what conditions, and by whom. One article forbade smoking within the fortress and instructed all soldiers to take the pipe away from any one violating that order. Other articles specified the hours for the opening and closing and the raising and lowering of doors and drawbridges of the fort.

The rigor of this order suggests that, upon arriving back in Vincennes, Daumesnil had found an unacceptable laxness in the control of the comings and goings of military and civilian personnel within the fort's confines, which may well have been exacerbated by the Emperor's orders to General Valée to augment the establishment's armaments, which would have brought large numbers of artillery officers and artisans to Vincennes. It seems probable that the risk of attempts at sabotage weighed on Daumesnil's mind.

On 25 May, in the midst of his efforts to reconstitute an army capable of meeting and defeating the immense Allied force being gathered north of the border, Napoleon nonetheless found the time to visit Vincennes in order to satisfy himself that the measures that he had prescribed for refurbishing the château's armaments were being put into effect as he had ordered. Nothing escaped his attention. He found 120 pieces of field artillery without carriages, and ordered that they at once be completed.

"The château must, above all else, be the principal artillery depot," he said. "Leave only indispensable housing. The chapel can contain another 200,000 muskets." A covered road was to be built around the entire curtain wall, thus providing additional shelter for troops and artillery pieces. In case of war, the roof of the keep should be replaced by a platform for cannon capable of reaching the gates of the capital." Vincennes must play an effective role in the defense of Paris," he noted.

Daumesnil soon discovered that his concern about security within the château had not been misplaced. While making his rounds on June first, he found two soldiers of the train, who had apparently broken into the tower of the reservoir, and had them placed under arrest. As he continued his rounds, he came upon a pile of straw and some burning rags near the battery at the Paris tower, adjacent to the door to the powder magazine in that tower. The following day he wrote to General Durrieu, on the general staff of the Minister of War:

> General,
> I take the liberty of observing, General, that the fort of Vincennes cannot be guarded by a single company of veterans 68 men strong, and that there should be at least 300 men permanently assigned.
> There are a number of entrances leading to the ramparts, and it would be necessary for the engineers to close them up without delay. None of the requests that I have made in this regard having yet been granted, I renew them today, assuming that the necessity for satisfying them will be appreciated.[12]

That got action out of the general staff. Durrieu told an aide to write to the minister explaining the situation, noting that "This affairs permits no delay, the fort of Vincennes being of the greatest importance." An order went to General Pierre Hulin, military governor of Paris, telling him to send a company of veterans from the Paris garrison to Vincennes. General Deponthon was instructed to send an officer to Vincennes to coordinate all these actions with Daumesnil, and to report to the minister.

When word of the disastrous outcome of the Battle of Waterloo reached Vincennes, there was no doubt in Daumesnil's mind as to what he should expect. On the 21st, he wrote to the Minister of War:

> *Monseigneur,*
> Your Excellency knows the devotion that I shall always hold for His Majesty. The enemy will only enter my fort when I am dead. I must ask Your Excellency to authorize me to have the woods of Vincennes cut down. It could be of a great advantage for the defense of Paris, and they are only a danger to that of the fort.

On the 24th, Daumesnil again appealed to the minister for orders and additional troops:

> *Monseigneur,*
> Not having any orders up until now regarding provisioning of the fort of Vincennes, and believing that in the present circumstances such a measure is necessary, I dare to ask you, Monseigneur, to inform me as to your intentions in that regard, and also to decide on

---

12 This, and the correspondence below, is in the S.H.A.T. archives, *Campagne de France, Correspondance*, C16 22 and *Correspondance Générale*, C16 23.

the number of troops which should make up my garrison, which, up until now, consists of two companies of veterans.

On 26 June the Minister of War's staff gave him this report:

The garrison of Vincennes consisting only of two companies of veterans, the general commanding the fort has requested, in a letter of 24 June, that he be sent additional forces. It is suggested to His Excellency that there be placed in Vincennes a battalion of retired soldiers, which has arrived in Paris from Dijon, consisting of 18 officers and 478 non-commissioned officers and men.

The circumstances seem to require that Vincennes immediately be prepared for an attack or surprise on the part of the enemy. The artillery and the engineering divisions wish to propose to His Excellency the measures necessary to complete the arming and the fortification of the fort. It would, in addition, be advantageous to declare it in a state of siege. A report to that effect for the executive commission of the provisional government is submitted for His Excellency's approval.

In turn, the minister wrote to the members of the executive commission of the provisional government on the same day:

Messieurs,
I have just given orders that the garrison of Vincennes be reinforced with a battalion of 500 retired soldiers, and that the armament and the fortification of the fort be completed as soon as possible. The importance of Vincennes and the present circumstances have seemed to me to require these precautionary measures.
I believe it would also be advantageous to declare this fort in a state of siege, and I have the honor to submit the attached proposal to that effect.

Although the Commission of Government prepared a decree declaring Vincennes to be in a state of siege, it seems not to have been signed. However, on 28 June Paris was declared to be. "Only the approaches to the capital will be defended."

On 27 June the Minister of War had ordered that a detachment of the 3rd company of pontoneers, consisting of 18 men, go to Vincennes. The next day he ordered that the battalion of retired soldiers from Dijon be sent to Vincennes. On the 30th, the commandant of the Fort of Vitry informed the Minister of War that that the munitions, which had been stored in the fort for the army, had been sent by ship to Vincennes the previous day.

The following day the minister wrote to Daumesnil to inform him that he was sending him the battalion from Dijon, but that order was changed so that it was the 2nd battalion from Cher, which was instead sent to Vincennes.

The critical event in the political background, against which Daumesnil was doing his best to prepare for a siege, was, of course, Napoleon's abdication on the 22nd. On the 21st he had given serious thought to appealing to the Chamber of Peers and the Chamber of Deputies to support him, or to setting up a dictatorship and declaring France to be in a state of siege, but Fouché and Lafayette had quickly moved to make any such moves on Napoleon's part impossible.

On the 25th Napoleon had left the Elysée and gone to Malmaison. Hearing that Blücher, two days march ahead of the British, had arrived at Gonesse with 50,000 men, Napoleon proposed to the provisional government that he be given an opportunity to crush Blücher before the British arrived on the scene. "I give my word, as a general, a soldier, and a citizen," he wrote, "not to retain the command one hour after the certain and brilliant victory that I promise to deliver." Fouché didn't bother to reply, although he did place a frigate at Napoleon's disposal, since he knew that Napoleon had thought of escaping to the United States. It was entirely in character of that endlessly devious individual for him to alert the British at the same time as to Napoleon's possible intentions.

There was one bittersweet moment during Napoleon's brief stay in Malmaison, when Marie Walewska came with her son to say good-bye and then begged to be able to accompany him. Saying, "We'll see," he put her off, not wishing to further complicate the already extraordinarily complex question of what his ultimate destination was to be.

Concerned that Napoleon might attempt to rejoin the army, the bulk of which was now beginning to arrive in the vicinity of Paris, the Commission of Government had given the unwelcome responsibility for ensuring that Napoleon remain in Malmaison to *général de division* Nicolas Beker, who was at that time the representative of Puy-de-Dôme in the Chamber of Deputies. Although Beker had had a falling out with Napoleon in 1809 over some comments he had made hostile to the war in Spain, after lingering in disgrace he had been restored to active service in 1814.

By the 29th, the Commission of Government decided that it was high time to get Napoleon away from the Paris area, and to move ahead with the process of removing him completely from French soil, whatever his ultimate destination. Consequently Beker was ordered to take the former emperor to Rochefort, on the coast of the Bay of Biscay, where, Fouché had said, a French frigate would be at Napoleon's disposal. Leaving Malmaison at five that afternoon and traveling via Vendôme, Poitiers, and Niort, they reached Rochefort on 3 July, only to find it blockaded by an English warship, the Bellérophon, and two smaller ships.

After ten days of indecision, on 13 July Napoleon wrote to the Prince

Regent, throwing himself, as he said, on the hospitality of the British people. Then, still hoping that he would be permitted to live out his days in England, on the 15th he thanked Beker for the consideration he had shown to his former emperor, and embraced him, saying that if he had known him better, he would have wanted him on his personal staff. Beker had great difficulty in restraining his emotions. Then General Bonaparte, as he would now be addressed, boarded the Bellérophon. He was to enjoy the hospitality of the British people, but not in the manner that he had hoped for.

The French army, which had been driven from the field of Waterloo, was far from being a band of tatterdemalions. Soult had collected some 55,000 troops of *l'Armée du Nord* in the vicinity of Philippeville. As many as 117,000 troops would be available for the defense of Paris by the end of June, not including the garrisons of the numerous fortresses between Paris and the northern frontier. Another 170,000 conscripts were undergoing training in depots in the northeast.

In late June there were 6,000 infantry, 2,000 cavalry, and thirty guns of the Guard at Soissons. When the Old Guard made camp at Charonne and Saint-Chaumont on the 29th, it totaled almost 10,000 men, including foot, cavalry, artillery and train, sappers, seamen, and artisans. Almost 3,000 men of the Young Guard were standing by. Although the provisional government was aware of these troop strengths and dispositions, the question of whether resistance to the Allies was still possible was further muddied when Ney, already hopelessly compromised in the eyes of the Bourbons by his promise to Louis XVIII to bring Napoleon to Paris in a cage and then going over to Napoleon, denied in the Chamber of Deputies that France any longer had an army with which to resist the invaders.

On other fronts, however, French armies were still full of fight. In Piedmont, Suchet's *Armée des Alpes* had given a trouncing to Field Marshal Frimont's Austrians, and a truce had been concluded between them. Suchet had also managed to preserve Lyon and its immense stores from Austrian depredations. In late June General Rapp had delivered a severe check to the troops of the Austrian commander-in-chief, Schwartzenberg, at Le Souffel, 50 kilometers north of Strasbourg, on the Rhine.

Within the fortress of Vincennes, Daumesnil was able to remain abreast of the rapidly shifting scene in Paris by virtue of a steady stream of officers coming and going in connection with the intensive effort to prepare the fortress for whatever contingency might be expected to arise in the coming days. Then, on the evening of 29 June, he had several surprising visitors. His old brother-in-arms, General Exelmans, had arrived in the vicinity of Vincennes, with 2,000 men of the two divisions of dragoons of the 2nd reserve corps of *l'Armée du Nord*. He was accompanied by a Major Brunneck, an aide de camp of Marshal Blücher's, who was bearing a draft proposal for an armistice to be delivered to Marshal Grouchy.

Unbeknownst to Brunneck and Exelmans, on the previous day Grouchy had turned over command of the army to Marshal Davout, who was also acting as the Minister of War.

Exelmans took Daumesnil aside and told him of a plan that he had conceived to deliver Napoleon from Malmaison, and to place him at the head of the army. He said that the previous day he had sent an aide de camp, Colonel Sencier, to Malmaison to persuade Napoleon to come away for that purpose, but that Napoleon had declined to go along with the plot, out of respect for his word of honor.[13] When he learned that Exelmans had recruited a squadron of his officers with whom to carry out this mad plot, whether or not Napoleon wished to go along with it, Daumesnil told Exelmans that it was too late: that Napoleon had already left Malmaison for Rochefort that afternoon, as indeed he had.

There was still the matter of the Prussian emissary to deal with. At midnight Exelmans wrote the following letter to Davout, in the latter's capacity as Minister of War:

Monseigneur,
I have the honor to inform Your Excellency that I arrived here this evening. I would have hurried to present my respects to Your Excellency if I had not been prevented by some service considerations.

I have the honor to tell Your Excellency what happened this morning to General Le Sénécal[14], who was crossing my column. That officer was seen in a chaise with a Prussian officer.[15] I did what I had to do to save General Sénécal from the fury of the troops, and I brought him here with the Prussian officer. I gave in to the urgings of Le Sénécal and let him go to Marshal Grouchy, because he said that he had been sent to General Blücher to negotiate a suspension of hostilities. General Le Sénécal was supposed to return to pick up the aide de camp of General Blücher, but since he didn't return, I am sending Major Brunneck to Your Excellency so that he may inform you regarding the purpose of his mission, about which Your Excellency will probably have a good laugh.

Tomorrow I will continue my movement toward Montrouge. I forgot to mention to Your Excellency that in the entire column of our troops they were saying that Le Sénécal was a traitor, and should be judged as such.

---

13 *Archives Nationales* AFIV 1670. It may well have been this plot, which prompted Napoleon to send General Beker on the next day to the provisional government, with his offer to assume command of the army long enough to smash the Prussian force then descending on Paris. That offer, in turn, seems to have decided Fouché that it was essential to get Napoleon on the road to exile immediately, as he, in fact, did.
14 Le Sénécal was the chief of Marshal Grouchy's general staff.
15 It was Major Brunneck, aide de camp to Field Marshal Blücher.

Having this Prussian officer on his hands, Daumesnil felt obliged to invite him to join them for dinner, although the Prussian's haughty, prideful manner scarcely commended him to Daumesnil, Léonie, or Exelmans. When Brunneck stated flatly during the dinner that on the following day Marshal Blücher would enter Paris, Exelmans stared him in the face, and said, "Before that happens, you'll taste the edge of our sabers." He was to give substance to those words two days later.

There must have been some fast galloping by couriers that evening, because, in a letter dated 29 June, Grouchy wrote to Davout regarding Le Sénécal's mission:

> As a result of his mission, he brought back a Prussian major charged with conveying the demands formulated by the enemy. By no means wanting to bring this Prussian into Paris, General Le Sénécal left him at Vincennes under the guard of a *chef d'escadron* of chasseurs, lent to him by General Exelmans, and came to report to me in Paris, where I happened to be.

On 30 June, Major Brunneck wrote to Prince Marshal of Eckmühl (Davout) from La Vilette:[16]

> It was at one o'clock on the morning of 29 June that I was ordered by the Prince Marshal Blücher to go immediately to the outpost to accompany the French general Sénécal to Marshal Grouchy, from whom he had been sent that morning.
> After General Exelmans had learned of all of the circumstances, he was kind enough to invite me to dine at Vincennes, and to permit me to return on one of his own horses to our outposts, providing me with his chief of general staff for security.
> Since Marshal Grouchy's situation had changed in the last 24 hours, I thought that I did not need to make the proposition for an armistice to Marshal Grouchy. That is why I have not had the honor of speaking to him.

So much for the Daumesnils' hospitality. Never mind: it would not be long before the haughty Prussian would realize that, among his fellow countrymen, he had been afforded a unique experience, which he would doubtless relate again and again to his children and grandchildren.

It must have been late in the evening of the 29th, or early the following day, that Daumesnil's brother-in-law, General Louis Vallin, stopped briefly at Vincennes. When General Maurin had been wounded at Ligny, Vallin had taken over command of the 7th cavalry division of the Fourth Corps, and had fought at Wavre and Limale. He had then been in command of

---

16 On the southern edge of today's Charles de Gaulle airport.

the rearguard of the retreating army. Now he had brought his hussars, chasseurs, and dragoons back to participate in the defense of Paris.

In his message to Davout, Exelmans had stated his intention of moving on Montrouge[17] on the 30th, which he proceeded to do that day. He had under his command General Piré's 2nd division, consisting of the 1st and 6th *Chasseurs*, Strolz's 5th, 15th, and 20th Dragoons, and Vallin's 6th Hussars. The 44th of Line was also at his disposition. Having learned that Blücher had arrived at Saint-Germain-en-Laye, and was pushing toward Versailles, with the apparent intent of "turning" Paris, Davout ordered Exelmans to drive from Versailles the enemy cavalry regiments that were leading the Prussian force.

On 1 July, Exelmans set out for Versailles with his men. General von Sohr, commanding a brigade consisting of the 3rd Brandenburg Hussars and the 5th Pomeranian Hussars, two of the most famous of the Prussian cavalry regiments, had imprudently started along the road to Montrouge, without having first sent out any patrols. Having arrived at the forest of Verrières, he found himself being assailed by four of Exelmans' regiments, led by the general personally. Thrown back to Versailles, pursued with sabers slashing at their backs, the Prussians galloped through the city's streets with the intention of reaching Saint-Germain via Rocquencourt. But Piré had set an ambush for the Prussians: the 1st and 6th *Chasseurs*, and the 44th of Line blocked their path. Stopped by a fusillade on the road from Vaucresson to Rocquencourt, de Sohr wheeled his men toward Chesnay, and now he found himself caught between two fires. His hussars were almost all killed or made prisoners. The two best light cavalry regiments of the Prussian army had ceased to exist. Exelmans continued to advance toward Saint-Germain, but when he encountered a considerable corps of Prussian infantry, he prudently withdrew to Montrouge. It would be the last Napoleonic battle, and its complete success may have served in some degree to rinse the bitter aftertaste of Waterloo from the mouths of those French troopers. Nonetheless, that victory was for naught, since an armistice was signed on 3 July. A plaque on the Place Exelmans in Rocquencourt, erected by the military historical society, *La Sabretache*, is dedicated "To the glory of the last combatants of the wars of the Revolution and of the Empire."

During those days, Daumesnil's efforts to prepare for the probability of a siege continued unabated. In the absence of a reply to his request to the minister for approval to clear fields of fire for the fortress by cutting trees in the Vincennes forest, he decided to go ahead with the necessary cutting. In doing so, he ran afoul of the administration of the public domain, in which category the Bois de Vincennes was included. When one of the forest guards saw the cutting beginning, on 30 June he wrote to his inspector as follows:

---

17 On the southern outskirts of Paris at that time.

I have the honor to inform you that General Daumesnil, governor of the château, yesterday began to have the elms of the *Cours Marigny* topped, and that he is giving the wood in payment to the wood-cutters. He is also having all sections of the old copses and plantings adjacent to the château, from the Avenue of Minimes to the Lake of Vincennes,[18] cut down. I don't know to what distance he intends to pursue this cutting, but if the 150 men who are doing the work continue as they are for eight days, they will approach the obelisk, cutting the copses to fifty centimeters from the ground. All the wood is still there. I think that General Daumesnil is fully authorized to have this cutting done. However, he hasn't notified me about this, and I didn't believe it was my duty to raise the least question about this with him, since I assumed that he would have written you about it. Furthermore, the circumstances are so urgent that it would be difficult to oppose such an operation, since it seems to be intended to contribute to the defense of the fort and the château of Vincennes.

Obviously the forester was hoping that his inspector had approved the cutting, so that he would not have to deal with this crusty general, who was notoriously impatient when mere *pékins* ventured to question his actions. The poor fellow was out of luck, however, because his superior instructed him ask the governor for an explanation of his actions. On 3 July the forester wrote this report to his superior:

The general could not have received me more badly, and said to me the most disagreeable things. I pointed out to him that I didn't deserve to be treated in such a manner. He replied by threatening to put me in prison as he had done with the guards Stette and Gaignand, who are at the moment being held in the château. I can't write the words that the general used with me. I will tell them to you in person. Suffice it for you to know that he told me that he had nothing to answer for to you, and that in these circumstances he was acting in accordance with the law. I think he meant, in the case of forts under siege.

Henri de Clairval comments that it's unfortunate that the guard didn't choose to transcribe Daumesnil's words, "since they must have been very tasty." It seems highly unlikely that the Domain inspector chose to cross swords himself with the governor, and the work went on. When it was finished, some 32 acres of woods bordering on the fortress had been cut down.

On 2 July, the pontoneers of the former Guard, the artillery artisans, the 4th regiment of foot artillery, and the 6th and 8th squadrons of the train went out of the fort and bivouacked on the glacis. They were

---

18 Subsequently re-named Lac Daumesnil.

replaced by the invalid gunners, four companies of the 8th regiment of foot artillery, and the 2nd battalion of the National Guard of the Department of Cher.

That same day Daumesnil had all the officers of the garrison assembled, and read to them a letter that he had just received from the Commission of Government. It instructed him "only to surrender the fortress to a French government recognized by the Allies, and, in the event of hostilities on their part intended to seize a depot as precious for France as that held in that fortress, he should defend it to the utmost extremity." That is exactly what Daumesnil intended to do.

With the signing of the armistice on 3 July, the Allies wanted to ensure that the still turbulent French army was safely removed from the vicinity of the capital. Davout was charged with the responsibility for moving it "behind the Loire," more than 60 miles south of Paris as the crow flies, and for discharging the greater part of it. It would be 9 August before the foot and cavalry regiments of the Guard reached Orléans, situated on the Loire.

The rebellious frame of mind in which the greater part of the officers and soldiers accepted the capitulation gave serious concern to the Commission of Government, whose members feared that they might face open resistance, or even revolt, from within the army's ranks, even as it began to make its way slowly south. In a session of the Commission in the Tuileries on 3 July, with Fouché presiding, there was discussion of a report that the commandant in Vincennes was disposed to use the garrison there to carry out a seditious action. Although it was agreed that it was not possible to have complete confidence in that accusation, it was nonetheless judged prudent to put the fortress under strict surveillance, and to give orders to that effect to the Minister of War, the military commander of Paris, and the Prefect of Police. That same day Fouché sent the following letter to those officials:

> It has been reported to the Commission of Government that the commandant of Vincennes is disposed to employ his garrison for a seditious movement.
> The charge may be unfounded, but its character is so serious that the Commission has not hesitated to charge you, as it does charge you, with applying to this matter the most exact surveillance.[19]

Davout attached little importance to that report. Such rumors abounded in Paris, and he was confident that the national asset represented by the contents of the fortress of Vincennes could not be better safeguarded than by Daumesnil. He was more concerned with the unwelcome task with which he had been charged—the orderly movement

---

19 S.H.A.T. archives, *Correspondance Générale*, C16 23.

away from the Paris region of the scattered and unhappy army. However, the secretary of Davout's staff, General Marchand, sent a copy of that letter to General Mouton-Duvernet, commander of the First military division, who replied promptly, "I don't know any other way than to change the garrison or the commandant."[20] That sharp response betrays an attitude on that general's part which was to lead to his downfall. He was proscribed later that year, and in 1816 he was shot.

The Commission of Government was aware that there was still one unresolved military matter that needed to be resolved: to wit, the manner in which the question of the fortress of Vincennes should be handled with the Allies, who would be sure to want to take possession of it. Fouché raised this question with Davout in the context of another letter to the marshal:

... [A] subject still much more important, on which the Convention[21] has not yet ruled, is the château of Vincennes. It seems that the château needs to receive a garrison and provisions until it is possible to negotiate regarding that installation. Inform the Commission what has been done and what can be done with respect to that fortress, filled with a great quantity of munitions entirely unprotected.[22]

Another individual wondering about the eventual disposition of the fortress of Vincennes was General Evain, chief of the artillery division of the Ministry of War. On 4 July he raised the matter with the minister in this note:

Monseigneur,
I have just read the capitulation decree for the evacuation of Paris. I note that there is no mention of Vincennes.
    I ask Your Excellency to inform me:
        1. If all the artillery materiel now there should be left there,
        2. If one should move there from here, on the 6th, all (the materiel), which time and the means did not permit being evacuated from Paris.[23]

On the same day, Daumesnil made another appeal for better quality troops for the fort's garrison:
Monseigneur,
According to what you did me the honor of telling my aide de camp with respect to the garrison of Vincennes, I beg Your Excellency to

---

20 S.H.A.T. archives, *Correspondance Générale,* C15 6.
21 The Convention concluded with the Allies. Its full text may be found in Annex C.
22 S.H.A.T. archives, *Correspondance Générale,* C16 23.
23 S.H.A.T. archives, *Correspondance Générale,* C15 6.

be so kind as to send me, as a replacement for the battalion of National Guards from the Department of Cher, a battalion of troops of the Line, the former not being battle-proven and in no condition to be of use to me. In the capitulation there is no mention of Vincennes, and, being responsible for its defense, I beg Your Excellency to give me all the necessary means.

On 5 July Davout replied to Daumesnil's request:

General,
I am ordering General Hulin, commander of the 1st Military Division, to send you today two of the best companies of *sous-officiers* veterans, who are in Paris, to reinforce the Vincennes garrison.

I don't know if you're satisfied with the battalion of National Guards of Cher, but if its disposition is doubtful as a replacement for the 2nd company of veterans, General Hulin is authorized to send you the numbers necessary to organize your garrison, and then he will withdraw the battalion of Cher, which will depart with the army.

Send an officer to General Hulin at once to coordinate with him these dispositions, which should be made during the day.[24]

In his invaluable "Journal,"[25] Adjutant Bénard gives the strength of the garrison, as of 1 July, as 77 officers, 1,325 *sous-officiers* and soldiers, and 303 horses. From the 1st to the 5th so many pieces of artillery were being brought to the fortress that some of them had to be parked outside its curtain wall, on the glacis.

During this time, further fortification measures were being implemented. The bays of powder magazines were being closed off with earth-filled sacks; the wood cutting on the park side of the château had extended to a distance of 1,200 feet; a covered and crenelated traverse[26] had been dug from the angle of the counterscarp at the Tour du Réservoir to the house at the nearest corner of the village; other traverses were being constructed within the fort, connecting to the counterscarp of the keep; and a circular demarcation line around the château and the village was being marked out in the park and open country, at a radius of 2,400 feet from the fort.

On 4 and 5 July, all of the artillery pieces and engineering equipment which could not be evacuated beyond the Loire were brought into the fortress. Then, on the 7th, the four companies of the 8th artillery regiment

---

24 S.H.A.T. archives, *Correspondance Générale,* C16 23.
25 Bénard, *Le Blocus de Vincennes en 1815.*
26 An embanked trench covered with wooden planking.

and the battalion of the National Guard of Cher left the fort, in accordance with Daumesnil's request to Davout, and were replaced by five companies of veteran fusiliers. This was to be the final composition of the garrison: 45 officers, and 974 *sous-officiers* and soldiers.

In emplacements on the four walls of the château, 55 artillery pieces of various types and calibers—cannon, howitzers, and mortars—had been set up. On the platform atop the keep, a battery of a French version of the English Congreve rockets, with a range of 4 kilometers, had been installed. Provisions calculated to sustain the garrison for 90 days had been brought into the fortress.

Outposts had been established around the fort's outer perimeter, and all roads leading to the village and the château, as well as the roads through the forest, were guarded. Within the fortress there now were, in addition to the guns mounted on the walls:

518 cannon
181 caissons
10 campaign forges
54 munition wagons
30 copper pontoons on carts
157,933 cannon balls
36,829 shells, 10,000 of them loaded
79,500 kilograms of powder
1,000,000 flints
50,000 cannon powder bags
50,000 infantry cartridges
1,000 Congreve-type rockets
53,350 muskets, 36,000 of which of foreign make
59,000 sabers
1,850 cuirasses,

plus thousands of engineering tools of all sorts. Everything that could be foreseen had been provided for, and the governor and his men calmly and resolutely awaited developments.

It was only on the evening of 6 July that the rear guard of the army, consisting of the Imperial Guard, had left the city. Many people had gone to the Champ de Mars to see them off, and there had been moving scenes of farewell. The first units of the Allied armies entered Paris on the 7th. At Arnouville, north of Paris, Louis XVIII waited impatiently to make his own entrance into the capital, but permitted himself to be persuaded that it would be better to let another 24 hours elapse, in which the excitement created by the army's departure could subside. Finally, at three in the afternoon of the 8th, Louis made his entrance without incident.

∽

With respect to Daumesnil's old regiment, there is an ironic footnote relating to its eventual disbandment. Like many of the other regiments of the Army of the Loire that were not to be incorporated in the royal army, the *Chasseurs à cheval* were sent on a seemingly aimless southward route into the heart of France. On 13 October, they arrived in Périgueux. Lieutenant Chevalier, who was still with the regiment at that time, comments that the inhabitants had been warned about them, so that they were received very coldly, and with an air of distrust. By a freak chance, Chevalier ended up being billeted with one of Daumesnil's sisters, and a niece. He was astonished to find that that sister, as well as Daumesnil's other sister, were fanatical supporters of the Bourbons, wearing large blue ribbons, from which depended enormous fleur de lys, and describing their illustrious brother as nothing better than a traitor, a brigand, a Bonapartist, a usurper, and a criminal, "capable of betraying our dear King and our dear Allies." Chevalier made haste to find other lodgings.

CHAPTER NINETEEN
THE BLOCKADE

1815

Before we follow the course of events during the second blockade of Vincennes, it is worth pausing briefly to draw a distinction between the Allied victory of 1814 and their subsequent occupation of Paris, and the Allied treatment of conquered France in 1815. In the former instance, the defeat of Napoleon, his exile to Elba, and the restoration of Louis XVIII to the throne had essentially satisfied Allied objectives. By early June, Allied troops had withdrawn from Paris. 1815 was quite a different matter, however. This time the Allies imposed themselves on France as complete masters.

With the capitulation of the French army and the return of Louis XVIII to the throne, the northern and eastern regions of France were divided into areas of occupation for almost all of the Allied armies, in much the same fashion as was Germany in 1945. In France there was even a "Free Zone," corresponding strikingly in its borders to that of Vichy France, and it was not until 20 November 1815 that the Treaty of Paris, formally ending the conflict, was signed. It provided that a certain number of cities, territories, forts, and frontiers were to be ceded by France. The occupations were to last for a minimum of three years and a maximum of five; a force of 150,000 Allied soldiers along the entire French frontier was to be maintained at French expense; and an indemnity of 1,636 million francs was to be paid by France.

It is understandable that the Allies, having thought in 1814 that they had settled the Napoleon problem once and for all, were dismayed and outraged to discover that, in fact, they were going to have to do it all over again. But once that painful process had been brought to a successful conclusion on the field of Waterloo, there was a significant difference between the English attitude, personified by the Duke of Wellington, toward their conquered antagonists of twenty-plus years standing, and that of the Russians, Austrians, and the Prussians, especially, the latter, as personified by Field Marshal Prince Blücher.

The reasons for that difference are not far to seek, the most obvious being that Great Britain had never been occupied by the French. On the other hand, the Austrians had repeatedly been trounced on a number of battlefields by the General/First Consul/Emperor, their capital occupied by his troops, and their own emperor obliged to wed his daughter to the "Ogre." For their part, the Russians had given as good as they'd taken in a number of ferocious battles over the years, but their Emperor had been deceived by honeyed words, their land invaded and devastated, and their capital captured and burned. So turn-about seemed to them fair play, although their Tsar was not a vengeful man. But the old Prussian hussar, nicknamed *Marschall Vorwärts* (Marshal Forward) by his men, had the names "Jena" and "Auerstädt" burned into his psyche, and would take them to the grave with him. His commanders felt no less strongly than did he about the humiliations that had been visited upon their country by Napoleon, and took every opportunity, as we shall see, to demonstrate to the French that they could not expect sweet reasonableness from their conquerors. In truth, the Bavarians, Württembergers, and Badois were no better.

Perhaps the single greatest single motivational difference between British and Prussian intentions with respect to France was that England did not want to crush France, but rather to permit it to regain sufficient status and power to contribute usefully, in the British view, to the Continental balance of power, whereas Prussia wished to reduce France to a level of weakness, which would ensure that it could not in the future pose a threat to Prussia.

A Wellington proclamation and Order of the Day promised that the British would conduct themselves as in a friendly country from the time that troops under his command set foot in France, whenever no resistance was offered, and when people abandoned the "usurper" and placed themselves under their legitimate sovereign.[1]

Wellington's General Order of 20 June, 1815, issued at Nivelle, expressed an intention and point of view in stark contrast with those of his allies:

> As the army is about to enter the French territory, the Field Marshal desires it to be understood by the troops of the several nations composing the army which he has the honor to command, that their Sovereigns are in alliance with the King of France, and that France must, therefore, be considered as a friendly country.
>
> No article is to be taken from any individual by any Officer or soldier without payment for the same. The Commissaries of the army will supply the troops with all that they require in the usual manner; and no requisition is to be made direct on the country, or its

---

1   Pasquier, *Mémoires*, vol. III, p. 343.

magistrates, by any Officer or soldier.

The Commissaries will receive directions either from the Field Marshal or from the Generals commanding the troops of the several nations (if these troops should not be supplied with provisions by the British Commissariat) to make such requisitions as may be necessary for the supply of the troops, for which they will give the usual voucher and receipt; and they will understand that they will be responsible to issue and account for what they will thus receive from the country in France, in the same manner as they would if they purchased supplies for the troops in their own countries respectively."[2]

A striking instance of the Duke's desire to make his army's presence acceptable to the French population may be seen in this letter of his of 27 July to the Paris Prefect of Police:

General Müffling has sent me your letter of the 26th, concerning your desire that soldiers be permitted to help with the harvesting.
I am sending you herewith a copy of the order that I have just given on that subject. You would do well to have it translated and sent to the neighboring communes, so that the inhabitants and the mayors may make their requests for assistance, which they need for that purpose.
I am also advising you that, if there is a need for it, I could lend army wagons for collecting the harvest."[3]

Evidence that there had been discussion among the Allies of attacking the fortress of Vincennes as early as 7 July is afforded by this letter of that date from the Duke of Wellington to Blücher:

Paris, 7 July, 1815.
Mein lieber Fürst,
I send you a letter which I have just received from Marshal Prince Wrede.[4] There does not appear to me to be any inconvenience in his taking up the position he proposes.
I have received a letter from the Commissioners appointed by you and me to carry into execution the convention of the 3rd instant, regarding the Château of Vincennes, upon which I shall be glad to have your opinion.
Vincennes' not being included by name in the convention, I believe the French Commissioners are right, and that we must attack that place.[5]

2 Wellington, *The Dispatches of Field Marshal The Duke of Wellington*, p. 378.
3 *Ibid*, p. 575.
4 Commander of the Bavarian army.
5 Wellington, *The Dispatches of Field Marshal The Duke of Wellington*, p. 547–8.

Although we have no record of a discussion of Vincennes between Wellington and the French Commissioners, a passage in Leonard Cooper's *The Age of Wellington* may shed some light on it, although in large part Cooper's story is fallacious. Cooper describes a meeting between the Duke and Fouché, during which the question of how to deal with fully armed and garrisoned French fortresses came up, with Vincennes being cited as a notable example. This is Cooper's account (p. 239) of that alleged meeting:

> When Wellington brought this deficiency to his notice, Fouché almost tearfully confessed that there had been an oversight, but protested his inability to control the commander of the garrison and begged to be told what he could do to ensure the evacuation and dismantlement of the fortress. Wellington replied without hesitation, "It is not my business to tell you what you are to do, but I will tell you what I am going to do. Unless the fortress is handed over to me by tomorrow morning, I shall take it by assault. Do you understand?" When Fouché attempted to argue, there was a brusque conclusion. "The fort must be handed over by ten tomorrow. If not, I shall assault it at noon.

Cooper goes on to describe a purely imaginary march on Vincennes by British troops, the deploying of cannon, the lighting of portfires, and the consequent evacuation and dismantling of the fortress of Vincennes. The notion of Fouché's "almost tearfully" confessing to anything is enough in itself to make this entire story suspect, and the rest of it is, as we very well know, absolute nonsense. It may, however, support Wellington's reference to the French Commissioners' having encouraged the Allies to attack Vincennes.

∞

When Daumesnil again took up his post as governor of Vincennes, his second in command was Colonel Jean Baptiste Varéliaud, a light cavalry officer, who had served as a captain in the Guard Chasseurs from 1807 to 1811. In March 1807, in the combat at Liebstadt, he had received 15 lance wounds, several of which in the breast. Altogether, he had been wounded an incredible 49 times. In accordance with the standard requirement for fortresses, Daumesnil had formed a defense council consisting of Varéliaud, Major Dérivaux, the artillery commander, artillery Captain Devarennes, Engineer Adjutant Bénard (author of the Journal), the five captains of the fusilier veteran companies, and Captain Chevalier, commanding the invalid gunners.

On 8 July the council met in order to make the final dispositions of the garrison before the anticipated siege could begin. To deal with the threat of fire, pumps were placed strategically, and 20 of the most intelligent veterans were assigned to the sapper officer to man them. 150 barrels filled

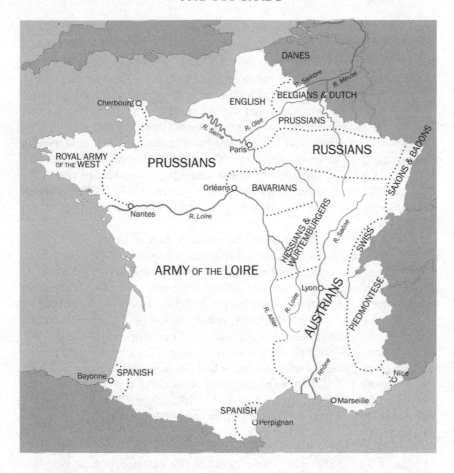

Allied zones of occupation of France, 1815. The map is by Alex Jamison.

with water were distributed throughout the fort. A hospital and pharmacy were set up, baking ovens were stoked, and food supplies were stored in easily accessible locations.

Outposts of fifteen or twenty men each were established around the fort's perimeter, posted at roads leading to Paris, at the village of Vincennes, and clockwise from there on roads leading to Montreuil, Fontenay, Nogent, Saint-Mandé, and on the north and south glacis of the fort. Those on the roads were to furnish sentinels positioned along the outer defense perimeter, generally at a distance of 400 *toises* (2,400 feet) from the fort. Thus, all approaches to the fort were guarded, so that any movement by enemy forces in the vicinity of the fort could be immediately reported to the governor. (See map)

At this moment Daumesnil did not know whether to expect an attempt by the Allies to seize the fortress by force, or a siege. It may be remembered that in 1814 a Russian colonel had first threatened to starve out the fortress, and then to "blow it up." Neither threat had had the least effect on *la Jambe de Bois*, and, not long afterwards, it turned out that neither threat was given effect. But now he had to be prepared for both possibilities: in the first case, to meet force with force, and in the second, to meet threats and pressure with patience and nerves of tempered steel.

On 9 July, it became clear that the villages beyond the perimeter that Daumesnil had established were going to be occupied by Allied troops. 40 caissons of munitions and several powder wagons, which had arrived at the fort the previous day, were still in the main courtyard. There was only time to place ten of the caissons in the underground spaces of two of the towers, while the powder wagons were brought into the keep. The other 30 caissons, contents and all, were dumped into the large watering pond for horses.

At ten that morning, men at the advance post on the road to Paris outside the village of Vincennes observed a large cavalry detachment approaching the village, and one of the sentries was sent to the fort to report this movement to the duty officer. One of the garrison's adjutants went to the post to determine the purpose of this activity. As he arrived on the scene, he saw a Prussian officer, accompanied by a trumpeter, riding ahead of the detachment. The Prussian officer stopped at the French sentry's post. His trumpeter blew on his trumpet, and announced that he was accompanying a *parlementaire*. When the adjutant approached him, the Prussian asked to speak to the governor. At the same time, the detachment had moved forward until they had come to the outpost at the 400 *toises* limit. When the soldiers of the outpost took up their arms, the Prussian cavalry detachment halted.

A moment later, the deputy commander of the garrison, Colonel Varéliaud, joined the other two officers of the garrison to hear what the *parlementaire* had to say. The latter stated that he came in the name of Marshal Prince Blücher to summon the governor to surrender the fort to him. Varéliaud replied that the fort would not be surrendered to Marshal Blücher, and requested in unambiguous terms that the Prussian officer withdraw and order his escort to pull back to a distance of 500 *toises*, adding that, if they did not do so, they would be fired upon. The Prussian and his escort withdrew, but almost immediately the officer returned alone to repeat his message. Word was sent to Daumesnil, who rode to the scene, accompanied by his aide de camp, Lieutenant Darribeau, and a detachment of the garrison. He spoke to the *parlementaire*, repeating to him what Colonel Varéliaud had said. With that, the Prussian officer departed.

Immediately afterwards, the Prussian commander withdrew his troops, but posted a large number of mounted sentinels directly opposite the sentries and the outposts of the fort. Daumesnil at once doubled the number of men at the fort's outposts. That signaled the commencement of the siege. Now both the fortress and the village of Vincennes were completely encircled by paired French and Prussian outposts, all roughly at a distance of 400 *toises* from the château.

Until 2:00 that afternoon, there were frequent contacts between the opposing forces, which did not, however, alter the situation. Shortly thereafter, two battalions of Prussian infantry appeared beyond Vincennes, and the cavalry detachment moved westward to Saint-Mandé. Then troopers from a squadron of lancers reinforced the Prussian outposts, and an artillery train came into view, dividing into two columns, one heading for Montreuil, the other for Saint-Mandé.

At three o'clock, Daumesnil, accompanied by Darribeau, went to the Prussian outposts, and was escorted to the headquarters, near La Tourelle, of the general staff of the Prussian general commanding the blockading troops, Lt.-General Hans Ernst Karl, Graf von Ziethen. After a half-hour of discussions, Daumesnil returned to the château, and the respective outposts resumed their previous positions. By that time, the Prussians had occupied the villages of Montreuil and Saint-Mandé, as well as all the other environs of the fortress. At four o'clock troops were seen emplacing two batteries near La Tourelle, each battery consisting of four 12-pounders and two mortars, all aimed at the fortress. From that time on, no person was permitted to pass beyond the Prussian outposts.

Within the fort, further measures to prepare for the possibility of an assault were undertaken. Then, at six on the morning of the 10th, a Prussian officer came to make the same demand for the surrender of the fort, and received the same answer as before.

Now let us cross over briefly into the "enemy camp," to take note of the Prussian view of this unexpected turn of events. Fortunately, a book entitled *Memoirs of Prussian Infantry General Ludwig von Reiche*, published by his nephew, Louis von Weltzien in Leipzig in 1857, affords us an invaluable insight into the Prussian reaction to the behaviour of this troublesome French general. I believe it's worth quoting *in extenso* from it, since I believe it provides confirmation of what has long been almost a doctrine of faith with the French—that in 1815 Blücher attempted to bribe Daumesnil to surrender the fortress of Vincennes. General von Reiche was General von Ziethen's chief of staff, and participated in von Ziethen's meeting with Daumesnil, so his credentials as a reporter of these events are impeccable.

Operation against the château of Vincennes, near Paris.

Our plenipotentiaries, Müffling[6] and Hervey,[7] had forgotten to specify in Article Eight of the Capitulation the surrender of Vincennes. The experience of 1814, when the same mistake had occurred, had not been noticed.

---

6 General Phillip Friedrich Carl Ferdinand, Baron von Müffling, Prussian liaison officer with Wellington during the Waterloo campaign, and military governor of Paris during the 1815 occupation.

7 Colonel Hervey, representing the Duke of Wellington.

Blücher, in his powerful and energetic manner, decided to have Vincennes attacked at once. Consequently, on the day after our entrance into Paris, 8th July, General von Ziethen received an order to that effect.

Vincennes was a well known state prison, with connected military establishments, which at that time contained a great quantity of arms and powder supplies, which had been moved there at the time of the occupation of Paris, the surrender of which now had to be compelled, since a peaceful attempt (to obtain its surrender) had been unsuccessful.

On the morning of the 9th, two battalions of infantry, a company of sharpshooters, a battery of heavy howitzers (10-pounders), a half-battery of 12-pounder cannon, and a detachment of cavalry, all under the command of the then colonel and brigade commander, von Rüchel-Kleist, appeared before Vincennes, and immediately put in place the blockade. During that night, emplacements for artillery were prepared, and the pieces were brought in.

The commandant rejected the summons to surrender, citing an order from Marshal Davout, according to which he should only surrender the fort to foreign troops at the express orders of the French government.

General Ziethen, with the intent of not neglecting any effort to achieve the objective, and without going to the utmost lengths, in the course of a reconnaissance of the château, invited the commandant to an oral discussion. The commandant appeared without an escort. It was General Daumesnil, with a wooden leg, at that time 38 years old.

All of General Ziethen's persuasive skills, even the *vortheilhaft-esten*[8] propositions, which were made to him, could not bring about his compliance. He referred constantly to his order from Davout, which, for him as a soldier, was the only guiding principle for his conduct. He gave Zieten a proclamation[9] as he called it, for Field Marshal Blücher, which Ziethen was unwilling to accept.

At this point in his document, von Reiche inserted this footnote, describing his personal efforts to win Daumesnil over:

At this opportunity I soon became very serious with him, one to another. Since we weren't getting anywhere with him and he kept referring to Davout's order, I said to him that he presumably had

---

8 *Vorteilhaftesten* can be translated as "the most profitable, beneficial, advantageous, favorable, lucrative, remunerative," all in the superlative form. In my judgment, the last two adjectives best fit the generally accepted belief that Blücher offered money to Daumesnil in return for the surrender of the fortress.

9 We have no record of the text of that document. Presumably it repeated Daumesnil's oral declarations to the Prussians.

some special (secret) orders for certain circumstances, which he might be kind enough to show us. This request almost sent him into a rage, and Ziethen had all he could do to calm him down.

We now revert to von Reiche's principal text:

Finally the conversation took on a serious character, in which General Ziethen gave him to understand, referring to Avesnes[10], that he would order the fortress bombarded with every caliber of gun: that he knew that important powder stores were contained in the fortress, and therefore he was making him (Daumesnil) responsible for all the resulting consequences. Since that had no effect, the conversation ended.

The threat of a bombardment was only a warning shot, which Ziethen, least of all, thought of carrying out, since he didn't trust the notorious population of the St-Antoine quarter, which in this connection was already demonstrating unmistakable symptoms. Furthermore, Blücher's vigorous measures, which he did not wish to encourage any further than military discipline required, were not entirely to the general's liking.[11] It is worth noting that he didn't want to rush ahead, and that he had in mind the imminent arrival of our king, whose aversion to exaggerated forceful measures was not unknown to him.

After a bombardment was discarded, and since there were neither time nor the means for a formal siege, and the blockade, which was already in effect, didn't seem to be bringing us any nearer to our goal, there remained only the breaching of the outer walls, and that's what General Ziethen decided upon.

However, we had at our disposal only the 12-pounders, the caliber of which the general considered inadequate for bringing down the strong walls at a distance greater than the weapons' range.

---

10 Where a border fortress had already been bombarded by the Prussians.
11 An event typifying Blücher's aggressively vengeful attitudes is cited by Henri de Clairval:
It was Blücher's intention to destroy all the monuments in Paris, the name or origin of which commemorated French victories, most notably the *Pont de Jéna*. Work on the mining of that bridge had begun on the day that the Allied troops entered Paris. Blücher replied to Talleyrand, who had sent him a note protesting this action: "The bridge will be destroyed, and I would wish that M. de Talleyrand would install himself on it beforehand." It was said that it was then that Louis XVIII wrote a letter to Blücher, ending, "As for me, if necessary, I shall place myself on the bridge; you may blow me up, if you wish."
It was the personal intervention of the King of Prussia, the Tsar of Russia, and the Emperor of Austria, all of whom arrived in Paris on the same day, that brought a halt to the preparations for the bridge's destruction. The *Pont de Jéna* was saved by losing its name, which was changed to the *Pont des Invalides*. However, a number of historians have denied the existence of that letter from Louis to Blücher, on the grounds that it was written after the fact to give substance to the legend of Louis XVIII's heroism.

Therefore, Ziethen asked Wellington's help with the eighteen-pounders of his army, which the latter promised, rather surprisingly, given his known views regarding Blücher's aggressive tendencies. However, the delivery of those guns was put off, first for one reason and then for another, from day to day, until finally nothing came of it, and in the end the matter became the subject of diplomatic negotiations, to Blücher's no little vexation, as one might imagine.[12]

Von Reiche added this footnote to his account. "The commandant had finally become so bold that he was refusing even more stubbornly to hand over the fortress, and swaggeringly threatened us with an attack, if we didn't pull back."

As we shall see, the Prussians did, however, pull back. In saying that Daumesnil quoted orders from Davout to the effect "that he should only surrender the fort to foreign troops at the express orders of the French government," General von Reiche misstates Daumesnil's position. It will be remembered that his orders from the Commission of Government were "only to surrender the fortress to a *French government* recognized by the Allies."

Now let us make our way invisibly back through the Prussian, and then the French outposts to see what has been happening within the fortress. Now we know that Daumesnil's otherwise unexplained visit to von Ziethen's headquarters was at the latter's invitation. The failure of that meeting to achieve the Prussian objective led to the delivery to Daumesnil, on the morning of 10 July, of the following letter:

10 July 1815

Monsieur le Gouverneur,
I have the honor to inform you that, by order of Prince Blücher, general commander in chief, you must surrender the château of Vincennes and join your troops with the French army under the orders of Marshal Davout behind the Loire, in accordance with the Convention. But if you do not wish to surrender the château, you will force me to take it with force, and that will only require several days, because it will not be possible to hold such a weak fort against an army of 200,000 men.[13] Your honor and the honor of your country cannot suffer by that capitulation, which will return brave soldiers to your country. You have often given proof of your courage, to which your wounds give witness, but at present you risk too much, when

---

12 Other of Wellington's subsequent responses to similar requests suggest that he never intended to lend those cannon to von Ziethen. In this case, on 11 July he sent the following letter—written in French, oddly enough—to von Ziethen: "General, I have just received your letter about the artillery for Vincennes. I am having it looked for at St. Denis at once, but I don't think it could arrive before tomorrow."

13 Blücher referred to the château as "a shack" (*Hütte*).

you want to oppose such an important force. You need also to take into account the fact that you will become prisoners of war, if you agree to capitulate after the commencement of hostilities, and that we shall carry out the laws of war, if we take the fort by force.

In short, I ask you to give me a decisive response, because I cannot accept any other declaration, even if you fly the white flag and recognize the Bourbons.

I have the honor to be, *Monsieur le Gouverneur*, your very humble servant,
von Rüchel,
colonel in the service of the King of Prussia
commanding the 3rd brigade of the troops before Vincennes.[14]

The face-to-face confrontation with Daumesnil having proved to be fruitless, von Ziethen apparently decided that it was time to establish a "paper trail" of his effort to resolve this thorny matter peacefully. Having a mere colonel write that letter to Daumesnil was obviously a psychological tactic by von Ziethen, intended to make clear to this unreasonable *maréchal de camp* with a wooden leg that he was in over his head in this matter, but von Ziethen had something to learn, when it came to psychological warfare. Daumesnil had no intention of letting himself be "put in his place" in that fashion. Having read von Rüchel's letter, he at once sat down and wrote to Blücher as follows:

Vincennes, 10 July 1815
Monseigneur,
As in the case of all of the forts of the interior, the one which I command was included in the convention concluded between the Allied forces and the French army. I therefore believe that I can only be attacked after ten days' advance notice. I ask you, *Monseigneur*, to let me know your intentions, and to believe that I shall only turn this fort over to the Allied troops upon the receipt of a positive order from the French government.
I have the honor to be, with the most profound respect for Your Excellency, *Monseigneur*,
Le maréchal de camp
Baron Daumesnil.

Colonel Varéliaud at once took that letter to the Prussian headquarters for General von Ziethen. A reply came back almost at once:

Paris, 10 July 1815
Monsieur le Général,

---

14 S.H.A.T. archives, *Correspondance Générale*, D3 1.

General Varéliaud has given me the letter that you wished to send to His Highness Marshal Prince Blücher. Since His Highness has given me the responsibility for negotiating the surrender of the fortress of Vincennes, I don't dare to forward your letter to him; I opened it because General Varéliaud wished me to do so. I have the honor to send you a copy of the Convention of 4 July for the surrender of Paris; you will see in it, General, that there is no question of any fortress having a cease fire. How could you expect that the fort of Vincennes, which is part of the city of Paris and which should be turned over the same day as the city, be treated more favorably than the other major fortresses? Consequently, I have the honor to inform you that I have the strictest orders to grant the garrison of Vincennes the same conditions as those of the French army under the walls of Paris, to wit:

1. The garrison has the right to retire behind the Loire.

2. The officers and soldiers will keep their baggage, horses, and other effects.

3. The garrison will take with it the materiel that belongs to it.

4. It will leave in Vincennes all the materials, whether powder, cartridges, arms, or cannon, which serve the fort, or as supplies for the army.

You see, General, far from wishing to take advantage of the position in which the Marshal Prince of Eckmühl has left you, I am acting toward you in a manner worthy of soldiers who have always fought with the greatest courage. I ask that you surrender the fort on these conditions, stating that your negative response will be the signal for the attack.

Please accept, General, the considerate thoughts with which I have the honor to be

your very humble servant.

Lieutenant General von Ziethen.[15]

Upon receipt of this letter, Daumesnil called together his Defense Council, and it was decided to send an officer to Paris to ask for orders from the French government recognized by the Allied powers. The governor then wrote to Colonel von Rüchel, the immediate commander of the blockading troops, telling him that he was sending an officer to the Ministry of War:

Colonel,

This officer will be under orders to report the deliberations of the

---

15 In transcribing this letter, I was reminded of that line in Kurt Weill's *Pirate Jenny* song: *"Und Sie wissen nicht mit wem Sie reden."* "And you don't know with whom you're talking." The source for the letter and the one below is S.H.A.T. archives, *Correspondance Générale*, D3 1.

Fort Council to the French government. You may recognize him, and believe that all of my officers will always follow the path of honor. If the fortunes of war go against us, at least our duty will have been accomplished. I ask that you assist the officer bearing the report of these deliberations so that his mission may be carried out as soon as possible.

At three-thirty, the Prussians cut off the supply of water for the fort coming from Montreuil. Two hours later Daumesnil sent off one of his adjutants with the letter for von Rüchel and the report to the Minister of War of the council's deliberations. That report concluded by referring to the instructions Daumesnil had received on 2 July from the provisional government and asking that he be told which government had been recognized by the Allies, finally stating that, when he was so advised, the fort was prepared to submit.

When the officer went to the Allied outpost, he was taken to Saint-Mandé, where he met Colonel von Rüchel, who refused to let him go on to Paris. When the adjutant informed von Rüchel of the contents of his letter, the Prussian replied, "The only government the governor of Vincennes has to do with is the one established by, and administered by, us. We will take the château. You only have food for three or four days. We'll starve you out."[16] With that, von Rüchel took possession of the letter to the French minister.

The adjutant returned to the fort and reported his inability to carry out his mission. Daumesnil sent him back to von Rüchel, but all that the officer received for his pains were more threats of hostilities. Seeing that his *démarches* were being rebutted, and that an attack by the Allies was imminent, Daumesnil warned the mayor of Vincennes, who sent a deputation to von Rüchel to ask for time for the inhabitants of the village to evacuate their houses and lead their animals away before any bombardment began.

At eight-thirty that evening, Daumesnil sent the troops of the garrison to their battle stations, manning all the positions which they would occupy during an attack. (The same procedure would be followed every night until the end of the blockade. At three in the morning the drummers would beat reveille.)

At four on the following morning, 11 July, Daumesnil learned that, during the night, in addition to having cut off the fort's water supply, the Prussians had emplaced some heavy caliber cannon west of the château, before Saint-Mandé. With the aid of a telescope it was possible to see a large number of ladders, which had been requisitioned from the villagers, collected behind a wall in preparation for an assault. Daumesnil ordered that three 12-pounders and two 24-pounders be added to the cannon

---

16 Clairval, *Daumesnil*, p. 203.

already emplaced on the fort's west front, facing the new Prussian battery.

At ten, a *parlementaire* appeared at a French outpost, and asked whether the governor's position was the same as previously. He was assured that it was. At two that afternoon, a second Prussian officer recommended to the mayor that he warn those inhabitants still in the village to evacuate their houses and lead their animals away, since a very heavy bombardment of the fort was going to begin at six o'clock. Almost at once, men, women, children, and animals began a hasty departure from the village.

At five-thirty, the call to arms was beaten in the fortress, and the infantry and gunners went to their posts, the gunners ready to open fire when the signal was given. At six, seeing that there was some movement among the Allied troops and that their outposts were advancing, Daumesnil led a small force out of the fortress to confront the Prussian troops, and as he did, the Prussians pulled back slightly. Both detachments then drew up facing each other in line-of-battle. Daumesnil asked to see the general commanding the blockade, General von Ziethen. He was informed that the general was away, but a colonel and several other officers appeared. Daumesnil told the colonel that, if he did not withdraw his troops to the demarcation line, and didn't turn on the fort's water supply and stop making preparations for an attack, he would be fired upon. The colonel gave his word of honor, and swore to him, as a Prussian officer, that his demands would be granted. The colonel added that he considered himself very fortunate to have had to do with an officer as brave and straightforward as the governor. The troops of both adversaries then returned to their previous positions, and the night passed peacefully.

At four in the morning on the 12th, the spigots in the water pipe from Montreuil were opened, and the Prussians withdrew the artillery pieces they had emplaced before Saint-Mandé during the previous night. A Prussian officer ruefully observed, "This devil of a fellow certainly wants to mix some water with his wine!"

It seems probable that the Prussians had only been attempting to intimidate the garrison. Daumesnil, evidently sensing that, had successfully called their bluff. At a time when the Allies were hoping to ensure that their entry into Paris, as well as the king's return to his capital, would take place in a positive atmosphere, a violent bombardment of a fortress on the city's outskirts was certainly not what they wished for.

Let us pause at this point to examine the circumstances surrounding what I believe to have been an attempt, initiated at the highest level of the Prussian command—which is to say, by Blücher—to bribe Daumesnil to surrender Vincennes.

From the time of that second siege of Vincennes, in 1815, it has been accepted by French historians and the French public alike that, during that second siege, the Prussians attempted to bribe Daumesnil into surrendering the fortress to them. That belief was embodied in the phrase employed by the president of the Chamber of Deputies in his eulogy on the occasion of Daumesnil's interment in the Vincennes cemetery: "He neither surrendered nor sold himself." By the same token, it has been accepted that Daumesnil's response to that offer was, "My refusal will be my son's inheritance," a turn of phrase entirely in keeping with Daumesnil's quick-thinking and articulate character.

Since, as has been previously noted, Daumesnil seems never to have had the impulse to write anything like a memoir, the only written statement of his that we have dealing with this question is contained in the document that he wrote to the General Staff in August of 1830, requesting promotion to the rank of lieutenant-general. In justifying his request, he writes:

I swore to serve the Emperor faithfully, I promised him that no foreigner would ever enter my fort, I kept my word.

Twice blockaded and attacked by the Allied armies, I knew how to repel them vigorously: I saved 90 millions of materiel for my country. All France knew of my defense and applauded it; twice I was removed from a post for having defended it too well. The offers that the foreigners made to me were dishonorable, I rejected them, and certainly they were of a character to tempt one's cupidity.[17]

When one combines that last sentence of Daumesnil's document with General von Reiche's account of Daumesnil's meeting with General von Ziethen, I am satisfied that an offer of a large amount of money was, in fact, made to Daumesnil by von Ziethen on that occasion.

In 1833, an old soldier, Jean-Bernard Canis, who had been a storeskeeper in the fortress of Vincennes during both sieges, wrote an account of what he said was a meeting between Daumesnil and Blücher on the glacis of the fortress, of which he, Canis, was a witness. We now know, however, that the attempt to "buy off" Daumesnil was, in fact, made by von Ziethen during that meeting on 9 July. But Canis had pieced together information about a number of other exchanges between the governor and the Prussians, and had the essence of those exchanges essentially correct. He says, for example, that the Prussian proposal to Daumesnil was made on "very advantageous conditions for himself." That seems to echo von Reiche's account of the meeting.

Another version of the bribe offer has it being made in a letter from Blücher, and that, in rejecting the proposition, Daumesnil had replied, "I will not surrender the fort which I command, nor will I return your letter. For want of other riches, it will serve as an inheritance for my children."[18] The notion that Blücher would have been so unwise as to make such a proposal in writing may be unhesitatingly ruled out.

---

17 Clairval, *Daumesnil*, p. 233.
18 *Ibid.*, p. 203. He had only one child at that time, his son, Léon.

Since we have no evidence of Daumesnil's having discussed with any one, including his wife, a Prussian attempt to bribe him, and since the nearest thing to a Prussian acknowledgment of such an action seems to be von Reiche's account of the meeting, who, then, could have carried away from it the story of that renowned retort? It seems highly unlikely that Daumesnil would have gone alone to a meeting of that importance. Therefore, I believe it is safe to assume that he took with him his aide de camp, Lieutenant Alexandre Darribeau. A sense of his own dignity, if nothing else, would have dictated that. Certainly Darribeau would have given his fellow officers of the garrison an account of that meeting, and the story would have quickly spread beyond that circle.

One final thought on this subject: why does it seem that Daumesnil was unwilling—or, at least, reluctant—to discuss this matter? Knowing his proud character, I believe the explanation is to be found in the phrase in his document of 25 August 1830—that dishonorable offers had been made to him. I believe he was implying that he was dishonored by the fact that his enemies judged him capable of selling out his country, and he didn't consider that gross misjudgment of his character to be something to which he wished to give currency.

∞

During the morning of the 12th, the work on the traverses joined with the counterscarps of the keep's moat was finished, and additional mortars were emplaced within them. Shortly after noon, a sentinel reported that some of the Prussian outposts were approaching the fortress, followed by several detachments. Daumesnil had the call to arms beaten, and left the fort by the main portal, with a small detachment. On the Paris road they found a Prussian officer, who had come to negotiate terms for the fort's surrender. That officer once again demanded the surrender of the fortress, saying that it was not tenable, and that, after due reflection, the governor would do well to give serious thought to the matter, because, if he persisted in his resistance, he would be attacked.

Daumesnil replied:

> I am awaiting you unwaveringly, but remember that you are going to be dealing with Frenchmen, who are ready to die for the sake of their honor, rather than to surrender like cowards to foreigners. The patience of the garrison is exhausted: for several days now they have wanted to attack.[19]

Both parties separated, and Daumesnil and his officers returned to the château, where he called together his council. Having heard their views as to how best to proceed, he wrote this letter to the Minister of War, who by now was Gouvion-Saint-Cyr:

---

19 Clairval, *Daumesnil*, p. 204.

Vincennes 12 July 1815
Monseigneur,
You cannot doubt that my intentions are to preserve for France the precious artillery objects that Vincennes holds, and that the sentiments of my garrison are the same. If Your Excellency will deign to send me his orders in writing, I beg him to believe that I will carry them out punctually.
I have the honor to be, with the most profound respect, the very humble and obedient servant of Your Excellency, *Monseigneur.*
Maréchal de camp
Baron Daumesnil[20]

The governor instructed his aide de camp, Darribeau, to go the Prussian outposts to ask for permission to take the letter to Paris for the minister. At a loss as to how else to resolve the impasse, the Prussians permitted Darribeau to proceed. When he reached the minister's office, the latter asked him whether the governor had received his letter of 10 July. He was told that it had not reached Daumesnil. Darribeau then went to Blücher's headquarters and asked what had happened to the minister's letter to the governor, and was told that the letter had been held there, and that some one had forgotten to send it on. He then asked what had happened to the governor's letter of 10 July addressed to the minister, and was told that no one knew anything about it. He was given a copy of the minister's letter of the tenth, which should have been delivered to the fortress.
The minister's letter of 10 July read as follows:

General,
You cannot be unaware of the fact that the King has returned to his capital to the acclamations of his people and has taken up the reins of power; you would therefore become guilty in the highest degree if you would put up a continued resistance; you will consequently raise the white flag at Vincennes and send an officer to make your submission and take the King's orders.
I have the honor, General, to greet you with great esteem,
The Minister of War
Marshal Gouvion-Saint-Cyr.[21]

Daumesnil called together his council and read the letter to them. It was decided that the governor should send an officer to the minister to ask for his orders, and to inform him that the fortress would submit to the king. Accordingly Darribeau left at ten o'clock, taking with him the record of the council's meeting and decision, signed by its members. He returned

20 S.H.A.T. archives, *Correspondance Générale,* D3 1.
21 Clairval, *Daumesnil,* p. 205.

at two that afternoon, accompanied by an aide de camp of General Dupont, bringing an order from the minister to raise the white flag of the Bourbons. (The same officer had come on the same mission on preceding days, but the Prussian outposts had not permitted him to pass.)

It seems probable that this officer informed Daumesnil of the result of a conference on 12 July among the Allied foreign ministers on the subject of Vincennes, the record of which included the following decision:

> It has been agreed to suspend the attack on Vincennes on the condition that the château surrender to the King, and that the military effects which are there will remain at the disposition of the Allies in conformance with the capitulation of Paris, except for those which are judged to belong to and to form the normal supply of the château; commissioners will be named by both parties to make the separation.
>
> The King will be asked to make the proposed demand.[22]

This document was signed by Castlereagh, Metternich, Nesselrode, and a Russian, whose signature is unfortunately illegible.

If that measure were to be carried out, it would, of course, render null and void Daumesnil's principled stand, that those highly valuable war materials should remain the property of the French government. Fortunately, Louis XVIII was not insensible to the desirability of retaining possession of that very considerable national asset, but he felt constrained to make a show of accepting the Allies' demand, so he resorted to a bit of tactical strategy. By the intermediary of one of his officers—most probably, Varéliaud—Daumesnil agreed with the Minister of War, Gouvion-Saint-Cyr, that he would ignore all demands or orders for the surrender of the fortress, even those coming from the French government.

Reassured by the knowledge that his course of conduct had the approval of the French government, Daumesnil continued his efforts to improve the fort's defenses. Among the additional artillery pieces, which Daumesnil had ordered be emplaced, on the walls of and within the château, were Congreve-style rockets of 3 and 3.5 inch caliber, which had begun to be produced in a Vincennes workshop as early as 1810, based on the design of British Congreve rockets captured at Boulogne in 1804, during the British attack on l'île d'Aix in 1809, and elsewhere.[23] He had these rockets mounted on racks on the platform of the keep, thereby significantly extending their range.

At four on the afternoon of the 13th the officer of engineers discovered that the water supply to the fort had again been cut off, and reported that to the governor. The remainder of that day passed without incident, however.

22 That is, for the surrender of the fortress. Archives of the Ministry of Foreign Affairs.
23 Information courtesy of the *Département Artillerie, Musée de l'Armée*.

At three on the morning of the 14th, Daumesnil had a white flag of the Bourbons, which had been hastily made, raised from the platform of the keep. The same day the *Moniteur Universel* noted that fact, commenting that it signaled the acceptance by the fortress's governor and garrison of the king's return and their rallying to His Majesty.

At four o'clock, those on that platform observed that the cannon, howitzers, and mortars, which the Prussians had emplaced in batteries on the hill before Saint-Mandé, were being withdrawn through the village of Vincennes, together with their munitions wagons, although the disarmed emplacements were still being retained. The garrison nonetheless remained on the alert against the possibility of an attack.

At ten that morning, Daumesnil sent his artillery commander, Major Dérivaux, and his aide de camp to the Prussian blockade commander, Colonel von Rüchel, to ask why the water supply to the fort had been cut off. At eleven, a Prussian captain appeared at the French outpost on the Montreuil road to inform the governor that he could send some one to turn the water back on, and that the individual in question would be respected and protected. At noon, the inhabitants of Vincennes, who had been prevented from returning to their homes or traveling to Paris, were once more permitted freedom of movement, although the lifting of restrictions did not apply to members of the fort's garrison, or to the dispatch and receipt of their mail. However, it was expressly forbidden to bring food or munitions to the village.

At two that afternoon Daumesnil sent Adjutant Bénard, with a plumber of the garrison, to the manhole on the Montreuil road, where the water had been turned off, and soon it was flowing once more. This inconsistent type of harassment of the garrison and its commander was to mark the Prussians' dealings with them throughout the period of the blockade, perhaps reflecting conflicting signals from the senior levels of the Allied command. The immediate blockading force at that point consisted of 600 infantry and 400 cavalry, with a similar number of both, as well as numerous artillerymen, at Saint-Mandé.

On 17 July Daumesnil wrote to the Minister of War, asking that two companies of veterans then in Paris be sent to him as reinforcements, explaining that he was experiencing desertions from soldiers serving in the fort's outposts, who had learned that men from the garrison would be accepted at the Hôtel des Invalides, and asking the minister to take action to prevent that practice. The minister replied that he could not send Daumesnil reinforcements at that time, but that he had written to the governor of Les Invalides, Marshal Sérurier, to ask him to arrest and send back to Vincennes any such deserters, since that was their post, which they should not leave.

On the same day, Daumesnil had written to the minister, telling him that a former artillery officer living near the arsenal in Paris had overheard some Prussian colonels, who were present at the arsenal when the saltpeter which had been stored there was taken away, discussing the need to seize the powder in Vincennes, since the workers in the powder factory at Essonnes had all departed. He went on to say:

> Without any concern for what these gentlemen might be able to do, I thought it my duty to inform Your Excellency, and to take all appropriate security measures, and to put my fort in the best possible state of defense. Since it would be possible to occupy an excellent position situated vis à vis the château, which, besides having the advantage of covering a part of the fort, dominates the entire village of Vincennes, I would hope that Your Excellency would deign to approve my doing so.[24]

He attached a plan for the proposed position, in the hope that it would convince the minister of the necessity for seizing it. The minister turned down the proposal, however, out of concern for provoking a violent Prussian reaction.

At noon on the 25th, Daumesnil received word from the Minister of War that the Allies, under the terms of the convention, wished to take possession of that artillery material that had belonged to the army when it was encamped outside Paris, but which it had not been possible to evacuate beyond the Loire, as well as muskets produced in various workshops in the capital. French and Allied commissioners were to come to the château to examine these materials, once the artillery commander in the fort had made up a list of them. That list was made, and sent off to Paris. Daumesnil had no intention whatsoever of turning over to the Allies anything more than a token of what the château contained, so the list was drawn up accordingly.

In a curious example of the character of the relationship which existed between the blockaded and the blockaders, on the 29th a Prussian officer came to one of the fort's outposts, asking to speak with the governor. It turned out that he wanted permission to lodge 600 Prussians in the village of Vincennes, which Daumesnil refused to grant, and the officer withdrew.

Since all appeared calm for the moment, men of the garrison continued cutting trees outside the fort, and bringing the wood into the fort to use in making *saucissons* (fascines), with which to strengthen the traverses. Villagers were now being permitted to bring food into the village but only for their own consumption.

At noon on the 6th, the commissioners—a French colonel, a Prussian major, and an English major—came to the fort to inspect the artillery materials that were to be turned over to them. Daumesnil went to meet them, and, after they had produced the orders of the Minister of War authorizing their mission, he admitted the three officers, but only into the

---

24 S.H.A.T. archives, *Correspondance Générale*, D3 3.

first courtyard. There 87 iron cannon had been arrayed, together with nineteen gun carriages in poor shape and 19,000 muskets needing repair, or incomplete. When the commissioners asked to see some munitions, Daumesnil took them to the horse watering pond and showed them the thirty caissons that had been dumped there. He then suggested that they go see the powder stored in the keep, telling them that he would deliver all 7,500 kilograms of it. With that, the commissioners left the fort. Their visit had lasted all of fifteen minutes.

This minimal concession to the Allies' demands not only failed to satisfy them, but it prompted the following letter to Talleyrand from the four foreign ministers:

It is evident from the report of the commissioners appointed to verify the status of the artillery objects and military effects that have remained at Vincennes in accordance with the Convention of 3 July, that the munitions manufactured there have been thrown into the water.

The destruction of these objects having been done in contravention of the cited Convention, the undersigned find themselves having to ask the French Ministry to give orders that the same quantity of munitions that were destroyed be produced and delivered.

The ministers of the Allied courts beg His Highness Prince Talleyrand to receive the assurance of their great consideration.[25]

The French government's reaction to that complaint was prompt. It was conveyed to Daumesnil in this letter to him from the Minister of War on 12 August:

General,
I have the honor to inform you that, in accordance with the Convention concluded with the ministers of the Allied Powers, France must turn over the materials placed in Vincennes from the 1st to the 7th of this past July, coming from the evacuation of Paris. These materials consist of:

27 24-pound cannon
4 12-pound cannon
46 8-pound cannon
10 6-pound cannon
11 gun carriages for 24-pound cannon
8 naval carriages for 6-pound cannon
7,500 barrels of powder

25 Archives of the Ministry of Foreign Affairs, *Mémoires et Documents France*, 690.

15,308 French and foreign muskets needing repair, or unservice-
able
337 carbines
3,157 musket barrels.

My intention is that these materials be delivered on Monday, the
14th of this month, at the place that will be designated in the Park,
and that the turnover be made to English and Prussian officers, who
will be responsible for receiving them. I instruct artillery Colonel
Doguereau to take the necessary measures for the removal of these
effects and their delivery to the officers of the Allied Powers. Since
some horses will be needed to transport (the effects), you should
give notice to the officer commanding the blockade so that there will
be no difficulty for their entry into the château. I have reason to
believe, moreover, that, with the delivery of these effects, the state of
blockade of Vincennes will be lifted.

Kindly give the orders for the necessary dispositions and
execution of these orders.[26]

In fact, the list of materials in the minister's letter seems to have been
simply a repeat of the list that had been prepared by the fort's artillery
commander and sent to the minister's office. The 7,500 "barrels" of
powder was presumably a garbled reference to the 7,500 kilograms of
powder that Daumesnil promised to the commissioners that he would
deliver in lieu of the munitions dumped in the pond. In any case, it
represented a very small fraction of the munitions contained within the
fortress, which the minister knew as well as did its governor. The former's
speculation that the delivery of these munitions would lead to the lifting of
the blockade proved to be considerably wide of the mark, however.

At six in the morning on 14 August, a French artillery officer and six
English and Prussian artillery officers came to the fortress to check on the
arms and munitions that were to be turned over to the Allies, saying that
they would return the following day to verify the count. At eight on the
15th, an English major and three Prussian officers, accompanied by 40
cannoneers of their respective countries, came to examine the materials,
which had been brought to the designated place, and to divide them.

At ten the same morning, Daumesnil and his artillery commander were
informed that French and Russian commissioners would be coming to the
fort to examine 10,000 new muskets that the French government was
transferring to the Russian government, for a fee of 40 francs each. At two
that afternoon a contretemps ensued, when those commissioners
presented themselves to the Prussian outposts at Saint-Mandé, and were
not permitted to pass. A Russian colonel sent for the Prussian colonel in

---

26 The Desclozeaux archives contain a copy of this letter.

charge of the blockade, and despite his protesting that the two countries were allies, the party was not permitted to continue to the fort. During the next few days, the English and Prussians worked to carry off their respective shares of the materials.

On 18 August, Talleyrand addressed this letter to the Allied foreign ministers:

> The Minister of His very Christian Majesty has the honor to inform Their Excellencies the Ministers of the four Allied Powers that the artillery materials, which had been transported from Paris to Vincennes from the 4th to the 8th of last July, have been completely turned over to the Prussian and English commissioners during the 14th and 15th of this month.
>
> The delivery of these materials must necessarily put an end to the state of blockade of Vincennes, since the demand for these materials was its cause. Nonetheless, the blockade still exists, and a Russian artillery colonel, who was authorized by the Minister of War to enter the château of Vincennes was not able to cross the line of the Prussian outposts.
>
> The Minister commits himself not to increase the garrison of this fort, but he asks that the blockade be raised, since there is no longer any reason to continue it, and the cessation of this blockade would appear to be a consequence of the delivery of the materials which were demanded.[27]

As for the Duke of Wellington, he evidently saw no need to put to use in the British army the arms taken from Vincennes. On 20 August he wrote to Prince Volkonsky, commander of the Russian forces:

> Prince
>
> There are in Montmartre 7955 muskets belonging to the army under my command, which came from Vincennes, and 1580 musket barrels. I need 250 of the former to arm the troops of Nassau; and I place all the rest at the disposition of His Majesty the Emperor.
>
> I ask that you coordinate with the officer, who will have the honor of giving you this letter, to take possession of these arms. I would wish that they were better.[28]

The following day Wellington instructed Lieutenant-Colonel Torrens to deliver "250 stands of the best French arms now at Montmartre" to the general commanding the Nassau troops.

Finally, on the 21st and 22nd, the Russians were able to take possession of their muskets, with some of which they immediately armed their troops.

---

27 Archives of the Ministry of Foreign Affairs, *Mémoires et documents, France*, 691.
28 Wellington, *Selections from dispatches ... of Field Marshal The Duke of Wellington*, p. 612.

However, Talleyrand's appeal for the lifting of the blockade was apparently ignored. In all likelihood, the Allies knew full well that the military equipment and supplies that they had received were a small portion of the château's contents, but, unable to think their way around the obstinancy of its governor while he was being covertly supported by the French government, they evidently decided to bide their time until the fortress, lock, stock, and barrel, would in due course fall into their hands.

On 24 August, Daumesnil ordered that a 21-gun salute be fired in honor of King Louis XVIII's birthday, sixteen from 24-pounders and five from 12-pounders, spread on all sides of the fortress, to demonstrate to the Allies that the château was well armed on all sides with heavy-caliber pieces.

From the middle of August on, there was a great deal of going and coming among the Prussian and Russian troops now sharing the blockading duty. The Prussians continued in various ways to test Daumesnil's resistance, or perhaps simply his patience, in a series of petty instances of harassment. For example, on 1 September, General Carl von Müffling, the Allied governor of Paris, for the first time put in his "two cents' worth," by requesting that the French outpost on the Paris road be withdrawn. Daumesnil sent back word that, as long as there were Allied outposts there, his would remain: that if the Allied outposts were withdrawn, so would his be.

By this time food supplies were running short within the fortress, since the Allies had prevented the passage of any provisions within its walls. Consequently, the governor wrote to the Minister of War asking for his help in this regard, and the latter charged a commisary officer with attending to the matter. In due course, adequate supplies were introduced into the fortress by various means, and from that time on until the end of the blockade. Surprisingly, the Allies seem never to have become aware of that penetration of the blockade.

∽

It is important to note the fact that the fortress of Vincennes was by no means alone in facing threats of, or actual assaults, by the Allies, although it remained, as in 1814, unique among all other French fortresses or besieged cities in that it was never surrendered. An examination of other instances of Prussian attempts to take possession of, and to destroy, French defenses will shed further light on the sharp split between Blücher and Wellington over the way to deal with such resistance.

When Louis XVIII returned to reclaim his throne, most French forts were flying the tricolor, although some commandants had replaced it with the white flag of the Bourbons, in the hope of avoiding a siege. Once Louis was installed on the throne, the Minister of War ordered all forts to fly the Bourbon flag, but some defied the order. Those whose commandants obeyed the order could hope for some tranquility and cessation of pressure, but it didn't matter to the Allies, who didn't consider a white flag evidence of submission to the Bourbons. All forts were blockaded, and some commandants defended them in the name of the king, and others, in the name of Napoleon. Not one opened its gates voluntarily to the Allies, but most replied with cannon shots to summations to surrender.

In July the French government laid down specific instructions for the procedures to be followed by the commandants of besieged fortresses, in the following terms:

Every commandant of a besieged fort, who, without having taken the advice of, or against the will of, the majority of the military council of the fort (in which the officers in command of artillery and engineering should always be members) will have agreed to the surrender of the fort before the enemy have made a practical breach, or will have sustained an assault, will be considered to be guilty of treason.

The governor will consult the commanders of troops, of artillery, of engineers, the *inspecteur aux revues* and the *commissaire des guerres*, individually or united in council.

In the latter case, the secretary-archivist will keep a record, and state in the record of the council's deliberations the general opinion, or the individual opinions respectively, of the members, who may sign it, adding whatever comments they believe may be appropriate.

But the governor, or commandant, alone will decide, by himself or against the advice of his council, which will remain secret. The council and its individual members should be told that it is expressly forbidden to let any subject of deliberation or their personal opinions on the situation within the fort leak out.[29]

At almost the same time, in an effort to establish some consistency in dealing with the question of the surrender of forts, in July the Allies adopted a model for their capitulation. A note of 17 July provided that regular garrison troops and departmental National Guards would move out of the forts and be replaced by local city guards, and there would be, in each case, an Allied commissioner to deal with whatever matters might arise. This action was justified on the grounds that all garrisons were loyal to Napoleon. The Allies would promise not to attack or blockade those forts which agreed to evacuate.

The Allies refused to allow French officers appointed by the king to enter the forts, however, and wouldn't permit the passage of orders from the commandant of the 2nd military division to be delivered to forts under his jurisdiction. Nor did the Allies always observe the conditions of the capitulation. In some cases, before lifting blockades the Allies demanded to know the destinations of the departing garrisons. In the case of forts

---

29 Wellington, *Supplementary Dispatches and Orders*, vol. II, p. 84.

they had occupied—Maubeuge, Landrecies, Avesnes, Philippeville—the Allies removed their artillery and prepared to destroy the fortifications. At Montmedy, an Allied officer devastated neighboring villages and had the inhabitants' animals seized, to be returned only when the people could persuade the fort's garrison to accept his demands. The commandant at Verdun reported that "exasperation with the Prussians was at a peak."[30]

By mid-July, Metz, Strabourg, and Lille were blockaded, the enemy not daring to lay siege to them. Arras, Condé, Valenciennes, le Quesnoy, Rocrois, Mézières, Auxonne, and Grenoble had been attacked, and had vigorously defended themselves. Some had forced their attackers to ask the king to order them to surrender.[31] In Longwy, a few hundred retired soldiers and volunteers organized a "free corps of Moselle." Led by General Meriage, they put the besiegers to rout, killing eight to nine hundred of them, wounding a larger number, and seizing several batteries. The Prussians were only able to resume their operations when the king dissolved the "free corps."

Rodemack, between Luxembourg and Thionville, was garrisoned by a small detachment of National Guards. Invested by the Prussians on 25 June, they resisted all attacks until 31 July. Another fort, near Briançon, had no garrison. The inhabitants of nearby Saint-Chaffre, men, women, and oldsters, went to defend it. An Allied force occupied their houses, and threatened to burn them, if the fort was not vacated. "Burn them!" was the reply, and the village was destroyed.[32]

Briançon itself was defended by the one-armed General Eberlé "with a few gunners and some 400 *douaniers* (customs clerks) and *Chasseurs des Alpes*."[33] In Thionville, the garrison's commandant, General Joseph Hugo, the father of Victor Hugo, succeeded in preventing the Allies from dismantling its fortress and carrying off its armament.

The defense of Huninge was under the command of General Joseph Barbanègre, who had 135 men at his disposal. Pillaging by the people of Basle had outraged the French townspeople, and when Barbanègre had fired on the pillagers, the latter had called on the Austrians to deal with the fort's garrison. On 25 June, the general called his men together and told them of his intention not to surrender the fort. On 14 August 25,000 Austrians began the siege, and on the 26th the fortress capitulated. When the small band of survivors marched out of the fort, they received full military honors, and the Archduke Jean embraced Barbanègre. (In 1892 Detaille immortalized this scene in his painting, *La reddition du général Barbanègre à Huningue,* in the Palais du Luxembourg (Sénat).)

Soissons capitulated on 6 August, Laon, on the 9th, and Philippeville on the 10th. At Mézières, where General Count Louis Lemoine was in

---

30 André, *L'Occupation de la France par les Alliés en Juillet-Novembre, 1815,* p. 109.
31 *Journal des Debats,* 14 July, Paris.
32 Vaulabelle, *Histoire des deux restorations, Tome III.*
33 Elting, *Swords Around a Throne,* p. 660.

command, resistance continued until the eleventh, but it was only on 1 September, on the orders of the king, that Lemoine signed the document for the disarmament of the town. Despite the terms of the capitulation, the fortress was pillaged by the Allies.

After Waterloo, all the French artillery that had not been captured during that battle had been placed in the fortress of Givet, just inside the Franco-Belgian border, where General Jean Bourke, a one-time aide of Davout's, was in command. Fearing that his communication might be intercepted, Marshal Gouvion-Saint-Cyr sent a courier to Bourke bearing a message written on a piece of paper no larger than a thumbnail, telling Bourke that the fort should only be surrendered when arrangements had been concluded with the French authorities to make the occupation as painless as possible.[34]

Things took an odd turn in Strasbourg, where General Rapp was the commandant. At the end of August, the soldiers of the garrison were told that they would be disbanded and sent home singly, without their arms and pay. They had not been paid for three months, and they refused to disband until they were paid. When Rapp told them that there was no money with which to pay them, on 2 September the soldiers announced that they were taking command of the garrison, and, putting aside their officers, they elected Sergeant-Major Dalhousie, of the *voltigeurs* of the 7th regiment of light infantry, as the commandant. The soldiers continued to resist the blockading force, and told the city's citizens that if they wished the blockade to end, they would have to raise 700,000 francs with which to pay the men of the garrison. By 4 September the money had been raised and the men paid, so they disbanded and went home.

Verdun, Toul, Lille, Metz, and Strasbourg were still in French hands when the Treaty of Paris was signed on 20 November 1815.

The stark difference between Wellington's and Blücher's views and intentions with respect to the French fortresses is made clear by the following correspondence. On 20 July Blücher sent this order to Lieutenant-General von Zeithen:

> Your Excellency will break camp tomorrow, the 21st, and, with two brigades, the 12-pounders, the howitzer battery, and as much cavalry as you judge necessary of the 1st Army Corps, you will march to La Fère and Laon in order to seize these two places. There can be absolutely no question of these commandants' wishing to raise the white flag in order to remain there; both places must be unconditionally under our control. In my position between the Seine and the Loire, and with the possibility of an operation across the Loire, I cannot tolerate having any fortified places across my communications being in foreign hands, least of all, French. Your

---

34 Pasquier, *Mémoires*, p. 352.

Excellency may therefore offer favorable conditions to the garrison and individuals, if we may thus be able to take possession of these places more quickly, but there must be no question of anything but our complete possession. Your Excellency will thereafter employ all measures in order to take possession as quickly as possible of La Fère, which is the most important thing. Do not execute any orders or messages that are not personally signed by me while my army is under my command, and I alone am responsible for everything. Your Excellency can use all supplies that are in the Château de Guise, and, as soon as the matter of Vincennes is settled, I will support you with the matériel that is there.

As soon as Your Excellency has taken La Fère and Laon, leave an appropriate garrison in them, until the Rhein Landwehr, which have been sent for, arrive.[35]

It is evident that von Ziethen, still not having the necessary heavy siege cannon with which he could be sure of being able to carry out the mission assigned to him by Blücher, had written to Wellington, asking to borrow some of the British siege train. On 27 July, the Duke replied to him as follows:

General,
A few days ago I received your letter of the 24th; and, as the question of the attack on La Fère had been discussed in the Council of Ministers of the Allied Sovereigns a few days previously, I thought it my duty to consult them before giving you an answer regarding the artillery; and it appears to have been decided that, for the moment, La Fère will not be attacked.

General Gneisenau, who was present at the conference, appeared to believe that you should have made your request to Marshal Prince Blücher, rather than to me; but I assure you that I would have had the greatest pleasure in giving you that assistance, if it had not already been decided that, for the moment, the attack would not take place.[35]

That was not the end of Prussian generals' asking to borrow heavy artillery from the British, as this letter of 5 August from Wellington to Colonel Sir Alexander Dickson, commander of his battering train, demonstrates:

Sir,
I have received your letter of the 30th July, in which you have informed me that His Royal Highness Prince Augustus of Prussia was about to attack Marienberg and Philippeville, and afterwards

---

35 von Prollius, *Militärisches*, p. 415.
36 Wellington, *Supplementary Dispatches and Orders*, p. 576

Givet; for which last operation His Royal Highness would require 150 pieces of ordnance.

I had always understood that His Royal Highness would proceed in these operations according to what had been agreed upon among the Allies here; and that he should not attack a place which it had not been agreed should be attacked, and would not attack any that should be found to have submitted to His Most Christian Majesty, and should have hoisted the white flag; and for this reason I had omitted to give you detailed instructions regarding the use of the battering train.

But as this does not appear to be clearly understood by His Royal Highness, I must now inform you that, consistent with the respect which I owe to the opinions and decisions of the Allies, I cannot allow the battering train to be employed to attack any place the commander of which has submitted to His Most Christian Majesty, and which has shown His Majesty's colors; and you will be pleased to communicate these instructions to His Royal Highness, and act accordingly.[37]

It does not require great powers of imagination to envision Blücher's reaction upon hearing of this principle that the Duke of Wellington was applying to this, and similar, cases. But there was nothing that he could do about it: for whatever reason, the Prussians simply didn't have their own heavy artillery.

∞

Let us now leave the broad stage of international political strategy for the narrower confines of the Château of Vincennes, where the tactical skill and unshakable determination of its governor continued to bedevil and frustrate the Allies.

On 1 August there had been published a royal decree stating that officers who had suffered amputations, and who were serving in forts or elsewhere, were without exception to be retired, the amount of their retirement to be set in accordance with the maximum amount allowable for the mutilation in question, without respect to their years of service. The Minister of War was to give effect to this decree on the first of September for all general officers of the army's general staff, (in command) of forts, and of military administration.

Daumesnil wrote to the minister, asking that an exception be made in his case, since he was dismayed at the idea of his being forced to leave his post for a purely administrative reason while the question of the fort's being kept in French hands was still in the balance.

On 17 August, General Maurice Castlenau d'Albignac, the secretary general of the Minister of War, replied to Daumesnil, saying that there could

---

37 Wellington, *Supplementary Dispatches and Orders*, p. 586.

be no exceptions to that general decree, while at the same time adding:

> The Marshal, with whom I discussed the matter this morning, is all the angrier about it, since he is persuaded that the fort of Vincennes could not be in better hands, but he told me that he would leave you in place as long as possible, and hopes that the Prussians will for the present leave you in peace.[38]

On 4 September, another royal decree specified that the retirement of generals with amputations would take effect as of 1 January 1816, and on the ninth, the order for Daumesnil's retirement on that date was written. He could only hope that, in the time remaining to him, a solution favorable to France could be found to the question of the control of the fortress.

Starting on 1 October, there was still further coming and going on the part of the blockading troops. At six in the morning of the 2nd, all the Allied outposts were raised, and only eight officers and 60 hussars were left in Saint-Mandé, and the batteries were no longer guarded. On the 3rd, the troops at Saint-Mandé departed, and 500 uhlans of the Prussian Guard arrived in Montreuil, and then *they* left the following day.

Daumesnil decided to profit by this seemingly disorganized pattern of movement on the part of the Prussians, and at eleven on the morning of the 4th , he ordered the officer of engineers to destroy the emplacements of the batteries on the hillside before Saint-Mandé. That officer took 60 veterans, furnished with tools, and 30 armed men, and left the fort, accompanied by Daumesnil. By two in the afternoon, the task had been accomplished, without any interference by the Prussians, who merely observed the progress of the work. Men sent on reconnaissance by the governor found that there were still a good many Allied soldiers in the vicinity, although not occupying the outposts that had been manned previously.

This seemingly random shifting of troops continued throughout the rest of October, the only new element being the addition of Silesian and Hanoverian troops. Then, on the 29th, *they* were all replaced by 4,600 soldiers from Brunswick.

All of this activity understandably gave rise to speculation as to the Allies' intentions regarding the fort. On 6 October, the Paris Prefect of Police, Count Anglès, sent this message to the Minister of War:

> *Monsieur le Duc,*
> I have the honor to inform Your Excellency that on the 4th I received the news that the Prussians had re-occupied the posts that they had abandoned around the fort of Vincennes; that the garrison was expecting to be attacked, the soldiers saying that they had been

---

38 Clairval, *Daumesnil*, p. 207.

warned by the Prussians; and that the inhabitants of Vincennes had abandoned their homes.

It was further reported that the governor had not let it be known that he had been warned of this attack, but movements within the fort had been noted.[39]

Daumesnil's continued presence in Vincennes was a source of bitter resentment on the part of the ultra royalists, who considered it disgraceful that such an obvious Bonapartist could be permitted to continue to occupy such a key post. On 7 October, the Prefect of the Seine wrote to the new Minister of War, General Henri Clarke, the Duc de Feltre, telling him that the governor of Vincennes and his *commandant en seconde* were known to have made observations insulting to the king and the government, and that officers being sought by the police were taking refuge in the château. Count Anglès, sent a very similar letter to Clarke, who reacted to these reports by sending this order to General Maison, governor of the 1st Military Division:

The Prefect of the Seine informs me that officers not part of the garrison of Vincennes go there every day for the presumed purpose of escaping searches being made for them.

I ask that you assure yourself of the accuracy of this report, and, for that purpose, send a general of your staff to that place, who should present himself at the gates of Vincennes *after retreat has been beaten*, with the orders and necessary authorization to visit the fort with care, and have brought to Paris all individuals there who do not belong to the establishment and who are unable to justify their regular positions.

In his turn, Maison sent General Vincent de Conchy, of his staff, to Vincennes to look into the matter. On the tenth of October, Conchy submitted this report to General Maison:

... I went to Vincennes after retreat had been beaten. After having acquainted *le Maréchal de Camp* Baron Daumesnil, the governor, with His Excellency's intentions, I asked him to inform me of the status of all the individuals employed in the service of the garrison, and had pointed out to me their lodgings, as well as those of the officers I visited, with an officer of the general staff. I didn't find any individual who did not belong to the garrison.

General Daumesnil and the *Commandant de la Place* gave me their word of honor that, to their knowledge, there had never whatsoever been any officer not part of the garrison permitted to

---

39 S.H.A.T., .*Correspondence Générale*, D3 10.

enter the fort: that the service was rigorously controlled; and that the surveillance was such that an individual of the garrison could not give asylum to any one without its being known immediately.

On 12 October, General Maison reported to the minister as follows:

> *Monseigneur,*
> I had the honor to submit to you yesterday the report of General de Conchy about the visit that he paid to the château of Vincennes, in conformance with Your Excellency's orders.
> I should not leave you unaware, Monseigneur, of the fact that the *Maréchal de Camp* Daumesnil has been deeply disturbed by this measure, which has seemed to him to be proof of a distrust of his fidelity to the service of the king and his correctness in fulfilling his primary duties. The reports given to you against him having been accepted as being false and lacking any foundation, General Daumesnil asks of Your Excellency the exemplary punishment of those making false allegations, and, I believe it is my duty to support his request, as a satisfaction justly due to this general.
> The governor of the 1st Military Division,
> Comte Maison.[40]

Obviously Daumesnil believed that the best defense was an offense. Equally obviously, some of his fellow officers were becoming increasingly irritated by the rumor-mongering of that *pékin,* the Prefect of Police. The chief of the Military Police Bureau of the 8th Division of the Ministry of War wrote to the Prefect, telling him that there was no foundation to his reports, and concluded by saying "your agents have led you astray." But the Minister of State, Prefect of Police, *le comte* Anglès, was not to be put off that easily.

On the 18th he picked up his pen once more, and wrote to General Clarke:

> *Monseigneur,*
> Your Excellency has already been informed of the repeated complaints occasioned by the bad spirit manifested in general by the officers and soldiers of the garrison of Vincennes. He has doubtless put into effect the measures and inquiries that this state of affairs makes necessary. I believe I should point out to him two soldiers, whom it would seem to be useful to question. Their names are Paul Bonté, an invalid, and Bertrand, a veteran.
> The former, who was part of the garrison of Vincennes, where he had been during the siege, and which he left under the protection of

---

40 All of this correspondence is in the S.H.A.T. archives, Daumesnil file.

the Duke of Duras, has said that he could no longer remain there because of the incendiary statements being made daily by the governor and the commandant of the fort. He states that he heard these officers say that, at the first indication of revolution in Paris, they would fire Congreve-type missiles on the château of the Tuileries.

The other, having shouted 'Vive le Roi!' in the citadel, is said to have been placed in a cell at the bottom of the moat for fifteen days.[41]

That this sort of nonsense was having some effect is indicated by a note by the minister in the margin of Anglès' letter reading, "Have them questioned. Propose the replacement of General Daumesnil by M. de Puivert." In fact, Puivert still considered himself the rightful governor of Vincennes, and he was readily available to the minister.

While a new inquiry was in progress, a Prussian colonel came to the château of Vincennes, and was brought to the office of the governor. There a cannon blocked the window, and beside it was a pile of cannon balls and grapeshot cartridges. Once again, the colonel demanded the surrender of the fortress and its arsenal. Daumesnil responded:

Unless I receive an order written in the hand of the king, I will not surrender the fort, the defense of which has been entrusted to me. I will repel every attack to the best of my ability, and if I see that I can no longer resist, this will be my final resource.

Indicating a trap door and opening it, Daumesnil showed the colonel that it was directly connected by a tin-enclosed chute he had had constructed, which lead to the main powder magazine directly below them. "I would only have to throw a lighted torch through that opening to blow up everything," the governor said.

The calm firmness with which Daumesnil made that statement deeply impressed the Prussian, who drew back instinctively from the menacing opening in the paved floor of the room, saying, "You're assuming a terrible responsibility."

"What responsibilities does a dead man have?" Daumesnil asked. The Prussian colonel saluted the French general, and withdrew without a reply.

It may have been that visit that prompted Daumesnil to write to the minister, again asking for reinforcements, and requesting that "someone important" come to the château so that Daumesnil could discuss with him an important project, which he didn't dare to commit to paper, being so closely blockaded. He had taken advantage of the trip of a woman in the fort, who was going to a nursing home in Paris, and who had agreed to conceal the letter in a garter. One of the sisters there had agreed to see that

---

41 Clairval, *Daumesnil*, p. 208–9.

the letter was delivered to the minister.

When Clarke received the letter, he at once thought of General de Rochechouart, the commandant of the Department of Seine and of the French military establishment of Paris, as being well suited to such a mission, and sent for him. When the minister asked Rochechouart how he planned to gain access to Daumesnil, and how he would disguise himself, the general replied that it would be ridiculous to try to go covertly to an establishment which was within his jurisdiction, and that he would instead go on horseback in uniform, and with an aide. He said that he would inform the Allied governor of Paris, General Müffling, of his intended visit to Vincennes, commenting that it would be interesting to see if Müffling opposed the visit.

When Rochechouart called on Müffling, whom he knew quite well, he was cordially received. The Prussian general posed no objection to Rochechouart's proposed visit to Vincennes, merely observing, "He's a tough man, that General Daumesnil of yours. I believe he doesn't care much for the Bourbons, because he doesn't like their allies." Rochechouart responded that he had no idea of his fellow officers' political views, being new in the army, and, with a *laissez-passer* for the château in hand, he left Müffling.

Early on the following morning, 24 October, Rochechouart set out for Vincennes with an aide and an orderly. In his memoirs, he writes:

> The account that I shall give of my interview with General Daumesnil has, as its principal purpose, making known the conduct, so deserving of praise, of this intrepid soldier in these circumstances. I consider myself honor-bound to give it all the publicity it deserves in recounting a doubly heroic feat, which has not only not been worthily rewarded, but the details of which have remained unknown, and that his biography has not mentioned. I count myself fortunate to be able to repair such an omission, and to add a branch of laurel to those which make up the crown of this valorous Périgourdin.[42]

Daumesnil greeted his visitor warmly, and took him to his apartment, where they at once began to discuss the governor's position. Rochechouart told Daumesnil that he had been charged by the minister with telling the governor how much his firm and courageous conduct was appreciated by the king, who, while congratulating Daumesnil, assured him of his satisfaction. He went on to say that he had been instructed to work out with Daumesnil the means by which the things that he needed could be provided to him, and to find out about the project, regarding which he had written to the minister. In his memoirs, Rochechouart then recounted his conversation with Daumesnil in the form of a dialogue. It

---

42 Rochechouart, *Le Général Comte, Souvenirs sur la Révolution, l'Empire et la Restauration,* p. 467.

seems worth reproducing in its entirety, merely simplifying the identities of the speakers from *Le Général* and *Moi* to "D" and "R."

D: For the moment, I have no need other than for additional men, since my garrison, which no one has sought to increase, probably because of the important events which have taken place and which have attracted the entire attention of the government, consists of 50 veterans, a few soldiers of the train, a small depot of a battalion of artillerymen and 20 men, some of whom are wounded, 35 dismounted troopers of different branches, 15 sappers, and some 40 line infantrymen from different regiments. So the total of my army doesn't exceed 200 sous-officiers and soldiers, with 20 officers of various ranks, not counting the staff of the fort.

R: I can't imagine how, with so few people, you have had the temerity to hold out against the forces which are opposed to you. Unfortunately, I don't see any way of sending reinforcements to you. The Prussians would never agree to it.

D: I'm equally convinced of that, but now that I'm certain of the support and approval of the Minister of War, I'll try to get along with what I have, in accordance with the resolution that I arrived at yesterday evening, which I conveyed to the Prussian colonel, who came to renew insidious propositions, which amounted to nothing less than delivering to him the château and its arsenal.

R: Can you tell me what that resolution is?

At that point, Daumesnil told General de Rochechouart of his meeting the previous evening with the Prussian *parlementaire*, and Rochechouart asked what effect the threat to blow up the fortress, as a last resort, had had on the Prussian.

D: The manner in which I had expressed it convinced him that I was fully prepared to carry it out. The colonel withdrew, saying to me that I was taking a terrible responsibility on my head. "That means little to me," I replied. "What responsibilities does a dead man incur? But I would perish gloriously, in giving my country the ultimate proof of loyalty at my disposition, because I would wish to die with all that is the dearest in the world to me."

R: That is sublime, my dear general. What does that last phrase refer to?

D: You shall see.

He rang for his orderly, and when the man appeared, he told him, "Ask my wife to come here with her son." A moment later, I saw a young and pretty woman enter the room, holding in her arms an infant of three or four years. Then, continuing, or rather finishing, his sentence, he went on:

"I could have sent this young spouse of mine, with our only child,

343

to Paris, but I knew her well enough to be certain that she shares my sentiments and my love for France. At the instant that I would be blown up, she would be by my side, holding her son as she is holding him now, and the same tomb would enclose the three of us."

My eyes filled with tears, hearing these simple and touching words, spoken without any pretension, and with the ring of truth, leaving no doubt as to their sincerity. As soon as I had mastered my emotions, I grasped his hand with all my strength, and, taking that of his young wife, I said to them that I hoped that it would not come to that extremity. "If we were at war," I said, "I won't say that couldn't happen, but, after all, we're not, and I'm convinced that your firmness and your courageous determination will impress them to such a degree that they will not push matters that far."

Then I had to take my leave of this courageous man, assuring him that I left him deeply moved by my esteem for his noble conduct and the devotion of his young and charming spouse, all of which I would report to the Minister of War.

As I was mounting my horse, General Daumesnil said to me, "Upon second thought, I think it's useless to try to send me reinforcements. That could lead to some angry exchanges, or encourage the Prussians to try to seize our materiel, the importance of which they might tend to exaggerate, in light of such an action by the French government. I don't need anything. I have enough supplies. As for munitions, I'm amply supplied. I'm happy to have the minister's approval. I hope that he'll remember it."

I went straight to the minister and reported what I have just written, and in terms most favorable to that intrepid General Daumesnil. I did not fail to say how advantageous it would be to the king to retain in his service a man capable of such devotion, motivated entirely by a determination to fulfill his duty to his country. The minister assured me that he would take care of him, and place him in a position suitable for his merit, and in recognition of the service that he had rendered. But, alas! in the end, it came to nothing. That promise—I should say, that obligation—was forgotten. Vain and irrelevant considerations, and Court intrigues, led to a result quite the opposite of what I had expected.

General Daumesnil must have been very handsome in his youth, because, at the time of which I'm speaking, he had preserved a remarkable figure; he was brown, as a man born in the Midi, his hair dark brown, a bit bald, although he was only 38. His wooden leg made him appear shorter than he had been before his wound. Everything about him gave an impression of strength of character.[43]

---

43 Rochechouart, *Le Général Comte, Souvenirs sur la Révolution, etc.*, p. 470–1.

In his report to the Minister of War on 24 October of his visit to Vincennes, General de Rochechouart said that the governor had told him that the village of Vincennes was full of officers and undesirable characters, who had gone there to escape the surveillance of the Paris police, and where they were able to find lodging because "the mayor is a rogue, and leaves them alone." Daumesnil had told Rochechouart that he was able to some extent to maintain order in the village during the day, but that at night he needed all his men to be able to guard against the almost nightly attempts by the Prussian to take possession of the fortress. Rochechouart ended by recommending that the minister send "an intelligent and dependable" officer to Vincennes for a few days to ascertain the facts.

It was now clear to Daumesnil that the more fervent royalists were looking for an excuse to remove him from Vincennes, and that, in consequence, he had more to fear from his own government than from the Prussians. It was unfortunate that the turbulent situation then obtaining in the village of Vincennes was playing into his critics' hands. Consequently, he felt the need to take the offensive in his own defense. On 26 October he wrote to the minister:

Monseigneur,
Some time ago I informed *Monsieur le Comte* Maison that several officers had come to Vincennes for lodging, on the pretext that food in Paris was too expensive. Since they couldn't show any authorization from General Maison, I forced them to leave. Today I have the honor to report to Your Excellency that the village is filled with individual soldiers, whom the mayor tolerates, and to whom the police pay no attention. On holidays, suspect men assemble in the cabarets, open all night long, sometimes crying out seditious expressions. Last Sunday, a white cockade was snatched from a hat and burned by some country folk, who were in a café one hour after midnight. I therefore beg Your Excellency to obtain some information on the mayor of the commune and the commandant of the National Guard. All the denunciations which take place are blamed on the château of Vincennes, while crimes are committed in the commune, which it would be very important to repress. Yesterday the captain who was arrested and is being detained can only be the victim of a false denunciation: his attachment to the king and fidelity to his august person have long been known to me. I hope that Your Excellency will be good enough to take these facts into consideration, and to convince himself of the accuracy of these reports, which have so often been repeated.[44]

Daumesnil must have now felt that his back was to the wall. If he did, he was far from wrong. The minister's reaction to Daumesnil's appeal, and

---

44 S.H.A.T., *Correspondence Générale*, D3 12.

to Rochechouart's report to him, was to write to the Minister of the Interior, *le Comte de* Vaublanc, informing of the undesirable situation in the village of Vincennes. He cited the fact that the commandant of the National Guard there had been discharged from the office of mayor a year previously, and had since been fined for having been caught in the act of smuggling. This argued for the responsibility for looking into the situation falling in the Minister of the Interior's sphere of responsibility, the Minister of War reasoned.

Events now began to move swiftly, with letters and notes passing back and forth, from one minister to another, each one seeming to paint a darker picture of the allegedly seditious activities centering in the fortress of Vincennes. On 30 October the Minister of War addressed this letter to Lieutenant-General Despinois, commandant of the 1st Military Division, the same man who had brought the Marquis de Puivert to Vincennes in 1814:

Monsieur,

Numerous reports are reaching me on the bad sentiments animating the majority of the troops of the garrison at Vincennes. Finally, the protection that different individuals brought to the attention of the police have found in the environs, and even within the fort itself, have decided me to give you the order to go there personally, and to satisfy yourself as to the state of affairs there.

In the event that the complaints that I have received on this subject seem to you to be well founded, I authorize you to order General Daumesnil to go to Paris, and to replace him immediately by a dependable and capable officer, who will retain the command until the arrival of the Marquis de Puivert, who had been the titular commandant before the last 20th of March.

You will also consider whether it would be to the advantage of the service of His Majesty to withdraw the veterans who make up the garrison of this fort (except for two or three companies that have been identified to me as being well led and motivated by a good spirit), and to establish there the depot of the Departmental Legion of the Seine, where it would be much easier to keep an eye on it than in Paris.[45]

On 30 October the Minister of War acknowledged Daumesnil's letter of 26 October, and informed him that General de Rochechouart had been asked to look into the matter of the captain—presumably from the fort's garrison—who had been arrested and was being held in the prison in the commune of Vincennes, and in whose fidelity to the king Daumesnil had expressed confidence.

---

45 S.H.A.T., *Correspondence Générale*, D3 12.

By this time, no rumor about supposedly subversive activities within the château of Vincennes was too fanciful to receive credence. Writing to General de Rochechouart on the subject of a further investigation of Vincennes, one Paulinier de Fontenille, of the 4th Division of the Minister of War's staff, mentioned to the general that one of the sources of information regarding activities within the fortress was a man who acted occasionally as Daumesnil's valet, and who "told everything" to his niece, who in turn was in touch with the minister's staff. The writer particularly urged Rochechouart to try to find out whether the governor of Vincennes had on the previous year delivered to the king 40,000,000 francs, which funds were known to have been stored in 105 barrels—in the fort, presumably. Moreover, he added, five days before the departure of Bonaparte, the governor had had 28,000,000 francs placed in chests, and it was important to know whether that sum had been turned over—again, presumably, to the king.

Finally, M. Fontenille wrote, it was known that a cannon had been placed in a tunnel, which led to a little house of the governor's between Charenton and Saint-Maur. It was not clear what de Fontenille wanted Rochechouart to do about that supposed sinister strategem.

During all of these "alarums and excursions," the fortress was still—in theory, at least—blockaded, but on 15 November, the Allies finally had had enough of trying to browbeat or circumvent that damned *Jambe de Bois,* and they lifted the blockade. On 20 November the Treaty of Paris was signed, formally ending hostilities between France and the Allies.

On 19 November, the Minister of War, *le Duc de Feltre,* wrote this letter to *Monsieur le Maréchal de Camp Daumesnil, Gouverneur de Vincennes:*

Monsieur,
I have the honor to inform you that, in conformance with the intentions of the King, *M. le Maréchal de Camp,* the Marquis de Puivert, has been named Governor of Vincennes and has received the order to take command of that château. You will kindly turn over the relevant papers and documents to him.

My predecessor has already informed you that, as an amputee, you would be eligible, in accordance with the edict of 1 August, for the maximum of the retirement pay for your grade. Please tell me where you will retire so that I may have paid to you the pension to which you are entitled.[46]

No foolish, sentimental expressions of congratulations for a job well done. Instead, "Please close the door behind you." The pension amounted to 5,000 francs.

For the second time, Daumesnil had prevented an important French

---

46 Desclozeaux archives.

national asset from falling into foreign hands. One determined and courageous man, with a handful of staunch veterans and devoted officers from the ranks of the Imperial armies, had faced down the armies of two kings, one tsar, and one emperor, and in the face of conflicting instructions, both overt and covert, emanating from his own government.

The Paris public was loud in its praise of the steadfast general, their acclamations no doubt serving to stoke the desire on the part of the royalists, within and outside the government, to see Daumesnil hurried off the stage as soon as possible.

On the day that the fortress regained its freedom, the king named the Marquis de Puivert its governor. In order for the marquis to be re-installed in Vincennes, some administrative juggling had to take place, because he was over the retirement age of 60, and had 42 years of service, the maximum allowable number being 34. That latter hindrance was overcome by subtracting from his total service the ten years during which he had been imprisoned. The age limit was dealt with by giving him the title and functions of governor, as Daumesnil had been, since the age limit didn't apply to governors. (In his earlier incarnation at Vincennes, Puivert had instead been *commandant de la place*.)

On 23 November 1815, the conclusion of Daumesnil's second assignment as governor of the château of Vincennes was finally signaled by this letter from General Despinois to the Minister of War:

> *Monseigneur,*
> I have the honor to report to Your Excellency that, in conformance with the arrangements of his letter of the 19th instant, I went yesterday to the château of Vincennes, and that I there re-established, and had recognized by the garrison assembled under arms, the Marquis de Puivert, in his capacity as governor, in replacement of the *Maréchal de Camp* Daumesnil, admitted for retirement.
>
> The latter has been ordered to cease his functions and to return to his home, as soon as he will have placed in the hands of his successor the responsibilities with which he has been charged.[47]

One might have thought that such an unceremonious dismissal of a man to whom France owed so much would have satisfied even the most vindictive spirits among the military and civil establishments of the new regime, but there was one more grotesque, little bit of theater to be played out before "the powers that be" had done with him.

When the people of the village of Vincennes learned that Daumesnil was to be removed from his position as governor, but before he had actually been sent into retirement, a number of the villagers agreed among

---

47 S.H.A.T., Puivert file.

themselves that it would be a fitting gesture to present Daumesnil with a sword of honor, in recognition of his heroic actions in the defense of the château and their village. Accordingly, a collection was taken up, and Emile Deschamps, a young lieutenant in the National Guard and friend of Daumesnil's, was chosen to contract with the famous armorer, Pirmet, for the delivery of such a sword.

When Deschamps brought the sword to Vincennes, the group of sponsors for the gift proceeded to the château and asked to meet the governor. When he appeared, it was evident to them that his normally calm demeanor had been ruffled by the recent turn of events. He had just received an order to leave the château immediately, and his apartments were in a state of disarray, with a sale of his furniture in progress. He quickly regained possession of himself, however, and the presentation of the sword was made. Then he remarked to Deschamps, "I fear that you're going to be pursued with this sword in your backs, you and those most involved in this matter."

It turned out that Daumesnil was right. The little party had scarcely left the château before they were taken into custody, and led to the prefect of police to account for a seditious action on their part—to wit, publicly honoring General Daumesnil on the very day of his official disgrace. Young Deschamps was repeatedly interrogated.

On 30 November, the chief of the bureau of military police of the general staff wrote this letter to Lieutenant-General Despinois, whom we have already come to know all too well:

General
I have the honor to inform you that several inhabitants of Vincennes have joined without authorization and have collected 1200 francs for the purchase of a sword that they have offered to General Daumesnil, former commandant of the Château of Vincennes. That step, taken at the moment of the installation of the Marquis de Puivert toward an officer who permitted the tricolor flag to fly for eight days after the return of the King, seemed to me appropriate for drawing to the attention of His Excellency, the Minister of War, and I believed that I should report it to you.

The Minister of State the Prefect of Police has already taken steps regarding this affair.[48]

Despinois passed this report along to the minister, commenting, "This event, of little importance in itself, is only worth noting as an indication of partisan spirit, and because the mayor, M. Champfort, a man devoted to the King, states that he has had nothing to do with it."

On the 7th, the minister replied to Despinois, telling him to look into

---

48 S.H.A.T., *Correspondence Générale*, D3 15.

the matter to determine whether this gift had been made in the name of the commune, or whether a few inhabitants had taken it on themselves to make the presentation of the sword as a purely private gift, so that he, the minister, could decide what action, if any, need be taken.

In this case, the wheels of justice ground slowly, for it was only on the 28th of December that Despinois informed the minister that a report on the matter by the mayor of Vincennes to the Marquis de Puivert indicated that M. (*sic*) Daumesnil had not solicited the gift of the sword himself, and that it was only the work of a few of the villagers, whose naïveté and simplicity had been played upon, rather than reflecting a spirit of partisanship. Some one—presumably the minister—wrote in the margin of Despinois' report, "Put in a report to the King, and inform the Minister of the Interior." In that way, that seemingly Machiavellian threat to the monarchy had been laid to rest. An air of calm once more settled over the Tuileries, and Louis XVIII could now sleep soundly, his dreams no longer haunted by visions of a uniformed, wooden-legged ruffian slashing with his engraved sword at the betasselled velvet hangings of his monarch's gilded bed.

Once the danger, which Daumesnil had valiantly held at bay for 129 days, had melted away, the Minister of War, his sycophants, the king and his counselors, all couldn't wait to rid themselves of the presence of that uncomfortable reminder of another day and another sovereign. One would have to search long and diligently to discover a more glaring example of ingratitude on the part of a government toward one of its country's heroes.

But that would by no means be the end of this regime's malevolent pettiness toward, and harassment of, Daumesnil, as we shall soon see.

CHAPTER TWENTY
YEARS OF SILENCE

1815–1830

Whatever Daumesnil's forced retirement from the service cost him in psychological terms—and no doubt that was a very great deal—it had a devastating impact on the family's fortunes, in a very literal sense. The consequences of his lifelong free-spending habits were now compounded by the deleterious results of his misplaced trust in the public notary in Périgourd, Fournier-Verneuil, to whom Daumesnil had, in effect, given a blank check in matters relating to the family's affairs. That rascal's betrayal of that trust had left the family saddled with a considerable debt, and it seemed that the only immediate solution to that problem was to raise the necessary funds by the sale of the furniture of their apartment in the château before leaving it. Once again, the burden of this painful task fell primarily on Léonie.

Now all the special endowments that had been given to Daumesnil by Napoleon were wiped out, and his entire income was that of his pension of 5,000 francs, amounting to about one-twelfth of what his yearly income had been at its maximum under the Empire. Léonie wrote in her Journal:

This time, we've lost everything—everything, including hope. My father came and took me in his arms.

"My child," he said, "you have nothing left in the world: position, endowments, all that has been taken away. Even your dowry has gone for foolish expenses, and you've lost it all. But your father's heart remains, and you will come there, you will live there, you and yours! I only urge one thing: never allow a word of reproach to pass your lips. Your husband is unhappy enough!"

There was only one solution for the now homeless little family—the apartments of the Banque de France, and there they were very warmly received by the Baron and Baroness Garat.

"I took possession once more of my old room," Léonie wrote. "It was in those fifteen square feet that I lived with my husband, during those fifteen years of retirement, during which his courageous resignation never faltered."

Now that the debts had been paid, the problem of the thieving notary had to be dealt with promptly. "He had even managed to extract my signature," Léonie wrote.

He was a Périgourdin and, because he was a countryman, my husband had a blind confidence in him. My father wanted to sue him, and take him to court. Daumesnil saw only one way to deal with him—to kill him. I wouldn't allow one or the other solution.

In June of 1816, Léonie gave birth to a second child, Marie. She was born in Sceaux, where the Baron Garat had a charming property, the English park of which, designed by Vautier, was one of the most attractive in the environs of Paris. After the child's birth, the family remained in Sceaux until 1818, when they returned to the Banque de France.

It was at that time that Daumesnil was assailed by a severe case of sciatic gout, his first illness other than his twenty wounds. The indispensable Dr. Larrey was called for and did his best to ease Daumesnil's great discomfort. The patient observed to his old friend, "My dear Larrey, the leg that you took off is doing better than the other, and serves me better. I think of you, when I'm resting on it."

For three months, Léonie gave loving care, day and night, to her ailing husband, surprising the celebrated surgeon by her ability to bear up under such an exhausting experience. "It even astonishes me that she takes such good care of me," Daumesnil said. In an effort to restore his health, in July 1818 he traveled to Baden to take one of its famous cures.

In December of that year, Daumesnil received a letter from the Grand Chancellor of the Royal Order of the Legion of Honor informing him that the King had authorized him to accept and wear the decoration of Knight of the Imperial Order of the Iron Crown of Austria, and forwarding the decoration itself, which had been received from Vienna.[1]

During the years since the end of the Empire, the watchful eye of the police had continued to be focused on Daumesnil, as well as on numerous other senior officers of the Imperial armies, who had not rallied to the regime, and were now living in retirement, all of them being regarded by the Bourbons as potential Bonapartist plotters. In a note of 20 September 1820 to Baron Meunier, the Director General of the Police Administration, the Prefect of Police of the Prefecture of Seine et Oise reported that he had been keeping a strict surveillance on the château of Plessis Picard, occupied by *le sieur* Roetier, a retired officer, who had served in the

---

1   Desclozeaux archives.

"ex-Guard." Observations over an extended period, he wrote, had not revealed the visits of any suspect individuals. He noted that "General Dosmenil (*sic*), with whom the Roetier family had a relationship, has left the nearby château of Fortoiseau."

In a following communication to the same addressee on the 22nd, the same prefect wrote:

It is evident from the information sent to me that all the officers living in châteaux in the environs of Melun, to whom you have called my attention, are now in Paris. These include General Dosmenil, the renter of the château of Fortoiseau, General Savary, General Durosnel, and *chef de bataillon* Roetier Duplessis.[2]

He goes on to mention other officers who are in touch with them, including General Sébastiani, at that time a deputy from Corsica. (That alone should have sufficed to make him a suspicious character.)

On 29 September, still in 1820, the Paris Prefecture of Police reported to Baron Meunier, that a passport for Villers-Cotterêts, which Daumesnil had requested, had been received. This is only worth noting because it illustrates how tight the control over such officers was: Villers-Cotterêts is only some 40 miles north of Paris.

In a note to Baron Meunier on 15 January 1821, the Minister of State, Prefect of Police, notes the previous reports, adding that "Dosmenil" lives in the apartments of the Banque de France, and rarely goes out. He concludes by saying, "To sum it up, there is no reason to suspect maneuvers against the government."

The news of Napoleon's death on 5 May that year was a painful psychological blow for Daumesnil, which served to drive him deeper into seclusion. He was soon drawn from his despondency, however, for the sake of going to the assistance of two old friends, Colonels Combe and Planzeaux. They had been arrested a year previously, and charged with a plot against the Duc d'Angoulême.

On 14 June 1821 the Paris Prefecture of Police reported to Baron Meunier that Daumesnil had been given a visa on his passport for travel to Riom. In a separate communication to the prefect of Puy de Dôme, the Paris prefect wrote:

General Daumesnil, who normally resides in the capital, has just obtained a visa for travel to Riom. I thought I should alert you to this travel, the purpose of which I do not know. If, however, the conduct of this general officer should give rise to some observations, I ask that you inform me of them.

---

2 *Archives Nationales. Police Générale. Affaires politiques 1814–1830*, F7 6903 carton B. The following extracts are from the same source.

On 29 June the prefect of Puy de Dôme, in Clermont Ferrand, replied to Meunier:

General Daumesnil, the subject of your letter of the 18th, was summoned to Riom as a witness in the trial concerning the Conspiracy of the East. In his deposition, this general officer stated that he considered it to be a great honor to be a friend of Colonel Planzeaux and of Colonel Combe, the two principals accused. His conduct since his arrival in Riom has not given rise to any observation unfavorable to him.

Apparently Baron Meunier was losing patience with that country bumpkin of a prefect, who couldn't see his duty when it was staring him in the face. (Fellow's probably a damned liberal himself: must look into that.) In any case, on 8 July he wrote back to the prefect in Clermont Ferrand:

Monsieur le Secrétaire Général,
I have received the confidential letter that you have done me the honor of writing to me in connection with General Daumesnil. The meeting in Riom of several individuals of interest must naturally attract the attention of the authorities. It is in that connection that I wish to be informed of the details relating to it. That is, the exact nature of the congratulations that some youths felt they should address publicly to the general; also, was it noted by the newspapers, which saw an opportunity to take advantage of it. I would have wished that at that time you had been better informed as to what happened, or, if you were, that you had taken care to report to me. To what class did these young people belong? In what name had they met? What was the effect of such a demonstration? I ask that you gather exact information, which will make it possible to judge matters at their proper value.

One may deduce that the prefect of Puy de Dôme was himself by now impatient with the paranoia of Baron Meunier, since the prefecture's reply to that sharp reprimand was signed by a lower ranking official, the *Maître des Requètes*:

I have the honor to inform you in connection with my report of the 5th that the liberals had in general received with signs of distinct approval those of the witnesses whose depositions appeared to be favorable to the accused. Among that number was General Daumesnil, who stated that he was honored to be a friend of Colonel Planzeaux. That declaration, in the mouth of a man known for his defense of Vincennes, could not fail to inspire a sort of enthusiasm among the people of that party. Several formed a project to give that general officer a serenade on the day of his deposition, and there had been sent to Clermont to look for some musicians. When General Daumesnil declared that he did not at all want to be fêted, and that he would regard such an idea with great distress, the serenade did not take place.

I don't know if it was this project, which was not carried out, that the journalists called "congratulations rendered publicly;" it is possible that some individuals went to General Daumesnil to congratulate him, but those visits did not give rise to any kind of gatherings and did not pose any threat to the maintenance of public order.

Some of these gentlemen went to Clermont, where the accused principals spent several days after the issuing of the verdict, including General Daumesnil and Colonel Grouchy. Each and every one of them conducted themselves in these circumstances with prudence and circumspection. Everything was limited to two or three dinners in some private houses. It does not appear that anything reprehensible took place.

How frustrating it must have been for the good Baron Meunier to see his potential prey slip out of his grasp so easily! In his *Mémoires*, Colonel Combe writes:

One hundred thirty-four witnesses were heard in this affair. The brave General Daumesnil made the trip from Paris to come to protest, with that elevation of soul which so eminently distinguishes him, against the injustice of the accusations, of which we were the victims for fourteen months, especially with respect to the arrest of the Duc d'Angoulême. He concluded his deposition by declaring energetically:

"I have always known M. Combe as a man of honor, and honor and a dagger are incompatible."[3]

A judgment of acquittal was rendered unanimously.

The Colonel Planzeaux, in whose favor Daumesnil had testified, was one of the closest friends of the former governor of Vincennes. An uncompromising old "grumbler," Planzeaux bitterly reproached Daumesnil, when the latter, having been approached by an old comrade who had rallied to the new regime, responded to the approach in an amiable manner.

"How can you even touch the hands of those cunning devils, General?" Planzeaux asked.

"And who is telling you, my dear friend, that they are not as worthy as us?" Daumesnil replied. "God alone sees into the depths of hearts."

---

3   Quoted by Clairval, *Daumesnil*, p. 221.

"And all we see is the bottom of our purse, which is not as full as that of those villains," was Planzeaux's grudging rejoinder.

Contrary to the police report saying that Daumesnil rarely went out of the apartment in the Banque de France, almost daily, weather permitting, he would go to the Boulevard des Italiens, where, at the Café de Paris or the Café Tortoni, he would meet with such famous heroes of the Empire as Exelmans, Pajol, Petit, and Lamarque, and the talk would be of the bygone days of glory.

Out of concern for the future of his son-in-law's family, Baron Garat tried to persuade Daumesnil to ask for a return to active service, even going so far as to draft applications for Daumesnil to sign, but the stubborn soldier steadfastly refused to do so.

"I simply cannot serve," he said. "I would always be seeing my past. It's fine that others serve, but I'm unable to do so. Besides, France doesn't need me."

Daumesnil's position was made awkward by the fact that his brother-in-law, General Vallin,[4] who had initially resisted the idea of serving under the restored royal regime, had ended up by rallying to the new government, and had been rewarded by being made inspector general of cavalry, promoted to lieutenant general, made a grand officer of the *Légion d'honneur*, and raised to the rank of vicomte and a gentleman of the King's Chamber. The Vallin family shared the apartments of the bank, as did the Garat's two sons, so they would frequently all find themselves together around the dinner table. As may well be imagined, this made for an uncomfortable situation for Léonie.

Léonie wrote in her Journal:

> The only thing that was prickly was most assuredly the contact between my husband and General Vallin, my brother-in-law, who had taken a completely opposite direction politically. Consequently, he was covered with dignities and honors, whereas Daumesnil, poor and forgotten, each day saw all that paraded before him. But he was never jealous. Vallin was ready to be adaptable, Daumesnil was all heart.

A number of Daumesnil's friends, who regretted seeing him inactive, wanted to intervene in his behalf with the government, and begged him to let them put his name on requests for positions, but he would have none of it. He never wanted to ask anything of the government for himself. One day, when he was walking in the gardens of the Tuileries, he encountered General de Clermont-Tonnerre, at that time Minister of War, who said to Daumesnil that the government would be happy to make itself agreeable to him. Daumesnil's only request was for a scholarship for his son, which

---

4   Vallin had married the Garats' older daughter, Saubade. The two Garat sons, Paul and Charles, followed their father's footsteps into the banking world.

was immediately granted.

At this time, Daumesnil's principal distraction was hunting. He would spend days at a time in pursuit of boar, wolves, and roebucks. But wherever he went during those days, the eyes of the police were on him. On 24 September 1882, the Prefect of Police of the Prefecture of *Bas Rhin* wrote to the Ministry of the Interior:

> General Daumesnil, who has been singled out to me for his negative opinions, and who has had frequent contacts in this Department with men known for their opposition to the King's government, went on the 21st of this month to Froment to visit M. Champy, deputy from Vosges. He is to leave Froment to go to Paris. I thought I should give you this information so that he could be surveilled, if Your Excellency deems it desirable.

On the 30th, the Ministry of the Interior asked the Paris Prefecture of Police to institute surveillance of Daumesnil. Here is one of the police reports to the Ministry of the Interior:

> Office of the Prefect of Police
> Paris, 30 October 1822
> General Daumesnil lives with his father-in-law, M. Garat, at the Bank of France. As that senior officer has had a leg amputated, he only goes to the Palais Royal, where he goes at nine in the morning. After having read the newspapers and chatted with a great number of persons, who are there almost every day, and with whom he appears to be on close terms, he lunches at the Café Lamblin, and goes to the book store formerly owned by Corréard, or to the reading room of *Sieur* Gauthier. Finally, he goes home at five o'clock, and doesn't go out again that day.
> The surveillance on him noted that, at noon on the 23rd of this month, he stopped before the door of the Bank of France, and talked in a very animated manner for a half hour with the officer who was guarding it.

Whew! Kind of makes you think, doesn't it?

The K.G.B. could not have done a better job. In all likelihood Daumesnil found such ham-handed spying on him more amusing than threatening, and he and his comrades, who were in all probability also objects of the paranoid regime's attentions, may well have entertained one another by comparing notes on the clumsiness of the police agents, who must have included some of their own domestics. After all, during his day, Fouché had trained thousands in the conduct of such activities.

Amid the constraints deriving from the family's sharply reduced income, and the awkwardness of their living arrangements, during these years the ties that bound the little family together grew steadily deeper and stronger. Léon was now a scholarship student at the prominent school, Louis-le-Grand, and Marie was attending the school of the House of the Legion of Honor, at Saint-Denis (over which her mother would preside in later years). Once or twice a week, Daumesnil went to see the children, accompanied either by Léonie or by a former officer, Captain Turpin, who was a devoted follower of the general's. Rather than spend money for a carriage, he would often make these trips on foot. Daumesnil had long since learned that necessity can be a stern mistress.

By 1827, Baron Garat had sold the property at Sceaux, and had replaced it with an attractive small château, la Briqueterie, on the banks of the Seine at Ris-Orangis, and it was there that the entire family was now spending the summers.

In March, a third child, Louise, was born, and almost immediately after the child's arrival Léonie became seriously ill. Daumesnil was constantly at his wife's bedside, or caring for the newborn child personally. Léonie later wrote:

> I don't know how many nights Daumesnil, a father and a mother at the same time, rose to appease the cries of our infant. He did just as many thoughtful little things for me, extraordinary for a husband at the end of twenty years, as he had on the first day.

When they were separated, for whatever reason, the letters, which the couple exchanged, were always of a most affectionate nature. In 1822, when Daumesnil was visiting M. Thurot, the mayor of Haguenau, in the Department of the *Bas Rhin*, Léonie wrote:

> I am sending my dear Daumesnil a letter that Léon has just written to him, quite quickly and without mistakes. I think you'll be satisfied with it. I'm always very pleased with him, and I spend a lot of time with him. He works with a zeal which gives me great pleasure. Don't worry, I'm not tormenting him. In a few days he will also write to M. Thurot. I think that you are now together with that excellent friend, and that you are forgetting the fatigue of the trip, and are only thinking of enjoying yourself. Yesterday Marie took three piano lessons, two with me. I pretended to be very upset that she was performing so well, saying, "My goodness, what shall I do? Here's a little girl who is going to ruin me with rewards. Marie, I beg you, don't play so well!" Marie was transported with joy, and renewed her efforts to play even better. Next time I'll have her write a little letter to her Papa. She and her brother speak of him often, and already are asking if he's coming home soon.
>
> I'm waiting for a letter from you. Take care of yourself when you're

hunting, and especially don't let yourself get cold afterwards. You will say that I'm always nagging you, but I don't care, it's for your own good. The children and I embrace you with all our hearts.[5]

In 1825, Léonie had gone to "take the waters" at Niederbronn, near Haguenau, and Daumesnil was missing her badly:

It's four days since you've written me, and if there isn't a letter this evening, I'll die. If you knew the pain that I feel when the cursed postman doesn't bring me anything, you'd write me every hour, because you wouldn't want to see me, who loves you more than my life, suffer. I won't say more now, because I hope to receive a letter this evening, and tomorrow I'll tell you the rest.
Adieu, too beloved, too cherished, I cover you with kisses,
Daumesnil.

Daumesnil's spelling and command of grammar left much to be desired, and inevitably his errors in such matters render translations of his letters seem awkward at times, but there can be no mistaking the depth of the love for his beloved Léonie, which shines forth from them. I believe that leaving his phrases as close as possible to his own way of expressing his deep emotions best conveys the warmth of his ardor. Sometime in 1825 he wrote these lines to Léonie:

How beautiful and good my dear Léonie is. Your letter is so kind, that I truly believe you will be as good for me as you wish me to be for you. Yes, my angel, I will make every effort to please you and to care for you and to love you forever. This morning I was right to tell you that I thought I would have your news this evening, so I was happy all day long, which hadn't happened to me since your departure. But a word from you makes me so happy, and especially today, so I will keep your letter very carefully. I'm glad that my little bouquet pleased you. I'll send you another, without worrying that you will forget the good husband who loves and embraces you so much. I'm very sorry that the lamp and the buckle didn't suit you. If you wish, just say so, and I'll send you something else. I'm very glad that you're enjoying yourself at Niederbronn. I've always told you that the waters would be good for you. Next year, if we have the money and you've enjoyed this year, we'll go there. Good night, my true jewel, I embrace you, with love from the very bottom of my heart.

One gets the impression that Daumesnil could never quite get over the fact that he had been so lucky as to marry this very exceptional young

---

5 Clairval collection.

woman, for indeed it was probably the most fortunate thing that ever happened to him.

At this time, some of Daumesnil's old brothers-in-arms were resuming their careers in the military. After thirteen years of inactivity, Exelmans had been named inspector general of cavalry. But Daumesnil did not seem to expect anything further from fortune. On 30 January 1830 he was prompted to make his voice heard by this article, which had appeared in the opposition newspaper, *Courrier français,* commenting on the fact that the Marquis de Puivert had been named a peer of France:

> We believe we've heard the name of M. de Puivert mentioned in connection with the defense of the château of Vincennes in 1815; it's a feat of arms which has been mentioned in contemporary songs, but not in a way that would open the avenues to the peerage to its author. If Vincennes were to convey such an honor to one of its defenders, the name of Daumesnil would naturally present itself.

The following day the same paper published this letter from Daumesnil:

> *Monsieur,*
> Despite the advantage that you kindly wish to give me in the comparison that you draw between M. de Puivert and me, for which I thank you, I confess that I experience a sense of repugnance in seeing my name figuring in such a parallel. I thought it my duty to defend Vincennes twice against enemies, and I would have died there with my brave invalids and veterans, rather than surrender it to them. M. de Puivert thought it his duty to surrender the fort on the 20th of March to General Merlin, accompanied by a gendarme and a domestic. Each of us is judged and rewarded according to his deeds. All that I ask today is to continue to live peacefully and obscurely in retirement, not envying M. de Puivert either his decorations or his peerage, or even his governorship.

Daumesnil wanted to remain apart from all political activity. It was in vain that the opposition party, which continued to grow from day to day, attempted to use his name with which to attract the discontented.

Some time before the Revolution of July 1830, when Daumesnil was walking in the gardens of the Palais Royal, he was approached by a group of individuals, who wanted to attach his name to some secret intrigues against the government. Daumesnil rejected these proposals indignantly. A few minutes later one of his friends encountered him.

"Would you believe," Daumesnil said in a highly irritated manner, "that those miserable creatures dared propose to me—to me!—that I sign my name on a list of people involved in a conspiracy? Let them get over it!"

CHAPTER TWENTY-ONE
GAME, SET, AND MATCH

1830

On the morning of the 26th of July, 1830, Louis Philippe, the Duc d'Orléans, was at home with his family in their residence in the Paris suburb of Neuilly. It was about eleven in the morning, and the Duke was wondering aloud why the official newspaper, *le Moniteur*, was late. Just then, the paper was handed to him. He had barely opened it to scan the headlines when he exploded with an oath. Spread across the first page were printed three royal edicts that had been published the previous day. One dissolved the recently elected Chamber, another virtually abolished freedom of the press, and the third was the new electoral law, which reduced the electorate to about 25,000 persons, almost all of them landed proprietors.

"They are crazy!" the Duke shouted. "They'll be driven out again!"[1]

Consternation reigned in the household. The Duke's sister, Princess Adélaïde, kept her wits about her, however. Having glanced at the paper that her brother had thrust into her hands, she exclaimed to the Duke's wife, Amélie, and the young princesses, "Quick—the cockades!" She ran to her wardrobe, and began pulling out clothes that were red, white, or blue. In a few minutes the floor was littered with scraps, as the ladies wielded scissors, thread, and needles, and before long a handsome array of Republican cockades had emerged from the cut and slashed garments, which had been tossed aside.

On the same day, and at the same hour, King Charles X was at the Château of St. Cloud, his mind on the prospect of a day of hunting. When *le Moniteur* was handed to him, he thrust it into a pocket without a glance and rode off in his carriage to Rambouillet.

On the following day, increasingly alarming reports of the unrest in

---

1   de Stoeckl, *King of the French*, p. 149.

Paris kept arriving in both Neuilly and St. Cloud. By that evening, the first shots had been fired in Paris. The Royal Guard had been put under arms, and three battalions had been deployed in the city's center. The mob had set up barricades and was assailing the troops with whatever hurtful objects came to hand.

By the morning of the 28th, it was clear that this was no passing rain shower, but instead, a cloudburst. The military commander of Paris, Marshal Marmont, the Duke of Ragusa, declared a state of siege. As further reports of the fighting in the city reached St. Cloud, the king remained unruffled, his advisors assuring him that the reports were exaggerated. That evening, while he was enjoying a game of whist with a member of his suite, an aide announced a visitor, who requested an audience. "Tell him to wait; I must finish my game," was the king's reply. When he had finished the game and the man was admitted to his presence, it was the deputy comptroller of the Military Household, who described to the king in bald terms the chaotic situation obtaining in the capital.

"Surely you exaggerate the danger, my dear sir," was the king's comment, and he sat down for another game of whist.

A considerable distance away, south of Paris on a small estate on the banks of the Seine at Ris-Orangis[2], Daumesnil lived with Léonie and their three children in a château, la Briqueterie (the Brickyard), which his father-in-law had bought after selling the place in Sceaux. When Martin Garat died in May of 1830, la Briqueterie became the little family's permanent residence. In the warm weather, Daumesnil frequently spent time seated on the grassy slope of the property, which extended to the bank of the river, often together with Léonie and one or more of the children. In that way, he had become a familiar figure in the eyes of the watermen passing up and down the river, who would often doff their hats to *la Jambe de Bois* as their craft glided by, and call out a greeting, which he would punctiliously acknowledge with a wave of his hand.

It was in the early evening of 28 July that Daumesnil first learned of the July Revolution, and then it was from some of those boatmen. He had heard a few of them shouting something, which at first he could not make out, but when he rose and made his way closer to the river, he could distinguish their cries: *"Vive Daumesnil! Vive la Jambe de Bois! Général, à Vincennes, à Vincennes!"* Although, as has been noted, this was not the first time that Daumesnil had been greeted by passing watermen, who knew well his fame and took pleasure in thus saluting it, these acclamations were clearly exceptional in nature. It says something for the affection in which Daumesnil was held by the common people that, even after fifteen years of his absence from the public's view, these boatmen were perceptive enough to connect at once the fall of a repressive regime with the rightful

---

2   South of today's Orly airport, and across the Seine from the forest of Sénart.

return of a well loved figure to the scene of his most memorable hours.

The explanation for these acclamations was not evident to the little household, however, until the following morning, when a youthful friend of Daumesnil's, Charles Schulmeister, came in haste to the little château to inform him of the extraordinary happenings in the capital. In a letter fourteen years later to Charles's father, Karl Ludwig Schulmeister[3], to extend her sympathy on the death of his son, Léonie wrote:

It was he, I recall with gratitude, who came in great haste to la Briqueterie to tell his friend, General Daumesnil, of the revolution of 1830. It is to his zeal, and to his attentiveness that my husband owes his return from oblivion to his position as governor of Vincennes, for the very day that the kind M. Charles came to inform us, Daumesnil, who immediately went to the Palais Royal, was received by the Duc d'Orléans, Lieutenant-General of the Kingdom, who embraced him, saying, "General, Vincennes awaits you."

There, dear Sir, are my memories, which can never be forgotten, for the 28th of July was assuredly one of the most wonderful days of my life.

One can easily imagine how infinitely rewarding it must have been for this young mother, now just 35 years old, to see her husband, so long the object of malicious suspicion and neglectful disregard, brought back into the sunlight of official favor once again, with the prospect of a peaceful fulfillment of his duty to his country stretching out before them both and their three children. During the sixteen years since the Emperor was first tumbled from his throne, she had borne uncomplainingly and with unbowed head "the slings and arrows of outrageous fortune" that had been visited upon her family in the wake of that momentous event, so now this unexpected upward course of fortune's wheel must indeed have lifted her heart with it. As for Daumesnil himself, he was never a bitter or vengeful man, but who could now deny him a quiet glow of vindication?

At that time General Vallin, Daumesnil's brother-in-law, was also living with his family at la Briqueterie. When young Schulmeister related the events of the previous day to the assembled household, and told Daumesnil that his comrades were calling for him to come to the city, the Vallin servants began applauding Daumesnil. He reproved them, saying that this political reversal of circumstances might cause the ruin of their master, so they would do well to await the outcome of these unpredictable events before celebrating them.

---

3   Schulmeister was a highly successful French double-agent of Alsatian origin, who, under Savary's direction, repeatedly penetrated the Austrian general staff. Perhaps his most notable achievement was planting in the mind of General Mack the notion that the *Grande Armée* was in retreat, and therefore that it was safe to remain in Ulm, where, of course, he and his army were trapped by Napoleon. See Chapter Seven.

Léonie insisted on joining her husband. She later wrote:
I wanted to go, too, for this day, unique in the annals of history, presented a marvelous spectacle: Paris with barricades, Paris with the debris of a recent battlefield, and yet, the capital illuminated as on its greatest holidays; Paris in elation and joy, because it only contained victors. From the barrier, we were already meeting friends, young people, some from the *Ecole Polytechnique* or other schools, who, recognizing Daumesnil, wouldn't let him pass without shaking his hand. In that way, at almost every step we were cordially stopped in our progress, even by complete strangers.

At St. Cloud the morning of the 29th, the news from the king's prime minister, the Prince of Polignac, had been reassuring, and, as he sat enjoying his tisane, Charles X was congratulating himself on not having taken seriously the alarming reports that had come flooding into the palace the previous day. His reveries were interrupted by the arrival of a carriage in the palace courtyard, from which emerged his ministers, looking pale and dejected. They had fled from the city, with a mob at their heels, calling out for vengeance.

Just then a deputy, the Marquis de Sémonville, asked to be received, and when he entered the room, he threw himself at the king's feet, and beseeched him to revoke the ordinances which had precipitated the crisis, and to dismiss his ministers. He warned that the king's failure to take both actions would cost him his throne. After hours of indecision, the king signed a decree dismissing his ministers, and authorized de Sémonville and others to inform Paris of his change of government. That evening, he played whist again.

In Neuilly, Louis Philippe was in a state of great uncertainty, despite the glorious news from Paris that the Royal Guard had been defeated, and that the tricolor was now floating over the Hôtel de Ville. He was far from clear as to how this was all going to work out, and knew that his own situation was delicate, as long as Charles was still on the throne. After actually considering flight, he collected himself, and remained for the night with his family in a small building called "the little château" in the surrounding park.[4]

The morning of the 30th witnessed unbridled acts of wanton destruction by the mob, as the Tuileries palace was ransacked, and where a macabre scene was enacted when the rioters placed the body of a dead insurrectionist on the throne and decorated him with bits of crepe. When Lafayette appeared in the midst of the turmoil, he was wildly cheered, and it seemed to him that the future course of France was, for a moment, in his hands. After a nearly sleepless night, he decided that the only solution to the crisis was to set Louis Philippe on the throne.

---

4   de Stoeckl, *King of the French*, p. 159.

At St. Cloud, the final desperate measures designed to avoid disaster were proving insufficient to dam the muddy flood that was creeping toward the palace. Marmont had been summoned to the Château to explain to Charles his failure to maintain control over the Paris rioters. The Duc d'Angoulême remarked bitterly to the discomforted Duke of Ragusa, "Are you going to betray us as you did the Other One?" "Prince," Marmont replied, "without traitors, you would never have reigned."

The king finally faced the inevitable, and at three on the morning of the 31st he seated himself in a carriage, which set out for Rambouillet, a patched-together column of *Gardes du Corps*, *Chasseurs à cheval*, and other regiments trailing behind. That same day, according to the *Courrier Français*, the garrison of the château of Vincennes made its submission to the new regime.

We need not detain ourselves further with the frantic comings and goings of the next 48 hours, as courtiers and politicians dashed from Paris to St. Cloud, and from Paris to Neuilly, and back again, while Charles continued to cling to the hope that the situation was not beyond salvage, and Louis Philippe steeled himself to take the step that he realized by now was being forced upon him. The scene at the Palais Royal on the 31st, where Louis Philippe, now declared to be the Lieutenant-General of the Kingdom, sat awaiting Lafayette and the deputies, who were to anoint him King of the French, was chaotic almost beyond description. After several hours of waiting, it dawned on the Duke that, instead, he was supposed to go to the Hôtel de Ville for that ceremony, so off he went. That office having been performed, he had to fight his way back to the Palais Royal through a riotous mob, finally arriving there in a state of psychological and physical exhaustion.

In Paris, Daumesnil found his old comrades-in-arms, Exelmans and Claude Pajol, who had been in the thick of things on the days of the revolution, and who were now helping to organize and lead a march of the Parisians to Rambouillet. Charles had abdicated on the second, and had gone through the charade of writing a letter to the Duc d'Orléans "requiring" him to proclaim the accession to the throne of Charles's grandson as Henri V, and appointing the Duke as Regent. When this absurd daydream had been politely brushed aside by Louis Philippe and his supporters, Charles had withdrawn his abdication in a rage. It was that final act of folly that prompted the Duke's advisers to conclude that Charles had to be frightened away. So the *générale* was beaten on drums throughout the capital, and by the thousands Parisians gathered, armed with whatever came to hand, and started marching to Rambouillet, to ensure that the deposed king took the highroad to the coast. When the mob straggled into Rambouillet at two in the morning on the 4th, there were no soldiers to confront them, and the château was empty. Charles had finally come to his senses, and was on his way to exile.

On 5 August Daumesnil received this order from the Minister of War:

Monsieur le Baron,

In conformity with the intentions of the Lieutenant-General of the Kingdom, I ask that, upon the receipt of this letter, you go immediately and by post to Vincennes to assume command of that fortress.

You will take the measures necessary to ensure the maintenance of tranquility at Vincennes, to see that the most exact discipline is observed among the troops, and for the conservation of the artillery materiel and the munitions, which are in that fort.

Inform me of your arrival and report to me everything that relates to this service.[5]

Leaving immediately on horseback, Daumesnil crossed Paris, gathering as he went an increasing throng of cheering Parisians, who escorted him all the way to Vincennes.

An Order of the Day published the same day by Lieutenant-General Maurin, commandant of the 1st Military Division, read as follows:

The troops of the division are notified that, conforming with the intentions of the Lieutenant-General of the Kingdom, *M. le Maréchal de Camp* Daumesnil has been named to the command of the château of Vincennes, in replacement of *M. le Maréchal de Camp* Marquis de Puivert, admitted to retirement.

On the 6th, the *Courrier Français* reported the change of command in these words:

Yesterday the château of Vincennes was turned over by the Marquis de Puivert to General Daumesnil. 'We were game to game,' the latter remarked gaily to the Marquis, 'but the match is mine.' The 2,400 men within the fortress burst into the liveliest expressions of enthusiasm. They have hoisted at least ten tricolor flags on the towers and the church, and mingled with citizens from the château's environs.

Whether it was at the new king's initiative or that of some protocol-minded officer in the Ministry of War, it was obviously deemed desirable to give Daumesnil's appointment more official recognition than that provided by Louis Philippe's "General, Vincennes awaits you" greeting of the heady days of the July Revolution. On 12 August he received a letter from the ministry informing him that the king would receive him the following day in the garden of the Palais Royal, and that he should be there by himself and in full dress uniform precisely at 12:30. He was further instructed to confide the command of the château, in his absence, to an

---

5 Desclozeaux archives.

officer invested with his confidence.[6]

So it was that, at the age of 54 and after fifteen years in comparative obscurity, Daumesnil found himself back in the post that he had occupied twice before with such exceptional distinction. His title of governor was restored.

His re-installation as governor in Vincennes must have seemed to Daumesnil to be an auspicious moment on which to claim a promotion he felt he should have long since received, so he wrote to the Minister of War, asking to be given the rank of lieutenant-general:

> I had sworn to serve the Emperor faithfully, I had promised him that no foreigners would ever enter my fort, and I kept my word.
>
> Twice blockaded and attacked by the Allied armies, I knew how to repel them with vigor. I saved for my country 90 millions of materiel. All France knew of my defense and applauded it. Twice I have been removed from my post for having defended it too well. The offers that foreigners made to me were dishonorable; I rejected them, and certainly they were of a nature to tempt one's cupidity.
> I have not betrayed either Louis XVIII or Charles X, I have never sworn an oath to them; I have never seen them. Charles X sent the Prince de Poix and the Duc de Gramont to me, I didn't want to accept anything from them, even the Cross of Saint-Louis, for which two nominations, which I can still show, were sent to me.
>
> During that time I lost 25,000 frs. for the governorship of Vincennes, 3,000 frs. on the Emperor's privy purse, 16,000 on the Little Notices, 4,000 on Illyria, 8,000 on Rome, and 2,000 on the Monte de Milan. I have borne all of these losses with resignation; I have never been at court and I defy all the ministers who have been in power to say that they have ever seen me with them; that I wrote to them, or made a request.
>
> Today, entirely devoted to Philippe the First, I claim my rights, based on the laws, such as the ordinances of Louis XIV (6 April 1705), the law of 26 July 1792, of 2 brumaire and the Imperial decree of 24 December formulated in these terms: "Every governor or commandant, who, according to the specific accounts received by us, will have defended his fort as a man of honor and faithful subject, will be presented to us by our Minister of War on the day of a parade and in the presence of troops; we will give him a grade above his, as evidence of our satisfaction."
>
> I therefore claim the rank of lieutenant-general, having already had that rank, as can be seen by the appointments which posted me to Vincennes, by reason of my services in the Imperial Guard.[7]

---

6 *Idem.*
7 Clairval collection.

Daumesnil had scarcely re-installed his family in the Queen's Pavilion of the château when he found himself charged with a very unwelcome task When the Parisians had risen in revolt against the ordinances decreed by Charles X and his government had fallen, the ministers of his cabinet had all fled. Under the pressure of public opinion, on 13 August the Chamber of Deputies had indicted the ministers who had signed the hateful ordinances. The new government rather hoped that all of the ex-ministers would successfully flee the country, thus saving Louis-Philippe from having to bring them to trial, with possible consequent death sentences. Three had, in fact, managed to escape abroad, but the Prince de Polignac, together with *Messieurs* de Peyronnet, de Chantelauze, and de Guernon-Ranville, had been caught by provincial police, apparently unwitting of the government's hopes that the men would safely get away.

The king was determined to save the ministers' lives, however. At first, it was proposed to place them in the *Conciergerie*, right in the center of the capital, but this solution was judged to be too risky, given the possibility of a mob's storming that prison of bloody memories. Vincennes seemed far safer, not only because of its removed location, but because of the absolute confidence that all concerned had in Daumesnil's ability to ensure the ministers' safety until their ultimate disposition could be decided upon.

On 27 August the four men were brought to the château under a heavy escort of *gendarmes*, and Daumesnil received them with the respect due to men whose fortunes were at a low ebb, and whose lives were hanging in the balance. Although he did not relish playing the role of a jailer, he accepted it as simply one more duty to his country.

At first he lodged the former ministers in rooms adjacent to his own apartment in the Queen's Pavilion, but the government instructed him to move them into the prison portion of the keep. By this time the garrison of the château was composed of the 4th battalion of the 5th legion of the National Guard. When the transfer of the prisoners to the keep was begun, a number of the guardsmen became very agitated, and one of them raised his musket and took aim at M. de Peyronnet, shouting, "Down on your knees, that miserable creature, who had the people fired upon! Let him beg for pardon!" Just in time, Daumesnil knocked up the man's musket.

The governor did what he could to lessen the rigors of the ministers' confinement. Usually he permitted them to meet with people who came to visit them, but one day, when de Peyronnet's daughter paid one of her frequent visits to her father, Daumesnil would not permit the minister to come down into the courtyard to see her. The former minister was furious, and dispatched his lawyer, *Maître* Hennequin, to ask the cause for that refusal. Without a word, Daumesnil led the lawyer into the courtyard of the keep.

"Do you know that man?" he asked, pointing to one of the guardsmen.

"Yes, no doubt about it," Hennequin replied, who had at once understood the reason for the governor's action, and he warmly shook his hand. The sentry to whom Daumesnil had pointed was none other than a mulatto named Bizet. He had been unjustly sentenced to be branded and exiled to Martinique under de Peyronnet, and, having learned that the latter was going to be coming down into the courtyard, the man had drawn his dagger.

"Ah! He's coming down!" he had exclaimed. "I'm going to get my revenge for the mark that I bear on my shoulder!"

In his *Journal*, Marshal de Castellane supplies a further insight into the problems arising from the presence in the château of these ex-ministers:

> The National Guard was very aroused against them. Despite the authority of his twenty wounds and wooden leg, *Maréchal de Camp* Daumesnil had the greatest difficulty in preventing them from imposing useless punishments on the prisoners. He says that the 4,000 men who have served as their guards are real cannibals.[8]

Daumesnil had been instructed to go to Paris, together with Colonel Greiner, his *commandant de la place*, on 14 September in order to take their oaths of loyalty in their new capacity.[9] That happened to be the day that the three Commissioners from the Chamber of Deputies were coming to Vincennes to interrogate the ex-ministers. Since Daumesnil had to be in the château to receive the Commissioners, both he and Greiner were obliged to swear fidelity to the King of the French, to the Constitutional Charter, and to the laws of the Kingdom in writing, which they did on that date. It was a far cry from the elaborate ceremony in the palace at St. Cloud in which Daumesnil had participated eighteen years earlier.

Leaders of the Paris street mob, still flushed with the success of their victory on the days of the July Revolution, were repeating the phrase that blood must be paid for with blood, and, fearful that the hated ministers might escape justice, they finally decided to take the law into their own hands. On the evening of 18 October a crowd gathered on the Rue Saint-Honoré, just off the Place de la Concorde, and after some inflammatory declarations from the leading agitators, which were greeted with roars of approval, the growing crowd surged along the narrow street to the Palais Royal, shouting "Death to the ministers! Death to Polignac!" As they approached the gate in the iron grilled fence surrounding the palace, the guards drew it shut in the face of the shouting and gesticulating mob.

After venting their frustration with angry cries and curses, when one of the leaders pointed out that the ministers were not in the Palais Royal, but in Vincennes, the mob at once took up the cry, "To Vincennes!" A ragged procession of seven or eight hundred men and a few dozen women set out

---

8 Quoted by Clairval, *Daumesnil*, p. 236.

9 Greiner was a former artillery officer, who had lost an arm at Wagram. He was a close friend of Daumesnil's, who had arranged to have him posted to Vincennes.

along the road leading to Vincennes, armed with swords, muskets, pikes, and whatever other weapons came to hand, and carrying a black flag bearing the inscription, "Death to the ministers."

It was close to eleven that evening when the mob arrived on the glacis of the fort, brought up short by a barricade barring its entrance. The flickering light of their torches threw the contours of the ancient, adamantine walls of the château in sharp relief as the raucous crowd pressed up against the crenelated wall of the triangular *flèche* protecting the bridge leading to the fort's main gate, which had arrested its progress. The approach of the mob had been detected by sentinels atop the keep while they were still at some distance, and it had not taken long for Daumesnil to be alerted, and for him to grasp the probable intentions of the mob. Making his way to the gate in the Tour du Village, he had the small footbridge lowered, stepped across it alone, and approached the threatening mass of tatterdemalions. They had no need to be told who he was, and their respect for him induced an almost complete silence in the throng, as they awaited his reaction to their presence.

In his haste, Daumesnil had forgotten his cane, and now he beckoned a boy to his side. "Come here," he said, "you can serve as my walking stick." Then, resting his hand lightly on the boy's shoulder, he addressed the leaders of the mob.

"What do you want?"

"The ministers or their death!" was the harsh response. With a calm and resolute air, the governor of the fortress responded,

Look here, my friends. I could only give up the prisoners on the orders of a higher authority, and since I have no such order, you shall not have them. Do you wish me to dishonor myself? You know me, and you know that Daumesnil never surrenders. Twice I was surrounded by allied armies, which never could enter here, so any attempt to do so now would be in vain. Don't you think the ministers are well guarded? Are you not aware that they must be judged by the law? You're asking for the heads of the accused, but you'll only have them with my life as well. My honor and my duty oblige me to protect them. Withdraw!

When the rioters were not to be put off so easily, and insisted that they would have the ministers, with a voice that cut through the night air like the flash of a chasseur's curved, steel blade, Daumesnil replied:

"You won't have the ministers, and if you try to enter this fort, I'll blow it up, together with the keep. Half of the *faubourg* Saint-Antoine will perish with it."

The crowd was under no illusions: they knew they were dealing with an old soldier of the Empire, whose determination and courage were legendary, and that he meant every word of his promise. At last, his unwavering stance had a calming effect on the rioters.

"I swear on my honor that the ministers will not escape," Daumesnil added, as it became clear that his words were bringing the rioters to their senses. After some muttering among the leaders, one of them shouted, "*Vive Daumesnil! Vive la Jambe de Bois!*" and the mob took up the cry. Some even pressed forward and embraced him around the knees and shook his hands.

Those few words from a man, whose appearance alone compelled a respect bordering on awe, had stilled the bloodlust that had brought the mob tramping through the night to the lowering walls of the château. Now they asked the governor to lend them a drummer and two National Guards to lead them back to Paris. When he willingly complied, off went the crowd cheerfully, trailing down the Paris road after the young drummer and his grinning escort.

By his action that night, Daumesnil had not only reaffirmed his absolute fidelity to the rule of law and the good of his country, but he had prevented the addition of another bloody page to the ledger of France's history.

There was a bizarre sequence to the events of that tumultuous day. A man who should have had better sense, and should have been a better judge of character, did an almost unbelievably stupid thing. He proposed to *la baronne* Daumesnil that "the lion who watches over Vincennes should put to sleep for an hour" so that the imprisoned ministers might escape. Here is her account of that extraordinary miscalculation:

> It was a question of nothing less than a property with 50,000 francs of rent as the price for my agreement. It was Prince Talleyrand who was the mover behind this plot, and who had sent. M. Charles Turpin to win me over. I have always suspected that this proposal originated higher up, since at that time the government was apprehensive about the outcome of the trial, and just wanted to be rid of the entire matter.[10]

When Daumesnil learned of this insulting proposal, he simply said to his wife: "Write to Turpin, telling him not to set foot in the fort again as long as the ministers are here, if he wishes to deprive me of the pleasure of having him thrown out of a window."

Shortly afterwards, the government was finally ready to put the ex-ministers on trial before the Chamber of Peers, and it was therefore necessary to transfer the prisoners to the prison of the *petit* Luxembourg for that purpose. Fearful that the movement of the accused might provoke another demonstration, when the transfer took place on 10 December, it was under a military escort made up of a squadron of the 8th *Chasseurs*,

---

10 Quoted by Clairval, *Daumesnil*, p. 237.

a platoon of National Guard horse, and a platoon of horse artillery from the Vincennes garrison. The procession took off at a gallop, and encountered nothing more threatening en route than a few shaken fists in the *faubourg* Saint-Antoine.

A problem had arisen at the last minute, when it was evident that M. de Chantelauze, who was suffering from severe rheumatism, was in no condition to be moved together with his former colleagues. When the members of the Commission insisted that he be brought along, Daumesnil objected, saying, "Leave M. de Chantelauze here until this afternoon, and I give you my word that by this evening he'll be at the Luxembourg. I'll take him there myself, and be completely responsible for it."

That afternoon, Daumesnil had de Chantelauze placed in his own cabriolet. Just as they were about to leave, observing that the ailing man needed to be more completely protected against the December chill, Daumesnil went back for a blanket in which he then wrapped the grateful man. Then, without any escort, the governor left for Paris with a man whom he would have defended against the entire world.

The four ministers of Charles X were tried in mid-December, and sentenced to life imprisonment. The *Courrier Français* of 16 December reported that Daumesnil had attended their trial on the previous day, accompanied by General Pajol, and had been seated on the bench usually occupied by the minister. When the prisoners were brought into the courtroom, M. de Polignac was the first to enter, and as he passed Daumesnil, he bowed politely.

At the conclusion of their trial, the convicted men were first taken back to Vincennes, but kept there very briefly, since there was serious concern that their presence so close to Paris might give rise to further demonstrations. It was therefore decided to transfer them to the fortress of Ham, on the Somme, to serve out their sentences.[11] The day of their transfer, as their carriage was passing out of Paris, the only cries that could be heard from the people in the streets were, "Death to Polignac!" M. de Chantelauze leaned forward in the carriage to his companion in misfortune, saying, "I see, Prince, that you're the most popular of us."

All four men retained a grateful recollection of the thoughtful attentions with which Daumesnil had surrounded them in their despairing moments. Perhaps his own experiences with fortune's reversals had made him more solicitous of men whose lives were at low ebb than another in his position might have been.

On 23 January 1831, the Count of Guernon-Ranville wrote to Daumesnil from Ham:

---

11 Some ten years later, another notable prisoner was incarcerated in the same old fortress —Louis Napoleon, later to become Napoleon III. All four men were eventually released, resembling ghosts more nearly than the men of consequence they had once been.

We were told recently that you were charged with conducting some sort of inspection, which would bring you to this dump.[12] Your former guests would be charmed by a circumstance which would provide them with the pleasure of seeing you and expressing to you how deeply touched they have been by the loyalty and the consideration with which you have discharged your painful duty towards them.

Still from Ham, on 3 April 1831 the Count of Peyronnet wrote to Daumesnil:

I was told yesterday that you still retain some memories of me, and that you continue to take an interest in the misfortune that has befallen me. I thank you from the bottom of my heart for those sentiments, for the esteem of a man of your caliber is the most precious and the most flattering thing in the world for me. I hope that my family has not failed to express to you its appreciation and mine, but I'm very glad to renew to you my expression of it.
The sojourn at Ham, although very sad, is however a bit less tumultuous and a little more favorable for studying than Vincennes. It's an advantage for those who love books, and who know how to find in them distractions and consolations. But all that does not wipe away the regret that I feel at no longer being in a place of which you are the commander.

During their imprisonment at Vincennes, Daumesnil often fell into conversation with one or another of the former ministers. On one such occasion, one of them observed to him, "In political discussions, the difficult thing is not to do one's duty, but rather to recognize it."

"Good heavens," Daumesnil replied, without a moment's hesitation, "I'm not so clever. My duty is the cry of my conscience. I don't march behind it; it pushes me, and I go right down my road, without caring what any one may say about it."

Whether in his words or actions, Daumesnil always went straight to the point. He was not one to play word games, and even less to hesitate when quick action was called for.

One day a gentleman, who had been a member of Charles X's entourage and had then gone over to Louis Philippe, thinking to please Daumesnil, was ridiculing the deposed king, with reference to a recent cartoon of him.

"I don't understand, Monsieur," Daumesnil remarked, in some irritation, "how, with an origin such as yours, you can forget the titles and favors that your family has received from the dynasty of an unhappy and

---

12 *Bicoque*, the same term that Blücher has scornfully applied to Vincennes.

exiled king."

With that, he turned his back on the man. Whatever Daumesnil thought of the qualities of the former king, his boyhood unwillingness to tolerate attacks on the defenseless had not left him.

Another time, an officer of the National Guard, seeing that several old cannons positioned on the ramparts of the château bore the fleurs de lys and initials of Louis XIV, expressed to Daumesnil surprise that those symbols of bygone royalty had not been obliterated.

"I will preserve them carefully," replied Daumesnil. "I have too much respect for cannons which served to conquer Flanders and Franche-Comté."

CHAPTER TWENTY-TWO
THE FINAL BATTLE

1832

W ith the matter of the prisoners' fate finally decided, life within the château settled down to a more normal pace than had characterized it for many weeks. Daumesnil was able to resume one of his favorite pastimes, having received a license for permission to hunt with a friend in the park of Vincennes. The license was valid for hares, rabbits, partridge, and birds of passage, and its holder was asked to destroy injurious animals, including boars, by reason of the damage that they cause.[1]

On 27 February 1831, Daumesnil was finally rewarded for his 25 years of active service and fifteen years of silent loyalty to the memory of one whom he had sworn to serve, by receiving a promotion to the rank of lieutenant-general.

Louis Philippe and his queen took an interest in the family of the governor of Vincennes, and on more than one occasion brought their children to Vincennes and within the grim walls of the fortress, where the seven-year-old Duc de Monpensier was at first a bit frightened by the sight of great pyramids of cannon balls. But when he perceived that the master of this rather fearsome place was not in the habit of eating small boys, he became quite brave in his manner, and produced presents for the two Daumesnil daughters; a doll and a little box for Louise, the younger girl, and several books from his library for Marie.

On another occasion the king, accompanied by Marshal Soult, the Minister of War, and several other generals, questioned Daumesnil about his resistance to the Allied armies in both 1814 and 1815. His reply was simple and to the point:

"Sire, in 1814 and 1815, the château contained materiel valued at 80 to

---

1 Clairval collection.

90 millions, which I had the good fortune to save for France."

A visit to Vincennes apparently became "the thing to do" for foreign visitors of any distinction. When Hussein Pasha, the Dey of Algiers, which had recently been "taken under the protection of France," was on an official visit to Paris, he was invited to attend firing exercises at the range in the Park of Vincennes. Once there, he asked to meet the valiant defender of the château, so Léonie received him in the Daumesnils' quarters in the Queen's Pavilion.

The constant stream of visitors, mostly friends of her husband's, began to be not only tiring for the young mother of three small children, but an expensive burden as well. In a letter to her mother, Léonie wrote:

> I am more and more disgusted with this proximity to Paris, which attracts entire processions to me. Happy are those who are able to maintain their household at what level they can afford, but there are positions in which one must do more than one is able to do. The number and expense of servants are killing me, and the cellar — oh, yes, the cellar!

Daumesnil liked to entertain well, and there were many ready to afford him an opportunity to do so. Skill in mastering the costs of maintaining a household had never been one of his strengths.

In March of 1832, a cool breeze briefly ruffled the otherwise tranquil waters through which the governor and his family were passing in comparative contentment. The Chamber of Deputies had been reviewing the budget with an eye to effecting some economies, and a proposal was made to eliminate the position of governor of Vincennes, thereby saving 22,000 francs. The further point was made that, as a lieutenant-general, Daumesnil was too senior to occupy such a post.

That observation prompted Colonel Jacqueminot, himself a deputy, to take the floor. "Gentlemen, in time of peace the château of Vincennes is nothing. In time of war, it is the soul of the kingdom. Napoleon was well aware of that when he confided it to General Daumesnil."

He went on to cite the record of Daumesnil's services, and concluded, "That, gentlemen, was the conduct of the brave General Daumesnil during that epoch. King Louis Philippe, immediately after his accession to the throne, hastened to give him the commandment of Vincennes. Would you take it away from him today?"

All the member of the Chamber denied any such intention, and one of them, M. de Marmier, exclaimed, "It's a painting of history that we should leave in its frame!"

The motion was rejected, with only one dissenting vote. The following day, General Bugeaud, a deputy from the Dordogne, wrote to Daumesnil, "Yesterday every one coveted the honor of defending the government of Vincennes. It was unnecessary. There was nothing to debate, no point of honor to be won. All associated themselves with Jacqueminot's words."

⌒

It was at that same time that a wave of cholera, which had been moving toward France from southeastern Europe, reached Paris, and its ravages were soon overwhelming the defenses of the city's physicians. Having seen the devastating effects of epidemics on armies in the field, Daumesnil was not one to make light of the threat posed to his little community by this insidious threat. "We'll treat it as an enemy," he said. "It will not enter this fortress."

Daumesnil took all possible measures to prevent the disease from making its way within the château's walls, in his characteristic style seeing personally that everything was done to his satisfaction, and for a time, it seemed that the legendary defender of Vincennes had once more put to rout a formidable adversary.

Early in August, two friends of Daumesnil had come to the château for dinner. One of them, a M. Appert, commented that doctors were recommending, as a means of protecting oneself from cholera, drinking very little wine, and no liqueurs whatsoever.

That drew a laugh from Daumesnil, who responded, "My dear fellow, you're afraid of dying! Come and spend a few days with us, and you'll be stronger than the cholera."

In his *Souvenirs*, Appert wrote: "We parted happily, promising to return soon to Vincennes, since the general had refused entry to the citadel to that horrible and merciless enemy, but, alas, within a week that jest had been given a cruel refutation."[2]

Daumesnil was only 56, but for some time his health had been declining. The effects of his wounds and the years of hard campaigning were beginning to tell on his previously robust constitution. In that vulnerable condition, he fell easy prey to the mortal infection.

By 15 August, he was feeling the first indications that the disease had invaded his body. The surgeon-major of artillery and Dr. Teyssier took every measure possible to stem the advance of the illness. But the one man, for whose intercession Léonie prayed, was beyond their reach. Other doctors were summoned for consultation, but they could do nothing more.

Sensing that he was dying, Daumesnil sent for the curé of the parish, the abbé Veyrinès, who administered the last sacraments to him on the evening of the 16th. Early the following morning, pressing to his lips a crucifix that had been given to him by Pius VII, Daumesnil quietly slipped away.

"I will not say with what regrets this father and this loving spouse released one another's arms," Léonie afterwards wrote, "nor will I speak of our powerless efforts to hold on to him, nor of our tears and our prayers. Who could still pray after that?"

---

2   Clairval, *Daumesnil*, p. 246.

On the 18th of August, the interment of this renowned soldier, who had run away from home as a boy after a fatal duel, and who had steadily won his way into the highest ranks of the most magnificent army of the age, took place with fitting military ceremony. His charger was led forth from the citadel, passing between beflagged ranks of artillerymen, infantry, engineers, and National Guards. The grinding sound of heavy cannon wheels rolling over stone paving blended with the rolling rhythm of black-draped drums and the echoing notes of brass fanfares.

Grasping the cords of the catafalque were long-time comrades of Daumesnil's—Generals Exelmans, Pajol, and de Belair, as well as the president of the Chamber of Deputies, M. Dupin. Then, behind Daumesnil's son, Léon, there followed a great number of the survivors of the Napoleonic epoch, together with civil and military personalities, deputations from the *Ecole Polytechnique* and Saint-Cyr, and a considerable crowd of the people of Paris and its suburbs, for whom Daumesnil was a hero.

At the Vincennes municipal cemetery, several eulogies were pronounced. In his turn, M. Dupin recalled that Daumesnil "Never wished to surrender or to sell himself." Alone at last in the family's apartment in the Queen's Pavilion of the château, on the 21st the young widow wrote to her husband's dear old friend, the surgeon Larrey:

> Texier has told me, Monsieur and excellent friend, what you could have done for us and what you regretted not having been able to do. Ah! That you were not able to come to our help, when we called for you! Perhaps you were the only one, you alone, to be able to save the one whom you had already so many times snatched back from death. Moreover, he would have found so much consolation in receiving the care of a friend such as you! Must my regret, already so great, be increased by so many other regrets ....[3]

Larrey wrote back to the grieving widow:

> Madame La Baronne,
> Yes, I confess to you the intense and very painful impression that I at first suffered at the news of the death of my old friend and companion of Egypt, the most profound regret at not having been able to receive his last farewells, and to have been deprived of the happiness of being able to administer to him the help of my art, but I was informed too late that I had been sent for, and, contrary to the truth, the porter had said that I was in the country. You must believe, Madame, that I share sincerely your sorrow and your regrets. Nevertheless, and without losing any time, I went Thursday

---

3   Clairval collection.

morning to our friend *Monsieur le Comte* Daure to beg him to request His Excellency the Minister of War to be kind enough to obtain the agreement of the King for the raising of a monument, at the expense of the state, in that fortress that he had saved for the country, with an immense artillery, scorning the gold that was offered to him to open the gates of that fortress. I also declared to him that he had left no other fortune to his family than his virtues and the name that he bore, associated from that time on with that of the great Captain, of whom he was one of the first lieutenants.

The minister informed me, via M. Daure, that he was going to acquaint His Majesty with the object of our solicitude. I have reason to hope, my dear Lady, that the memory of our illustrious friend will be consecrated by an act of the government, and that it will carry its paternal regards for the tearful family, which inspires so great sympathy.

Believe, Madame, in my sympathy and in the affectionate respect of your deeply devoted

D. Larrey[4]

If the porter at Larrey's residence had not mistakenly told the urgent messenger from Vincennes that his master was away in the country and Larrey had been able to reach the bedside of his old friend in time, could the eminent surgeon have saved the old soldier's life? That will remain one of the innumerable unanswerable questions that an enigmatic history poses to us. One can easily appreciate, however, the bitter regret with which this unkind quirk of fate afflicted both widow and surgeon.

The Marquis de Puivert had been bested by Daumesnil in yet another sense. He had died in January of that same year, and was also laid to rest in the Vincennes cemetery, not far from where the château's staunchest defender lies.

---

4   Clairval collection.

EPILOGUE

With Daumesnil's death, all but 1,500 francs of his pension disappeared, leaving Léonie, at the age of 37 with three children to raise, in a precarious financial position, but the courage that she had consistently demonstrated during her twenty years of marriage never failed her for a moment, and her many friends were determined that she should not be left to fend for herself. In his funeral oration, M. Dupin, the president of the Chamber of Deputies, had committed himself to asking of the legislature in it next session that it grant an additional pension to *la baronne* Daumesnil and her children.

At the time of Daumesnil's death, his old friend and comrade, Baron Thurot, was an honorary *maréchal de camp*, and, in that capacity, was in command of the 14th Legion of *gendarmerie* in Carcassonne. He had promised to assume the role of father for the Daumesnil children, but now found himself at a disadvantage in fulfilling that promise, because of his distance from Paris. He therefore asked that the Minister of War either confirm him in his rank, or transfer him to the command of the 1st Legion in Paris, or the 22nd in Nancy, so that, as he said in his letter to the Minister, he could be closer to his adopted children. In fact, there was never any question of Thurot's adopting the Daumesnil children. Clairval believes Thurot invented the story to explain his request for approval of the subscription, and to justify his request for a move closer to Paris, adding that Thurot had a reputation as a braggart.

Obviously Thurot's request was not granted, because on 10 July 1833 he wrote the following letter to the Minister of War, Marshal Soult:

Monsieur le Maréchal,
I read in the *Echo français*, of 4 July, the following passage:
    "The *Constitutionnel* of Loire-et-Cher, of 2 July, announced that
    Marshal Soult, in a recent circular to the colonels of the army,

invites them—which, in ministerial terms, means he orders them—to oppose in their regiments any subscription in favor of the children of the brave Daumesnil. It adds that, as a consequence of that strange circular, the subscription, which had been opened in the 31st of Line by the officers of that brave regiment, had to be cancelled."

Your paternal benevolence, for all military, convinces me not to give any credence to that article.

I am, *Monsieur le Maréchal*, the adoptive father of the children of my late friend, Lieutenant General Daumesnil; it is in that quality that their mother has sent me a subscription to open in Carcassonne.

I did it, *Monsieur le Maréchal*; I ask you to believe that it was without any intention of showing opposition to the will of the King or of his government, to which I am devoted, heart and soul, whatever happens.

If I still possessed the fortune that I have lost, it would belong to the children of my friend, and I would not be responsible for a popular subscription, always humiliating for the person who is its object.

I thought it was my duty, *Monsieur le Maréchal*, to inform you of what I have done in this regard, rather than to permit some impression of hostility toward the chiefs of the government to cast doubt on my position.

Thurot probably knew, when he wrote that letter, that the newspaper report about Soult's order was accurate, but nonetheless felt that he had to take that action to protect himself, which is rather saddening, if understandable. Given Soult's reputation for being hard on his inferiors, it is discomforting to see Thurot crediting him with "paternal benevolence" toward the troops, even if Thurot was trying to prick Soult's conscience, probably a well-nigh impossible task.[1]

In the session of the Chamber of 12 January 1833, true to his promise, Dupin presented a proposal for a pension of 6,000 francs for the widow Daumesnil and her children, which would continue in effect until the death of the last of the children. In the session of 2 March the proposal was put forward in the form of a law making special exceptions to the standard retirement pension of 1,500 francs for officers of that rank, in favor of the widows of three generals—Daumesnil, Duhesme, and Decaen—granting pensions of 6,000 francs in each case. Then, in a session of 1 June, the Chamber approved the proposal in its normal public session, but then, in a secret ballot, rejected it, for reasons which are not clear, and to the indignation of many members of the Chamber, and to the public at large.

---

1   Paradoxically, however, Soult granted an allowance to Léon Daumesnil, then a student at Saint-Cyr.

Almost immediately, the commune of Vincennes reacted to that action by undertaking, under the leadership of Mayor Lejemptel and the municipal council, a public subscription in behalf of the widow Daumesnil and her children. Dupin, stung by the defeat of his proposal in the Chamber, quickly associated himself with the Vincennes initiative, pledging 500 francs to the fund, and the mayor added another 500 from the Vincennes municipal treasury to launch the drive.

Soon offerings in varying amounts, from a few francs to much more considerable sums, began to arrive in the Vincennes town hall. Emmanuel de Las Cases, who had accompanied Napoleon to St. Helena and was now a deputy for the Department of the Seine, wrote:

> I ask that you associate me with your generous thought in the amount of 50 francs annually during my lifetime for the children of the hero of Vincennes. That will be my humble contribution for the widow, and a remembrance for Napoleon, from whose mouth I heard at St. Helena that the brave Daumesnil had saved his life at Saint-Jean-d'Acre, at the peril of his own.[2]

As soon as he heard of the subscription, M. Segond, the former mayor of Vincennes, who had been at crossed swords with Daumesnil at one point over trivial matters, and whose house adjoining the curtain wall of Vincennes Daumesnil had refused to destroy, wrote:

> It is with great pleasure that I add my name to the list of subscribers. I owe it, in every respect. The brave General Daumesnil was my very sincere friend; he became so after an act of generosity toward me, which saved my little house, which I had not expected of him. The operations of 1814 required the destruction of my house; three or four shots from a cannon would have sufficed. Everything was ready, but at the last moment, the governor stopped it, and said to an officer, who later told me, "M. Segond is very happy to be my enemy; it will be said that I wanted to revenge myself."[3]

A printer in Paris promised to contribute ten francs annually to the fund during his lifetime. In August, the prefect of Orne, in Alençon, sent out an appeal to the inhabitants of that department to participate in the subscription. The principal newspapers in Paris and in the provinces opened subscriptions as well, and private commissions were formed in Paris and throughout the country to receive contributions from the citizens. Notwithstanding Soult's "invitation" against such subscriptions, collections were taken up in many military units.

In January 1834, contrary to the general expectation, the Chamber

2 Deschamps, *Biographie du Générale Daumesnil*, pp. 44–5.
3 *Ibid*, p. 8.

again rejected a proposal for the increase of *la baronne* Daumesnil's pension. On the 23rd of June, the final results of the subscription were published in an astonishing record, which provides the name and trade, or profession, of every individual who contributed, and the amount given, for every department in France. It constitutes a sociological cross-section of the country, much as a modern census does. The total collected was 57,126 francs 52 centimes.[4]

In 1838, the Chamber of Deputies took up the matter of a pension for Léonie once again, and that time voted a pension of 3,000 francs to the widow Daumesnil, in the form of a national reward.

In 1851, Léonie wrote to Prince Louis Napoleon, at that time President of the Republic, asking that she be appointed superintendent of the *Maison de la Légion d'honneur,* in Saint-Denis, one of three such schools for children of members of the *Légion d'honneur.*[5] (The post had recently become vacant.) Her request was supported by the old family friend, General Exelmans, now Grand Chancellor of the *Légion d'honneur,* who had just been made a marshal of France by Louis Napoleon. When she received a reply from Prince Napoleon, in which he noted that there were many others making the same request to him, she asked for an opportunity to be received by him, which was granted. In a letter of 11 June 1851 to her daughter, Louise, she related part of the conversation in the audience with "*Le Président:*"

> I can well imagine, Prince, that many people are making the same request, but there is only one Daumesnil, as there is only one Vincennes. You also know that there are circumstances in which favor is justice, and that favor and that justice are what we expect from the nephew of the Emperor. The opportunity for acquitting France's debt has been reserved for you.

She was granted the appointment, and for the next eighteen years she presided over that institution with a grace and distinction, which continuously augmented the respect and admiration with which she was regarded by the most prominent personalities of the day. She personally participated in the care of the sick, remaining at their bedsides night and day when necessary, and assisting in operations. She founded a fund for former students in need, and couldn't bear to see hungry or abused children. Having heard that a boy, who hadn't eaten for a day, had said to his mother, "We must hope that we'll eat tomorrow," she couldn't rest

---

4 Deschamps, *Biographie du Générale Daumesnil.*
5 The schools of the Legion of Honor had been established in 1805, under the patronage of Queen Hortense. There were supposed to be five, but only three were created. The original intent was that their students would be daughters of members of the Legion killed in action, but this limitation was later expanded to include daughters of living members, and finally twenty per cent of the enrollment were paying students.

until she had heard that mother and son were cared for.

In 1870, her health no longer permitted her to carry the burden of her position's responsibilities, and she submitted her resignation. Napoleon III, as Louis Napoleon had now become, made her an honorary superintendent of the school. She was to live for another fifteen years, and when she died in April of 1884, at the age of 89, in accordance with her wishes she was buried in the white dress that she had been wearing when she had held her dying husband in her arms 52 years before. Her love for her Daumesnil still burned undimmed in the slightest degree.

In her 89th year, she wrote an Epilogue of her own:

Stop, time.

How long I've lived! What suffering I've seen, and yet my course has been rapid!

Stop, time, I still have to pray, to love my children, to bless my children!

I have seen my father die, a man of goodness and love.

I have seen the last of the hero, my husband, I have seen his great courage expire in my arms, and my mother, a consoling angel, make me a widow for a second time in returning to Heaven.

I have seen my daughter die, in her best years, leaving me her child, all she had!

I've seen three kings reign, two empires crumble. How many wars and republics have passed before my eyes? Have I indeed seen the last of them?[6]

She was buried beside her husband in the Vincennes communal cemetery, where a small obelisk rises above their tombs. It bears this inscription:

AU
GENERAL
DAUMESNIL
LA COMMUNE DE
VINCENNES
RECONNAISSANTE
MDCCCXIV
ET
MDCCCXV

In 1867 an Imperial decree approved the decision of the municipal council of Vincennes to erect a statue to the glory of General Daumesnil on a square of the commune. In 1869 money for the support of the project was collected by a public subscription, and the sculptor Louis

---

6 *Biographie de la Baronne Daumesnil*, by *la vicomtesse* Thérèse de Clairval, grand-daughter of *la baronne* Daumesnil.

Rochet was chosen to execute the design and casting of the monument. The fall of the Second Empire delayed the execution of the project, so it was only in 1873 that it was brought to fruition. The statue was dedicated on 26 May 1873 with an appropriate military and civil ceremony. Among the speakers was Baron Larrey, the son of the famous surgeon of the Imperial Guard who had performed the amputation of Daumesnil's leg.

On 28 September of the same year, a bronze replica of the Vincennes statue was erected in the square in front of Daumesnil's birthplace, in Périgueux. On the base of the statue's pedestal is the inscription:

A
DAUMESNIL
NE A PERIGUEUX
SES CONCITOYENS
SEPTEMBER 1873[7]

On each side of the base are incised: 1814–1815.

∞

Early in 1909, the Paris newspaper, *le Petit Journal*, ran a contest entitled *"Vote pour le Panthéon,"* which it described as "a true national consultation on the French glories of the 19th century." It was intended to identify the popular choice of those individuals deemed worthy of having their names enshrined in the French national memorial building, the *Panthéon*. Among the twelve men who topped the list, with Pasteur heading it, were Pierre Curie, Dumas, *père*, and Ampère, the physicist and mathematician. Marshal Ney is number fourteen, Lafayette is seventeen, General Cambronne, of Waterloo fame, is twenty-five, and then General Daumesnil makes his appearance as number twenty-eight. He's in very good company. The composer, Gounod, the photographer, Daguerre, the novelist, Balzac, the painters, Ingres and Corot, and scores of other famous men are lost in the crowd.

When the 200th anniversary of Daumesnil's birth was celebrated in Périgueux in 1976, an article in the *Dordogne Libre* recalled another instance in which, the writer asserted, Daumesnil once again had, in effect, refused to surrender. During the German occupation of the city in World War Two, the statue of Daumesnil had been earmarked, along with other statues in the town, for consignment to the foundries of the Third Reich as scrap metal. The town fathers would have none of that, however, and a local mover was given the task of spiriting the statue away. He accomplished the task successfully, and the statue was safely hidden away. Some fragments of a broken bell were left in its place. On the day of the Liberation, the conspirators triumphantly brought forth the statue and reinstalled it on its pedestal, looking exactly as it had for some 70 years, except for the fact that now the statue of Daumesnil had a brassard of the F. F. I. (*Forces Françaises de l'Intérieur*) on one arm.

---

7   To Daumesnil—Born in Périgueux—His Fellow Citizens—September 1873.

ANNEXES

ANNEX A

DAUMESNIL'S SERVICE RECORD

27 July 1776	Born in Périgueux, France, the son of Jean-François and Anne Pietre Daumesnil.
10 November 1793	Enlisted as a private in the *Légion nationale des Pyrénées*, which on 21 November was incorporated in the newly formed 22nd *Régiment de Chasseurs à cheval*.
14 June 1797	*Brigadier* in the *Guides à cheval* of General-in-Chief Bonaparte.
28 October 1797	*Maréchal des logis. Idem.*
3 January 1800	*Maréchal des logis* in the *Chasseurs à cheval de la Garde des Consuls* (which became the *Chasseurs à cheval de la Garde Impériale* on 10 May 1804).
3 May 1800	*Adjutant sous-lieutenant. Idem.*
18 July 1800	*Lieutenant. Idem.*
1 August 1800	*Capitaine*: *Idem.*
18 December 1805	*Chef d'escadron. Idem.*
13 June 1809	*Major. Idem.*
2 February 1812	*Général de brigade,* Commandant of Vincennes.
11 February 1812	Marriage to Anne-Fortunée-Léonie Garat.
20 March 1812	Governor of Vincennes.
31 December 1814	Senior Commander of the *arrondissement* of Condé-sur-l'Escaut.
27 March 1815	Commander of the Fort of Vincennes.
8 April 1815	Governor of Vincennes.
9 September 1815	Retired in accordance with the royal ordnance of 1 August 1815.
End of November, 1815	Ceased his official functions.
1 January 1816	His name removed from the roll of active officers.

5 August 1830	Recalled to active duty and named Governor of Vincennes.
27 February 1831	Promoted to lieutenant-general.
1 November 1831	Senior Commander of the Fort of Vincennes.
17 August 1832	Died at Vincennes.

Campaigns

1793, 1794, and 1795, Army of the Eastern Pyrenees. 1796 and 1797, Army of Italy. 1798 and 1799, Army of the Orient. 1800, Army of the Reserve, in Italy. 1804, Army of the Ocean Coasts. 1805, *Grande Armée*, in Austria. 1806 and 1807, in Prussia and Poland. 1808, in Spain. 1809, in Austria, 1814 and 1815, in France.

Wounds

He was wounded twenty times, including six times by musket fire and by a cannon ball; a bullet wound in the thigh at the combat at Elne, 19 August 1794; a saber blow to the head in the assault of Saint-Jean-d'Acre; a wound at the Battle of Austerlitz, 2 December 1805; a bullet in the thigh at Madrid, 2 May 1808; a lance wound at the Battle of Eckmühl, 22 April 1809; and a cannon ball at the Battle of Wagram, on 6 July 1809, which necessitated the amputation of his left leg.

Decorations

June 1804	Member of the Legion of Honor.
14 March 1806	Officer of the Legion of Honor.
17 November 1808	Knight of the Order of the Crown of Iron.
17 January 1815	Knight of Saint-Louis.[1]

He was awarded two *sabres d'honneur,* one for his exploits during the Egyptian campaign, on 10 November 1799, and one by King Joseph Bonaparte of Spain, during that monarch's brief reign, for his conduct during the campaign of 1808–1809.

General Baron Pierre Daumesnil's name is inscribed on the north wall of the Arc de Triomphe, between those of Cambronne and Gouvion.

Title

Baron of the Empire, by a decree of 13 August 1809, and by letters patent of 9 March 1810.

Pensions and endowments

The record of these awards to Daumesnil is useful for two reasons: it reflects the generous favor that Napoleon extended to an officer for whom he had a special affection; and it indicates, in theory, the degree to which Daumesnil's base pay was augmented by the recognition of his feats of arms in a material manner. It is probably unrealistic, however, to simply add up the amounts of these various awards and to assume that the total represented regular annual income for

---

1   Although the Cross of a Knight of the Order of Saint-Louis was awarded to Daumesnil by Louis XVIII, in a gesture evidently intended to deflect criticism of Daumesnil's being forced into early retirement, he never wore it, because doing so would have required him to sign the award certificate, thus implying an oath of allegiance to the king, which he was unwilling to make.

Daumesnil, in addition to the pay of his rank and the additional allowance he received as governor of Vincennes.

A pension of 600 francs from the Cisalpine Republic, for his action at Arcole on 15 November 1796.

A pension of 3,000 francs on the privy purse of the Emperor. 7 September 1807.

An annuity of 2,000 francs on Monte Napoleone, Milan. 1 February 1808.

An annuity of 8,000 francs on property in Hanover (replaced in 1813 by an annuity of 8,000 francs on property of the department of Rome). 15 August 1809.

Shares on the *Petites Affiches*. 18 August 1811.[2]

An annuity of 4,000 francs on property in Illyria.

Sometime after 1 April 1814, he was given 2,000 francs as *secours* (relief), probably for the loss of his left leg.

In addition to these pensions and annuities, both presumably intended to be paid annually, along with many other officers and soldiers Daumesnil received periodic bonuses from the Emperor after notable actions and campaigns. For example, in addition to the pension of 3,000 francs on the Emperor's privy purse awarded him on 7 September 1807, he was also given a bonus of 6,000 francs.

The pensions, or emoluments, were drawn from various properties in conquered territories, and, as such, were the fruits of conquest. They represented indemnities paid by the conquered countries, or tribute imposed by the establishment of new states on their enthroned sovereigns. In the case of Monte Napoleone, in Milan, this was documented by a "*Diplome en faveur de M. Daumesnil. Rente de 2,000. f.*" This was a decree in the name of Napoleon, signed by Berthier. The decree instructs Napoleon's Minister of Finance of the Kingdom of Italy "to have inscribed on the *Grand Livre* of the said Monte-Napoleone[3] the sum of 2,000 francs on the funds of 1,200,000 francs that we have set aside for recompense to the brave men of our army."

It would be an error to think of these various awards as nineteenth century equivalents of government checks being deposited electronically in one's checking account. Pensions, or annuities, based on taxes levied on foreign properties had to be collected by French representatives in those countries, not all of whom were of the highest probity. Judging by the complaints of many of the beneficiaries of these pensions, the payments were irregular, and often significantly in arrears.

It seems logical to assume that, as happened in 1815 with Napoleon's final fall from power, all of Daumesnil's above-mentioned pensions and annuities were also cut off in 1814. Whether the bureaucratic machinery was efficient enough to cut them off when Napoleon went off to Elba, and then to restore them during the Hundred Days, is impossible to say. In 1814 Daumesnil's financial situation was better than in 1815, however, because then he was then continued on active duty, and presumably had some special allowance as the commandant of the Condé *arrondissement*.

One final note respecting Napoleon's generosity towards Daumesnil: it was generally believed by the people in the Dordogne, where Daumesnil bought the château and property of Nanthiat, that the Emperor provided the money to make that purchase possible.

---

2   Money collected by the government by taxes on "small advertisements," presumably in newspapers and other printed matter.

3   Presumably a bank.

ANNEX B

BONAPARTE'S PROCLAMATION
TO THE ARMY OF ITALY.

Soldiers! In fifteen days you have carried off six victories, captured twenty-one flags, fifty-five cannon, several fortified places, and conquered the richest part of Piedmont; you have taken 17,000 prisoners, killed or wounded more than 10,000 men. Until now, you had fought for sterile rocks, rendered illustrious by your courage, but of no use for our country; by your services, today you are the equal of the Army of Holland and the Rhine. Lacking everything, you have provided for everything. You have won battles without cannon, crossed rivers without bridges, made forced marches without shoes, made camp without eau-de-vie, and often without bread. The republican phalanxes, the soldiers of liberty were alone capable of suffering what you have suffered. Thanks are owed to you, soldiers! A grateful country owes its prosperity to you; and if, conquerors of Toulon, you foresaw the immortal campaign of 1794, your victories presage an even more splendid one.

The two armies that you of late attacked with such audacity were terrified of you; the depraved men who laughed at your misery and rejoiced in their hopes for victories of your enemies are astounded and trembling.

But, soldiers, you have done nothing, since there remains more for you to do. You don't hold Turin or Milan; the ashes of the conquerors of Tarquin[1] are still trampled by the murderers of Basseville[2].

You were deprived of everything at the beginning of the campaign; today you are abundantly provided for; the storehouses taken from your enemies are numerous; siege and field artillery have arrived. Soldiers, the country rightly expects great things from you; will you justify its expectations? No doubt the greatest obstacles have been overcome; but you still have battles to win, cities to take, rivers to cross. Is there one among you whose courage is weakening? Are there those who would prefer to return, across the summits of the Apennines and the Alps, to patiently wipe away the abuses of this soldierly slavery? No, there is not one among the conquerors of Montenotte, of Millésimo, of Dégo and Mondovi. All of you are burning to carry afar the glory of the French people; all of you wish to humiliate the proud kings, who dare to contemplate putting us in irons; all of you wish to grant our country a glorious peace, and to indemnify it for the immense sacrifices that it has made; all want to be able to say with pride, when returning to their villages, "I was in the conquering Army of Italy."

Thus it is that I promise you that conquest, but it is on a condition that you swear to fulfill; to respect the peoples that you free, and to repress the horrible plundering committed by criminals led on by your enemies. Without that, you would not be liberators of peoples, you would be their scourge; you would not bring honor to the French people, they would disavow you. Your victories, your courage, your success, the blood of your brothers died in battle, all would be lost,

---

1   The seventh and last legendary king of Rome, who, upon his accession, repealed the recent reforms in the constitution, and attempted to set up a despotism.

2   Nicolas Jean Hugou de Bassville, a French journalist, whose death in Rome at the hands of a mob was exploited by the French Revolutionary government as a grievance against the papacy.

even honor and glory. As for myself and the generals who have your confidence, we would blush to command an army without discipline, without restraint, which would only know the law of force. But, invested with national authority and empowered by justice and the law, I would know how to make the small number of men, without courage or hearts, respect the laws of humanity and honor that they were trampling under their feet. I would not tolerate brigands' soiling your laurels; I would execute rigorously the regulations that I have had put into effect. Plunderers will be pitilessly executed; already several have been; I have had occasion to note with pleasure the willingness with which the good soldiers of the army conduct themselves in carrying out orders.

People of Italy, the French army has just broken your chains; the French army is the friend of all peoples; come with confidence to meet it; your properties, your religion, and your customs will be respected.

We make war as generous enemies, and we only wish harm to the tyrants who subjugate you.

General Headquarters, Cherasco, 7 *floréal an IV* (16 April 1796).[3]

∞

ANNEX C

CONVENTION OF PARIS

A General Order published at the Duke of Wellington's headquarters at Gonesse, on 4 July, 1815, included the full text of the Convention, which brought to a close hostilities between France and the Allied Powers.

Convention of Paris

This day, 3 July, 1815, the Commissioners, named by the Commanders in Chief of the respective armies, that is to say, the Baron de Bignon, holding the portefeuille of Foreign Affairs, the Count Guillemenot, Chief of the General Staff of the French Army, the Count de Bondy, Prefect of the Department of the Seine, being furnished with the full powers of His Excellency the Marshal Prince of Eckmühl, Commander in Chief of the French Army, on one side; and Major General Baron Müffling, furnished with the full powers of His Highness the Field Marshal Prince Blücher, Commander in Chief of the Prussian Army, and Colonel Hervey, furnished with the full powers of His Excellency the Duke of Wellington, Commander in Chief of the English Army, on the other side, have agreed to the following Articles.

Art. 1. There shall be a suspension of arms between the allied armies, commanded by His Highness the Prince Blücher and His Excellency the Duke of Wellington, and the French army under the walls of Paris.
Art. 2. The French army shall put itself in march tomorrow, to take up its position behind the Loire. Paris shall be completely evacuated in three days; and the

---

3 Pigeard, *Les Campagnes Napoléoniennes*, p. 23.

movement behind the Loire shall be effected within eight days.

Art. 3. The French army shall take with it all its materiel, field artillery, military chest, horses, and the property of regiments, without exception. All persons belonging to the depôts shall also be removed, as well as those belonging to the different branches of the administration which belong to the army.

Art. 4. The sick and wounded, and the Medical Officers whom it may be necessary to leave with them, are placed under the special protection of the Commanders in Chief of the English and Prussian armies.

Art. 5. The military, and those holding employments to whom the foregoing article relates, shall be at liberty, immediately after their recovery, to rejoin the corps to which they belong.

Art. 6. The wives and children of all individuals belonging to the French army shall be at liberty to remain in Paris. The wives shall be allowed to quit Paris for the purpose of rejoining the army, and to carry with them their property and that of their husbands.

Art. 7. The Officers of the Line, employed with 'Les Federés,' or with the tirailleurs of the National Guard, may either join the army, or return to their homes, or to the places of their birth.

Art. 8. Tomorrow, 4 July, at mid-day, St. Denis, St. Ouen, Clichy, and Neuilly shall be given up. The day after tomorrow, the 5th, at the same hour, Montmartre shall be given up. The third day, the 6th, all the barriers shall be given up.

Art. 9. The duty of the city of Paris shall continue to be done by the National Guard and by the corps of the Municipal Gendarmerie.

Art. 10. The Commanders in Chief of the English and Prussian armies engage to respect the actual authorities as long as they exist.

Art. 11. Public property, with the exception of that which relates to war, whether it belongs to the government or depends upon the municipal authority, shall be respected; and the allied powers will not interfere in any manner with its administration and management.

Art. 12. Private persons and property shall be equally respected. The inhabitants, and in general all individuals who shall be in the capital, shall continue to enjoy their rights and liberties without being disturbed, or called to account, either as to the situations which they hold or may have held, or as to their conduct or political opinions.

Art. 13. The foreign troops shall not interpose any obstacle to the provisioning of the capital; and will protect, on the contrary, the arrival and the free circulation of the articles which are destined for it.

Art. 14. The present Convention shall be observed, and shall serve to regulate the mutual relations, until the conclusion of peace. In case of rupture, it must be denounced in the usual forms, at least ten days beforehand.

Art. 15. If difficulties arise in the execution of any one of the Articles of the present Convention, the interpretation of it shall be made in favor of the French army, and the city of Paris.

Art. 16. The present Convention is declared common to all the allied powers, provided it be ratified by the powers on which these armies are dependent.

Art. 17. The ratifications shall be exchanged tomorrow, 4 July, at six o'clock in the morning, at the bridge of Neuilly.

Art. 18. Commissioners shall be named by the respective parties, in order to watch over the execution of the present Convention.

Done and signed at St. Cloud, in triplicate, by the Commissioners above-named, the day and year before-mentioned.

(Signed) The Baron Bignon
Count Guilleminot
Count De Bondy
The Baron De Müffling
F.B. Hervey, Colonel.

Approved and ratified the present suspension of arms at Paris, 3 July, 1815.

(Signed) Marshal the Prince d'Eckmühl
Prince Blücher
Wellington.

ANNEX D

BLÜCHER *vs.* WELLINGTON
re NAPOLEON'S FATE

During the Waterloo campaign and subsequently, Major-General Philipp Friedrich Carl Ferdinand, Baron von Müffling, served as the principal liaison officer between the Duke of Wellington and the Prussian high command. After the Allied occupation of Paris, he became the city's military governor. Four letters that Blücher's chief of staff, General August Wilhelm Anton, Count Neithardt von Gneisenau, wrote to Müffling at Blücher's instructions will serve to illustrate the great disparity between the Duke of Wellington's views regarding the ultimate disposition of Napoleon and Blücher's, and may serve to explain why von Ziethen felt an obligation to try to temper Blücher's more violent impulses.

These letters are quoted from the Appendix to *The Memoirs of Baron von Müffling*, Greenhill Books, London 1997. Although they are all signed by von Gneisenau, it is clear that he is, for the most part, simply quoting from Blücher's dictation. No doubt this was clear to Müffling.

1. To the Royal Major-General von Müffling, Grand Cross, &c., &c.
   The French General de Tromelin is at Noyons, with the intention of proceeding to the head-quarters of the Duke of Wellington to treat for the delivering up of Bonaparte.

   Bonaparte has been declared under outlawry by the Allied Powers. The Duke of Wellington may possibly (from parliamentary considerations) hesitate to fulfill the declaration of the Powers. Your Excellency will therefore direct the negotiations to the effect, that Bonaparte may be delivered to *us*, with a view to his execution.

   This is what eternal justice demands, and what the declaration of March the 13th decides; and thus the blood of our soldiers killed and mutilated on the 16th and 18th will be avenged.
   Compiègne, June 27th, 1815.

(Signed) "von Gneisenau"

2. To the Royal Major-General von Müffling, Grand Cross, &c., &c.
Your Excellency will give notice to the Duke of Wellington that we have sent an officer to the five Deputies from Paris, in order to accompany them to the head-quarters of the Sovereigns.

A halt and armistice is denied them, but it has been declared that after the Conquest of Paris, we Prussians would agree to a truce under the following conditions:

1. The delivering up of Bonaparte alive or dead.

2. The cession of the fortresses of the Sambre, Meuse, Moselle, and Saar, including Longwy.

3, The occupation of the provinces of the Marne, including Château Thierry and Epernay.

4. The cession of the Castle of Vincennes.

5. The restoration of the treasures of art to the nations from which they were taken.

6. Indemnification for the costs of the war.

Your Excellency will inform the Duke on these points, in order that no scruple may arise respecting them on his part, which however I do not expect.

Perfect liberty is left to the Duke to stipulate for *himself* to act as he pleases, according to the views of his Cabinet.

Guiory, June 27th, 1815.

(Signed) Count N. von Gneisenau

3. To the Royal Major-General Baron von Müffling, &c., &c.
I am directed by the Field-Marshal to request your Excellency to communicate to the Duke of Wellington, that it had been his intention to execute Bonaparte on the spot where the Duc d'Enghien was shot; that out of deference, however, to the Duke's wishes, he will abstain from this measure, but that the Duke must take on himself the responsibility of its non-enforcement.

It appears to me that the British will feel embarrassed by the delivery of Bonaparte to them; your Excellency will therefore only direct the negotiations, so that he may be delivered up to us.

Senlis, June 29th, 1815.

(Signed) N. von Gneisenau

4. To the Royal Major-General, Baron von Müffling, &c., &c.
When the Duke of Wellington declares himself against the execution of Bonaparte, he thinks and acts in the matter as a Briton. Great Britain is under weightier obligation to no mortal man than to this very villain: for the occurrences whereof he is the author, her greatness, prosperity, and wealth, have attained their present elevation. The English are the masters of the seas, and have no longer to fear any rivalry, either in this dominion or the commerce of the world.

It is quite otherwise with us Prussians. We have been impoverished by him. Our nobility will never be able to right itself again.

Ought we not , then, to consider ourselves the tools of that Providence which has given us such a victory for the ends of eternal justice? Does not the death of the Duc d'Enghien call for such a vengeance? Shall we not draw upon ourselves the reproaches of the people of Prussia, Russia, Spain, and Portugal, if we leave unperformed the duty that devolves upon us?

But be it so!—If other will assume a theatrical magnanimity, I shall not set myself against it. We act thus from esteem for the Duke and—weakness. Senlis, June 29th, 1815.

(Signed) Count von Gneisenau

∞

ANNEX E

THE "ADDRESS" OF 23 MARCH 1815

The text of this address (see p. 69 above) is preserved in the Archives Nationales:

The Colonel, the Major, battalion commanders, officers, sous-officiers, and the soldiers of the 42nd Regiment of Infantry of the Line, to His Majesty the Emperor Napoleon the Great:

Sire,
The brave men of the 42nd Regiment, although the most distant from the point where Your Majesty made an appeal to French soldiers, have not heard your proclamation without trembling with joy. Bound by their duty and the honor of defending a frontier fort of the greatest importance, they have sworn to preserve it for France; they will be faithful to their oath.

All Frenchmen recognize today, in Your Majesty, the Prince who alone can save their dignity, make their laurels flourish once more, and return to their glory, tarnished by treason, the luster with which it was surrounded during the course of your reign.

The 42nd Regiment, imbued with this noble enthusiasm, unites its wishes with those of the great nation and of all its brothers in arms, and with one unanimous voice makes the air resound with shouts repeated a thousand times of 'Long live Napoleon, Long live our Emperor, Long live the liberator of France.' The tricolor flag floats over the ramparts of Condé; we are wearing the National cockade and the Eagle.

Long live the Emperor!

Signatures follow, and it is signed: *Le Général Commandant supérieur à Condé Baron* Daumesnil.

∞

NOTES ON ILLUSTRATIONS

1   *The Charge of the Mamelukes*, by Goya. In this dramatic painting the artist has vividly conveyed the hatred aroused among the *madrileños* by the slashing scimitars of the "pagan" Mamelukes, an emotion presumably shared by Goya himself. The Mamelukes were attached to Daumesnil's squadron at the time of the Revolt of *Dos de Mayo*, and he and his Chasseurs were in the middle of the mêlée. Although there were no dragoons involved in this affray, Goya has chosen to place one in the scene, either being unaware of the role played by the Chasseurs, or possibly because he thought that a brass dragoon helmet made for a better image. (There were Guard dragoons in Madrid at that time.)

2   *Survey of the Park of Vincennes, and of the Bridges of St. Maur and Charenton*. The red dots indicate the outposts established around Vincennes by Daumesnil on 7 April 1815, which formed a defensive perimeter at distances ranging between 250 and 400 *toises* – 500 to 800 meters – from the château. As may be seen, the then small village of Vincennes was entirely included within that perimeter. Almost at once, the Prussian blockade commander posted his own outposts, directly facing those of the garrison.

3   *Le Général Daumesnil à Vincennes*. On the morning of 1 April 1814, a Russian *parlementaire* delivered to Daumesnil the Russian commander-in-chief's summons to surrender the fortress. The artist has depicted Daumesnil giving the Russian cuirassier officer his defiant response to that demand, gesturing with his cane to his wooden leg as he does so in order to give added emphasis to his ringing declaration. For whatever reason, Mélingue has set this scene at the gate of the Tour des Salves – the Saluting Tower – rather than at the gate of the Tour du Village, the main gate of the fortress, where the confrontation actually took place.

4   *Daumesnil*, by Maurin. The handwritten text reads: *Il n'a voulu ni se rendre ni se vendre* (He did not wish to surrender or to sell himself). The signature is that of Dupin, the president of the Chamber of Deputies, who invoked that phrase in his eulogy at Daumesnil's funeral. The artist has symbolically placed beneath Daumesnil's *jambe de bois* a crumpled letter, on which is supposedly written an offer to Daumesnil from Field Marshal Blücher of a large sum of money – one-and-a-half or three million francs, depending on which version

you prefer – in return for the surrender of the fortress. An offer of a substantial sum was, in fact, made, but it was made orally, as described in the text, and not by Blücher personally.

5 *Les Uniformes du Ier Empire. Les Guides de Bonaparte.* Cdt Bucquoy. The *Guides'* green coats and breeches, with their scarlet collars, cuffs, and vests, would give way in 1800 to the first hussar-style uniform of the Consular Guard Chasseurs. The trumpeter's uniform seen here is distinguished only by its gold lace collar and cuffs.

6 *General View of Vincennes,* seen from the forest side. The keep rises on the west side of the château, and behind it the Village Tower may be seen. In the center foreground is the King's Pavilion, behind which stands the chapel. Beyond the Gate of the Woods is the Queen's Pavilion.

7 *Interior View of the Château of Vincennes.* The ramparts of the keep and its tower gate are located in the west side of the château. Barracks, stables, and workshops are dominated by the Village Tower at its northernmost side.

8 *Plan of the Château of Vincennes in Relation to the Projects of 1818.* North is at the bottom of the plan, where the main gate to the château, over which the Tour du Village rises, opens out on the Route de Paris. The east side of the château is bounded by the Cours Marigny, while the gate on the south side opens on to the Bois de Vincennes. Cultivated fields flank the western side of the château. The village of Vincennes clusters along the north face of the château.

The principal fortifications are: (a) *Tour du Roi* – the King's Tower; (b) *Tour de la Reine* – the Queen's Tower; (c) *Tour du Réservoire;* (d) *Tour de Paris;* (e) *Tour du Gouverneur;* (f) *Tour des Salves* – the Saluting Tower; (g) *Tour du Diable* – the Devil's Tower; (h) *Tour du Village;* (i) *Tour du Bois;* (k) *Donjon* – the keep; (l) *flèches crenelées* – crenelated flèches

The principal buildings within the fortress are: the Pavilion of the King (A), the Pavilion of the Queen (B), the chapel (D), barracks (G, N, R), stables and sheds for horses and vehicles (F, L, M, O, P, Q), the armory (S), quarters for *sous-officiers* (H), and workshops and forges (J, K). In 1812, Napoleon ordered that the King's Pavilion be made into a barracks for 1950 men. The Governor's residence was in the Queen's Pavilion. The horse watering pond, into which the caissons of powder were dumped in 1815, is near the northeast corner of the ramparts surrounding the keep. The underground aqueduct, the lead to which the Prussians twice cut off, is at T.

9 *DETAILS SUR LE GENERAL DAUMESNIL. (La Jambe de Bois de Vincennes), mort de choléra.* Paris, Imagerie Chez Garson, Fabricant d'Images. This print appeared the day after Daumesnil's interment. The costume in which the artist has imaginatively dressed the image is explained by the text beneath it:

Fearless, beyond reproach, o! modern Bayard!

You refused a foreigner's gold.

Faithfulness, constancy to your flag;

Your spotless integrity follows you to the tomb.

The reference is to the legendary 16th-century hero, Pierre Terrail Bayard, *le Chevalier sans peur et sans reproche.* The text below the sheet's title reads:

Brilliant discourse pronounced at his tomb. — Reply that he made to the Cossacks, in refusing to surrender the fortress of Vincennes, of which he was the governor. — Other interesting details respecting this brave general. — The tomb of Daumesnil. — The Emigrés.

BIBLIOGRAPHY

Abrantès, la Duchesse d', *Mémoires de Madame la Duchesse d'Abrantès*, Ladvocat, Paris, 1893.

Ambert, Général Baron Joachim, *Gens de guerre. Portraits. Le Général Daumesnil*, Paris, 1863.

Ambert, Général Baron Joachim, *Trois hommes de coeur. Larrey – Daumesnil – Desaix*, Alfred Mame et fils, Tours, 1895.

André, Roger, *L'Occupation de la France par les Alliés en Juillet-Novembre 1815*, E. De Boccard, Paris, 1924.

Appert, B., *de la société royale des prisons de France, Dix ans à la cour du roi Louis-Philippe et souvenirs du temps de l'Empire et de la Restauration*. 3 vols, Paris, 1846.

Aubry, Octave, *Napoléon*, Flammarion, Paris, 1961.

Balagny, Commandant D. E. P., *Campagne de l'Empereur Napoléon en Espagne (1808–1809)*, Berger-Levrault, Paris, 1902–1906.

Baschet, Roger, *Le Général Daumesnil, 'L'Ange Gardien de Napoléon'*, Librairie Hachette, Paris, 1938.

Baudus, Lieutenant-Colonel de, *Etudes sur Napoléon*, Debécour, Paris, 1841.

Bénard, L'Adjutant, *Le blocus de Vincennes en 1815. Journal Rédigé par l'Adjutant Bénard*, Albert Philippe, Charavay Frères, Paris, 1881.

Bernede, Colonel Allain, "Une armée de diversion sur un théâter d'opérations secondaire, Bonaparte et l'Armée d'Italie, mars-avril 1796" *Carnet de la Sabretache*, Nouvelle Série No. 131, 1er Trimestre 1997, pp. 5–6.

Bigarré, *général de brigade*, *Mémoires*, edited by A. Debidour, Paris, 1880.

Bourdeau, Colonel E., *Campagnes modernes, Tome 1. L'Epopée républicaine 1792–1804*, Henri-Charles Lavauzelle, Paris, 1912.

Buat, Commandant E., *1809. De Ratisbonne à Znaïim*, Chapelot, Paris, 1909.

Castellane, Maréchal Boniface de, *Journal du Maréchal de Castellane, Tome III*. 5 vols, Paris, 1895–97

Chandler, David (ed.), *Napoleon's Marshals*, Macmillan, New York; Weidenfeld & Nicolson, London, 1987.

Chandler, David, *The Campaigns of Napoleon*, Macmillan, New York; Weidenfeld & Nicolson, London, 1966.

Chandler, David, *Dictionary of the Napoleonic Wars*, Macmillan, New York; Arms & Armour Press, London, 1979.

Chevalier, Lieutenant Jean-Michel, *Souvenirs, mémoires, campagnes et voyages en Europe depuis l'Egypte jusqu'au désastre de Waterloo, par Chevalier (sous lieutenant) Maréchal-des-Logis en chef des Guides et Chasseurs à cheval de la Garde Impériale*, MS, Bibliothèque Thiers, mark 230, Masson Collection.

Chlapowski, Captain Dezydery, *Memoirs of a Polish Lancer*, translated by Tim Simmons, Emperor's Press, Chicago, IL, 1992.

Chuquet, Arthur, *Dugommier (1738–1794)*, R. Roger & F. Chernoviz, Paris, 1904.

Clairval, Vicomte Henri de, *Daumesnil*, Librairie Académique Perrin, Paris, 1970.

Clairval, Henri de, "Léonie, l'unique amour du général Daumesnil," *Historama* No. 235, June 1971, pp. 106–20.

Clairval, Henri de, "Schulmeister, Espion de l'Empereur," *Histoire pour tous*, January 1973, 58–65.

Clairval, Thérèse de, *Biographie de la Baronne Daumesnil*, Ethiou Pérou et Fils, 1887.

Combe, M., *Mémoires*, Plon, Paris, 1896.

Cooper, Leonard, *The Age of Wellington*, Dodd, Mead & Co., New York, 1963.

Correspondance inédite de Napoléon Ier conservée aux Archives de la Guerre, Ernest Picard, Paris, 1912.

Cronin, Vincent, *Napoleon Bonaparte. An Intimate Biography*, William Morrow & Co., N.Y., 1972.

Daumesnil, la Baronne *Journal de mes souvenirs*. Bibliothèque Nationale, Nouvelles acquisitions françaises 12794.

Dautancourt, General Baron, *Manuscrits du général baron d'Autancourt*, annotated by General Delaître (1829), and General Duvivier, former *adjutant major* of the Polish Light Horse, 1830. S.H.A.T. Archives de la Guerrre, Vincennes, MR 2331.

Deschamps, Emile, *Biographie du Général Daumesnil surnommé La Jambe-de-Bois de Vincennes – au bénéfice de la souscription*. Chez Paul Dupont, Paris, 1834.

Dupont, Marcel, *Cavaliers d'epopée*, Editions Lavauzelle, Paris, 1985.

Dupont, Marcel, *Guides de Bonaparte et Chasseurs à cheval de la Garde*, Les Editeurs Militaires Illustrés, Paris, 1945.

Elting, John R., *Swords Around a Throne*, The Free Press, New York; Weidenfeld & Nicolson, London, 1988.

Enaud, François, *Le Château de Vincennes*, Caisse Nationale des monuments, Paris, 1964.

Esposito, Brigadier General Vincent J. and Colonel John R. Elting, *A Military and History Atlas of the Napoleonic Wars*, Praeger, New York; Greenhill Books, London, 1999.

Even, Commandant E., 'Un brillant fait d'armes: la sortie victorieuse de la garnison de Bayonne le 14 avril 1814', *Carnet de la Sabretache*, two parts, Nouvelle Série No. 69, 4e Trimestre 1983 and Nouvelle Série No. 71, 1er Trimestre 1984.

Foissac, Dr. P. *La Chance ou la destinée*, Paris, 1876.

Fossa, François, *Le château historique de Vincennes à travers les âges*, vol. 1, chapter X, Paris, 1929.

Gallaher, John G., *The Iron Marshal. A Biography of Louis N. Davout*, Southern Illinois University Press, Carbondale, 1976; Greenhill Books, London, 2000.

Gerbaud, Capitaine. *Le Capitaine Gerbaud, 1773–1799: Documents published by Maxime Mangerel*, Plon, Paris 1910.

Goepp, Edouard, *Les Grands hommes de France. Hommes de Guerre. Daumesnil, Kleber*, etc., P. Ducroq, Paris, 1872–1874.

Gourdin, Jean-Luc, *L'Ange Gardien de Bonaparte. Le Colonel Muiron*, Editions Pygmalion/Gérard Watelet, Paris, 1996.

Grandin, F. (ed.) *Souvenirs historiques du Capitaine Krettly, ancien trompette-major des Guides d'Italie, d'Egypte et des Chasseurs à cheval de la Garde Impériale*, Berlandier, Editeur, Paris, 1839.

Grasset, A., *La Guerre d'Espagne*, Berger-Levrault, Paris, 1914–32.

Griffon de Pleineville, Natalia, "Le Général Exelmans, dernier vainqueur en 1815 (2)", *Tradition* no. 183, Nov. 2002.

Grivel, Vice-Admiral Baron J-B., *Mémoires*, Plon, Paris 1914.

Guyot, Général Comte, *Carnets de campagnes (1792–1815)*, Librairie Historique F. Teissedre, Paris, 1999.

Hanoteau, J (ed.), *Mémoires de la reine Hortense – publiés pare le Prince Napoléon, Tome I*, Librairie Plon, Paris, 1927.

Houssaye, Henry, *1814*, Librairie académique Perrin et Cie., Paris, 1918.

Jacquemart, René, "Blocus de la Ville de la Fère", *Bulletin de la Société académique de Chauny*, 1894–1895, pp. 33–95.

Jéhan, Philippe, *Rapp le sabreur de Napoléon*, Preface by Jean Tulard. La Nuée Bleue, np, after 1933

Johnson, David, *Napoleon's Cavalry and its Leaders*, Batsford, London; Holmes & Meier, New York, 1978.

Johnston, R. M. (edited by Philip Haythornthwaite), *In the Words of Napoleon*, Greenhill Books, London, 2002.

Jones, B. T. (ed.), *Napoleon's Army*, the military memoirs of Charles Parquin. Longman, Harlow; Greenhill Books, London, 1969.

Lachouque, Henry, *The Anatomy of Glory*, adapted from the French by Anne S. K. Brown, Brown University Press, 1961, Percy Lund, Humphries and Co., Ltd., London; Greenhill Books, London, .

Lachouque, Henry, *Napoleon's Battles. A history of his campaigns*, E.P. Dutton & Co., Inc., New York, 1967.

Lachouque, Henry, *Napoléon à Austerlitz*, G. Victor, Paris, 1960.

Larrey, D. J., *Mémoires de chirurgie militaire et campagnes de D. J. Larrey*, chez J. Smith, Imprimeur-Libraire, Paris, 1983.

Las Cases, E., Count de, Le *Mémorial de Sainte-Hélène*. Flammarion, Paris, 1951.

La Tombelle, Henri de, *Gens de plume et d'épée du Périgord*, Périgueux, Fontas, 1946.

Lejeune, General Baron Louis François, *Mémoires ... De Valmy à Wagram*, Paris, 1895.

Lucas-Dubreton, Jean, *Napoléon devant l'Espagne*, Librairie Larousse, Paris, 1969.

Macdonald, Maréchal Jacques Etienne Joseph Alexandre, *Souvenirs du Maréchal Macdonald, duc de Tarente*, Paris, 1892.

Maddin, Louis, *Fouché 1759–1820*. Librarie Plon, Paris, 1923.

Manceron, C., *Austerlitz*, George Allen & Unwin, London, and W.W. Norton, New York, 1966

Marbot, J., *The Memoirs of Baron de Marbot*, translated by Arthur John Butler, Longmans, Green, London, 1913; Greenhill Books, London, 1988.

Masson, Frédéric, *Cavaliers de Napoléon*, Boussat, Valadon et Cie, Paris, 1895.

Mazade, C., *Correspondance du Maréchal Davout*. Librarie Plon, Paris, 1885

Merme, Jean-Marie, '*Des Pyramides à Moscou.' Souvenirs d'un soldat de Napoléon Premier*, L'Academie de la Val d'Isère, Moutiers, 1978.

Müffling, Baron Carl von, *The Memoirs of Baron von Müffling*, Introduction by Peter Hofschröer, Greenhill Books, London, 1997.

Murat, Prince, *Lettres et documents pour servir à l'histoire de Joachim Murat*, Paris, 8 vols, 1908–1914.

Oman, Carola, *Sir John Moore*, Hodder & Stoughton, London, 1953.

Oman, Carola, *Napoleon's Viceroy. Eugène de Beauharnais*, Hodder and Stoughton, London, 1966.

O'Meara, Barry Edward, *Napoleon in Exile*, Simpkin Marshall, London, 1822.

Pasquier, Etienne-Denis, Chancelier, *Mémoires du Chancelier Pasquier*, Librarie Plon, Paris, 1894.

Pelleport, Pierre Vicomte de, *Souvenirs militaires et intimes du Général Vte. de Pelleport de 1793 à 1853*, Didier et Ce., Librairie-Editions, Paris, 1857.

Phipps, Colonel R. W., *The Armies of the First French Republic and the Rise of the Marshals of Napoleon*, 5 vols., Oxford University Press, London, 1931.

Picard, Commandant L., *La Cavalerie dans les guerres de la Révolution et de l'Empire*, Librairie Militaire S. Milon, Fils, Saumur, 1895.

Pigeard, Alain, *Les Campagnes Napoléoniennes 1796–1815*, Editions Quatuor, Entremont-le-Vieux, 1998.

Pigeard, Alain, *Les Etoiles de Napoléon*, Editions Quatuor, Entremont-le-Vieux, 1996.

Portail, Félix, *La Chute de Napoléon 1er et la Crise Française de 1814-1815*, Paris, 1943.

Prollius, von, *Militärisches*, Vol. 1, Brückner & Niemann, Leipzig, 1896.

Rabel, André, *Le Maréchal Bessières, duc d'Istrie*, Calmann-Levy, Paris, 1903.

Rapp, General Count J., *Mémoires*, Paris, 1821.

Reinhard, Marcel, *Histoire de France, volume 2*, Paris, 1954.

Renaud, *Souvenirs de jeunesse du général Daumesnil*. MS, Clairval collection.

Rembowski, Alexandre, *Sources documentaires concernant l'histoire du régiment des chevau-légers de la Garde de Napoléon I*, Warsaw, 1899.

Rochechouart, de *Le Général Comte*, *Souvenirs sur la Révolution, l'Empire et la*

Restauration, Librairie Plon, Paris, 1933.

Rossetti, General, aide de camp to Murat, *Journal inédit,* Archives Nationales, Murat Collection, 31 AP 10.

Saski, Lieutenant-Colonel Charles-Gaspard-Louis, *Campagne de 1809 en Allemagne et en Autriche,* Paris, 1899–1902.

Savary, General Anne Jean Marie René, *Mémoires du duc de Rovigo pour servir à l'histoire de l'Empereur Napoléon, Tome 3,* Paris, 1900–1901.

Ségur, Philippe Comte de, *Histoires et mémoires,* Paris, 1837.

Stoeckl, Agnes de, *King of the French – A Portrait of Louis Philippe 1773–1850,* G. P. Putnam's Sons, New York, 1958.

Teissèdre, Editions Historiques, *1814 Résistance et occupation des villes françaises,* Paris, 2001.

Thomassin, Général, "Blocus de la Fère par les Prussiens en 1815." *La Sabretache,* 2er sér., vol. VII, 1908.

Tranié, Jean, *Les Guerres de la Révolution,* Editions Quatuor, Entremont-le-Vieux, 2000.

Tranié, J and J-C Carmigniani, *Les Polonais de Napoléon,* Copernic, Paris, 1982.

Triaire, Paul, *Dominique Larrey et les campagnes de la révolution et de l'empire,* Tours, 1902.

Tulard, Jean, *Pasquier – Préfet de Police et son administration (1800–1830),Ville de Paris Commission des Travaux historiques,* Paris, 1976.

Vaulabelle, Ach. de, *Histoires des deux Restaurations, jusqu'au l'Avenement de Louis-Philippe,* Garnier Frères, Paris.

Verillon, Commandant M. *Les Trophées de France,* J. Leroy, Paris, 1907.

Veron, Louis Desire, *Mémoires d'un bourgeois de Paris,* Paris, 1853–5

Weltzien, Louis von, *Memoiren des königlich preussischen Generals der Infanterie Ludwig von Reiche, zweiter teil, 1814–1855,* F. A. Brockhaus, Leipzig, 1857.

Wellington, Arthur Wellesley, Duke of, *The Dispatches of Field Marshal the Duke of Wellington, 1799–1818,* ed. John Gurwood, London, 13 vols, 1834–39.

Wellington, Arthur Wellesley, Duke of, *Supplementary Dispatches, Correspondence and Memoirs,* ed. the Second Duke of Wellington, John Murray, London, 15 vols, 1858–72.

Willing, Paul, *Napoléon et ses soldats de Wagram à Waterloo,"* Collections Historiques du Musée de l'Armée, Arcueil, Paris, 1987.

Wood, Walter, *The Dispatches of Field Marshal the Duke of Wellington, selected and arranged,* E. P. Dutton & Co., London, 1902.

INDEX

Note: I have not attempted to index the names of Bonaparte/Napoleon or Pierre Daumesnil, since the entire book is essentially about the two of them.